CHANZEAUX

CO-EDITORS

William Christian   Mary L. Felstiner
George de Menil   Judith Herman

CONTRIBUTORS

Evelyn Ackerman   Stephanie Krebs
Frederic Ballard   Roger Lewin
Whitley Bruner   David McGranahan
William Christian   William Reilly
Richard DeAngelis   Suzanne Tollinger
George de Menil   Peter Winship
Mary L. Felstiner   Jonathan Wylie
Elizabeth Fox   Laurence Wylie
Judith Herman   Thomas Yager

CHANZEAUX

A VILLAGE IN ANJOU

EDITED BY

LAURENCE WYLIE

HARVARD UNIVERSITY PRESS

Cambridge, Massachusetts

1 9 6 6

Distributed in Great Britain by Oxford University Press, London

Library of Congress Catalog Card Number 66-18258
Printed in the United States of America

TO CLARENCE AND C. DOUGLAS DILLON

Preface

THIS BOOK is the cooperative effort of eighteen authors to describe a small rural community in western France, a village in Anjou. A traditional township in one of the most traditional regions of France, Chanzeaux has nevertheless undergone striking transformations in its long history. Even in the eight years the authors have known it there have been important changes. Yet Chanzeaux as a social entity, as a personality, seems to persist. The fundamental question is to see how Chanzeaux retains this personality and at the same time evolves within itself as well as with the rest of France.

Originally we had no intention of writing a book. We started as an undergraduate seminar, studying the dynamics of a French community. We discussed our projects and problems in common, but we wrote individually and only for each other. Gradually we felt the need to write as well as to study as a group. We realized that we all had different views of Chanzeaux, based on our special interests and experiences, but that collectively we had posed some basic questions, and we wished collectively to suggest some answers as they relate to the community of Chanzeaux. Consequently we have synthesized our material and believe we have expressed it through our collective personality. Except for this preface, our book was composed so jointly that each of us feels himself involved on almost every page. To achieve this complex common product, we have had to devote enormous good will and patience and work to the project. How our group evolved and functioned would have been an interesting study in itself. We thought it best, however, to emphasize our collective authorship.

We have tried to look at Chanzeaux in three ways — as a unit with a life of its own, as a cell forming part of a larger organism, and as a "personality" seen at certain critical points in its history. In some parts of our book one view is stressed more than the others, but throughout we have tried to keep all three in mind to achieve an integrated picture of how Chanzeaux lives and evolves. We think we may have more information about this community than has ever before been had for any community. But as one accumulates information, one becomes humble. We do not have the illusion that we have fully answered the basic question we have posed. Still, we feel that the answers we do have and the information on which these answers are based ought to circulate beyond the confines of our group.

Our project would have been more efficient had it been carried out in accordance with a previously defined master plan and written by a single person. However, our varying perspectives, the cooperation and conflict inherent in group work, the eventual synthesis we forced ourselves to achieve as this project spontaneously evolved, most certainly gave us insights into our subject we could not otherwise have had. Since the composition of our book was not imposed on us, grew rather from the shared curiosity and excitement inherent in true learning, its creation has been more an adventure than a chore.

Our concern with a village in western France grew from the experience of 1950–51 when my family and I made a study of a southern French village in the Vaucluse. In Roussillon ("Peyrane") the people voted characteristically to the left, and a small proportion of the population was active in the church. When in 1957 the time came for my next sabbatical leave, I wanted to undertake a companion study. This time we would live in a community resembling Roussillon in many respects, but unlike it in political and religious behavior. I wanted to find a community where most people attended Mass and where the majority of political expression was overwhelmingly to the right.

French Catholic sociologists and political geographers have produced atlases showing geographical variations in the political and religious behavior of the French people. By studying the maps one can see at once the regions where I might have found the sort of community I wanted to study. I might have gone to the southeast Massif Central or to the Alps, but both are fairly near the Vaucluse, and I wanted to become acquainted with a different part of France. Most of the other regions characterized by conservatism and piety are also distinguished by linguistic and cultural differences from what we might like to consider the core culture of France. Catholicism and conservatism have been especially strong in the Basque country, in

Brittany, in Alsace, in Flanders, but I wanted to avoid the complicating factors of linguistic and cultural distinction.

After talking to a good many people in France who understood my problem, I chose finally to look for a community in the region called *le pays des Mauges,* roughly the southwest quarter of the old province of Anjou, which is about as traditionally French as one can imagine. After visiting many communities in the Mauges and talking with political and diocesan authorities, journalists and *notaires,* teachers and rental agents, priests and town secretaries, my search for a specific village ended eventually in Chanzeaux. We settled in a house in the center of the village, and our two sons, ten and twelve years old, were accepted in the Catholic school. The people immediately put us at ease with their cordial acceptance of probably the only Protestants who had ever lived in the community. The year was happy and fruitful. I collected what I thought at the time was a great amount of information, much more certainly than I had had on the village of Roussillon. However, hepatitis, apparently endemic in Chanzeaux and which I contracted at the very end of our stay there, kept me from using the material I had gathered when I returned to Haverford College the following year.

An unexpected event made my information on Chanzeaux useful in a way I had never anticipated. At Haverford I was a French teacher and utilized my sociological material only incidentally in my courses, but in 1959 I was invited to fill the newly created C. Douglas Dillon Chair of the Civilization of France at Harvard University. Here I had the opportunity to give a course on French social structure in the Department of Social Relations. In an undergraduate seminar, a dozen or so students began working with the primary materials I had collected on Chanzeaux. Since 1959 this seminar has been given every year, so that by now almost a hundred undergraduates have spent a semester digging into — as well as adding to, as we shall see — the Chanzeaux material.

A majority of the students in any course do their work and move on, but there are often a few who become really interested. After the second year I very much wanted some of the students to be able to visit the community they had been studying. Clarence Dillon accepted this idea, and in the summer of 1962 made it possible for three students to carry on their research and writing in Chanzeaux. Two other members of the seminar were there, supported by their parents. In 1963 three more students benefited from Mr. Dillon's generosity, and the next summer Douglas Dillon made it possible for four students to make the trip. In that year there was a total of eleven students in Anjou, however, for seven others were supported in their research by grants made through the Undergraduate Science Education Program of the National Science Foundation. In 1965 six students spent the summer in Chanzeaux, another was in nearby Saint-Lézin, and another was in a rural community of Brittany — recipients of aid from Mr. Dillon, from a Ford Foundation grant made to Harvard, and through assistance offered by the Harvard Social Relations Laboratory.

When students return from Chanzeaux they inevitably want an opportunity to interpret the information they have brought back. After the first summer, since there was no suitable course in the university curriculum, we organized an informal seminar: some students received permission from their departments to carry out independent research in the place of a regular course; others were utilizing their material for senior theses. As the Chanzeaux group grew year by year, our relationship became more complicated and more fluid. The veterans became as important as the teacher in helping new students. A class or seminar situation no longer sufficed. In the autumn of 1963 we began to meet informally for lunch every Saturday.

It was at one of our first lunches that the idea occurred to us to write a book together. We were all working on different aspects of the same problem. It seemed logical that each of us should write a chapter and that, by putting all these chapters together, we should have a well-rounded description of the community of Chanzeaux. We set to work enthusiastically. But writing a book jointly is at best complicated and, besides, we soon found we were not content with a collection of separate though related essays. A further difficulty lay in the fact that since we had begun our book, our knowledge of Chanzeaux and the number of students capable of saying something important about it had increased considerably. We risked being lost in the number of contributors and in the mass of our own material. Also, some of the authors had graduated and moved on to graduate or professional schools. Working as a group became increasingly complicated.

In the spring of 1964 we held a crucial conference to decide whether to drop the book. The result was renewed determination as well as, on the practical side, more formal organization and a working plan. Each of us made a financial contribution to secure editorial and stenographic help. Katherine Bruner was persuaded, partly because of her professional interest and competence, partly perhaps because her son was one of the authors, to be the shepherdess for our flock — keeping us in touch with each other, harrying those who were not meeting deadlines, making sure our manuscripts were in the proper form, and generally providing a nerve center for our rapidly scattering group. Certainly this book owes its existence to Mrs. Bruner's tactful and persistent concern.

As an example of how the book has developed, let me sketch the history of the section on social organization. The original version consisted of chapters by Fox on social structure, Herman on secular organizations, Christian on political organization, and myself on religious organizations. After lengthy discussion and mutual correction of manuscripts, we decided that there should be only two chapters, one on secular organizations and one on religious organizations. The Fox, Herman, and Christian contributions were combined and rewritten by Christian, and the religious organizations remained separate. We were then troubled, for we saw that our division between secular and religious was false, or at least misleading. We decided to combine the sections and rewrite them with attention to all of the organizations, their function, growth, and death, in their relationship to changing problems and personalities. By that time, the summer of 1964, Christian was on the island of Saint-Pierre, Herman was at Tougaloo, Mississippi, Fox was in New Haven, Mrs. Bruner was in Cambridge, and I was in Michigan. It was Judith Herman, finally, on a two-week vacation in New Hampshire, who rewrote what we thought was the final draft. But meanwhile life in Chanzeaux brought further changes. The development of the Syndicat d'Initiative and of farmers' cooperative groups during the summer and the following year, and the municipal elections in the spring of 1965, gave us additional insights into the social organization of the community. Eventually it was Herman and Christian who, in June of 1965, gave new meaning and final form to the whole section in the light of these developments.

We could follow the growth of other sections in the same way. Each has its history. The section on economy originally consisted of separate chapters by five of us, but it was always considered the weakest part of our work. Eventually the interested authors decided that more unity, more information, and sounder theory were needed. David McGranahan made a special trip to Chanzeaux to fill the gaps in our knowledge, and George de Menil took all our data and with tremendous energy and concentration wrote the entire section — helped in whatever ways we could by those of us who stood at the ready. Finally, the section was again completely rewritten by Thomas Yager and Roger Lewin, on the basis of information they obtained in the summer of 1965. The chapters on population movement, originally the work of George de Menil, were reworked by Bruner, Christian, and Yager; but since ideas in these chapters were involved in other sections of the book, there was considerable consultation among the rest of us. Whether this sort of composition improves the quality of a book is not the point here; we are simply stating that to understand this particular book it is essential to know that, for better or for worse, the joint authorship is real.

It would be difficult to describe adequately the final burst of energy and cooperation that brought our product to its conclusion. The four co-editors, William Christian, Judith Lewis Herman, Mary Lowenthal Felstiner, and George de Menil, called for an all-out effort to finish the manuscript by July 1, 1965, after which most of the authors would disperse for fairly long stays to many parts of the world. June was a month of frantic work, in the shadow of what seemed at times an impossible deadline. Finally, most of the crew spent the entire night of June 30 at William James Hall, putting the finishing touches on each section so that the bulk of the manuscript could be finished on time. The following week a complete manuscript was presented to Harvard University Press, almost exactly eight years since the first of us visited Chanzeaux.

During this period how has information been gathered? What sources were open to us? What kinds of data did we accumulate?

Our main tool has been that of participation-observation. We lived in Chanzeaux and recorded what we learned. Several of us kept journals and field notes, which are now at the disposal of our whole group (as is all the information we have gathered). We also have data obtained from formal interviews and from questionnaires developed for specific projects. A few students have sought specific information on the basis of which they have written their senior theses. Most students who have been to Chanzeaux have written not only a formal paper on their summer projects but also a more personal account of their relationship with an individual or with a family in the community.

Information basic to this book has also come from research in archives. The town council and the curé have given us access to the archives of the commune and of the parish of Chanzeaux. M. and Mme. Delbosc, chatelains of Chanzeaux, have let us work in their *chartrier*, which contains records dating from the fourteenth century to the present. Maître Milon and Maître Galland have opened their notarial archives to us. In Angers we have worked in the archives of both the department and the diocese. From the offices of the Institut National de la Statistique et des Etudes Economiques in Paris and Nantes, we were given any information we sought, provided that it was of an anonymous, statistical nature. Professor Victor Savary of Nantes helped several generations of American Chanzeans by making available copies of his maps of Chanzeaux; we are grateful to him.

From all these sources we have information about the past as well as the present. We have large cadastral maps on which we have noted who owns and works each field in the commune. We have copies of all the censuses since 1836, of all land ownership and land transactions since 1825, of all the election results since 1881, of all the marriages (with considerable data about each party to a marriage) since 1845, birth records since 1845, lists of Chanzeans who since 1800 have become priests, a list of all living nuns born in Chanzeaux. We have a copy of the *fichier* (file) — the main working tool of the town secretary — containing vital statistics and residence data for every individual living in Chanzeaux. We know who has not voted — and why — in each of the last seven elections. We know who goes to Mass and who takes communion and with what regularity. We have a list of all adults in France who were born and raised in Chanzeaux but vote elsewhere, and we know a good deal about these people — their age, marital status, address, when they left Chanzeaux, and in many cases the reason commonly given for their departure. We know the children whose education is being continued beyond the Chanzeaux grade school. We have drawings, based on the draw-a-man test, made by all the schoolchildren. We have a file of the plays put on at the parish house, including the manuscript of the local historical drama written by a former schoolteacher. We have a series of themes writ-

ten by the schoolchildren on their conception of the Vendée Rebellion. Naturally we have a great deal both of information and of
hearsay of a more intimate nature, too, which for ethical and legal
reasons may not be included in our book. Nevertheless it has helped
us to formulate questions and suggest answers of more general significance about human relationships in Chanzeaux.

Besides many hours of interviews and conversations on tape, we
have more than three thousand still photographs, taken by Paul
Williams and by me. The illustrations for this book were chosen
from among them. We have a movie made in the summer of 1964 by
Paul Williams and Thomas Yager. Much of our information is
hoarded in our files in 1420 William James Hall, but much is available
in more modern and sometimes more efficient form. Essential demographic and land-tenure data, as well as a great quantity of historical
documents, are recorded on microfilm. A large amount of data has
been recorded on IBM cards. The "print-ups" now available contain
masses of information in convenient form and have been especially
helpful for students going to Chanzeaux. On one long sheet they may
now have with them much of our accumulated statistical knowledge.

We have also had the information gathered by other people, for
France — and especially Catholic France — has developed a passion
for sociological research. Chanzeaux has been included in studies made
by several organizations. Every year the Catholic youth movements
in the region make a concentrated investigation of some aspect of
local life as part of their leadership-training program. In the adult
Catholic Action groups the leaders, former members of the youth
movements, continue to carry out research projects. We have had
the results of these inquiries at our disposal. J. P. Vagneur, a graduate student at the Jesuit agricultural college in Angers, is making a
study of thirty farms in Chanzeaux, chosen because the regional head
of the farmers' union lives there and offered to help persuade the
local farmers to cooperate. We have given Vagneur our information,
and in turn he has given us data on local farm operations. We have
also had access to the information gathered by sociologists of Economie et Humanisme, a Dominican research organization, who were
engaged by a regional economic expansion committee to survey the
social and economic state of the Maine-et-Loire. Diocesan officials
have let us use the data from their statistical study of religious behavior in the region. The Chambre d'Agriculture gave us a copy of

the report which they commissioned from a Parisian sociological research organization, Synergie Roc. We also have the information gathered by several governmental agencies, notably the study of Maine-et-Loire agriculture made by the departmental Services Agricoles.

There are relatively few printed sources to which we owe acknowledgment. The classical references for Anjou are the works of three great scholars of the nineteenth century — Célestin Port, the Abbé Uzureau, and A. Le Moy. To these we add three scholarly works of recent years — Joël Le Theule's *Vignoble du Layon* (Xerox copy of manuscript in Widener Library), Paul Bois's *Les Paysans de l'Ouest* (Le Mans, 1960), and Charles Tilly's *The Vendée* (Harvard University Press, 1964). Certain periodicals have been useful. The only strictly local Chanzeaux publication is the parish bulletin, mimeographed and distributed sporadically by M. le Curé. The bulletins published by the Nantes office of INSEE provide statistical information of many sorts for the region. The best source of news of communities in the Maine-et-Loire is the *Courrier de l'Ouest*, published in Angers. Since 1957 we have received a free subscription, and we have kept not only the file of the newspaper but also a file of every item relating to Chanzeaux.

Mention of the *Courrier de l'Ouest* at once brings to mind the friendly assistance offered over the years by Paul Fleury, business manager of the newspaper, by Michel Poinot, and by other members of the staff. Through benevolent references to "les Américains de Chanzeaux," they have made it clear to their readers that we were not spies asking impertinent questions for nefarious purposes. Other officials and dignitaries of the Maine-et-Loire have also lent their aid whenever we needed it — Monseigneur Bouin, Pierre d'Herbecourt (Archivist Emeritus of the Maine-et-Loire), Canon Tricoire (Archivist of the Diocese), Maître Milon and Maître Galland (who control our most pertinent notarial archives).

It is, of course, the entire population of Chanzeaux that deserves our deepest appreciation. The Chanzeans have the reputation of being especially "acceuillants," and we have seen this reputation for cordiality justified again and again. They took us into their homes, shared countless bottles of wine in their day-to-day hospitality, and sacrificed precious bottles of '47 to "arroser" our many arrivals and departures. More important, they have taken infinite trouble, shown great understanding, and devoted hours of their time to our questions and interviews, which must often have seemed quite silly or, worse still, impertinent.

We should like to thank everyone by name, but we must be satisfied by mentioning only representatives of the commune and asking them to extend our thanks to the whole community: the mayor and the former mayor, the members of the Conseil Municipal, the former curé of Chanzeaux (now Dean of Lion d'Angers), the present vicar, the secrétaire de mairie, the officers of the Syndicat d'Initiative, the regional representative of the BNCI, and the teachers of Chanzeaux. We should have liked to mention specifically the families who were kind enough to feed and lodge the Americans, but it seems best to keep them anonymous. We have changed the names of all the individuals mentioned in the book, adopting new names from nineteenth-century censuses.

Among our list of authors we should like to be able to include members of Social Relations 108 who have given us substantial assistance but were unable for one reason or another to participate fully in our project. We have been helped by the ideas of the more imaginative students of the early days of the seminar before this book was conceived: Waud Kracke, who spent the summer of 1962 living in hamlets of Chanzeaux; Nicholas Hopkins, who studied Chanzeaux's relation to the regional community; Christopher Boehm, who tried to define the ideal characteristics of the Chanzeaux town councilor; and Richard Solomon, who emphasized the use of aerial photographs as source material.

From first to last Harvard University has cooperated in every possible way — the best way being simply its chaotic, permissive nature which allowed Social Relations 108 to evolve from a traditional seminar into what students say is a state of mind. We thank Harvard for letting this state of mind develop despite departmental limits, despite faculty regulations and administrative efforts to keep things neatly compartmentalized. Four members of the Harvard faculty have helped and advised us on our long and often circuitous road to our goal: Philip Dawson, Patrice Higonnet, Charles Tilly, and Harrison White. We express our appreciation for their interest and their help.

Of course, our class, our research, and this book have all depended on several sources of financial support. My first year of research was made possible by sabbatical leave granted by Haverford College and by a fellowship from the Guggenheim Foundation. We are grateful to the National Science Foundation whose grant in 1964–65 under the Undergraduate Science Education Program enabled several members of our seminar to go to Chanzeaux and then to work further on their projects after their return. We thank the Social Relations Laboratory and the Ford Foundation, through its grant made to Harvard for International Studies, for support given in 1965.

Finally and above all we are grateful to Clarence and Douglas Dillon, who have from the beginning found value in what we were doing and expressed their faith by their generosity in helping make the project materially possible. It is right that we should dedicate our efforts to them.

Laurence Wylie
Paris
March 1966

CO-EDITORS' NOTE

For all the people who have worked on this project, Chanzeaux has been much more than a normal undergraduate course of study. In our studies, all of us were teachers; all were students. The result, we believe, is an experiment in sharing that is rare in the university environment. This exchange would have been inconceivable without a man willing to share years of research with our unsteady explorations. Despite the time and effort expended on it, this book is but a narrow portion of what we have learned from Laurence Wylie.

CONTENTS

CHANZEAUX

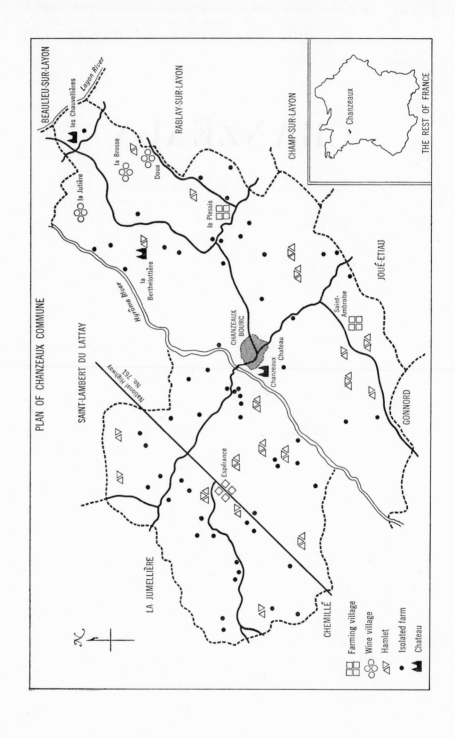

PLAN OF CHANZEAUX COMMUNE

BEAULIEU-SUR-LAYON

Layon River

les Chauvellières

la Jutière

la Brosse

Doua

RABLAY-SUR-LAYON

le Plessis

CHAMP-SUR-LAYON

la Berthelottière

Hyrôme River

SAINT-LAMBERT DU LATTAY

National Highway No. 761

CHANZEAUX BOURG

Chanzeaux Chateau

Saint-Ambroise

JOUÉ-ÉTIAU

GONNORD

Espérance

LA JUMELLIÈRE

CHEMILLÉ

Chanzeaux

THE REST OF FRANCE

⊞ Farming village
○○○ Wine village
◁ Hamlet
● Isolated farm
▲ Chateau

Introduction

CHANZEAUX's twelve square miles of villages and fields and its population of 1,150 cannot compete for recognition on an ordinary map of France. Still, as one of the 36,000 rural communities that have shaped the character of the French countryside and are now participating in its transformation, Chanzeaux is important. To understand the structure of this village, and in turn have some insight into the individual inhabitant's involvement in the community, is to increase our understanding of both the culture of France and the dynamics of small communities.

On a detailed map, the definition of the commune of Chanzeaux is clear: somewhat kidney-shaped, a well-defined mass, large compared to the neighboring communes, about six miles long in its longest dimension and a mile wide at its narrowest point. The lines are made clearer on two sides by the Hyrôme and Layon rivers that form the boundary. From the *Dictionnaire des Communes* our impression of Chanzeaux's being easily defined is reinforced: it covers 3,000 hectares (about 7,500 acres), has a population (according to the 1962 census) of 1,159 people who live in 327 dwellings. But Chanzeaux is a living cell, and in neither definition nor inner structure is it a static unity. As we come to know it, we become increasingly aware that it has a complicated internal organization whose parts are dynamically related to one another as well as to the world outside. Generally speaking, the functioning of these parts is the subject of our book.

Located about two thirds of the way from Paris to the Atlantic, Chanzeaux is fifteen miles southwest of Angers, the capital of the old province of Anjou in the heart of traditional France. The fact that Chanzeaux is southwest of Angers is significant, because Anjou is a peculiar province, divided into four regions, each with its own personality. Anjou straddles the Loire Valley, and first of all there is a marked difference between the halves of the province on the left and right banks. It is also a transitional area between the Parisian basin and western France. Its eastern half has strong cultural ties with the bordering provinces of Touraine, Poitou, and Orléans and has its own cultural capital, Saumur. The western half, in which Chanzeaux is located, is closely related to the neighboring regions of Brittany and the Vendée and feels the influence of the Atlantic port city of Nantes. Angers lies near the point where the four quarters of the province meet: it counteracts the divergent influences and exerts a centripetal force to give the province unity.

Except for the city of Angers, the traveler's acquaintance with Anjou is usually restricted to the Loire Valley. He knows the levee roads between Saumur and Angers, with their several churches and monasteries now so successfully illuminated on summer evenings — Blaison, Saint-Rémy, Le Thoureil, Saint-Sulpice, Cunault. From Saumur he may drive into the country to the monastery of Fontevrault, where Richard the Lion-Hearted and Eleanor of Aquitaine are buried. He may even visit the chateau of Brissac. But beyond these places the countryside of Anjou has few obvious lures; the tourist usually turns and goes east to the great chateaux of the Loire, to Mont Saint-Michel in the north, or to Brittany in the west. On the other hand, the tourist who heads toward the Atlantic Ocean and the beaches of Sables d'Olonne, only a hundred miles southwest of Angers on a straight, fast road, goes through what is called the *pays des Mauges,* a part of France scarcely mentioned in the guidebooks or in that basic compendium of information about France, *Le Petit Larousse.* It is here in the Mauges that Chanzeaux is located.

There is nothing startling about the landscape of this part of France. At its center is the highest point in Anjou, a hill only six hundred feet above sea level. From the top of this hill — flattered by the name of Le Puy de la Garde — one sees little but green fields, enclosed by hedges, rolling away to the horizon. Dozens of church spires mark the towns and villages, but the churches — like the one on Le Puy de la Garde itself — were almost without exception built after 1800. The traveler seems justified indeed in not stopping on his way to the Atlantic.

For anyone interested in understanding France and the French people, however, the Mauges is one of the fascinating areas of France; some of the most interesting and maddening puzzles of French history are actually before the traveler's eyes, even though he may be unaware of what he sees. The very hedges surrounding the fields, for instance, have to do with that baffling question in European history of why, in some parts of Europe, farmers have traditionally lived on isolated farms while in others they have lived in villages. This distinction is a feature of two contrasting ways of life, manifested by the presence or absence of the hedges. A rather sharp line running north and south through England and France divides the hedge country (*le bocage*) from open-field country, and no one has ever found an explanation for exactly how or when or why the two systems developed.

A traveler to the Mauges can actually see the abruptness of this change if he comes from the Loire Valley or from the open-field country to the east. The horizon suddenly disappears. The hedges — dense thickets of brambles and trees growing atop mounds of earth packed solidly to a height of three or four feet — block the view and give the impression that the countryside is heavily wooded. The contrast with the open fields of wheat and vines to the east is remarkable. This book will be concerned partly with the implications of this contrast, since Chanzeaux lies on the line dividing the two regions.

Another difference, quite as remarkable though easily explained, is that on entering the Mauges one leaves behind the limestone houses of the Loire Valley, with their steeply slanting slate roofs, for ones typically built of grey fieldstone and covered with stucco, trimmed with brick, and usually roofed with rounded Roman tiles. This distinction may be explained geologically. The Saumurois is in limestone country and the building stone is tufa; excellent slate comes from the mines north of the Loire. The Mauges is in granite country, and good clay is available for making brick and tile.

The line that divides the Mauges from the Parisian basin is also the invisible boundary separating two distinct patterns of religious practice. In the Mauges one notices immediately that each village church is huge. It stands in the center and dominates the community, and is well filled for every service. The typical village church in the eastern part of Anjou is small and, in spite of its size, rarely crowded on Sundays. When French Catholic sociologists made a map showing the religious practice of France, they found that a line could be drawn between cantons where a large majority of the people take an active part in religious activities and cantons where few people ever go to church. Gabriel Le Bras writes:

If you travel from Luçon to Bayeux, following rather closely the line of the hedge country, you have constantly to your left a population of whom seventy to ninety-five percent go to Mass regularly; on your right twenty percent practice regularly. I have taken this trip several times myself to establish the points of geographical separation. Sometimes in a village divided by a small stream you find on the right bank twenty percent of practicing Catholics among the population and on the left bank ninety percent. And this proportion is found consistently over an area of fifty or one hundred kilometers in depth.[1]

The usual explanation for this difference is historical. In 1793 the bocage country in western France was the scene of a violent rebellion against the revolutionary government in Paris. The causes for this uprising — called the Vendée Rebellion — are obscure. Apologists for the rebels have said that the people of the west rose spontaneously to defend their religion, their king, and their nobles against the Parisian regime. Apologists for the republican government have said that the western priests and nobility stirred up the peasants to defend the very social order by which the peasants were being outrageously exploited. Both explanations are extravagant oversimplifications, but, for whatever cause, a bitter ideological conflict developed between the Vendée and the rest of France. The Vendeans south of the Loire and the "Chouans" north of the Loire attacked the blue-uniformed republican soldiers, "les bleus," with the savagery characteristic of all civil wars. Eventually the republican forces put down the rebellion, but with such cruelty and violence that for generations the Vendeans remained especially fervent in defense of their priests. They chose as representatives men — often of the nobility — who favored a conservative government and opposed the predominantly anticlerical majority of the French people.

The effects of the Vendée war may be seen concretely in the relative newness of the churches, chateaux, and houses in the Mauges. Between 1793 and 1795 most of the buildings in the area were destroyed; everything had to be rebuilt. The chateaux are mid-nineteenth-century versions of Renaissance buildings; the churches are mostly late-nineteenth-century gothic or romanesque — or a mixture of both. Chanzeaux's church dates from 1900, and only three of its prerevolutionary houses remain.

Chanzeaux is on the eastern border of the rebel Vendean country. Traditionally this limit has been recognized as the valley of the Layon

River, which flows southeast to northwest through southern Anjou and divides the bocage country of the Mauges from the plains of the Saumurois. Like most border towns that have had to defend their way of life, Chanzeaux from the first has had the reputation of being more extremely Vendean than the towns lying securely toward the center of the Mauges. In 1793 Chanzeaux was a focal point of rebel sentiment, and one of the first attacks that committed the people to rebellion took place there. The revolutionary government massed its troops in the village of Saint-Lambert du Lattay to attack the Vendeans of the Mauges. One of the republican soldiers wrote in his journal as his regiment bivouacked there just to the north of Chanzeaux: "Demain nous entrons dans le pays des boeufs." Chanzeaux was the outpost of this alien grazing country, and throughout the rebellion it suffered the brunt of attack and counterattack.

Because the northeast corner of Chanzeaux touches on the Layon River, the commune is officially included with the other Layon communities in the canton of Thouarcé in the arrondissement of Saumur *sud*. Although most of Chanzeaux's area and population have relatively little in common with these wine-growing communities to the east, a geographical accident means that administratively Chanzeaux is considered a part of this traditionally republican and revolutionary segment of France. Even the church of Chanzeaux is attached to the east, for church districts normally follow governmental administrative divisions. The priest of Chanzeaux is directly under the authority of the curé doyen of Thouarcé.

With the exception of the small corner of the commune touching the Layon, however, Chanzeaux's economic and sentimental ties are with the communities to the south and west — Gonnord, Joué-Etiau, La Jumellière, Chemillé, and the communities of the Mauges. Ecologically they are alike and contrast with the limestone plains of the Saumurois. The Mauges farms have the same lime-poor, clay soil on a schistous base that makes for adequate though not particularly desirable agricultural land. This part of France receives the fresh winds from the Atlantic Ocean, however, and enjoys a somewhat mild climate with frequent and not too violent rains, favoring the growth of grass and fodder crops. Consequently the region has always depended primarily on the production of wheat and dairy products for its livelihood. Sometimes the farmers of the Mauges have the problem of too much or too little water. When it rains hard, the water either collects on the impermeable soil or runs off, carrying a load of top soil. Fortunately droughts are not common but, since good wells and springs are fairly rare, the ground cannot store sufficient water for periods of drought, and the wells soon run dry. Each farmhouse typically collects water in its "mare," or little pond, as a supplementary supply for the cattle as well as for household use. When the ponds are emptied during a prolonged drought, the farmers cart water in tank wagons from the Hyrôme River. Then they joke somewhat bitterly about living in "Chanzeaux sans eau" and complain because the town council has not done something about a public water supply. [Something has been done now. In 1965 Chanzeaux began receiving water pumped in from the Loire.]

Because labor is relatively cheap in the Mauges, farmers supplement their incomes by growing a few crops requiring special care but bringing relatively high returns — tobacco, flower seeds, medicinal plants. This is the camomile center of the world, and in Chanzeaux tons of mint are grown each year. In early summer one sees groups of women, children, and old people picking the mint leaves from the stems. Their hands are stained green, and the odor is overpowering.

The systems of transportation and communication reflect the economic ties of Chanzeaux to the Mauges rather than to the east. In fact, there is no means of direct public transportation from Chanzeaux to Thouarcé, but this is unimportant since essentially no one goes there except on administrative business. On the other hand, there is constant coming and going between Chanzeaux and the Mauges. The main highway is the one passing through the Mauges that connects Angers and the Atlantic, so buses and express trucks must enter Chanzeaux from the west. The grazers of Chanzeaux sell their cattle in the Chemillé market on Thursday mornings, and their wives go there to shop and to sell their butter, eggs, chickens, and rabbits.

Nor is it surprising that the affinity of Chanzeaux to the Mauges is equally apparent in its kinship patterns. It is rare, for instance, for a young man or woman from Chanzeaux to marry someone from Rablay or the other towns to the east. The kinship network ties people to the west. Some 55 percent of the people living in Chanzeaux but not born there come from the Mauges, from the neighboring towns of Chemillé, La Jumellière, Joué-Etiau and Gonnord, or from communes deeper in the region.

The nucleus of the *commune* (township) of Chanzeaux is the *bourg*, the village by the same name. It is the home of about a quarter of the population and the administrative center of the commune. Its location on the southern slope of the bank of the Hyrôme River was no doubt at first strategic, as the etymology *cancelli* (enclosure) implies. Perhaps it was a fortress guarding a key passage. Since there were no highways in this part of France until the nineteenth century, the river valleys were used as roads. Cut deep into the underlying granite and at points forming little canyons that were impassable during the spring floods, the valley roads were a confusing maze; and when the republican invaders came to the region in 1793, they were forced to depend on local guides. The rivers were also important to run the mills for grain raised in the region. Along the Hyrôme in Chanzeaux were seven mills at half-mile intervals; for each, a hilltop windmill overlooking the river provided supplementary power during droughts. In the nineteenth century the river was also used for soaking the flax then grown in the community, and we know that there was constant conflict among cattle grazers and flax growers, millers and fishermen, who accused each other of polluting and abusing the stream. In the early twentieth century the valley was still a lively part of the commune. M. Forget says that when he was a boy, there were refreshment stands along the lane in the valley; on Sunday afternoons one walked along the river, met one's friends, and drank at the stands. Today the mills are in ruins and the valley is deserted; on Sundays one sees only an occasional fisherman.

The national highway that cuts across the western part of the commune was projected in the eighteenth century, but was not actually built before the first half of the nineteenth. Since then the focus of life has shifted farther away from the valley — and consequently from the bourg. As means of transportation have improved, the bourg has lost its earlier economic and commercial functions. Today it serves primarily as the administrative and social center of the commune. The most prominent men actually living in the town are engaged primarily in maintaining channels of authority and communication with the farm families that constitute most of the population of Chanzeaux.

The danger we risk in describing Chanzeaux is that through our generalizations we create a mythical community. We are tempted to conclude too easily: "The Chanzeans do this and believe that." Certainly we cannot talk about Chanzeaux without arbitrarily creating categories, but we do not intend to give them an importance they do not have in reality. For example, when we speak of "the Chanzeans," it may seem that we have in mind a well-defined group of people. Statistically this is true, for we have adopted as a working definition the group of individuals listed in the private file of the secrétaire de mairie of Chanzeaux. This file contains a card for each ménage, giving the vital statistics for all official residents of Chanzeaux. But if we tried to make a list of the individuals who belong or do not belong to the community of sentiment that we call Chanzeaux, it would be distressingly difficult to be precise. The difficulty is readily seen in specific cases.

M. and Mme. Delbosc, the gentry who now own the chateau, live most of the time in Paris, and their membership in the community as a sentimental unit is tenuous. Still, they are registered voters in Chanzeaux, and M. Delbosc was until recently a member of the town council. They are listed in the *fichier* and are included in our statistics. On the other hand, the owner of the Chateau de la Berthelottière is not included because he is officially a citizen of Nantes; yet as a property owner he has had considerable influence in Chanzeaux, as have other city capitalists whose land in Chanzeaux is worked by tenant farmers. In a description of Chanzeaux as a "community of interests," these landowners would be properly considered Chanzeans. Then there is the case of the dozen or so girls who live in other communes but come to Chanzeaux to work in the basket factory and spend all day in the bourg, dining at noon *chez* Mme. Gaudin. They help to create the atmosphere that gives the community its personality. Undoubtedly some of them will marry Chanzeaux men and become official Chanzeans; still, they are included in none of our statistics except those relating to the factory. We know, however, that these young women are more a part of the community than the grandsons of Mme. Dutertre, who inherited and maintains a residence in the bourg. The two young men spend only a few days during their vacations in Chanzeaux and will presumably never live there. Although they did not vote in the last election, they are on the voting list and recorded in both the census and the *fichier:* they are therefore included in our figures.

The disparity between the official and sentimental Chanzeaux may be seen even in the case of farmers who have lived in the region all their lives. Included in our statistics are the farmers living in the hamlet of Les Bretêsches because their homes are within the limits of the commune. In fact they come to the bourg only for official business. Most of their fields lie in the neighboring commune of Chemillé, and most of their friends live there. They send their children to school in Chemillé, and there they do all their marketing. Excluded from our official Chanzeaux, however, is M. Lopin, whose house stands across the brook separating Chanzeaux from Saint-Lambert. All of Lopin's sheds and barns and most of his fields are on the Chanzeaux side of the brook. The only way to get to his farm is by the Chanzeaux road; he must even pass through the bourg (two kilometers from his house) to go the eight kilometers to Saint-Lambert to transact administrative business. Lopin's economic as well as kinship ties are all with Chanzeaux. His children went to school there and married there. He even goes to Mass there, though technically he is not a member of the Chanzeaux parish. Nevertheless, to the extent that we depend on official statistics, Lopin is not a Chanzean.

The practical solution to the problem of definition is to accept the fact that we are dealing with a shifting, dynamic population within arbitrarily set boundaries. Our attempt to avoid creating a static Chanzeaux by stressing its constantly shifting human boundaries is basic to our interpretation of the community. We see Chanzeaux as a system, but a living system — complex, indistinct, constantly evolving, essentially related to larger systems. We first show how Chanzeaux was functioning in periods of crisis: in the 1790s, in the 1850s, and then at about the turn of the century. In the rest of the book we are largely concerned with Chanzeaux in its grave trials of the 1960s. How do Chanzeans now earn their living? What resources are available to them, and how are these resources organized? In what ways are the Chanzeans dependent on markets? on government? We then analyze the community's social organization and describe its relationship to the larger systems of which it is a part. Finally, and basically, we are concerned with the involvement and participation of the individual Chanzean in his community.

Part One

HISTORY

At first sight, Chanzeaux is a village left behind by history. Off the main road, its approach guarded by the towered chateau, its square dominated by the massive stone church, it seems like a picturesque survival from the Ancien Régime. But to give the lie to this early impression, one need only stop at the Café Lambert off the square. There the *patron*, who is a bit of an anarchist, will quickly dispel one's illusions. For Chanzeaux's historical monuments are of disappointingly recent origin. The church is no more than seventy years old; only its belltower is an authentic relic of the Middle Ages. The chateau was an insignificant building before it was rebuilt to conform to the florid taste of a nineteenth-century lord. The four pointed towers at its corners are the result of a construction boom in the 1840s, which saw the transformation of many *maisons bourgeoises* in the region into structures of loftier pretensions.

These images of the past, then, are anachronisms that becloud both the present and the history of the village. Yet the village without its history is inconceivable, if only because of the apparent survival of a traditional way of life. Paradoxically, we must search for the origins of a tradition in a past that tradition has itself obscured.

Three historical situations have had a lasting effect on the village. All are bound up with the national life of France; all are commemorated in the architecture of Chanzeaux. The first was the shock of the Revolution and the counterrevolution — the Vendée Rebellion — in which Chanzeaux participated. The second was the domination of the region, during most of the nineteenth and early twentieth centuries, by a nobility that was increasingly estranged from national politics. The third was the intermittent revival of the political and religious conflicts of the Revolution. The belltower of Chanzeaux is the scene of a legendary battle of the Vendée Rebellion; the latter-day chateau is a symbol of the power of its builder; and the church itself, with its murals depicting the martyrdom of Chanzeaux's rebels, is a testimonial to the revived memories of war a century after the event. In this sense, they are clues to the critical moments in the village's past.

1

Chanzeaux at the Time of the Vendée Rebellion

W HEN the sun rose on Tuesday morning, March 12, 1793, over the town of Chanzeaux, most of the inhabitants of the parish were already about their routine morning chores. Jacques Rozé, the "constitutional" sacristan of the church, must have been walking to the church to ring the angelus that would wake any Chanzean still in bed. In the countryside, most of the farmers must have already finished an hour's work. At the Mill Point, the miller and baker, Pierre Bureau, might have been asleep while his apprentices built the fires for the day's first batch of bread. Those who lived in town, like Mme. Coustard, wife of the notaire, could be more leisurely in rising. But soon Maurice Jouslain, the shoemaker, would be about his work in the shop in front of his house, and Mme. Forest, the wife of the innkeeper, would be sweeping the front room of the café.

Despite its calm beginning, March 12 was to be unlike any other day in the history of Chanzeaux. By the middle of the afternoon, a gendarme had dispersed a disorderly crowd milling about the Forest café, just off the square. There René Forest, nephew of the owner, had rallied the young men of the town to protest the draft that had been scheduled for the end of the week. At the same time, the mayor and the municipal council were meeting at the house of the notaire. They had watched the restlessness of the young men grow as the date set for the draft approached, and they feared that the young men would start a pitched battle. An incident earlier in the day had alarmed the town officers. René Forest had broken into the house of one of the town officers and made him hand over the guns he had previously confiscated. Forest left with the guns, swearing that it was time the young men took over the governing of the town. That afternoon, when the crowd at the Forest café was dispersed, the young men split up into groups to scour the surrounding countryside for more guns. They had planned to meet in the evening and compel the officials at gun point to burn the lists of potential draftees.

One group, led by René Forest, captured a town officer in the hamlet of Vauchaumier and forced him to accompany them back to town. At the mill of Chapître they were joined by another band led by Maurice Ragneau. The combined group made its way back to town along the Chapître road. They stopped suddenly as Claude Godelier, a municipal officer, stepped out of the bushes and told them to "disperse in the name of the law." Someone shouted, "Fire!" and three shots rang out. Godelier fell, mortally wounded. Maurice Ragneau was blamed for the shooting, but no one knew for certain which young man had fired the first shot of the Vendée Rebellion in Chanzeaux.[1]

By midnight of that day, the young men from Chanzeaux and the surrounding towns had gathered in the Bois de Chemillé to plan further action. They exchanged news of the day's events in Joué, the town next door, and in Cossé and Saint-Florent nearby, where insurgents had also taken over. By Thursday, March 14, a group of several hundred men, led by the peddler Cathelineau, had stormed a republican garrison at Jallais. Within a week the counterrevolution had spread throughout the area bounded by Nantes, La Rochelle, Poitiers, and Angers. The towns of Vihiers, Cholet, Chemillé, Beaupréau, and Saint-Florent were in the hands of the insurgents. By this time the heterogeneous mass of inhabitants, armed with ordinary working tools, pitchforks, scythes, and an occasional hunting gun, had found leaders in the nobles d'Elbée and Bonchamps, and in Cathelineau. They called themselves "the Catholic and Royal army," and it was by this title that the people outside the Mauges came to know them. The gap seems great between a group of disorganized young men trying to avoid the draft and a disciplined army fighting for the re-establishment of religion and the monarchy. But the change was illusory, as local patriots who called their rivals "brigands" knew. The men could not be drilled and disciplined in a matter of weeks: they took leaves to go home and work on the farm, to see their wives, to tend their affairs. In Chanzeaux, although the young men were fine combatants, they seemed to have best enjoyed a nonmilitary incident that took place shortly after the outbreak of the rebellion: they seized and banqueted gleefully in the home of the hated republican, Coustard.[2]

Nevertheless, the Vendeans, as they were now known, were experts in guerrilla warfare. For six months the republican troops sent against them were baffled by the tactics of men fighting in their home country, the impenetrable bocage. By the end of 1793 the republicans had effectively destroyed the Vendée army, but sporadic conflicts were to continue through 1795. The republican troops came through Chanzeaux several times. At each visit more men, women, and children were killed. The town of Chanzeaux itself never again reached its pre-Revolution population (see graph). Over a third of the people, 700 of 1,800, emigrated or were killed between 1793 and 1795. Of 100 houses in the bourg, only 21 were left standing.

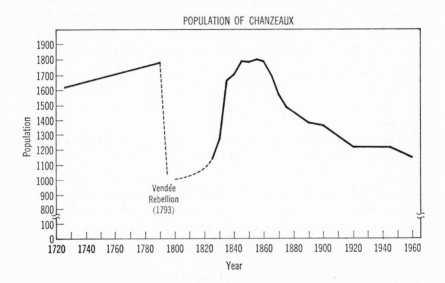

Who were the Vendeans, and what were they fighting for? More than a century and a half after the event, these questions are by no means answered. Both the republicans and the Vendeans have had their partisans among French historians, for the issues of the counter-revolution did not die when the rebellious territory was pacified. In recent years, however, studies have appeared that for the first time elevate the Vendée Rebellion from polemic to social history. Paul Bois and Charles Tilly have rediscovered the regional differences in economy, urbanization, and power structure that prepared the terrain for war, and the class conflicts that did so much to precipitate it.[3] It is unlikely, of course, that the Vendean guerrillas thought in terms of these abstractions. The conflicts that resulted in counterrevolution were first played out within each village as personal antagonisms, and the first outbreaks of war everywhere were acts of personal vengeance.

Let us turn, then, to Chanzeaux on the eve of the Revolution, in an effort to discover how the announcement of a draft might precipitate civil war.

The Neighborhood

The republican foot soldier, making his journal entry as he stopped just beyond Chanzeaux, needed no special perspicacity to perceive that the Mauges "cow country" was very different from the Saumurois. The rich open fields and vineyards of the Saumurois bespoke an important and prosperous agricultural economy. Eighteenth-century Dutch traders came up the Loire to buy wine. The other agricultural products of the region, wheat and hemp, were also sold on the national market. Rich abbeys, the first civilizers of the region, efficiently cultivated extensive tracts of land, while legions of peasant proprietors worked small vineyards around villages and towns. Population centers spread out along important roads.

In contrast to the Saumurois, life in the Mauges was rude and poor. Inferior soil and small enclosed fields restricted the farms to subsistence levels. Here were no large population centers, but only fragments of villages, hamlets, and isolated farms. Devoid of natural resources, the Mauges offered few rewards to enterprising nobles or bourgeois. There was a modestly developed cottage industry in linen centered in Cholet,[4] but linen and the cattle of the Mauges were the only products traded with other regions of France.

Potential investors, visitors, and eventually the republican army were discouraged by the lack of highways and other means of transportation. This crucial difference between the Mauges and the Saumurois can be seen on the maps of the period. The prosperous regions of France lay along rivers, the major routes of trade, but the Mauges had not a single navigable river. Furthermore, no sizable roads had been constructed within its boundaries. The fate of the Mauges is graphically shown on the General Map of Post Roads of 1785. A main artery runs from Paris to Angers for the coaches carrying passengers and mail between Paris and the provinces. For passengers who wished to continue south of Angers, the coach proceeded by a circuitous route. To arrive at Oulmes in the south, for example, the coaches skirted the Mauges, turning either to Poitiers in the east, traveling through the Saumurois, or to Nantes in the west. The one important highway through the Mauges, the Angers-Cholet road, was so inferior to other regional routes that the excellent maps and Cassini atlases of the epoch usually omit it. Since the mail had to go through, it was along this road that it traveled, not by coach but by courier on horseback.

Chanzeaux lies on the border between the Mauges and the Saumurois, and its system of agriculture, containing elements of both regions, gave it a distinct character. Wheat, a cash crop for the large markets, was a primary crop in the Saumurois. Rye, used for making poorer dark bread consumed at home or sold in the local market, was grown in the Mauges. All in all, Chanzeaux grew slightly more wheat than rye, in this striking respect resembling the Saumurois. On the other hand, the greater part of Chanzeaux land was devoted to pasture and grain and not, as in the Saumurois, to vines. The northeast corner of Chanzeaux, one sixth of the land, was planted in vines, but, according to an examiner's report in 1789, it produced wine of only "passable quality."

Despite the apparent ambiguity of Chanzeaux's agricultural position, it was a commune more closely tied to the Mauges than to the Saumurois. Personal contacts, markets, and marriages created a community of interest between Chanzeaux and the Mauges towns. When the Revolution drew a mixed response from the people of southern Anjou, Chanzeaux threw in its lot with the insurgent villages. It was the paucity of natural resources which determined that Chanzeaux's principal relations should be with the Mauges. The parish supplied only its own food, most of its own fuel, and its basic building material — the soft, low-grade stone mortared with mud. The few woods in the parish certainly could not provide timber for beams, or even large logs for heating. A report of the church council listed among the expenses for the year 1774, "six cartloads of wood taken from the forest of Joué for heating church buildings." Smaller timber for carts, barrels, and farm implements also had to be imported. A report on the economy of Chanzeaux in 1789 reveals that the town had no textile factory, no iron mill or lime kiln, and no means for establishing them.

This natural poverty forced the artisans of Chanzeaux to seek raw material outside the parish. The plowmaker, the blacksmith, the nailmaker, and the locksmith needed iron. The chandler had to import his tallow, and the ropemaker his hemp. Since very little flax was grown here, the weavers also had to go elsewhere to get their supplies.

Most of these raw materials, as well as limestone and slate, could be obtained in the vicinity of Chalonnes. To arrive in that town, ten miles to the northwest in the Loire Valley, the Chanzeans passed along the main commercial thoroughfare of the Mauges, the road from Chalonnes to Vihiers. It was undoubtedly with this fact in mind that the Chanzeans demanded in 1789 that the road be made practicable, "in order to export chalk, coal, flax, hemp, slate, limestone, iron, and grain to Poitou." [5]

Economic activity was by no means restricted to the environs of the village, but the preponderance of trading and transporting was carried on with the Mauges. A handful of thread merchants supervised a busy textile production, making thread and yarn and weaving it into wool and linen cloth; their work supported a considerable inflow of flax and wool, and an outflow of finished cloth to the textile centers of Chemillé and Cholet. Merchants might also hope to sell their products at seasonal fairs or markets. Many towns like Chanzeaux held a yearly fair lasting one or two weeks; others held weekly or monthly markets, such as Chemillé's cattle market.

Merchants were not the only people to travel beyond Chanzeaux. Occupational opportunities encouraged many young men to migrate; job and government obligations forced other Chanzeans to make at least short trips away from home. Apprentices followed their trade, and seasonal workers followed the crops. A certain number of *domestiques* moved from their own towns to others: these were usually young men who worked temporarily for a farmer in exchange for room and board. They often found work in neighboring parishes, stayed to marry a local girl, and eventually took over the farm on their own account. Apprentices to craftsmen were equally mobile and willing to become master craftsmen in an adopted parish. Seasonal hands often worked in several parishes. Even the substantial tenant farmers of wealthy proprietors might be called on to help with the harvest on one of the proprietor's farms in another parish. The corvée, that hated obligation of all peasants to work a few days at repairing state roads, might take a farmer several miles from his home. Although they complained that their own roads were in sore need of repair, the Chanzeans were forced to fulfill the corvée of 1785 on a road near Brissac, eight miles away — and, worse, a road little used for the trade of Chanzeaux itself. With few exceptions, this economic activity was contained within the boundaries of the Mauges. These connections, of course, encouraged more lasting ties: the inhabitants of Chanzeaux often married into the Mauges. Laborers and apprentices moved into a neighboring parish and stayed.[6] Fairs, church outings, and group cooperation at harvests and vendages introduced the youth of various parishes.

More than half the marriages of Chanzeans in the decade preceding the Vendée Rebellion involved a spouse from another parish.[7] A familiar pattern emerges when we look at these marriages. The "outsiders" come mainly from the contiguous parishes, particularly Saint-Lambert, Thouarcé, Beaulieu, and Chemillé, in that order. Unfortunately the parish registers do not specify the location of the homes of the bride and the groom within the parish. It is likely, though, that people who married into other parishes lived near the Chanzeaux border of these parishes. Thus the inhabitants of the wine villages would tend to marry people in Beaulieu, Thouarcé, and Rablay; the people on the southern border would marry the inhabitants of Chemillé.[8] When a Chanzean took a spouse who lived more than ten miles from the bourg of Chanzeaux, the "outsider" was invariably from the Mauges, never the Saumurois. This leaning toward the Mauges is repeated in the list of witnesses to weddings in Chanzeaux. Even when the bride and groom were both natives of Chanzeaux, their list of witnesses almost always included relatives living in other parishes. Over 20 percent of their siblings, 15 percent of their aunts and uncles, and 30 percent of their cousins were not residents of Chanzeaux. Most of them lived in contiguous parishes; several were from the Mauges; none lived in the Saumurois. This information would suggest that immigration and emigration followed the same lines.

Thus, by virtue of the ties of kin and commerce, Chanzeaux belonged to the neighborhood of the Mauges. A common economic structure further strengthened these personal ties.

Land and Farming

In 1790 Blondel de Rye, the curé of Chanzeaux, reported that the terrain of his parish was "mountainous, unproductive, and sterile in great part." Although Blondel exaggerated (the land is hardly mountainous), there is truth in his statement. Chanzeaux lies in a region of rolling hills, where bluffs and steep slopes rise above the Hyrôme stream, and small ravines lead off from this valley. The slopes, too difficult to cultivate, were left to the yellow broom flower and an occasional hardy sheep. Most of the flat land was cultivated, but farmers complained that some areas were too difficult or too boggy for their teams. It is impossible to determine exactly how much land was actively cultivated; but whatever the figure, it must be divided by three. The wasteful system of *jachère*, crop rotation in which the land was left fallow for two years out of three, drastically reduced the amount of land cultivated in any one year.

Although the land of the parish was assessed by an impartial observer in 1789 as "good enough," the generalization is not very helpful. The large number of sheep suggests that much of the land was quite poor. On the other hand, we know that the northeast corner along the Layon produced acceptable wine, even if the soil and exposure were inferior to those of other Layon communities. The remaining land resembled that of the Mauges, fairly poor soil lacking in lime and other important minerals. Although farmers did use manure as fertilizer, they were limited by the number of cattle they could raise. In order to improve their yields they needed more manure, which meant more cattle, which required more fodder that only fertilizer could produce. Without chemical fertilizers, this vicious circle was unbreakable.

Yields, then, were limited; and sale of crops outside the commune was further hampered by the uncertainty of roads and the difficulties of storage. It is mistaken, of course, to imagine that the village operated on an absolute subsistence economy. Even with a poor wheat crop in the worst years, the farmer might sell two or three head of cattle at the Chemillé market. Still, these sales were incidental to the primary business of farming: to provide food for a family, and to keep the farm going for another year. No Chanzean could depend so heavily on the market as the farmers of the Saumurois plains could.

The land of Chanzeaux was unevenly divided into large farms of 35 to 120 acres, smaller farms of 4 to 25 acres, and scattered fields. Only a few of the smallest farms were worked by the person who owned them. Instead, the farmers rented them for periods of five, seven, or nine years.

The *métairie* was the largest and most important type of farm. The sixty or so métairies of Chanzeaux covered slightly more than half of the 7,500 acres of the parish, and represented about three fifths of the arable land. Consisting of a bloc of fields attached to and usually surrounding an isolated farmhouse, the average métairie of Chanzeaux was composed of about 50 acres of fields and 10 acres of meadows.

Although the métairie has often been associated with sharecropping in other areas of France, the rent in Chanzeaux consisted of a fixed amount of cash and produce. Just before the Revolution, the métayer of La Haute Lande paid the owner 330 livres in cash, 160 bushels of wheat, 8 bushels of rye, 2 hens, and 3 pounds of thread. In addition he agreed to carry two loads of goods to a place specified by the owner. The métayer of the smaller Basse Lande paid only 45 livres and 8 bushels of rye. In addition to these rents, each métayer agreed to keep the land "en bon père de famille," making necessary repairs, trimming the hedges, and maintaining the ditches along them. Although he was required to plant a number of fruit trees each year, the métayer was not permitted to chop trees down.

The size of the métairie required that the farmer work with a team of oxen. Indeed, it was not unusual for a métayer to own eight oxen: two working pairs, one pair too young to work, and another being fattened up for the market. Since the animals and their harnesses and equipment represented a large outlay of capital, only fairly wealthy farmers could afford to work métairies. In other areas of France, notably the Gâtine Poitivine on the southern border of the Mauges, few farmers could afford such an outlay; instead they rented their teams and equipment from enterprising nobles and cattle merchants, who took advantage of the métayers' poverty to keep them in debt. The métayers of Chanzeaux, on the other hand, owned their own oxen and equipment. Called *laboureurs* because they labored the land with oxen, these farmers of large métairies were the richest of the farming community.

The houses attached to the smaller farms of 4 to 25 acres were located in villages and hamlets, never in isolated spots. These small farms called *closeries* (more rarely, *borderies*) consisted of the usual combination of fields and meadows. Just how many closeries there were in Chanzeaux is uncertain, but their number probably equaled that of the métairies. The rent for a closerie was relatively small and often restricted to a cash payment of 25 to 50 livres. With less land to work, the closiers were definitely less prosperous than the métayers and rarely possessed their own oxen and heavy equipment. The farmers who worked the smallest closeries and those who worked scattered fields were hard pressed to earn a living. Many of them were artisans as well as farmers, and those who had no other trade were often forced to work as *journaliers* (seasonal or day laborers).

In a class apart from these farmers were the *vignerons* who lived in the northeast corner of the parish. Leading a life very different from that of the ordinary farmer, the vignerons of Chanzeaux resembled more the vintners in the neighboring towns of Rablay and Beaulieu. They lived in the villages of La Jutière, La Brosse, and Doua. Although the vignerons, too, mainly rented their land, for a comparably small amount of land they received much greater yields.

These various farmers shared one common feature: almost all leased the land that they worked. Most of the land was owned by nobles, professional men, merchants, craftsmen, or religious orders, each group owning a characteristic type of land or farm. The nobles owned almost all the métairies; the religious orders, principally the mills; the professional men, merchants, and craftsmen owned most of the closeries, the scattered fields, and the vineyards of Chanzeaux. But land ownership was not so simple as this listing might imply, for these owners were themselves tenants of the seigneurs and religious orders that had once settled the region. All the land in Chanzeaux belonged to one or another of these large seigneuries.

Let us look at the *châtellanie* of Chanzeaux in 1789. Covering half the land in Chanzeaux, the estate had its seat in the chateau of Chanzeaux. The seigneur of Chanzeaux was patron of the parish and possessed certain honorific rights — those of hunting and of fishing in the Hyrôme, and the right to receive communion ahead of others. More lucrative rights included the right to require certain tenants to bring grain to be ground in his mill, the right to try the crimes and cases concerning his tenants, a tax levied on wine and merchandise sold at Chanzeaux's annual fair, and a certain tax on all transactions involving land in his domain.

The pecuniary benefits of the possession of the estate of Chanzeaux were small. While the seigneur paid 379 bushels of grain to the County of Chemillé, the Barony of Bohardy, and several religious orders, he received only twice that much grain from all his tenants. The seigneur of Chanzeaux had gradually lost control of his land over the centuries: rents converted into money payments at the end of the sixteenth century had lost all their value by the middle of the eighteenth. For example, for a bloc of several fields the seigneur received "seven sous, two chickens, one hen, and a day of work during the harvest." What rents had remained substantial by 1767 were amortized by the tenants; that is, the tenant paid the seigneur a fixed lump of cash in return for which his rent was reduced to a few sous per year. Over the centuries these tenants had gained the right to buy and sell the land as they wished, paying the seigneur only a small fee for the transaction. In this way the tenants were able to work their farms with a minimum of interference from their landlords.

In 1769 the seigneur of Chanzeaux, Guy Poulain de Brétignolles, sold the estate of Chanzeaux, including the title of seigneur and all the dues and honorific rights, to his chief tenant, Jacques-François Gourreau. Former mayor of Angers, Gourreau was a member of an old, but lesser, noble family with a town house in Angers. This purchase united the honorary titles of the seigneur and the actual possession of the land, thus re-creating an eighteenth-century equivalent of the former power of the lord. It soon became obvious, however, that M. Gourreau was interested in Chanzeaux land only as an investment. He continued to buy métairies in the parish, concentrating his holdings there, until he owned more land in Chanzeaux than any other individual. Only rarely, however, did he stay at his "chateau," which was little more than a hunting lodge.

Religious orders, which had once owned perhaps a sixth of the land in the village, had lost their control of the land in much the same fashion as the seigneur of Chanzeaux had. The abbess of Ronceray, the head of a powerful religious order located in Angers, had thus turned over to her tenants all practical control of the vinelands in the northeastern section of Chanzeaux. But several small religious orders had retained direct control of the mills that they had founded along the Hyrôme.

The pattern of land tenure in Chanzeaux reflected the wider pattern of the Mauges. Like Gourreau, the noble and ecclesiastical landlords of that region were absentees who had little to do with the life of the communities in which they held the predominant share of the land.

The local professional men and merchants, on the other hand, took a more active interest in the lands of their own villages. Their share of the holdings was not inconsiderable — perhaps 20 percent would be a fair estimate — and they undoubtedly wanted to own much more. In general, they were excluded from the largest and most profitable type of farm, the métairies, which the nobles kept in their own hands.

Their acquisitions were restricted to the closeries and vineyards in the parish and the many scattered fields. Charles Fougeray the chandler, for example, owned a house in the bourg, many plots of vines and parcels of land both in Chanzeaux and in Saint-Lambert, half the métairie of Tremblaye, and two closeries. He leased these scattered but extensive holdings to five farmers. Similarly, the notary, the doctor, the more prosperous artisans, the millers, and the merchants were landlords to the poorer farmers of their parish.

Village Elites

The small minority of Chanzeans who did not work the land but who sought to acquire it were set apart from their fellow villagers in several ways. They had greater contact with the neighboring cities and towns than most farmers — the tradesmen by virtue of their commerce, the professional men by virtue of their education. Conscious of their position as intermediaries between the village and the greater world outside, they tended to consider themselves a group apart. They lived in the bourg rather than the countryside, married their children to the children of other professionals and tradesmen, and aspired to the dignity of the bourgeois. Many imitated the bourgeois of the cities by prefacing their names with the title "sieur."

It would be a great mistake, however, to consider this group homogeneous. No villager in 1789 would have considered Sieur Bureau, miller at Le Point, or Sieur Fougeray, chandler of the bourg, in the same class as Sieur Coustard, notary. Wealth alone could not fully account for the difference, for certainly the miller and the chandler were among the most prosperous men in the village. Bureau employed no fewer than ten domestiques to run his mill, and Fougeray was, as we have seen, a substantial landowner as well as a craftsman. What distinguished them from the professional men was the range of their outside contacts. The millers and merchants were a more or less indigenous elite. Generally natives of Chanzeaux, they tended to marry and remain within the village. The families at the mills along the Hyrôme, for instance, were almost all interrelated. Pierre Bureau was married to a Blanchard girl, whose family ran three of the mills. The Bureaus and Blanchards were still millers in Chanzeaux fifty years later, and some of their descendants are there yet. The professional men, on the other hand, often came to the village from outside, married outside, and traveled outside.

Jean-Nicolas Coustard was Chanzeaux's only notary. Born in Chanzeaux, he followed in the footsteps of his father, who had been notary before him. He had married well, and his wife was known for the charity she gave to the needy parishioners. As *notaire royal*, he drew up most of the legal contracts in Chanzeaux: land sales, rent contracts, marriage contracts, guardianship papers. Coustard had many additional duties. He served as agent for the abbey of Ronceray and the seigneurie of La Tarpinière, which held land in Chanzeaux and most of the contiguous parishes. Just after the Revolution, he became judge of the canton of Chanzeaux. Thus from his several jobs Coustard knew more about the personal affairs of his fellow citizens than anyone else but the curé. His intimate knowledge of land transactions in the parish had undoubtedly helped him to amass the considerable amount of land he owned.

The only other professional men in Chanzeaux in the eighteenth century were the *chirurgiens*, who, like the notary, had a city education. With less training than doctors, the chirurgiens nevertheless performed the functions of doctors in rural areas. There were three chirurgiens in Chanzeaux on the eve of the Revolution — a master and two younger men who had come to Chanzeaux to establish a practice. One of the latter was Claude Godelier, son of a master chirurgien in Saint-Lambert and an important landholder there. The family had followed the same profession for generations; Claude's brother practiced in Saint-Lambert, and his uncle in Gonnord. Coustard and Godelier were to become the staunchest supporters of the Revolution — which brought them to unprecedented power in the village — and the first victims of the counterrevolution.

Power Structure

Although the "sieurs" of Chanzeaux possessed social prestige and respectable wealth, compared with the priest Blondel and the seigneur Gourreau they wielded little political power. M. Gourreau, by virtue of his position as landlord of the largest farmers, was potentially the most powerful individual in the parish. As seigneur of Chanzeaux he had a certain moral obligation to intercede for his parishioners with the government. Thus when the parish assembly wished to rebuild a bridge over the Hyrôme, it was Gourreau who lent them the money and also wrote to the intendant asking for government aid. In most local affairs, however, Gourreau showed little interest. A city man, used to city ways, Gourreau and his family lived in Angers and rarely came to Chanzeaux.

That the local affairs of Chanzeaux should seem unimportant to a noble who had been mayor of the provincial capital is understandable. Yet the central government seemed equally uninterested in the parishes of the Mauges. The poverty of the area, its lack of large cities, the inadequate means of communication — all help to explain this administrative neglect. To be sure, an administrative framework existed, even in the Mauges. Chanzeaux, for example, belonged to several overlapping districts; the generality of Tours, the province of Anjou, the bureau of Brissac, and the "grenier de sel" (salt-tax area) of Cholet. Yet the government officials responsible for these areas simply did not penetrate as far as Chanzeaux. For the administration of parish affairs they relied upon the curé and upon the offices of the *huissier*, and *notaire royal*, all of which were purchased by local inhabitants. The office of tax collector proved so unpopular that the assembly was forced to elect a collector for the salt and other taxes every two years. The tax collectors of Chanzeaux complained that it was impossible to collect the village's prescribed quota and that they were always forced to pay the deficit out of their own pockets.

The notaire and the huissier were the only permanent government positions in the parish. More than a simple constable, the huissier was a kind of sheriff, delivering writs and seeing that court orders were enacted. He was invariably present at parish assemblies, and his name appears as witness on all important documents. The name from 1770 to 1787 was that of François Picherit. In a parish where only one third of the men could sign their own names, Picherit wrote with a flowing hand. A capable person, he also assumed the post of *procureur fiscal* of the seigneurie of Chanzeaux, taking charge of seigneurial dues and keeping the accounts of the seigneurial tenants. He gained his living managing the lands of an absentee landlord in Chanzeaux. When François Picherit died in 1787, it was natural that the position should pass to his son Julien. Although the position effectively disappeared two years later with the Revolution, Julien was by then able to assume new posts that the Revolution had created.

The huissier, though important, was not so prominent as the notaire. M. Coustard possessed considerable power from his combined positions as *notaire royal* and *procureur fiscal* of several seigneuries.

He served also as judge of the seigneurie of Chanzeaux until he was appointed judge of the canton of Chanzeaux in 1790.

Coustard and Picherit were able partially to fill the power vacuum left by the lack of administrative controls. There was a similar vacuum in the ecclesiastical sector of Chanzeaux life, this one completely filled by the local curé, Blondel de Rye, who in the process also assumed some of the power and influence that the judicial leaders failed to grasp. With the help of two *vicaires* (curates) the curé governed the parish without paying much attention to subtle distinctions between his role and Caesar's. In truth, the government almost invited the curé to assume the two roles: if there was a government edict, Chanzeans first heard about it when their curé read it to them from the pulpit. The word of God and of king was revealed by one man, and he was appropriately respected.

By the outbreak of the Revolution, Blondel had been an integral part of the community for over a generation, having come to Chanzeaux in 1760 from a small town in northern Anjou. Over the years Blondel had come to know the Chanzeans better than any other man in town. He heard confession, officiated at Sunday and weekday Mass, and performed most of the parish's forty-five or so baptisms a year, an equal number of funerals, and about ten marriages. He led the special processions on festival days, such as the day of St. Fiacre, Chanzeaux's patron saint.

His administrative chores were equally important. He appointed the midwife, supervised the parish school, presided over the parish assembly. He kept the parish registers — the record of the birth, marriage, and death of every inhabitant in Chanzeaux. Because of his administrative ability and his position of trust, many Chanzeans named him executor of their wills. When a Chanzean had business with the central government, it was the curé who served as liaison. In affairs of general importance to the region, it was again Blondel who represented Chanzeaux. When the inhabitants of the towns bordering the Layon River sent a letter to their intendant protesting its canalization, Blondel signed it, along with important government officials.

Another function of the curé was the administration of charity, for he was expected to use part of his salary to dispense alms to the poor. Since his salary was largely in kind, this meant that he too shared in the good and bad fortunes of his parishioners. In 1791 the inhabitants reported only four old people who were forced to live entirely by charity; yet the curé helped many more. He lent money and grain, gave bread to the sick, poor, and aged. He helped to support a widow left with many children and advanced a farmer grain to plant his field after a poor harvest. Blondel's personal qualities admirably qualified him as spiritual and temporal governor of the parish. For his position and his ability he was respected; for his dedication he was revered. The story was often repeated how, when an epidemic struck the village in 1769, he had worked tirelessly to care for the sick. During the first years of the Revolution, his fame was to spread beyond the village to the borders of the Mauges.

The parishioners of Chanzeaux participated in the affairs of the community through the church. All heads of family were eligible to take part in the parish assembly and the *fabrique* (vestry). Theoretically these were separate institutions. The fabrique was supposed to concern itself with the material interests of the church — its property and buildings — while the parish assembly was to deal with matters of more general interest. In practice, however, the heads of family met together after Sunday Mass to perform both functions. On a busy Sunday the priest might call on them to settle such questions as rents on church property, the ordering of a new confessional, the sale of flax given to the church, repairs to the church, upkeep of the parish roads, and arrangements for Chanzeaux's annual fair. For an affair requiring intercession with the intendant, the regional governor, the curé would draw up a letter that all those present then signed.

The parish of Chanzeaux, then, was at once a religious and a political unit, a miniature theocracy. The limited affairs that were considered a matter of common interest were settled in common, under the leadership of the curé. Blondel was thus virtual governor of a village that the larger government neglected. The Revolution was to put an end to this neglect and, in time, to the rule of Blondel.

Revolution and Rebellion

In 1787, in the course of reorganization of the provincial government of Anjou, all parish assemblies were replaced by municipal assemblies. The parishioners of Chanzeaux continued to refer to "the assembly" and saw little difference in the way they were governed, since the priest was an automatic member of the new assembly. In fact, the change in the governing body was very real. No longer was the parish government to be made up of all heads of families: it was to be composed of representatives elected from among those who could meet certain property qualifications. Participation in the communal affairs of the village, previously open to all, was for the first time formally limited on the basis of wealth.

The membership of Chanzeaux's new governing body could have surprised no one. The municipal assemblymen were the substantial and the respectable, the *responsables*. Of the ten members, six were dignified with the title "sieur." One of the ten, M. Cresteau de la Motte, was a bourgeois of Angers who spent little time in the village; the others, probably all residents of Chanzeaux, included Pierre Bureau the miller, Charles Fougeray the chandler, and Jean-Nicolas Coustard the notary.

Late in 1789, the municipal assemblies were in turn replaced by municipal councils, and new elections were held. Eligibility for both candidacy and voting was again restricted by a property qualification. In Chanzeaux, the most prominent members of the assembly were returned to office, and other substantial citizens were elected to join them. Jean-Pierre Blond the locksmith was a man to be trusted, since he had a key to every cabinet and chest in town. Julien Blanchard took a place on the council beside his brother-in-law, Bureau. Also elected were Julien Picherit the huissier, Pierre Forest the innkeeper, and Claude Godelier the new chirurgien. These were the men who made up a government that no one suspected would be different from the old one. But the very fact of separation of the powers of the commune from the powers of the parish implicitly threatened the position of the curé. In the next two years, this threat was to be realized.

The first major problem the council faced was economic. In the face of poor harvests it was the duty of the council to reimplement old taxes, restrict wheat transportation, and regulate the activities of the millers. Within the town council a particularly zealous minority led by Coustard was singled out as being responsible for these unpopular measures. Later Coustard was chosen to be the justice of the peace of the area around Chanzeaux, an appointment that made him a government agent. Although he could hardly be blamed for accepting a post for which he was well qualified, his performance at the sale of church lands made even such innocent acts seem blameworthy.

The sale of church lands, suggested by many of the *cahiers de doléances*, offered the revolutionary government an excellent source of revenue to bolster its finances. All the property of the church, secular and monastic, in every part of France, was to be confiscated. It was the responsibility of the municipal council to draw up a list of all such property, stating its approximate value. There seems to have been no disturbance in Chanzeaux when the list was made public in 1790.[9] The lack of opposition in Chanzeaux is understandable, since the *soumission* did not represent a direct attack on the community. The land was taken from monasteries and orders such as the Chapter of St. Leonard de Chemillé and the Chapel of St. Denis, which were based outside the community. Only a small portion of the curé's lands was cited, and this accounted for only 3,000 livres of the total 60,000. The religious orders owned métairies and mills and large tracts of land, while the curé owned only scattered bits of *terre, pré,* and *vigne*. Men like Blond and Fougeray, who later became ardent Vendeans, could sign the soumission with no qualms, since they could reason that the only losers would be the rich and corrupt religious orders. They probably hailed a move that took land from strangers and offered it to the inhabitants of the town.

When the land was put up for sale in the following year, Chanzeans noticed that more lands were included than the 1790 list had indicated, especially more of Blondel's lands. The sale of these properties particularly alienated the townspeople, perhaps because of their affection for the curé, perhaps also for more material reasons. The curé's lands were in small parcels, which many Chanzean farmers might have hoped to buy. Their hopes were disappointed, for Godelier and Coustard, who had been appointed commissioners for the sale of church lands, also took part in the bidding and buying. Their inside position clearly gave them the advantage, and they made use of it to acquire the most valuable plots. Others, outsiders, who bought large métairies were not condemned at the time, but these few patriots had offended by snapping up the choice bits of land from under the noses of the farmers. Less than two weeks after the second period of land sales, the electors of the district met in Vihiers to name replacements for the curés who had refused to swear an oath of allegiance to the revolutionary government. Chanzeaux was among twenty-five out of the forty-three communes in the district that had nonjuring priests. Among those who nominated Blondel's replacement was Coustard, *procureur fiscal* of Chanzeaux, commissioner and purchaser of church lands. It must have seemed a mockery to the more religious people of

Chanzeaux that, instead of the bishop, men like Coustard should select their next priests. The nominee, M. Chatelain, refused to accept the position of curé of Chanzeaux, as did the five succeeding nominees.

As the weeks went by, more and more nonjuring priests were replaced by "constitutional" curés. In many cases the new men did not have the qualifications of their predecessors. Curés and vicaires were brought in from other parishes, especially from the Saumurois region, which was the only area with an excess of juring priests. As Blondel became more and more an anomaly, people from the neighboring parishes began to flock to Chanzeaux for the Masses of this venerable curé. At the same time, a sort of priests' underground was formed in the neighboring commune of La Jumellière. The vicaires of the neighborhood became the leaders of this movement, whose aim was to provide traditional Masses, baptisms, burials, and marriages for the loyal inhabitants. Chanzeaux became one of the focal points of these activities, which have left their traces on the parish registers. From February 7 to March 20, 1792, for instance, five women "visiting friends" or "passing a few days in Chanzeaux with their families" gave birth to children who were subsequently baptized by Blondel. The five women all came from different communities around Chanzeaux, in each of which a disturbance had occurred because the regular priest had been replaced with a constitutional curé.[10] The women evidently came to Chanzeaux when they knew they were due to give birth, so that their children might be baptized by Blondel.

By early 1792 the group of perhaps a dozen men, led by Coustard, had been identified with the most unpopular aspects of the Revolution. As a result, Bureau, Fougeray, and Blanchard were returned to the council in that year, but Coustard and his band were excluded. In a letter to the district commissioners in April of 1792, Coustard and four others described themselves as "the only men in town faithful to the government."[11] They blamed Blondel for the unrest in the parish and demanded his removal from Chanzeaux as the only way of quieting popular discontent. Blondel, now the only priest in the area who had not been replaced by a republican curé, had become a rallying point for all the dissatisfied elements of the region. From many towns in the Mauges, people came to hear Blondel's sermons. Since support for a curé who had refused to swear the oath of allegiance to the government was an open defiance of government orders, these processions had a clear political character.

Blondel was removed from office two days after the secret letter was sent by Coustard. If anyone had any doubts about the identity of Blondel's opposition, the ambiguity was soon removed when Coustard and his friends actively supported Blondel's replacement, a republican curé. When all the rest of the inhabitants shunned the church, they attended his Masses. When the sacristan resigned rather than serve a government appointee, two of Coustard's friends took over the office. The new curé praised them for "their knowledge, their piety, their patriotism, their gentleness," and for the courage they displayed in exposing themselves to "the nasty looks and perhaps the hatred of the majority of their fellow citizens." Although the townspeople of Chanzeaux threatened the soldiers who came to arrest their priest, there was no violence on the day that Blondel was led away. The curé did not give the signal for rebellion; that signal awaited younger, more reckless leaders, and an incident that involved the neighboring communities as well as Chanzeaux.

Coustard and his men were out of power at the time the curé was removed; they were soon reinstalled, against the will of the majority. In November 1792 another election was called, in which only those who swore allegiance to the republican government were allowed to stand as candidates. Since Bureau and all the moderates refused to swear the oath, the elections saw the return to power of Coustard, Godelier, Picherit, and ten other patriots, including the new sacristans, both of whom worked for Coustard as his secretary and his assessor. Although now in command of the local government, Coustard and his friends had already lost effective control over their fellow citizens. The November elections excluded just those moderate Vendeans who might have prevented conflict. Perhaps the elders of the village would not have resorted to armed combat, but their sons had no such scruples; and now the elders had no more voice in the town than their sons. A resistance group was organized around two young deserters from the republican army: René Forest and Charles Fougeray. These two young men urged defiance of the draft scheduled in all the towns of the Mauges for March 12, 1793. In neighboring communes, similar bands were being organized. The date of conscription thus set the date of the rebellion.

Although this protest precipitated the outbreak of the Vendée war in Chanzeaux, after the first days of the insurrection the draft was never mentioned again. Only 25 men, at the most, were threatened —

a small fraction of the 160 young men of draft age.[12] There had been drafts before that had occasioned no violence. The source of the young men's apprehension thus went deeper than a mere aversion to the draft. They were an integral part of the Vendée Rebellion. It was their youth that precipitated the explosive incident and made compromise impossible. But the towns had already been split, along personal, social, and economic lines, by the legislation of the Revolution.

The removal of Blondel, the sale of church lands, the deportation of the nonjuring priests, the installation of the constitutional priests: all the unpopular aspects of the revolution had been attributed to a small group of loyalists. The inhabitants of Chanzeaux, used to working out their own problems with no interference from the outside, saw the developing conflict in terms of the personalities of the leaders of their town. Thus the Revolution divided the inhabitants much as they had once been earlier divided in their attitude toward the outside world: the more city-oriented men became loyalists; the men oriented toward the country — the millers and many of the artisans, as well as most farmers — became Vendeans.

Although the Vendée Rebellion was ultimately suppressed, it achieved many of its purposes. The reforms of the Revolution, drastic elsewhere in France, remained a dead letter in the Vendée. The church and gentry lands, which elsewhere found their way into the hands of peasant and bourgeois proprietors, tended in the Vendée to revert to their former owners. In fact, the counterrevolution may have helped to consolidate the nobles' estates in the region. The curé, it is true, never regained the position of power he had enjoyed in the Ancien Régime village. In many of his civil functions he was replaced by the elected town council. But the small, energetic, middle-class element that had briefly monopolized the newly created municipal governments had been definitively banished from power. Finally, the rebellion left the region filled with the language of a holy war. It gave the villages of the Vendée an idiom and an ideology that would last a century.

2

Chanzeaux under Quatrebarbes

In the fifty years following the end of the rebellion that had devastated Chanzeaux, the battle scars of the village healed. Houses were rebuilt, and a new generation grew up to live in them. The population of the village increased — slowly in the first years of recovery and then, in the 1830s, precipitously. By the 1840s, it almost equaled that of prerevolutionary days and was approaching a maximum of 1,800 souls, never to be attained again. A degree of prosperity, too, had returned; every piece of arable land was under cultivation, and at mid-century the town councilors could boast of the varied and bustling activity of the little commune.

The war, however, had left its legacy, to Chanzeaux as to the nation. As long as the Revolution remained the great unsettled issue in national politics, it could not be forgotten in the villages of the Vendée. During the half-century elapsing since the rebellion, the force of outside events had constantly impinged on Chanzeaux to revive memories of the past. Under the Bourbon Restoration, the nobility had returned to demand their old power and privileges, the restoration of their estates and their milliard in indemnities for the property confiscated during the Revolution. In the west, especially in the Vendée, they had been particularly successful in regaining their former properties. Revolutionary land reform, whatever its success elsewhere in France, effectively bypassed the Mauges. The seigneurie of Chanzeaux, which had been confiscated after the Gourreau family emigrated in 1791, had become the property of a notable Vendean family, the Soyers of Saint-Lambert. The lands were promptly restored to the Gourreau family when it returned.

When the July Revolution forced the Bourbons out of power once again, the legitimist nobility withdrew in great numbers to their provincial estates, hoping by this boycott to undermine the regime of the "bourgeois monarch." One such disaffected aristocrat was Count Théodore de Quatrebarbes, a young career officer who, on receiving the news of the abdication of Charles X in 1830, resigned his commission and retired to his native Anjou. Soon after, he married Mlle. Gourreau, thus becoming the heir to the estate of Chanzeaux. In 1832, when the Duchess of Berry attempted to incite the Vendée to arms against Louis-Philippe, Quatrebarbes took part in a conspiracy in her behalf, as did most of the noble families of the region. The rebellion was a notable failure. For his participation in the fiasco, Quatrebarbes received a token prison sentence, and, upon release, he took up residence on the estate of Chanzeaux. There, except for a brief period late in the 1840s when he served as his region's representative in the Chamber of Deputies, he spent the remainder of a long life.

While behind bars, Quatrebarbes began writing a romantic narrative in the style of the provincial historical novels of Walter Scott. In this book, later published under the title *Une Paroisse Vendéenne sous la Terreur,* he recounted the history of his adopted village during the Vendée Rebellion. To Quatrebarbes, that war was not yet over; he was determined not to let the people of Chanzeaux forget it so that, when the time was ripe, they might rise again. The officials of the July Monarchy, however, alarmed by the fitful outbreaks of violence in the Vendée, were equally determined to prevent future uprisings. During the Revolution, the extremely poor communications in that hilly, neglected, hedge-enclosed country had crippled the operations of the republican troops and greatly favored the guerrillas. The restored Bourbons, like their predecessors, had shown little interest in the region that had served them so well, and the roads and bridges in the bocage had remained in a deplorable state. Yet distrust proved a more effective motive than gratitude, and the improvements the Bourbons had denied to the Vendée were accomplished under the regime of the House of Orléans. In the 1840s six major roads were constructed in the arrondissement of Beaupréau, the administrative district corresponding to the Mauges region.[1] It was hoped that these strategic roads would serve not only to render future rebellion impossible, but also to put an end to the spiritual isolation of the bocage country and to reintegrate the area with the rest of France.

Thus outside influences were at work to keep the issues of the Vendée war alive. Whereas the administration attempted to change the political complexion of the region by means of a program of public works and the careful surveillance of prefects, the provincial aristocrats fought to consolidate and preserve the political control of the villages in their territory. The government machinery was powerful, but remote; it could accomplish little against the influence of the noblemen living on their estates, against the local power of men like Quatrebarbes. Like many of his peers, Quatrebarbes devoted his wealth, his unquestioned social position, and the energy of a frustrated military career to the attempt to create, in his village, the image of the Ancien Régime as it existed only in retrospective myth. In *Une Paroisse Vendéenne*, he portrayed Chanzeaux as an idyllic survival of the feudal system, a stable, patriarchal, entirely agrarian community in which peasant and nobleman lived in perfect harmony. Until he died, in 1871, he did everything in his power to make the people of Chanzeaux live in accordance with his ideal.

Land Tenure and Use

The village in which Quatrebarbes was to play the role of feudal lord did retain essential features of life under the Ancien Régime. The land remained the basis of economic life and social structure. The uses of the land, it is true, had changed somewhat in the preceding fifty years. In the Maine-et-Loire, as in France as a whole, the first half of the nineteenth century had seen such agricultural improvements as the clearing of previously uncultivated land and the replacement of the old triennial system of crop rotation with more sophisticated sequences. The spread of such crops as clover, alfalfa, and potatoes permitted the continuous cultivation of fields that had previously lain fallow for one year in every three. Wheat rather than rye had become the most important crop of the department, in terms of both production and consumption, an indication of the relative prosperity of the region.[2]

By the 1840s, probably one fourth to one third of the arable land in Chanzeaux was planted in wheat, in rotation with fodder plants such as clover, potatoes, and turnips. The crop was not, of course, a stranger to the area; under the Ancien Régime, wheat had been grown in Chanzeaux as a cash crop. This increase of wheat production did not imply an increasing dependence on the outside market, for the old distrust of cash crops remained. Instead, wheat had replaced rye as the staple of diet and was grown largely for local consumption. The fodder crops, too, were consumed locally.

In the region of the bocage, it was the introduction of lime as a fertilizer which led to the possibility of cultivating wheat in large areas where it could not have grown previously. By mid-century, the mining of limestone had become a large industry in the area of the confluence of the Loire and Layon rivers. The center of the industry was the town of Chalonnes sur Loire, about ten miles north of Chanzeaux, and lesser mines could be found in several communes that bordered Chanzeaux to the northeast. Quatrebarbes himself invested in a small mine in Saint-Lambert. Chanzeaux, however, had no limestone deposits and was thus obliged to import most of its fertilizer.

The increased use of lime was in turn made possible by the development of roads, and the construction program under the July Monarchy undoubtedly did a great deal to further the progress of agriculture in the Mauges. But because strategic considerations rather than regard for the economic needs of the region had been the primary determinant in the laying out of the roads, the new highways did not always follow already existing currents of trade. Thus although Chalonnes, the source of the much-needed limestone, was more than ever an important commercial center for the entire Mauges region, the roads running south from Chalonnes remained in disrepair. Chanzeaux's main transportation problem, then, had not changed in fifty years. The national highway from Angers to Cholet bypassed the bourg of Chanzeaux, and travel on the local roads was still a doubtful proposition. In 1836, the town council of Chanzeaux met in extraordinary session to request that a departmental road be built from Vihiers to Chalonnes, passing through the bourg of Chanzeaux. Such a road was of the utmost importance, the council declared, because of the "transport of great quantities of fertilizer from the furnaces of St. Lambert, Beaulieu, St. Aubin . . . and Chalonnes, which goes on continually during seven or eight months of the year." Year after year the council repeated its request, in vain. When Quatrebarbes became a member of the Conseil Général of the department, the council enlisted his support for their petition. In order to keep the existing road at least barely passable, the council voted yearly impositions of three days' labor on all property-owners in the commune. Still the road remained in poor condition until 1847, and, as will be seen, it was Quatrebarbes who eventually found the means to improve it.

In spite of the general improvements in the agriculture of the region, the means of exploiting the land had not changed much since the Ancien Régime. Total production had increased, especially under the July Monarchy, but it had not increased radically and the rural population had also grown, absorbing the benefits of improvements in agricultural technology. In the late 1840s, the Maine-et-Loire, like much of rural France, must have been in a situation analogous to that existing at the eve of the Revolution, when population pressure had reached a maximum point. Prices were still unstable, fluctuating from year to year and from region to region, and the specter of local famine had not yet entirely disappeared.[3]

Nowhere was this state of affairs more evident than in the west, and part of the reason lay in the system of land ownership and use. The west (as we have seen) had remained an area of great noble estates. If these consolidated holdings had been exploited as single economic units, the revolution in agriculture might have come to the area much sooner. The owners, however, did not generally supervise the working of the property themselves, even when they lived on their estates. Instead, the lands were divided into medium-sized farms that were rented to a large number of tenant farmers. Although this system provided a rural way of life at a subsistence level for a great many people, in terms of production it was hardly the most efficient form of land utilization. The greatest progress in total production during this period was to be observed in areas of small proprietorship and intense cultivation, like the Loire Valley, or on the few noble estates operated as a unit by their owners. On the large rented estates, increase in production was minimal.

The structure of property in Chanzeaux exemplified that of the region, for the village's three large seigneuries — les Chauvellières, la Berthelottière, and Chanzeaux — had survived the Revolution intact. Quatrebarbes' estate overshadowed all others, with close to 1,200 acres, or almost one sixth of the land in the commune. Count Auguste de Kersabiec of les Chauvellières, Chanzeaux's other resident nobleman, was the second largest proprietor living in the village. Between them, Quatrebarbes and Kersabiec owned about one fifth of the commune.

Nonresident proprietors owned an additional third of the land in Chanzeaux, and again, the largest holdings belonged to members of the nobility. M. de la Perraudière of Angers owned about 300 acres in the village, and M. de la Grandière, the seigneur of la Berthelottière, owned almost 1,000. His property was second in size only to that of Quatrebarbes. Although he was not an official resident of the commune, he probably spent his summers there. His presence is recorded in the minutes of occasional town-council meetings and at special village ceremonies. Two other large estates in contiguous communes, one owned by M. de Caqueray in La Jumellière, the other by M. de la Sayette in Joué-Etiau, cut into Chanzeaux and accounted for another 300 acres. Altogether, half of the land in the village was in the form of large property (holdings of over 100 acres).

The concentration of property appears even more striking if we consider the fact that many of the largest landowners of Chanzeaux were related. La Perraudière was a cousin or nephew of Mme. Prévôt of les Chauvellières, the wife of Count de Kersabiec. De la Sayette was a kinsman of Quatrebarbes and was involved with him in the conspiracy of 1832, as were the families of Kersabiec and de Caqueray.

In short, land tenure in Chanzeaux revealed the overwhelming predominance of the legitimist nobility and was typical of the pattern throughout the bocage. The subprefect of the region, reporting to his superior in 1837, could find little occasion for official optimism. In his estimate, political control of the territory remained a corollary of land ownership, and the nobility still owned the land:

> The political climate has not improved . . . although the region has never been so prosperous. This strange situation is attributable to the ignorance of an ill-disposed clergy, and to the absence of bourgeois property, which puts the people at the mercy of a nobility which is hostile to the government. The fifty to sixty proprietors who compose the nobility of the region are almost all legitimists and were almost all more or less directly involved in our disturbances of 1832.
>
> The worst canton of all is Chemillé, which is dominated by MM. de Caqueray, de Quatrebarbes . . . etc.[4]

Such an absence of bourgeois property was also strikingly evident in Chanzeaux. Only two notable families, the Forests and the Fougerays, held fairly large tracts of land in the commune and lived in the bourg on the income of their land. The Forests, parvenus, owed their fortune to their association with the royalist cause in the Vendée war. The Fougeray family, though better established, seemed to be on the decline. The head of the clan, Pierre Charles Fougeray, who owned over 100 acres in Chanzeaux, had served as mayor of the commune during the Hundred Days. His lack of principle alienated the local nobility, who branded him "un type de caméléon peu commun."

Probably in consequence, the family had lost their position among the town's leading citizens. During the 1840s, no member of the family served on the town council, while the Forests were well represented.

Independent farmers owning an entire viable farm (roughly, a property of 25 to 100 acres) were almost equally rare in Chanzeaux. Only twenty people living in the village in the 1840s owned a farm of this size and, even of these twenty, not all worked their own land. Members of the two notable families, the Forests and the Fougerays, accounted for seven of the owners, and they lived in the bourg as rentiers. Only about ten of the owners were independent farmers (*propriétaires exploitants*). The nonresident owners of properties of this size were bourgeois of neighboring communes or, even more frequently, of Angers. Altogether, medium-sized holdings accounted for a quarter of the land in the commune, a much smaller fraction than that of the large holdings.

Many Chanzeans did own land, but in the form of very small parcels. Over a hundred people owned less than 2.5 acres each, and close to another hundred owned between 2.5 and 25 acres. These plots were large enough to supplement the income of a family, but rarely enough to support it entirely. A large number of people who were not residents of Chanzeaux also owned small scraps of land in the village, but most of them lived in the neighboring communes, probably for the most part near the borders of Chanzeaux. Small proprietors in all held about 18 percent of the land (see Tables 1 and 2).

Table 1. Land Tenure, 1841

Size of holding	No. of resident owners	% of commune owned	No. of nonresident owners	% of commune owned
Small (less than 25 acres)	201	13.4%	89	4.6%
Medium (25–100 acres)	20	11.3	22	16.8
Large (over 100 acres)	3	20.0	8	31.0
	224	44.7%	119	52.4%

Note. Communal land equals 0.1% of indexed total; 2.8% of the indexed total is unaccounted for.

The main economic unit for the exploitation of the land, then, was the rented farm. This system is reflected in the distribution of agricultural occupations (see Table 3).

Table 2. Nonresident Landowners, Land Tenure and Residence, 1841

Residence	Small proprietors (less than 25 acres)	Medium proprietors (25–100 acres)	Large proprietors (over 100 acres)
Neighboring commune	68	7	3
Angers	2	10	4
Other	15	5	0
	85	22	7

Note. Nonresident landowners account for 52.4% of land in the commune.

Table 3. Occupational Breakdown of Active Population, 1851

Occupation	No.
Proprietor	81
Fermier	178
Domestique	169
Journalier	86
Vigneron	32
Herdsman	8
Total agriculture	554 (64.5%)
Artisan	80
Miller	21
Tradesman	35
Rentier	11
Professional man	11
Textile worker	125
Servant	18
Total nonagriculture	301 (35.5%)

Note. Fermier (tenant farmer); domestique (hired hand); journalier (day laborer); vigneron (vintner)—see text for description of terms.

Occupations and Social Hierarchy

The proprietors were a heterogeneous lot, ranging from the big land-owners who lived on the income of their properties to the owners of a tiny house and garden. The few who owned more than 25 acres generally did not farm the properties themselves. Most of those who owned less found it necessary to farm rented land in addition to their own. The main type of agricultural entrepreneur of the village was thus the *fermier* (tenant farmer). Although a certain number of fermiers did own some land of their own in addition to the rented farm, almost always such a holding was insignificant in comparison to the amount of rented land. The average size of a rented farm was between 50 and 75 acres.

Although it was not profitable to operate farms on a smaller scale than 40 or 50 acres, a farm of over 50 acres' size required much more labor than that of the fermier alone. A farmer working 75 acres might require three full-time hands (two men and one woman), plus additional labor at harvest time. For this labor, the fermiers preferred to rely as much as possible on their own families. Thus they tended to have many children and to keep them on the farm as long as they could (see Table 4). Often their sons remained on the farm until well into

Table 4. Family Size and Occupation, 1841

No. of dependents	Fermier	Proprietor	Artisan, shopkeeper, professional	Vigneron	Journalier, textile worker
3 or more	43%	20%	20%	18%	10%
0–2	57%	80%	80%	82%	90%
No. of household heads (married men, widows)	98	50	75	23	148

their twenties, and sometimes one or more sons continued to work on the family farm even after marriage. It was not uncommon to find a two-household farm operated by one patriarchal three-generation family.

Almost always, however, a tenant farmer found it necessary to employ at least one *domestique* (hired hand), and some employed as many as four. The wages of a domestique were relatively low but the job was secure, for he was hired for an entire year and lived on the farm with his employer. A *premier garçon de ferme* earned about 200 francs per year, plus room and board. Domestiques, usually single men and women in their twenties or teens, were the most transient members of the community and the owners of the least land. Being a hired hand was often a temporary stage in life for people who would afterwards find farms of their own. Of the fifty-seven men and women who had been working as domestiques in 1841 and still lived in Chanzeaux ten years later, fewer than half were still working as domestiques. But there were many domestiques, also, who had no hope of finding the necessary capital to rent a farm, whether they stayed in the village or moved elsewhere. These people, when they married, became *journaliers* (day laborers).

Farmers greatly preferred to hire year-round hands than to employ day laborers, and generally turned to the journaliers only during the summer. Hence theirs was the least desirable of all agricultural occupations. Not only were their wages low, but their employment was seasonal. Wages in winter were 90 centimes per day plus meals, or between 1.25 and 1.50 francs without meals. In the summer, wages were higher by 25 to 40 centimes. A day laborer could just about support himself and his wife in seasons of full employment. If he had children, the situation became more uncertain. About one in five day laborers owned a small piece of property, usually no more than a house and garden, with which he could supplement his wages; still, his economic position was precarious. The majority kept their families small (see Table 4), and those who did not had frequent recourse to the charity of their neighbors.

Thus the system of land exploitation gave rise to a four-stage occupational hierarchy of proprietor, fermier, domestique, and journalier. In addition, there was a small class of farmers in Chanzeaux who operated in an almost entirely separate economic system. These were the thirty-odd *vignerons* (vintners), living in the northeastern section of the commune near the banks of the Layon. A high proportion of these people owned their own land, and, though the majority of the holdings were small, they were still viable in terms of land use. Wine-growing land had about three times the value of ordinary arable land of good quality, and, since the vines required more intense culture than other crops, a small holding was in any case desirable. The wine growers, with their small families, employed very little outside labor; they were the closest thing in Chanzeaux to a class of small independent proprietors.

Altogether, about two thirds of the active population of Chanzeaux derived its living directly from the land. The remaining third of the labor force was employed either in providing various goods and services to the village or in domestic textile production. At least 15 percent of the working population of the village was employed in the textile industry. The center of the cottage textile industry in the region was Cholet, about twenty miles south of Chanzeaux. Before the Revolution, Cholet had been a prosperous center, but under the July Monarchy its trade, like that of the rural textile industries generally, was reported to be much depressed. Nevertheless, the industry was still able to provide employment for a score of men in Chanzeaux who worked as weavers, and a large number of single girls and widows who took in spinning. Salaries were low. A weaver might earn 1 franc per day on the average, a spinner about 80 centimes. A widow who owned a little garden besides might support herself adequately on these wages; a large family could not. The weavers, like the journaliers, were undoubtedly among the first to feel the pinch of hard times.

The remaining 15 percent of the population — those employed in the trades and professions — were among the most prosperous people in the village. Considering the size and relative insignificance of this commune, through which no main road passed, the specialization of functions was elaborate. In 1851, seventy-three people made their living as artisans. Several of the larger villages still had their own blacksmiths and masons, while in the bourg one might find a number of "luxury" craftsmen as well — shoemakers, a watchmaker, and a wigmaker. Their presence testifies to the relative well-being of at least a part of the population.

In a position intermediate between farmer and artisan were Chanzeaux's fifteen to twenty millers. Several millers' families had benefited from the sale of church lands during the Revolution. They had become proprietors of their own mills and enjoyed a much higher social position in the town than any fermier. The miller of Frogeroux, François Gallard, served as deputy mayor of the commune until 1848, and three other millers served with him on the town council. At that time one could become eligible for membership on the council only by meeting a high property requirement; so the millers must have been among the wealthiest citizens of the town. Mill families tended to intermarry, and the owners of several of the largest mills were relatives. The Blanchard and Bureau families had been millers in Chanzeaux since before the Revolution.

Another thirty-five people in the village made their living through commerce. Included in their number were five butchers, four bakers, and as many as eight innkeepers. Their presence again reveals the degree of complexity of the village economy.

Finally, the village required the services of a priest and vicaire, a schoolteacher, a notary, a doctor, a veterinary, and a constable. These were the elite of the commune. The doctor, M. Lheureux, was wealthy enough to employ a servant, a luxury that only the genteel families of the bourg, the Forests and the Fougerays, also enjoyed. The notaire, M. Aimé Thomas (whose wife's family, the Beaurepaires, held a position of prestige in the neighboring commune of Joué-Etiau analogous to that of the Forests in Chanzeaux or the Soyer family in Saint-Lambert), did a large enough business to require the assistance of a clerk as well as an apprentice. The schoolteacher, M. Sellier, who had married into a family of Vendean heroes, had a guaranteed income of 600 francs per year.[5] He was therefore a well-established member of the community, though probably not on the level of the doctor, the notary, and the notable families.

The general occupational structure was relatively stable, and jobs were, as a rule, passed on from father to son. In the 1840s, about two out of every three young men who remained in Chanzeaux when they reached working age followed in their father's profession. The only exceptions were those who began work as domestiques; among these, one could find an equal number of sons of journaliers and sons of fermiers, with a handful of artisans' sons as well. But this was temporary work; no permanent occupation recruited new men from such a wide variety of backgrounds (see Table 5).

Table 5. Transmission of Jobs from Father to Son, 1841–1851

Occupation	No. of sons of Chanzeans entering occupation	% following occupation of father
Proprietor	8	87
Fermier	52	87
Artisan, miller	15	87
Journalier, domestique, textile worker	30	33

The differentiation of occupations within the community was reflected in various types of settlement, each with its own character. The bourg, or village proper, sheltered about one fourth of the inhabitants of the commune; another 20 percent lived in villages of over ten households; and most of the rest lived in small hamlets or on isolated farms, while the people in the wine-growing area of the commune had their own distinctive form of settlement (see Table 6).

Within this one village, at least three types of society coexisted. The bourg, as the administrative, religious, educational, and commercial

Table 6. Population by Residence, 1851

Type of settlement	% of total population
Bourg	24.5
Villages (10 or more households)	20.3
Wine villages	13.3
Large hamlets (5–9 households)	7.7
Small hamlets (3–4 households)	7.2
Two-household farms	10.5
Isolated farms	11.7
Mills	3.6
Chateaux	1.2

center of the commune, was the locus of greatest contact with the outside world. There, living side by side with the poorest inhabitants of the commune, the weavers and day laborers, could be found the wealthiest and the best-educated people in Chanzeaux. The number of signatures on acts of the civil register is one indication of the extent of literacy. Between 1841 and 1851, about half of the fathers who came to declare the birth of a child could sign their names, a figure slightly below average for France as a whole. In the majority of cases, however, it is clear from the rudeness of the signature that the signer did not otherwise know how to write. Only about fifteen people signed in a fluent hand, and only two among them were farmers; others included the doctor, the veterinary, a merchant, a butcher, a shoemaker, a mason, a carpenter, two innkeepers, a tailor, and the sexton — all bourg residents.

In social composition, the elite of the bourg resembled the "sieurs" of prerevolutionary days. In political temper, the two groups could not have been more dissimilar. For the few families that could be called bourgeois had risen to their present status on the crest of the Vendée Rebellion, and they were not liable to forget on which side their fortunes lay. Relations between Quatrebarbes and the village notables were on the whole cordial — so much so that, when M. Forest the elder retired as mayor in 1846, he wrote a letter to the prefect on behalf of the town council warmly recommending Quatrebarbes as his replacement.[6] (The prefect, naturally, could have welcomed nothing less.)

The second type of Chanzean society was exemplified by the wine villages, the distinguishing feature of which was the predominance of self-sufficient small proprietors. Although a majority of the inhabitants of these villages made their living from agriculture, they probably had more in common with the bourg residents than with the fermiers. Wine producing, then as now, was more commercialized than wheat-and-cattle culture, since a much smaller proportion of the produce was consumed locally. The wine villages, like the bourg, must have been accustomed to relatively frequent contacts with the outside world. Like the bourg, too, the wine villages were generally prosperous. The hamlets were poor cousins to them, as the villages themselves were to the bourg.

Finally, there was the society of isolated farms, which alone manifested clearly traditionalist characteristics: tenant farming rather than proprietorship, large families and patriarchal family organization, and low literacy. It was this type of settlement that corresponded most closely to Quatrebarbes' ideal of the society of the Ancien Régime; but only about one third of the people of Chanzeaux lived on such farms.

The social stratification based on occupation, on land ownership, and on residence was undoubtedly more elaborate and more rigid in this period than it is today. The gap in the style of life between the notary and the tenant farmer, or again between the farmer and his day laborers, was as wide as the distance between the village notables and the chatelains. The majority of the people, then as now, found themselves on the relatively amorphous middle level, leading a quite modest but fairly secure existence; still it is likely that Chanzeaux never again harbored as large a marginal class, or as large and as well-defined an elite, as at mid-century. The village notables, as we have seen, lived in certain comfort and with some pretense of elegance. We know less about the standard of living of those unfortunates at the bottom of Chanzeaux's economic hierarchy, at least in normal years. Since we do, however, have a record of the effect of the great depression of 1847 on the village, we can infer what proportion of the population led a precarious existence in normal times.

When in the winter of 1846–47 the fear of famine spread over a large part of Europe, Quatrebarbes, newly elected to the Chamber of Deputies for the district of Beaupréau, showed his solicitude for his constituency by organizing his own private survey of the local grain supply. To Chanzeaux he sent his nephew to make a house-to-house tour of the village and prepare an inventory. The mayor of each commune in the district was asked to do the same for his village and to send the results of the inquiry to Quatrebarbes. We do not have the report on the grain supply of Chanzeaux, but we do have the replies of mayors from nearby communes, where the situation must have been similar to that in Chanzeaux. Most of the mayors complied with Quatrebarbes' request, some with expressions of gratitude for his concern, others with an admonition that such an inquiry could only generate panic, since what the farmers feared most was the forced export of grain. The prefect, on hearing of the survey, sent Quatrebarbes a furious letter, requesting him with the utmost politeness to mind his own business and to leave the matter to the appropriate authorities. Quatrebarbes' gesture, however, ineffective as it was in concrete terms, did not lack color. To many a village mayor, he must have appeared a public benefactor. Most communes reported that there was enough grain in the region to feed the population, but that the prices were extremely high and there was suspicion of hoarding. Those who had a farm, whether owned or rented, were relatively secure; it was the marginal class of people who earned their wages by the day who suffered most severely.

The number of people in this desperate situation had grown so great as to constitute an emergency. In Chanzeaux in January 1847, the town council, meeting to discuss the means of complying with the prefect's "invitation" for the establishment of an *atelier de charité* (workhouse), recorded in their minutes that out of a population of close to 1,800, about 450 people "have nothing to live on but the daily wage of the head of the family; and this salary, which is almost always insufficient, is even more so this year because of the high prices and the lack of employment." At the inspiration of Quatrebarbes, in whose hand the report was written, the council decided to employ the indigent quarter of the village population to accomplish the long-desired improvement of the road to Chalonnes. A loan of 1,000 francs was requested from the prefect's office, and this sum, together with an allocation of 360 francs from the commune, was set aside to pay the wages of the road gang. M. Gallard (the deputy mayor), Bureau (another miller), Thomas (the notary), and Charles and François Forest were among those named as overseers of the workhouse. Thus the more prosperous citizens of the commune were able to turn the effects of the depression to their own advantage.

In normal years, when the commune provided no public charity, the main source of poor relief was the chateau. Quatrebarbes was a wealthy man, his income being something upwards of 60,000 francs per year, which would be equivalent to about 120,000 in France today. Of this amount, between 12,000 and 15,000 francs came from the farms of Chanzeaux alone. Since Mme. de Quatrebarbes kept a scrupulous account of every sou she spent, we can calculate the amount that found its way back from the chateau to the village each year in the form of charity. By a standing agreement, between 400 and 800 francs worth of flour from the storehouse of the chateau was supplied annually to a baker in the bourg, who made it into bread and distributed it among the poor. In addition, almost every day Mme. de Quatrebarbes recorded a gift of perhaps one or two francs to some "pauvre honteux." Over a year, she generally spent between 1,000 and 1,500 francs in this manner. In an average year, then, the poor of Chanzeaux received up to 2,000 francs in largesse from the chateau. Although this sum may seem trivial as a fraction of Quatrebarbes' income, it was certainly enough to make him the major source of poor relief in the village.

If indeed a quarter of the inhabitants of Chanzeaux were living in poverty in the 1840s, the economic structure of the village could not remain stable. The depressed class was still too small, then as now, to wield power; we have seen that any measures undertaken for relief of the poor were organized and controlled by the village notables. At the same time, the village could not continue to support this large group. So it is not surprising to find during this period signs of future change in the village population, and in particular a sizable amount of migration. During the decade 1841–1851, 465 people left Chanzeaux, and about 410 moved in. The fact that the total population actually fell slightly between 1846 and 1851 suggests that the greater part of this migration occurred during the lean years. Most of the emigrants were young and single. We do not know their ages exactly, since age was not entered on the 1841 census. We do know, though, that 41 percent of those who left were dependent children in 1841 and thus would probably have been in their teens or twenties by 1851. About as many women left as men. The immigrant population also was young, composed mainly of people in their twenties and thirties (see Table 7).

Table 7. Immigration by Age Group, 1841–1851

Immigrants	Age				
	22–31	32–41	42–51	52–61	62–71
No.	96	80	34	21	15
% of age group in Chanzeaux	36.5%	31.7%	20.2%	13.6%	12.2%

A breakdown by occupation shows that the emigrants were primarily agricultural and textile workers; artisans, shopkeepers, rentiers, and professional men tended to remain in the village. In agriculture, only certain occupations were particularly mobile. Foremost among the migrants were the domestiques, who alone constituted 44 percent of the emigrant population (as opposed to 18.5 percent of the total village population). Proprietors and even day laborers were less likely to move, with millers, vignerons, and fermiers still less disposed to leave the village (see Table 8).

Table 8. Emigration Rates by Occupation, 1841–1851

Occupation in 1841	% emigrating
Proprietor	
Rentier	
Fermier	
Miller	0–15
Vigneron	
Tradesman	
Artisan (incl. apprentice)	
Textile worker	16–30
Journalier	
Servant	31–60
Domestique	Over 60

A great number of immigrants to Chanzeaux were also domestiques, so that the movement of hired hands in and out of the commune was almost complementary. The greatest volume of migration tended to occur on the isolated farms and small hamlets, where the demand for hired labor was greatest. The wine villages and large hamlets, on the other hand, the two types of settlement that counted a large proportion of small proprietors among their inhabitants, were the most stable; while the villages, which were less prosperous than the bourg but offered more opportunities for employment, experienced more migration. Whether the migrants were entering the village or leaving it, whether they were young people in search of a temporary situation or families with children, they had this in common: almost without exception they owned no land. Ninety percent of the emigrants, and an even higher percentage of the immigrants, were landless, while only slightly more than 60 percent of Chanzeaux's stable population owned no land.

Although the volume of migration was much greater in the 1840s than it is today, the major part of this population movement was undoubtedly circumscribed. Most of the people who left Chanzeaux went no farther than the next village, just as most of the new arrivals had not traveled far. This type of short-distance mobility between contiguous villages followed well-established and familiar patterns. A young man might come from a neighboring commune to work as a domestique on the farm of a relative in Chanzeaux; at the end of a few years, he might marry a Chanzeaux girl and return with her to his hometown. This system, in fact, provided the most important opportunity for young people of nearby towns to meet. More than half of the marriages celebrated in Chanzeaux during this decade were between native Chanzeans and outsiders, but in the majority of cases both partners had been living in Chanzeaux at the time of marriage.

The local and traditional currents of immigration and emigration probably balanced out. The phenomenon of *net* emigration was very likely recent in Chanzeaux; considering the village's meteoric growth in the first part of the century in spite of a low regional birthrate, it may actually have occurred for the first time since the Ancien Régime in the 1840s. This new kind of population movement reflected the beginnings of a more permanent emigration, over greater distances, to more urban areas. Domestiques who despaired of saving enough money to rent a farm began to try their fortunes in the towns, rather than remaining in the village to lead the unenviable life of a day laborer. Journaliers themselves began to consider moving to the cities; most of the married men who left with their wives and children during the 1840s were day laborers. Although the gross census figures still give no sign of the effects of emigration, the depopulation of the village was already beginning at this early period.

In this process, the village followed the pattern for rural France as a whole. In the first half of the nineteenth century, the rate of migration from the country to the towns slackened by comparison with the eighteenth century.[7] Urbanization did continue, in a certain sense, but it often took the form of the development and specialization of bourgs within rural areas. By mid-century, Chanzeaux, like villages all over France, had reached both its maximum density in terms of population and its maximum complexity in terms of social organization. This was not a durable situation. If we are to believe the reports of the town council, a quarter of the population of the village lived at least on the verge of poverty, with no hope of improving their situation within the community. The only way out for these people was to leave — a drastic solution, but one that was to become more conceivable and more tempting as the century progressed. In the next fifteen years until about 1865, as an industrial boom provided an ever-greater promise of city jobs, as improved agricultural techniques continued to reduce the amount of manual labor needed on the farms, and as the rural textile industry dwindled and disappeared, the population of Chanzeaux began its long, uninterrupted decline. It was undoubtedly the marginal class that was the first to disappear.[8]

From the vantage point of the chateau, Quatrebarbes recognized the signs of future change and fought it bitterly. All outside contact, in his view, threatened the integrity of the self-contained rural society of which Chanzeaux was the prototype; but the greatest danger of all was exactly the kind of permanent emigration to cities that he could see beginning in his own village and all over France. In the closing pages of his history of Chanzeaux, he addresses an impassioned plea to the "good inhabitants of the countryside" not to abandon their ancestral homes and occupations:

Remain laborers like your fathers, and conserve religiously their customs, their probity, their love of work. The earth is the source of all wealth. Let your sons not abandon the plow, nor your daughters their spindles for the factories. Beware of deceiving words; and if ever someone seeks to awaken your ambition, offering you the lure of gold, arrest your glance, before you leave, on the roof of your cottage and on the old church where you were baptized; walk in those bountiful fields and fertile pastures where your flocks are frisking, consider the healthy appearance of your children and compare them then to those of that pale, sickly, and irreligious population who pass their lives in the factories, far from the sun and the fresh air, whose existence is consumed in mechanical gestures, who know neither the joys of the family, prayer, nor Sunday rest, but who get drunk on Mondays, blaspheme every day, and plunge into debauchery as a diversion from work. Choose, then, and see on which side lie virtue and happiness! [9]

In order to combat the rural exodus, Quatrebarbes did not shrink from certain practical measures, but none went far beyond the conception of palliative charity. The miniature public-works program in Chanzeaux was his model for the kind of reform he envisioned for all of France. In 1847, shortly after he had organized the road gang for Chanzeaux, Quatrebarbes proposed to the Chamber of Deputies a law that would have enabled town councils to vote a yearly tax in cash, rather than a certain number of days' labor, for the upkeep of local roads and to hire workers especially for that purpose. The cardinal virtue of the proposal, to his mind, was that by providing more jobs in the country it would prevent the rural day laborers from being forced to migrate to the wicked cities in search of work: "It is necessary, vitally necessary, to stop the deplorable uprooting of the rural population. We must attach the people to the soil by giving them the well-being that the cities falsely promised them, for in the cities they find too often nothing but disappointment, immorality and ruin." [10] The proposal was promptly quashed. Quatrebarbes' project was illusory, and the Chamber recognized it as such. The creation of municipal workhouses was hardly the kind of measure to prevent emigration from an overpopulated countryside.

In a sense, however, it was fortunate for Quatrebarbes that he could do nothing to stem the flow of emigration, for, paradoxically, the stability of the social system that he was determined to preserve depended on population movement. The patriarchal, hierarchically organized isolated farms that corresponded most closely to Quatrebarbes' ideal were the locus of the greatest mobility in Chanzeaux, while the more democratically organized wine villages and hamlets and the bourg (that urban intrusion into Quatrebarbes' rural paradise) were the most stable sections of the commune. If the estates of the west had been divided among peasant owners during the Revolution, if, instead of the hundred-odd fermiers of Chanzeaux, there had been twice the number of small proprietors in 1850, the village might have experienced less turnover and maintained its peak population longer. Conversely, if all the people who could not be absorbed into the economic system of Chanzeaux had not been able to move away, the traditional hierarchy might have been strained to the breaking point. The condition of permanence for the prosperous fermiers, the notables of the bourg, and the chatelains at the apex of the pyramid was just this transience of an anonymous populace of landless laborers. Luckily for Quatrebarbes, the people who could not survive within the old forms moved away; the forms remained.

Politics

If Quatrebarbes' attempt to control population movement in his village was a patent failure, in other respects his control of the village was effective and secure. Particularly when it came to politics, his domination was unchallenged. In this matter too, though, Quatrebarbes was actually more successful in preserving institutional forms than in influencing the majority of the people of Chanzeaux. In his idealized vision of what a rural community ought to be, a perfect identity of political convictions and aspirations existed between the nobility and the peasantry; the seigneur was simply the fittest person for expressing these common beliefs. In fact, however, although the people of Chanzeaux accepted the leadership of Quatrebarbes, they demonstrated a most lamentable indifference to his ideology.

Until 1848, Quatrebarbes' political fortunes depended very little upon the people of Chanzeaux or of the region, for only substantial property owners could vote. That revolution, however, swept away all property requirements and instituted universal male suffrage. All at once, it was no longer sufficient for Quatrebarbes to regard himself as the natural spokesman for his people; he was obliged to appeal to them for a mandate. To the people of Chanzeaux he presented himself and a chosen slate (which included several members of the Forest family) as candidates for the town council. On election day, in spite of his confidence in the natural and spontaneous rapport between himself and his peasants, he found it worthwhile to have his overseer distribute prepared ballots among his tenant farmers. To make doubly sure that the voting proceeded as it should, he himself supervised the committee that supervised at the polls. On the whole, then, the elections were of a peculiar sort. In the words of one angry citizen of Chanzeaux, who was moved to protest the results of the election: "Many other irregularities we will not even mention here, notably in the conduct of the board which supervised the election. Many were absent from the room so often that only M. de Quatrebarbes was left, eating lunch in the midst of ballots and official papers." [11] Nevertheless, the prefect found no reason to annul the election. Undoubtedly Quatrebarbes had done nothing that was strictly illegal or even uncommon in 1848, and it is quite possible that many people voted for him without being instructed or "advised" to do so; after all, he could not have won on the strength of the votes of his tenants alone. It is clear, however, that a somewhat crude form of social blackmail did play its part in the election of Quatrebarbes' slate.

On a departmental level, where he was unable to coerce voters as he had in his village, Qutrebarbes did not fare so well and was not reelected to the Chamber. We do not know how many votes he got in Chanzeaux and cannot arrive at a good estimate from the votes of the immediate region, for, not surprisingly, Chanzeaux was situated on the borderline between two sharply opposed political districts. Like other legitimist candidates, Quatrebarbes received his greatest support deep in the bocage country, and his proportion of the popular vote decreased as one approached the Loire Valley. In the canton of Chemillé, bordering directly on Chanzeaux to the southwest, Quatrebarbes obtained almost twice as many votes as in his home canton of Thouarcé.[12]

But we do have concrete evidence of at least some opposition to Quatrebarbes in the neighborhood of Chanzeaux. In the summer of 1848, Quatrebarbes started a lawsuit against Jean-Jacques Hérard, a coach proprietor in Saint-Lambert, for slander. M. Hérard was alleged to have said that "he was amazed that anyone was voting for M. de Quatrebarbes, when it was common knowledge that he was a grain speculator who starved the poor people and who was responsible for the high prices in 1847." The court established that the accusation was absurd, "in the midst of a region where the plaintiff has generously employed his time and fortune to make sure that the people had adequate provisions." Hérard was ordered to have the court decision published at his own expense and posted in all the communes around Chanzeaux. If Hérard's had been an isolated voice of opposition in a neighborhood that solidly supported Quatrebarbes, it is not likely that so trivial an offense would have been prosecuted.

Having lost his seat in the Chamber of Deputies, Quatrebarbes began to draw closer to the extreme right faction that favored restoration of the Bourbons by force of arms. In 1850 he paid a visit of homage to the pretender and brought with him a quixotic plan for the mobilization of the west. The scheme included the novel recommendation of the use of village fire brigades, led by loyal legitimist mayors, as the nucleus of a clandestine military organization. (Quatrebarbes had in the meantime superintended the formation of his own brigade in Chanzeaux.) The rural populace hardly figured in his plan at all, for the essential ingredient of a new Vendée Rebellion, popular support, was conspicuously lacking. The people who had given Quatrebarbes their votes so half-heartedly were certainly not on the point of rising *en masse* to don their firemen's helmets and join the heroic battle to restore the pretender to the throne. Though Quatrebarbes did not entirely abandon hope of a new rebellion in the Vendée, he was sensitive enough to the political temper of his region to realize that such an uprising would be out of the question except as a response to an extreme and immediate threat: "The present temper of the Vendée does not justify the hope of an energetic initiative *at the first sign of anarchy*. All the men who know and live in the Vendée are agreed that action is not possible except under two conditions: anarchy in the capital, and not only in Paris, and pillage in the countryside." [14] But this danger, like so many outside threats, existed only in Quatrebarbes' imagination.

As the hope of a restoration faded, so did Quatrebarbes' political career. After the coup d'état of Louis Napoleon in 1852, Quatrebarbes resigned from all public offices, even his position as mayor of Chanzeaux, and retired once again to his chateau; as the years passed, it was the chateau that came to symbolize his real political achievement. It had been little more than a hunting lodge when he inherited it. He himself designed the octagonal turrets that were added to transform his ordinary mansion into a Renaissance castle, and he himself ordered the enclosing wall that changed the land around the chateau into a private park. In the process of resurrecting this manor, he evicted tenants, tore up public property, and generally antagonized the village — but what did it matter? The people of Chanzeaux might resent the imposition, but they had to swallow their resentment as best they could. When the hostility had died down, Quatrebarbes' symbol of faith in the Ancien Régime remained. Although the people of Chanzeaux did not share his ideal of the past, they acquiesced in it, as they acquiesced in the building of the chateau.

Even if they would not follow Quatrebarbes into battle for his cause, they had little objection to re-enacting the legendary episodes of *Une Paroisse Vendéenne sous la Terreur* in the pageants that he organized. There was no M. Coustard and no ambitious bourgeois clique to challenge his control. Chanzeaux's notables now had to content themselves with a partnership in which control of communal affairs was shared with the lord of the estate. Indeed, the "better families" were only too pleased to cooperate with Quatrebarbes and to enjoy the benefits of his patronage.

After all, the community depended on him: the tenants for their farms, the artisans for trade, the poor for charity and casual employment. He was one of the few residents of Chanzeaux who could represent the village to the outside and deal with the machinery of the administration. His initiative and support were essential in any large communal undertaking; the village had to turn to Quatrebarbes for financing the renovation of the church or the building of a girls' school. There was the government, perhaps, but the people of Chanzeaux had learned by experience that the government was not likely to be of much assistance. It mattered little, then, that Quatrebarbes insisted that the school be run by Ursuline nuns or that the church preserve monuments of the Vendée war. Without his endowment there would have been no girls' school, and the church might have fallen into ruins. In short, because Quatrebarbes' social predominance in the village was an unquestioned fact, the people of Chanzeaux accepted its concomitants: they recognized him as their political leader and suffered him to be the interpreter of their past and the architect of the traditions of their future.

3

Chanzeaux at the Turn of the Century

Chanzeaux, June 2, 1892

M. le Curé:

I can do none other than respond to the wishes of the population in demanding your replacement.

This demand is based upon facts which I will communicate to you at your convenience.

I have the honor to remain, M. le Curé, your respectful servant,

H. P. R. Milon
Mayor of Chanzeaux

Thus, a century after the outbreak of the Vendée Rebellion, the people of Chanzeaux were witnessing what appeared to be a re-enactment of their own history. Once again, a republican town official had confronted a defiant priest. The particular incident that led to the mayor's letter turned out to be trivial; the conflict, and the general situation that gave rise to it, were not.

For France was again a republic, and once again the republic was at odds with the church. Created as a temporary expedient, the Third Republic had survived the denunciations of the Pope and the serious threats posed by the army and the royalists to become an established government. Although royalist hopes for a restoration of the monarchy fell sharply with the death of the last Bourbon pretender in 1883, the leaders of the Third Republic were periodically reminded of the strength of the opposition, first by the threat of a coup d'état in 1889 and later by the Dreyfus case. After each crisis the republican politicians temporarily buried their differences in a campaign to consolidate their position and to curb the power of the church. Each of these campaigns served to revive the old antagonisms of the Vendée controversy.

The republican government was not without support in the Mauges. As the regime proved durable, it slowly gained in respectability, and by 1906 the subprefect of the second electoral district of

Angers, which included Chanzeaux, reported that the region, "although entirely rural, is not absolutely subservient to the reaction." [1] One quarter of the communes, in fact, had republican town councils. The region consistently elected royalist delegates to the Chamber of Deputies, but the prefect saw reason for optimism in the considerable minority vote that republican candidates polled in certain years. In 1910, the republican candidate in the second electoral district lost by only 250 votes, and the prefect conjectured that with a genuinely secret ballot he would have won. "The voters are subject to the pressure of the clergy and the big proprietors, and risk losing their work if they vote republican." [2]

The people of Chanzeaux, however, encountered relatively little political pressure from local nobles during this period. From the death of Quatrebarbes in 1871, until 1905, when Colonel de Kerdouec retired from the army in protest over the separation of church and state, the seigneurie of Chanzeaux had no resident chatelain. Quatrebarbes' heirs showed little of his solicitude for the village, and Chanzeaux's town council soon found itself involved in a dispute with the Quatrebarbes estate over sums that Mme. de Quatrebarbes had designated in her will for the building of a new church. Many other communal responsibilities that Quatrebarbes had to a large extent fulfilled during his lifetime, such as the provision of poor relief, now through neglect also fell to the lot of the town council.

The absence of the chatelain not only necessitated a stronger municipal government, but also permitted a new faction to gain control of it. Ever since 1852, when Quatrebarbes resigned as mayor of Chanzeaux, members of the Forest family that he protected had held the mayoralty in unbroken succession. By the early 1890s, however, this family had apparently lost much of its credit with the townspeople of Chanzeaux. In 1891, the last of the Forests lost the mayoralty by a narrow margin to the republican notary Milon, and in the following year Milon was re-elected by a large majority. With Milon's sudden death a year later, another republican, Henri Pellerin, was elected to succeed him. Pellerin in turn served as mayor until his death in 1912. Chanzeaux was thus among the minority of communes with republican town councils, a fact that the prefect often noted in favor of the village and its mayor.

Thus, while the church and the landed nobility remained the most powerful political forces in the region at large, republicanism had made considerable inroads into the district, particularly into the village of Chanzeaux. At times, the gradual expansion of republican power seemed to proceed with little conflict, and many local politicians like Mayor Pellerin undoubtedly found it quite possible to combine a pragmatic acceptance of the existing regime with personal loyalty to the church. But this slow evolution of village politics was interrupted during periods of crisis, and then compromise between the opposing factions was all but impossible.

The two great periods of aggressive republican anticlericalism occurred in the early 1880s and the early 1900s. The first period produced the famous Ferry Law of 1882, which made primary education free, secular, and compulsory. The second period culminated in the law separating church and state. These measures raised bitter opposition in conservative and Catholic circles everywhere; in the Vendée, they revived memories of armed resistance. The republican offensives were not, however, of sufficient magnitude to provoke a second rebellion. At its most aggressive, the government ceased to pay the salary of the curé; it did not attempt to remove priests as the First Republic had done one hundred years before. Even Monseigneur Freppel, the arch-conservative who was bishop of Angers from 1870 to 1891, conceded that it was futile to imagine a second Vendée rebellion. "Alas, not a single rifle would be raised in protest. Let us found private schools, let us demand the repeal of the law and call attention to its excesses, but for pity's sake let us not start a revolt in which no one will follow us." [3]

Although violent opposition to anticlerical legislation was limited to a few riots, local resistance often took subtler forms. Many villages did their best to circumvent the new laws and to outwit the prefects' zealous attempts to enforce them. The extent of popular dissatisfaction in the region can be measured by the results of the legislative elections. Throughout the west, the percentages polled by the republican candidates fell sharply during or immediately following these periods of crisis. [4]

Electoral results in Chanzeaux proved no exception to this rule (see graph below). The vote fluctuated with the intensity of the church-state conflict. In the years of détente (1893, 1898, 1910), republican candidates were able to obtain as much as 30 to 40 percent of the vote. In years of increased antagonism, royalists either ran unopposed in the district or trounced their republican opponents: in

1889, for instance, the royalist candidate received 69 percent of the vote, with 31 percent abstentions.

Chanzeaux's town records for the 1880s reveal little additional evidence of conflict between clerical and anticlerical factions. In accordance with the provision of the Ferry Law, a public school for boys was established in the village, under a loan authorized by the prefect. There is no record of opposition to the new school. The departmental inspector of schools, in recommending the granting of the loan, reported that Chanzeaux had about 100 boys of school age,

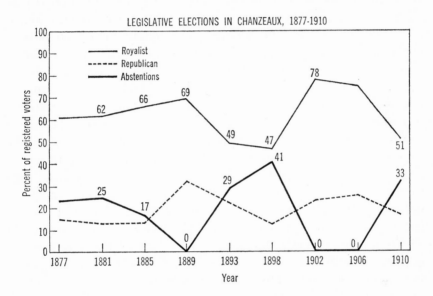

LEGISLATIVE ELECTIONS IN CHANZEAUX, 1877-1910

and estimated that about half would attend the public school.[5] Diocesan officials, on the other hand, reported in 1890 that about 60 boys were enrolled in the Catholic school and about 20 in the public school.[6] Allowing for this understandable discrepancy in the reports, we can conclude nevertheless that republican families were an appreciable minority in the village.

The commune put up a more vigorous resistance to their prefect's repeated demands for the creation of a public school for girls. The first time that the matter was broached, in 1888, the town council pleaded poverty and added that the existing girls' school, founded by Quatrebarbes, charged no tuition and was "entirely in conformity with the wishes of the population." The subject was dropped for several years, then revived in the early 1900s, whereupon Mayor Pellerin answered with the same protests as his predecessors. When it became clear that these objections were useless, the commune resorted to delaying tactics. Even the inspector of schools intervened with the prefect on Chanzeaux's behalf, asserting that Mayor Pellerin was a good republican who gave "energetic support to the public school teacher in his competition with the private school for boys," [7] and that his objections were probably legitimate. The issue had still not been resolved at the outbreak of the First World War. Chanzeaux's reluctance to build the school was undoubtedly motivated in part by a genuine lack of funds and in part by respect for the tradition of religious education for girls, which was strongly rooted not only in the village but in all of France.

Chanzeaux's most aggressive anticlerical official was not elected mayor until after the first national crisis in church-state relations had passed. Had Mayor Milon's tenure in office coincided with a national offensive against the power of the church, his effect on the village might have been extremely disruptive. Instead, his one-man attack on the curé, undertaken without the backing of higher officials, provoked little more than a tempest in a teapot. The quarrel apparently began over irregularities in the budget of the *fabrique* (vestry) and was eventually brought to the diocesan level, where Mayor Milon and the bishop's secretary exchanged insults and threats to expose one another's behavior to the newspapers. Just as the dispute was threatening to turn into a scandal, it abruptly ended with Milon's death in the summer of 1893. His successor, Pellerin, did not resume the quarrel, and the fabrique's accounts never again caused any comment. In this period of improved relations between the church and the republic, such quarrels were definitely out of season.

The Dreyfus case, however, put an end to any possibility that may have existed for reconciliation. With the advent of the Waldeck-Rousseau ministry in 1899, anticlericalism once more became a major government policy. In July 1901, a law was passed requiring religious orders to obtain authorization from the government and denying any nonauthorized congregation the right to teach. Waldeck-Rousseau presumably did not intend to use the law to prohibit all teaching congregations. But by the time the requests for authorization were filled, Waldeck-Rousseau had resigned from the premiership and had been replaced by the more radical Emile Combes. A militant atheist, Combes enforced the 1901 law with rigor.

The two teaching orders serving Chanzeaux's Catholic schools, the men's order of Ste. Croix and the Ursulines, duly registered their requests for authorization, with the unanimous approval of the town council. They were perhaps among the fifty-four orders whose applications received a blanket refusal in March 1903, for in April, Frères Emile and Judicaël, the teachers in the Chanzeaux boys' school, were required to leave. Chanzeaux's parish almanac fulminated against the injustice of the new laws: "Our atheistic freemason governors want all the children of France to be atheistic freemasons like themselves, and to attain this infamous goal they are preparing schoolmasters of their own mentality for our poor children." [8]

Chanzeaux's experience was repeated all over France; by October 1903, 10,000 schools taught by members of religious orders had been closed. In order to keep religious teachers in the classrooms, Monseigneur Rumeau, who had been bishop of Angers since 1898, asked many members of teaching orders to defrock themselves, considering this "the only practical means of preventing the closing of the schools." [9] In Chanzeaux, Frères Emile and Judicaël were replaced by M. Paillet, a monk who had left his order so that he could continue teaching. Of M. Paillet the parish almanac reported: "Piety was his first preoccupation. As a layman he took great pains to remain faithful to the rules of his order. Convinced that piety is the necessary base of all moral life, he never missed an occasion to speak of it to his students." [10] In this manner, the schools of Chanzeaux submitted to the letter of the law and defied it in spirit.

The legal separation of church and state in 1905 imposed even more serious difficulties on the commune. The *conseils de fabrique*, which held title to church property, were dissolved by law; hence the commune was faced with the problem of disposing of the church's possessions. A subsequent law gave the free use of the "édifices du culte" to the curé and the faithful in each parish. In Chanzeaux, as in most other villages, the church and the rectory were the property of the commune. It was necessary, then, to form a contract for the curé's free use of the church (the commune was to see to its upkeep) and to find somebody to rent the rectory from the commune.

One town-council meeting held a week after the promulgation of the law sufficed to settle the question of Chanzeaux's church. The free use of the building was given to Abbé Braud for eighteen years, and the free use of the church was also to be accorded to his successor. The mayor closed his reading of the contract, which was accepted immediately and unanimously, by forbidding himself and his successors any interference in the management of church affairs. The token leasing of the rectory was accomplished smoothly as well. In February 1907, Baron de la Grandière of the chateau of la Berthelottière offered to rent it. The town council, after discussing the decrepit state of the building, agreed to lease it to the baron for 50 francs annually and stipulated that he would have to pay the taxes, insurance, and repairs. Apparently the rectory was not in such a poor condition, and the prefectoral office saw through the ruse easily, for it annulled the decision in March. The next month, the mayor told the assembled town council that the baron had offered to rent the rectory for twice the price, and the deal was finally transacted.

Had the property of Chanzeaux's parish council been limited to the church building and the rectory, its disposal would have been relatively simple. But the fabrique of Chanzeaux, as well as that of most other communes, had amassed a considerable amount of property in the form of land, vineyards, and investments. To determine the extent of such property, the separation law required an inventory of every church in France. In less devout regions, this maneuver was executed with little difficulty; but in the Vendée, it often provoked riots. In neighboring Saint-Lambert, for example, the official assigned the task of taking the inventory was greeted at the church doors by the curé, the vicaire, the whole parish council, the mayor, and a "crowd of a hundred men and boys and three hundred women," [11] who successfully prevented him from entering. Chanzeaux's church was inventoried two days later, although it is noted that there had been a previous, unsuccessful attempt at which the curé of Chanzeaux appeared to read a protest and to refuse entry to the church.

Why did Chanzeaux permit an inventory to be made while Saint-Lambert obstinately refused? A partial explanation may lie in the differences of conviction and personality of the mayors of the two villages. Paul Saudreau of Saint-Lambert was a convinced legitimist and ardent Catholic. Considering the causes of God and King to be intimately linked, he felt that it was his duty both as a Catholic and as a public official to stave off the onslaughts of the atheistic republic.

His energetic defense of his principles, in fact, led to his defiance of a prefectoral order in the following year, and to the subsequent revocation of his position as mayor. Mayor Pellerin of Chanzeaux, although a good Catholic whose curé spoke of his "loyauté personnelle bien connue," also believed that republicanism need not be godless. He too was acting on principle when he did not use drastic measures to prevent the taking of the inventory.

The inventory, taken at six in the morning in order to discourage any onlookers and objectors, revealed that the fabrique, in addition to the church furnishings, owned a tiny vineyard for the use of the curé valued at 400 francs, a small piece of land valued at 200 francs, a one-acre orchard for the curé's use worth 2,000 francs, all located in Chanzeaux, and two pieces of land worth 400 and 1,500 francs located in the neighboring village of Rablay. The fabrique was also credited with 127 francs in rents, and the actual grounds were valued at 500 francs. An inventory of the *mense curiale* made on the same day produced a small field worth 400 francs, which had been bequeathed by Curé Peltier to his successors.

Although the fabrique no longer held legal title to the church properties, it was not at all clear who did. The separation law had proposed the establishment of *associations cultuelles* to fill this role, but the idea did not meet with ecclesiastical approval and none was formed in Chanzeaux. In 1906, the property was sequestered, by order of the prefect, for passage to the Bureau de Bienfaisance of the commune. This body, however, heeding the still small voice of conscience or perhaps the louder voice of financial reality, declined the property. At a meeting in 1907, it issued a statement that was also endorsed by the town council: "The members of the Bureau de Bienfaisance, considering that this property is under heavy mortgages contracted by the fabrique, refuse to accept this property. They consider moreover that they are unable to accept the property of the fabrique for reasons of conscience." For the fabrique was some 20,000 francs in debt as a result of a loan it had contracted to pay for unforeseen construction expenses. A prefectoral order of September 1909 set up a list of twelve creditors; about half of them were spinsters and widows from especially religious families of Chanzeaux, so it is difficult to imagine that they would have pressed their claims on the church. They undoubtedly returned any money they received.

In 1910, a prefectoral order confiscated the fabrique's rents, which were used to pay some of the creditors; it also stipulated that the fabrique's lands and vineyards be sold. A price list was drawn up and public posters advertised the sale. No Chanzeans were interested in buying land usurped, in their eyes, from their church, but members of neighboring communes showed no such scruples. Three buyers were found in Le Champ and one in Angers. It is worth noting that no buyers came from the Mauges.

Having learned its lesson in the matter of the fabrique's property, the Bureau de Bienfaisance did not repeat its mistake when the field bequeathed by Curé Peltier to his successors devolved upon them. They accepted the property, under protest:

> The undersigned members of the Bureau de Bienfaisance protest the transfer of this property, which is as unjust as the Separation Law that requires it. In the full possession of his faculties M. Peltier bequeathed this field to his successors. At his death they became the legitimate proprietors, and there is no human law which can legitimately annul such a gift.
>
> Catholics above all, the undersigned members can not accept this transfer of property condemned by civil and religious laws alike. But considering that acceptance is imposed upon them by virtue of the office they hold, they will attempt to fulfill as far as possible the intentions of M. Peltier by returning the field in question to its legitimate owner as soon as circumstances permit.

If the government's objective in passing the law of separation was to reduce the power of the church, the success of the measure is questionable. Since the republic no longer offered legal privileges and financial support to the church, the church no longer found it advantageous to seek accommodation with the republic. Instead, the church was forced into a relation of greater dependence upon the conservative and often overtly antirepublican elements of French society. Thus the government lost one of its principal means of control over the church.

Certainly this was the case in Chanzeaux. The implementation of the separation law and the disposition of church property not only provoked general indignation, but also drove the parish to seek other means of support. It found its new protector in the person of M. de Kerdouec, seigneur of Chanzeaux, who had retired from the army in protest against the separation law. Kerdouec found waiting for him a position of leadership that the government, by withdrawing its support from the church, had created. Someone was needed who was willing and able to supplement the salary of the curé, to maintain the Catholic schools, and to support the activities of the church. Kerdouec, in assuming the role of village patron, assured himself of a dominant position in the town government. By 1908, in the first municipal election since his arrival in the village, he was elected first assistant to the mayor; by 1912 he was mayor, and Chanzeaux's period of republican leadership had come to an end.

Once again, the village seemed to be repeating its own history, as the heir of Quatrebarbes reclaimed the chatelain's position of ascendency. Once again, under Kerdouec's leadership, the old legends of the Vendée were revived and made to fit the context of contemporary conflicts of church and state. It is at about this time that Chanzeaux's new church was built, largely with Kerdouec's money. Its walls bear murals depicting the martyrdom of Chanzeaux's rebels, and its windows carry the inscription, "Your ancestors died for their faith and their country." In a real sense, this new monument to the past was the tangible form of the village's resistance to current attacks on the position of the church.

In general, then, in Chanzeaux the republic's offensives against the church achieved exactly the opposite of what was intended. During periods of relative calm in church-state relations, we can discern a gradual evolution in the village toward a less anomalous, more realistic political position. This slow change paralleled the general movement in France toward permanent acceptance of the republican form of government. The implementation of anticlerical laws, however, far from accelerating this trend, periodically disrupted it. The republic's campaigns to reduce the influence of the church could only appear in Chanzeaux as outside intrusions into an accustomed way of life. These inroads infused new meaning into the legends of the village's past, strengthened the most conservative elements of leadership, and confirmed the village's sense of identity as a fortress defending the faith.

*   *   *

In order to understand Chanzeaux's present, one must recognize what remains of its history. The past endures in Chanzeaux in many forms: in the configuration of the land, in the tradition of autocratic leadership, in the persistent memory of religious conflict. This inheritance has shaped every aspect of the present life of the community.

One of the most marked continuities in Chanzeau's history has been in its system of land tenure. The basic features of this system can be traced back to the Ancien Régime. Before the Revolution, the greater portion of the land was owned by absentee nobles, who rented the land in relatively large and compact units, the métairies. The smaller parcels of land, owned by villagers, were scattered about the commune in the form of closeries. The land reforms of the Revolution, which elsewhere in France accelerated the breakdown of large holdings, produced little basic change in the system of land tenure in the Vendée. If anything, the bitter resistance to the Revolution and all its works may have helped to consolidate the large estates in this region. In the middle of the nineteenth century, eleven people owned over half the land in Chanzeaux. This system persisted with little modification until after the First World War. Although the large holdings have now been divided among a larger number of owners, the size of the functional units, the rented farms, has changed only slightly in the last hundred years.

Chanzeaux's history has also determined that the land remains the predominant means of livelihood. Since the Vendée Rebellion, when the people of the countryside massed to attack the cities and drove out the bourgeois who were the chief importers of the Revolution, there has been little development of industry and little growth of cities in the region. As a result, those people whom the agricultural economy of the village could not support were obliged to emigrate. Since the 1840s, the village has been slowly losing population to larger towns and cities.

Another form of emigration also affected Chanzeaux's history: the "émigration à l'intérieur" of the nobility. Most notably in 1830, but also on subsequent occasions, French aristocrats, outraged at the political situation, retired in numbers to their estates in the provinces. Among them were Quatrebarbes and Kerdouec. Throughout most of the nineteenth century and well into the twentieth, resident noblemen presided over Chanzeaux. As absentees, these men might have had little influence on the commune; as residents, they dominated it. Their ownership of the land gave them unrivaled power in the village, and the services they performed for the town made the exercise of this power appear legitimate. Over many decades, the people of Chanzeaux became accustomed to acquiescing in the leadership of the chatelain.

Finally, Chanzeaux's relationship to the rest of the country has been conditioned by periodic challenges to the political structure of the village. During the Revolution, this challenge came from a small faction within the community, backed by the strength of the central government. After the Vendée Rebellion, however, the power of the church and the leadership of the nobility met with no effective opposition within the village or in the region. The prefects attributed this general lack of opposition to the absence of urban development in the Mauges, and to the consequent weakness of the middle class. The nineteenth-century offensives against the church and the aristocracy originated not in the villages but in the cities. Initiated in Paris, they came to Chanzeaux through the orders of the prefect's office in Angers. As a result, the conflicts, which during the Revolution had been an internal affair, became externalized and the village responded to attacks on the church as to an intrusion from the outside. Because the attack on the power structure of the village always involved the position of the church, the conflict repeatedly took on the character of religious controversy; faith became a political issue.

History has thus given Chanzeaux a basic pattern of economy, a traditional form of social organization, and an inherited ideology. How the village lives with its inheritance, and how it deals with change, is the subject of the remainder of this book.

Part Two

FARMING

On June 26, 1961, fifty Chanzeaux farmers descended on Angers to join a mass protest against the agricultural policies of the de Gaulle government. The Chanzeaux contingent brandished signs bearing bitter slogans: "Agriculteurs à Part Entière, Debréons-Nous" (Farmers want all their rights now. Do away with Debré!). Once in Angers, the farmers listened approvingly to syndicalist leaders who filled the day with fiery speeches accusing the government of having betrayed the French farmer. The nasal voice of Chanzeaux's own outspoken André Blond rang over the public-address system for more than an hour. Two and a half years later, on January 30, 1964, Angevin farmers, including a group of Chanzeans, barred the gates to the Chemillé meat market. About seven hundred sullen men milled about the entrances to the market for the greater part of the morning. The Chemillé demonstration was part of a nationwide effort by beef producers to force up the price of beef by artificially limiting the supply. The effort did not succeed, and the government granted the farmers no important concessions. In fact it responded by importing a large quantity of Argentine beef to compensate for what the farmers were holding back. The ultimate result was a temporary glut on the beef market and a drop in the price of beef cattle, exactly what the demonstrators most wished to avoid.

Six months after the strike in Chemillé, Eugène Bourdelle, the president of the Chanzeaux farmers' syndicate, concluded, "No one is interested in demonstrations any more. They are useless." But such protests are certainly indicative of the farmers' mood. Since World War II their expectations have risen dramatically. The realities of their economic situation — the average size of a farm in Chanzeaux is 53 acres — stand in harsh contradiction to their desires. Caught between rising aspirations and static prices, the Chanzean farmers' first reaction, like that of their fellows throughout France, was to protest the government's agricultural policy. They have, however, been quick to perceive the ineffectiveness of protest. Since the motivating forces behind the present evolution in French agriculture are basic economic ones, the most the farmer can hope to receive from the government is a reprieve. Nor are the Chanzeans unaware of this. André Blond emphasized the fact in his 1961 speech when he insisted that farmers did not wish to become charity wards of the state.

Once again, as in 1789, 1793, and 1905, Chanzeaux faces the necessity of adapting to changes coming from outside the community. Those most resourceful in meeting the challenge have been precisely the young, progressive, relatively prosperous farmers who led the 1961 and 1964 protests. These men are deeply committed to farming as a way of life. It is they who have taken the initiative in modernizing Chanzeaux's agricultural economy. They have adopted new fertilizers and types of seed, initiated new rotation patterns. They have begun to take measures to rationalize breeding and have experimented with new crops. They have gone deeply into debt to begin mechanizing their farms. Finally, they have introduced a new institution for cooperative farming, the Association d'Entr'aide du Plessis. Yet there are limits to the effectiveness of any response to the present situation. Since demand for agricultural products is relatively static, the agricultural population must decrease as productivity rises. Already Chanzeans look with apprehension to the day when farmers in their prime will be forced to abandon their farms.

4

Land Tenure

IN LOOKING at Chanzeaux's farms, the first characteristic that strikes the observer is their diversity. Pierre Amelin's farm, at la Berthelottière, belongs to a garage owner in Nantes. The farm of Joseph Barbot, a man who lives in the hamlet of les Touches in Chanzeaux, is owned by Barbot himself and six other people. Pierre Chalonneau's farm covers 140 acres, while that of his next-door neighbor covers only 27. Half of Jean Mercier's farm is three miles away in Rablay; the whole of Louis Binet's farm neatly surrounds his farmhouse. To understand these contrasts, we must look to the past.

The history of land tenure in Chanzeaux is the history of the evolution of two distinct systems, each with its own rules and problems. The first is that which has evolved on noble and bourgeois holdings: the *fermier* system. According to this scheme, lands are divided into sizable farms that are run by tenant farmers. According to the second arrangement, the *propriétaire-exploitant* system, the farmers own their farmhouses and some land but usually also rent land from relatives or minor landholders who live in the bourg or in neighboring communes. The two systems are quite separate: only one farm out of the 124 in Chanzeaux in 1962 shared features of both. The fermier system was the dominant one in the past, but it has changed radically since World War II (see Table 9).

The Fermier System

To placate the nobility in the Vendée, the Bourbons saw to it that the lands sold by the republic were restored to the nobles, unless they were compensated for the loss. In Chanzeaux, the lands of two of the three chateaux had been confiscated; the other family had given its allegiance to the republican government. Of the land confiscated, a good part of it was not sold and, after the amnesty, Gourreau was able to return from exile in the United States to reclaim most of his lands.

Table 9. Comparison of Fermiers and Proprietors, 1962

Farms (acres)	Fermiers	Proprietors
Farm size		
Under 25 (5–10)[a]	0	23
25–39 (11–15)	5	21
40–50 (16–20)	3	17
51–75 (21–30)	16	12
76–100 (31–40)	18	1
Over 100 (over 40)	8	0
	—	—
	50	74
Total land farmed	3,700 (1,480)[a]	2,600 (1,040)
Aver. size of farm	76 (30.2)	37 (14.9)

[a] Numbers in parentheses after acre designations represent the equivalent in hectare designations; 1 hectare equals 2.47 acres.

Similarly, the chateau of la Berthelottière, with its lands, was restored to the de Jourdan family.

Thus in 1825, the year of the first systematic, governmental record of landholdings in Chanzeaux, the nobility owned about 3,000 acres of Chanzeaux's total 7,500 acres. Included in their numbers were the seigneurs of the three chateaux and owners of chateaux in the neighboring Mauges communes whose estates extended into Chanzeaux. The noble estates were usually well over 1,000 acres in size. (Les Chauvellières, which covered less than 500 acres, was the only exception.) Throughout the nineteenth century and all the way up to 1926, these estates remained much the same size, passing from one owner to another without being divided among several inheritors. Then in 1926 M. de Kerdouec, the chatelain of Chanzeaux, split his lands among his sons, and at almost the same time the Berthelottière estate was divided between two relations. In this one year, then, the system of landholdings that had dominated Chanzeaux collapsed.

The demise of the great estates was the result of financial pressures. After the First World War France, like many European countries, experienced a prolonged period of rapid inflation. Rents, as fixed sums from the beginning to the end of a lease, lagged behind the rising prices. Inflation eroded whatever wealth landlords had in bonds and other fixed-income securities. With the depression came surpluses on most agricultural markets, which reduced even further the real value

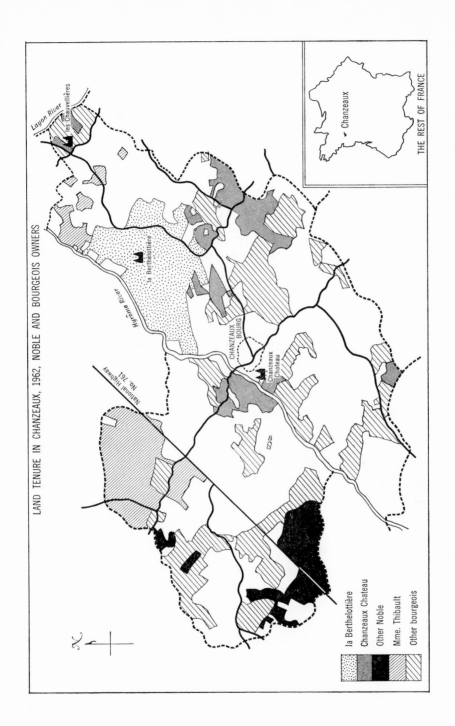

LAND TENURE IN CHANZEAUX, 1962, NOBLE AND BOURGEOIS OWNERS

la Berthelottière

Chanzeaux Chateau

Other Noble

Mme. Thibault

Other bourgeois

Layon River

les Chauvellières

la Berthelottière

Hyrôme River

National Highway No. 761

CHANZEAUX BOURG

Chanzeaux Chateau

Chanzeaux

THE REST OF FRANCE

of land rents. The nobles were forced to find occupations, move to the city, and become absentee owners. The seigneuries thus lost their social and political significance.

The present chatelain of Chanzeaux, if one can call him that, owns but 118 acres, a far cry from the 1,200-acre estate of his predecessors Quatrebarbes and Kerdouec. The estate of la Berthelottière is owned jointly by two sons-in-law of the last chatelain. Their lands combined are only 420 acres, less than a third the size of the estate in the nineteenth century. Les Chauvellières was completely sold. A widow from Paris, Mme. Rondeau, owns the chateau and has started an apple orchard on a portion of her 50 acres (see land-tenure map).

The other group of large property owners in Chanzeaux is the bourgeois (see Table 10; we are defining a bourgeois to be a nonnoble

Table 10. Evolution of Noble and Bourgeois Landholdings

	1825		1913		1939		1962	
Type of owner	No. of owners	% of commune owned[a]	No. of owners	% of commune owned	No. of owners	% of commune owned	No. of owners	% of commune owned
Resident[b]								
Noble	7	35.4%	3	30.8%	3	8.0%	0	0.0%
Bourgeois[c]	15	17.3	8	11.3	8	8.7	8	14.1[d]
Nonresident								
Noble	1	4.0	3	8.1	7	22.5	14	19.5
Bourgeois	9	11.6	11	13.7	13	20.2	18	16.5
	32	68.3%	25	63.9%	31	59.4%	40	50.1%

[a] Expressed as a percentage of the commune's total 7,500 acres (3,000 hectares).

[b] A resident owner is an owner who lives in Chanzeaux or in one of the communes contiguous to Chanzeaux. Except in terms of his political participation in the town itself, an owner living a few miles away cannot be considered an absentee.

[c] Bourgeois here includes nonfarming owners of over 50 acres (20 hectares) and heirs of land; millers are thus included.

[d] Includes 510 acres (207 hectares), or 6.9% of the commune's land, belonging to Mme. Thibault, who lives in Saint-Lambert.

who owns more than 50 acres but does not farm the land). Originally this group of landowners was a secondary one. Bourgeois properties were smaller than noble properties; in only one or two cases did they exceed 250 acres. The aftermath of the Revolution found 30 percent of Chanzeaux in the hands of bourgeois and millers. Some of the land had been bought during the sale of church lands and the lands of the noble émigrés. But much cannot be traced and probably belonged to the bourgeois before the Revolution. Although some of these people were Chanzeans — the Forests and the Fougerays — most were from Angers or from neighboring communes (see Chapter 2, Tables 1 and 2).

After the turn of the nineteenth century, most of the bourgeois, unlike the nobles, were able to keep their property. Many, in fact, added to it by buying up the land of the nobles. About half of the 1,500 acres of noble estates sold outright have been bought up by bourgeois from Angers and the surrounding region. Today the bourgeois as a group own more than the nobles. Mme. Thibault, widow of a Parisian doctor, owns more land in Chanzeaux (510 acres) than anyone else (see map).

Today the relative legal positions of a tenant and his landlord are almost the opposite of what they were before the 1930s. The political, economic, and social power concentrated in the hands of men like Quatrebarbes and Kerdouec was first substantially reduced in the 1920s, when the estates were divided. Such economic power as the landlords retained was abolished in 1945 by legislation, the Statut de Fermage, which created a completely new system of state-supervised rent control.

At the turn of the twentieth century, however, the situation was quite different. In those days, de la Grandière used to gather all his tenants at his chateau every Sunday before Mass. He would line them up behind his carriage and then drive off to church — they followed like a group of children trailing their teacher from the schoolhouse. After Mass they followed the carriage back to the chateau, where the chatelain questioned them on the sermon. In neighboring Saint-Lambert at the height of the church-state crisis the largest landowners, who were republicans, required their tenants to send their children to the public school.[1] This kind of social and political dependency was compounded by economic uncertainty. Louis Pinier's father, for example, sharecropped a 160-acre farm near Cholet. When the First World War broke out, it happened that his contract was up for renewal. In the face of imminent draft, he hesitated to commit himself and his five employees to even a year's service, and asked for time to think and follow the news. Before he acted, however, his worried landlord had sold the farm to an outsider, who then divided it into five parcels and sold it to five land-hungry "paysans." Pinier *père* and his employees were out of work, their families homeless.

Even when there was no immediate threat of eviction, a fermier before World War II was not fully his own master. The final decision on which crops to grow was the landlord's. Any plans for improvement that the fermier might consider were discouraged by two factors: first, the knowledge that an important share of the return would eventually be absorbed in rents by the landlord; and, second, the fear that he would not be compensated for the value of his investment, should his lease not be renewed. But the law passed in 1945, the Statut de Fermage, made the tenant farmer the master of his own farm, free in his decisions on crop planting, rotation, construction, and such matters. It established a mechanism of rent control distinctly in his favor and drastically reduced the landlord's power to remove him. Moreover, the standard rent for a department — expressed in quintals of wheat or some other commodity — was fixed by the administration; the original intention was that the rate be fixed at its 1939 level. The changes in the rental rate and the selling price of arable land in Chanzeaux in the last seven years demonstrate the effect of the statute. During a period in which advancing techniques and increasing productivity have raised the demand for land, the selling price of an acre has doubled — from 1,000 francs in 1958 to 2,000 in 1965 — while its rental price has risen by only 50 percent.

If, during negotiations for renewal of a lease, the landlord demands a rental figure that the tenant considers excessively high in terms of the departmental standard, the tenant has recourse to a district parity commission, SAFER (Société d'Aménagement Foncier et d'Etablissement Rural). This commission is probably the most interesting product of the Statut de Fermage. Like American labor-management relations boards, it aims at adversary representation. It includes one farming tenant, one representative of the nonfarming landowners, and a third "neutral" party drawn from the civil service, the judiciary, or a respected professional circle. Impartial in theory, the commission actually functions to introduce the government on the local scene as a third party to disputes and to give effect to the latest governmental policies regarding the balance between the contending groups. Local observers all agree that in the recent past the commission has been decidedly in favor of the tenants.

According to the provisions of the Statut de Fermage, all leases are automatically renewable at the end of nine years unless: (a) the landlord and tenant agree to break the lease; (b) the tenant fails to pay or ruins the farm; (c) the landlord or his son wants to take over the farm and run it himself. In the last case, the landlord must not be operating another farm elsewhere and must live on the farm. A few years ago in Chanzeaux, M. Delattre, chatelain of la Berthelottière, tried to evict all of his tenants and to transform his estate into a sheep farm. Two farmers were ready to retire, but a third, Pierre Amelin, took his case to the regional tribunal. Delattre was unable to prove that he intended to make la Berthelottière a permanent residence. Amelin won the case and remained on the farm. All dealings between him and Delattre now take place through the tribunal.

If a landlord decides to sell his land, under the Statut de Fermage his tenants have the first option to buy.[2] Thus if this law had been in effect in 1914, M. Pinier would have had the right of first purchase and a three-month period of grace in which to reflect on his decision or to accumulate the necessary funds. If Pinier had found the asking price excessive, he could have gone back to the paritary commission for adjudication. And whereas in 1914 an outsider could have bought the property for purposes of subdivision and resale in smaller parcels, today's law prohibits the division of a 150-acre farm in the Maine-et-Loire into more than two plots. Very likely SAFER would intervene to prevent such parcellization. The same commission would freely loan Pinier up to 50 percent of the purchase price on easy terms. It is even conceivable that SAFER itself would exercise Pinier's right of first option, buying the farm and holding it for five years while Pinier remained as tenant and accumulated enough money to repurchase the farm. Such an arrangement has occurred more than once in the Maine-et-Loire. Needless to say, the mere presence of this ponderous potential ally of the fermier causes speculators to shy away from agricultural property.

The other side of the coin, however, is that in exchange for helping to correct an inequitable distribution of land, the Statut de Fermage has introduced rigidity and inflexibility into the fermier system. In the nineteenth and first half of the twentieth centuries, the nobles and bourgeois divided their large tracts of land into farms whose average size fluctuated from about 50 to 75 acres. Given time, they could increase the size of the lots. Today each tenant is almost frozen into his lease. An enterprising landlord would have great difficulty consolidating farms.

The Propriétaire-Exploitant System

The half of Chanzeaux's land that is not owned by bourgeois or nobles is owned by a great number of people with rather small holdings. Since most of them farm the land themselves, they are *propriétaires exploitants;* they own a quarter of the land in the commune and actually farm a third of it. The people they rent from are primarily residents of Chanzeaux's bourg or inhabitants of neighboring communes. Among the village residents who own land, one finds artisans, shopkeepers, civil servants, and retired farmers, almost all of whom have inherited their 25 acres or so of land. Beyond a few exchanges between farmers, there is not much trading of this land.

The base of land ownership in the proprietor system is the farmer himself. These farmers generally do not own much land: nearly four out of five own less than 30 acres; only four own more than 50 acres. Twenty-seven farmers own less than 18 acres each and must rent more to achieve a minimum standard of living. (For the following list, a farm holding is defined as the amount of land owned by the farmer and his parents or in-laws.)

Size of holding	No. of owners
0–2.4 acres (0–0.9 hectares)	7
2.5–12.2 (1–4.9)	15
12.3–24.9 (5–9.9)	29
25.0–49.9 (10–19.9)	19
50 and over (20 and over)	4
	74

One of the important developments in the pattern of land tenure in Chanzeaux in the last fifty years has been the doubling of the total area owned by the proprietors. During the period between the two wars, when the nobles were selling land, Chanzeaux farmers bought about 750 acres, one half of what the nobles sold. This was before the passage of the Statut de Fermage, at a time when the risk and the political pressure associated with tenancy made owning one's own farm seem preferable to renting it. A number of farmers, like Jean Arrial's father, gave up leases on farms of 50–75 acres in order to buy farms of about 35 acres. Today, with the Statut de Fermage in effect, Jean Arrial rues the day that his father terminated his lease on the 60-acre farm of le Verger in order to buy the 27-acre Laujardière. Since the increases in the total number of acres owned by farmers was matched during the 1920s and 1930s by an increase in the total number of owners, the average size of a proprietor's farm remained nearly constant. Thus the average amount of land owned by *propriétaires exploitants* rose only slightly, from about 18 acres to 25.[3]

Another feature of the proprietor system is a marked tendency among farmers to subdivide their land among their heirs. René Lusson came to Chanzeaux in 1930, immediately after marrying. His wife was the only child of François Challain, a farmer in the hamlet of La Hutte, near Saint-Ambroise. Lusson was fortunate enough to be able to take over the farm when his father-in-law retired; but since Challain owned only 12 acres, Lusson had to struggle to extend the size of the farm. Over the years Lusson has bought what land he could afford, when it was up for sale; and his additional 7.5 acres, together with the 12 acres of Challain and about 15 acres he rents, go to make up his tiny farm. He had a son and a daughter who is now married and lives in a house the family built nearby.

Lusson is worried about the fate of small farms. If asked, he will tell you that most of the small farms in Chanzeaux will have to go and be replaced by a few consolidated cooperative farms. Even so, Lusson plans when he retires to divide the farmland between his son-in-law (who already farms some of Challain's land) and René his son, keeping a few acres for himself to live on. This means that to each will go less than 12 acres of farmland. How are they expected to live on this? They are not, he says; they can rent land as he did.

Lusson's determination to split his property among his children, all reasoning to the contrary, is shared by most of Chanzeaux's proprietors. To some extent, equal division of an inheritance is required by French law.[4] But the tenacity with which Chanzeaux's proprietors continue to divide farms from one generation to the next goes beyond the letter of the law. The practice is one of the heaviest burdens on the agricultural system. In every generation, three or four proprietors have been able, through continuing acquisitions, to raise the size of their farms to over 50 acres each. Inevitably the succeeding generation has split up these holdings. In the same way, the farms of the four proprietors who today own more than 50 acres of land (all of them having acquired most of it from nobles and bourgeois) will last no longer than the rest.

M. Lusson's farm, les Noyers, is not only small but, to make matters

[86]

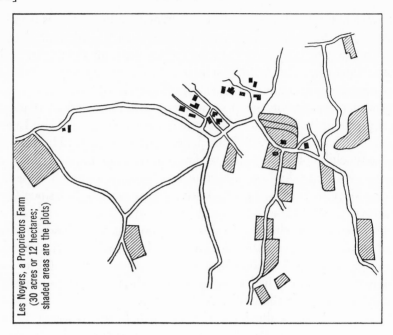

Les Noyers, a Proprietors Farm (30 acres or 12 hectares; shaded areas are the plots)

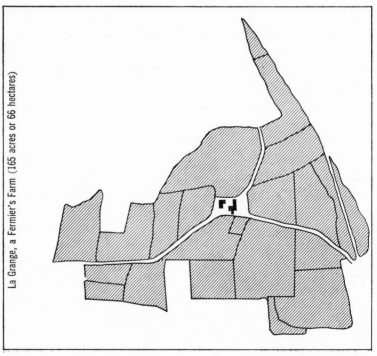

La Grange, a Fermier's Farm (165 acres or 66 hectares)

worse, it is composed of a number of small parcels scattered over a wide area (see figure opposite). Again Lusson's situation is typical of that of all proprietors, some of whom farm plots that are miles apart. The result is that endless time is lost in getting from one field to another, the use of tractors is limited, and farmers frequently interfere with each other's activities. Such fragmentation may go back even to the Middle Ages. Chanzeans today say that the land is split up because its farmers live in hamlets and villages, as opposed to isolated farms. With each farmer's house next to that of another, lands cannot be grouped compactly around the farmhouse. In fact, the division of the land and the residential pattern have both resulted from the character of the original settlement.

More important than the origins of fragmentation, however, are the reasons for its persistence. The first is, again, equal inheritance. When farms are divided, concern lest any one inheritor get a better lot than another inheritor often overrides every consideration of efficiency. Fields are carefully carved up so that each heir gets the same amount of sandy soil, rich soil, vineyard, and pasture. If the father has two plots of different value a half mile apart, each heir may get a piece of both. Why, then, do Chanzeaux's farmers not make exchanges of land from time to time in order to rationalize their farm locations? Why has the market for such obviously desirable exchanges never sprung up?

One obstacle is that the government collects a very high transaction tax on sales of land, amounting to about a third of the price. Although this practice clearly discourages sales, it does not discourage trade of land through mutual renting agreements. Rental of small plots of land is arranged on an informal basis, not subject to governmental control or taxes. Since the last war, moreover, the government has tried to encourage exchanges of land by suspending the tax under certain conditions. Initially about four or five "échanges à l'amiable" took place in Chanzeaux each year. The number is now thinning out, and in any case it always represented far fewer transactions than would have been optimally profitable.

The basic reason for the persistence of fragmented land is distrust. Given the atmosphere of jealousy and suspicion that exists in many of Chanzeaux's hamlets and villages, not much exchange takes place. Claude Chaillou has two triangular fields that meet at only one point, and he must go around the road to get from one to the other. Since the contiguous plots are the same size as his own, Chaillou proposed an exchange. The owner's response was: "You would not be making this offer unless you hoped to profit from it. You're trying to take advantage of me. I won't have anything to do with it." The effect of this individualism is to limit sales and even rental of small plots of land to the few transactions that result naturally from migration patterns and the deaths of original owners. If M. Lusson, eager to extend the size of his farm, had waited for the right parcels to come up for sale or rent, he might have had to wait until their owners died or left Chanzeaux. Because it was better to have a plot of farmland a mile away than not to have one at all, Lusson bought whatever land became available, land not always adjacent to his other parcels. The land he inherited was likewise composed of scattered parcels, partly because Challain also had to buy land when and where he could get it.

In both the fermier and the proprietor systems, the market for land is sluggish. The Statut de Fermage discourages sales of rented land or changes in the lease; distrust prevents sales and exchanges between proprietors. In the fermier system, the inactivity of the market is new; before 1946 farms did change hands and even size occasionally. In the proprietor system, the market has never been active. The government's failure to change the character of the latter system has been almost as striking as the success of the Statut de Fermage. To be effective, the statute had simply to regulate an already fluid market. The units with which it deals — large, compact farms — are relatively easy to keep track of. To interfere with the proprietor system, on the other hand, the government would not only have to cope with numerous owners of myriads of small plots, but it would have to create channels for exchange that do not now exist. It is much easier to regulate existing economic activity than to induce individuals to initiate exchanges where there were none before.

Rather than changing the law, the government has attempted to alleviate the problem of divided inheritance by establishing semiautonomous regulating commissions. It has always been possible for one son to preserve the farm intact by convincing the other heirs to accept payment in place of their share. What the new provisions do is to strengthen this custom by allowing the son to appeal to a government commission for intervention to prevent fragmentation of an "economic unity." The maximum area subject to the provisions of this law is set by the Ministry of Agriculture at 75 acres for the department of the Maine-et-Loire.

The usual pattern in case heirs cannot agree on succession is for the farming heir who has remained with the father to invoke the aid of the government. He asks for a ruling that the farm would not be viable if it were to be divided equally among the claimants. The second, and more risky, step is for one heir to have himself adjudged the most capable of maintaining the undivided farm. A complex institutional mechanism exists that will offer financial aid to a deserving heir, loaning him sufficient sums on easy terms with which to run the farm and to make payments to the other heirs. The law even provides for a governmental commission to purchase the farm from the heirs and to hold it, for periods up to five years, while the heir who has been chosen as farmer borrows (often from the same commission) or accumulates sufficient capital with which to buy the farm. During the interim no apparent change in status occurs, since the chosen farmer remains on his father's (the government's) land as nominal tenant. The weakness of the new provisions lies in the fact that one of the heirs must appeal to the commission before it can have any jurisdiction. In Lusson's case, it looks as if the division of the farm will be settled amicably within the family. Unless either the son or the son-in-law decides to abandon farming, or unless antagonism develops between them, the likelihood of an appeal to the commission is a remote one. Some people feel that, though there have been few appeals in the region around Chanzeaux, the mere existence of the legal mechanism influences heirs to agree among themselves on a reasonable compensation. But even that implicit pressure operates only when at least one of the heirs does not want the farm to be split.

The government's approach to the problem of parcellization has been much more direct. The current laws on land reform (*remembrement*), the most audacious of all the modern agricultural legislation, predate the Statut de Fermage of 1946 by a full five years. Indeed, if they had not been already in force, it is doubtful that the lawmakers of the immediate postwar period would have assumed the risk of further agricultural discontent that land reform involves. The crux of the new law is the assignment of full power for redistribution to a departmental commission headed by the prefect. The intention is not merely to straighten out boundaries and to regroup distant parcels, but to redistribute property in order to permit a more efficient use of machinery.

The first initiative in appealing for a land-reform project is still left to the tenant farmers and landowners in the commune. In the Maine-et-Loire, where only a few communes have been regrouped, as in departments like Seine-et-Marne and Eure (where regrouped communes number in the hundreds), the usual procedure has been for the farmers themselves to promote a project after study and recommendation by the Génie Rural. The final decision is the prefect's. Two projects will be undertaken in the Loire Valley near Chanzeaux: one at Mesnil en Vallée, the other at Saint-Georges sur Loire. The prefect of Maine-et-Loire took a careful sample of local opinion in both cases before giving his approval to the projects. Once a project is approved, it is carried out by a communal commission appointed by the prefect. This includes four members of the administration and four representatives of local interests — usually the mayor, his deputy, and two prominent farming owners. A justice of the peace presides. The pivotal figures are a surveyor, who assesses the values of each plot of land, and the mayor, who follows the surveyor over every parcel in the commune. The surveyor and the mayor then assign classifications to the land according to value. After the results of the classification are posted, the haggling begins and complaints are heard. Next, the new lots are tentatively assigned and posted, after which there is another period of review. Finally, the lots are actually redistributed, farmers are recompensed for any losses, and the public work of razing hedges and building ditches and roads begins.

The question for Chanzeaux is when *remembrement* will come. Successful projects are widely publicized in France. Recently fifty projects have been executed in the department of Deux Sèvres on the southern border of the Maine-et-Loire, and many Chanzeans feel that a redistribution project will be started in their commune. But they do not expect it for about ten years. Neither at the Chambre d'Agriculture in Angers nor at the mairie in Chanzeaux is it considered a pressing item of business. The Chambre d'Agriculture feels that there are other communities in the Maine-et-Loire where the situation is more critical and the need greater. M. Gardais, Chanzeaux's mayor, speaks guardedly about *remembrement*. His reticence is understandable, for a successful project requires a strong mayor, and Gardais is new in office. The actual period of classification is grueling for the communal commission; elected officials are often turned out in the middle of a controversial project. Chanzeaux's grain merchant, one of the most acute analysts of the commune's economy, predicts that land reform will not come until a succession of bad harvests or an abrupt decline in prices dramatizes the tenuousness of an economy based on the farming of small plots.

One hundred years ago there would have been just cause for disagreement about whether it was better to be a fermier or a proprietor. The tenant farmer had the advantage of working on a relatively large farm and of not being forced by the tradition of equal inheritance to divide the farm. If the lease passed from father to son, that was by the decision of the landlord; no title to property was involved. On the other hand, the tenant always lived under the potential threat of eviction, and his economic insecurity dampened any initiative to improve the farm. He had little freedom of action, in any case. Every decision, from what to plant in what field to when to go to church, was at the discretion of a paternalistic landlord. In exchange for political and social submission, however, the fermier received certain benefits. In periods of crop failure, the landlord might come to his assistance. The proprietor had a small farm with the land inconveniently dispersed in parcels. He could barely get by, but at least he could do as he pleased.

In the past thirty years, as the noble estates have been broken up with their owners going to the cities, the constraining paternalistic order has dissolved. A national government with a philosophy of social welfare has taken over the position previously held by the nobility. Compensation in times of crop failure now comes from the central government, through its price-regulating functions; rents too are controlled, and far lower than they would be on the free market. A fermier cannot be removed unless he has been grossly negligent or unless the rentier wants to farm the land himself. The fermier is now his own master.

Meanwhile the proprietor system has not changed. Although it now covers a larger area of Chanzeaux than it did in the past, the average size of farms has barely increased. The central government has tried to reform this system as well, but so far without success. Unable to effect structural reforms, it has resorted to indirect supports and subsidies. The system of *allocations familiales*, first initiated in 1937 and greatly intensified ten years later, gives welfare payments to families in proportion to the number of their children. Governmental support of agricultural prices has also, until recently, supported marginal farming, only postponing the inevitable. Today the proprietors are far less independent than the fermiers. Almost every aspect of the *propriétaire-exploitant* system as it stands today works against the farmer. His holdings are small and in scattered lots. The tradition of divided inheritance prevents the consolidation of his farm. The type of settlement he lives in — the hamlet or village — reinforces his natural desire for independence and his distrust of his neighbors.

Some of the proprietors try energetically to cope with their problem; Jean Arrial, for instance, makes up for the paucity of his land by growing intensive cash crops. Others, usually the older and the poorer, seem to lose hope. Their goal is just to keep their heads above water; often they become bitter and suspicious. When a student dressed in a corduroy shirt and jeans (an unlikely looking tax collector) went up to one of these farmers to ask the size of his farm, the first reaction was, "C'est pour les impôts?"

The position of the proprietors resembles the classic example of the four gasoline-station owners at a crossroads, not one of whom gets adequate business. The gas station needs customers; the farmer needs land. Each farmer hangs on, in the knowledge that, if his neighbor retires and he himself can get some of the land, he will be able to survive for at least a while.

5

Crops

FARMING in Chanzeaux is based on the cow. Of its 124 farms, 111 depend on cattle for the principal portion of their income. Nearly four fifths of the commune's farmland is used to raise feed for cattle. Chanzeaux's herds are dual-purpose, designed to produce both milk and meat. Generally, large farms tend to concentrate on meat, while smaller farms specialize in dairy products. Since cows will not give milk unless they give birth regularly, the dairy farmer is inevitably in the meat market. If he does not wish to expand his herd, he will sell his better calves to be raised as soon as they are weaned. Before they complete their first year, the lesser breeds are sold to be slaughtered for veal. Aged dairy cows also find their way to the slaughterhouse. The farmer who puts the emphasis on meat is still likely to produce some milk: in order to renew his herd, he must keep a number of cows. Even if he does not sell their milk, he will use it, combined with water and a dehydrated feed mix, to feed his calves once they have been weaned (see Table 11).

Providing nourishment for cattle is the most important activity on most Chanzeaux farms. The haying season begins in early June and lasts much of the month. After the hay has been cut, it is left to dry for a few days, then baled and stored in the barn. The recent introduction of silage, which can be cut early and stored while damp, promises to revolutionize this system. Today, if he works swiftly and is favored by good weather, the Chanzeaux farmer can hope to cut his hayfields twice. With silage he may get an extra cutting. Haying is exhausting work, compressed into a short, full period of time. Fodder beets and fodder cabbages require more effort than hay does. It is a different kind of work — not strenuous, but slow, steady, and tedious. Beets and cabbages are planted in late June and early July. Once the field has been prepared, the seedlings must be uprooted one by one, often from earth baked hard by the sun. Some oldtimers insist on transplanting by hand. They advance with astonishing speed, one

Table 11. Chanzeaux Products, 1963

Product	Chanzeaux			Total production, Maine-et-Loire	Total production, France
	No. of producers	Quantity sold	Value of sales (1,000 francs)		
Beef (tons)	114	210	1,400	28,207	1,238,000
Veal (tons)	114	8	44	3,272	423,000
Lamb	15	n.a.	85	n.a.	14,926
Wheat (1,000 quintals)	124	4.2	250	1,827	102,490
Milk (1,000 hectoliters)	114	25	710	3,876	246,000
Wine (1,000 hectoliters)	201	3.2	200	940	57,596
Camomile	78	n.a.	120	n.a.	n.a.
Mint	11	n.a.	25	n.a.	n.a.
Pansy seeds	27	n.a.	25	n.a.	n.a.
Tobacco (tons)	7	n.a.	75	1,769	40,615

Sources. For France and Maine-et-Loire: Ministry of Agriculture, *Statistique agricole, 1963*. For Chanzeaux: townhall records; Office National Interprofessionnel pour les Céréales; estimates.

Note. The Chanzeaux columns in this table are intended only to give an indication of the proper orders of magnitude. Most of the figures are gross estimates. The only hard figures are for sales of wheat and wine (1963), both of which are closely regulated by the government. The values of cash-crop sales are derived from the land area devoted to each crop in 1964 and estimates of average money yield per hectare for each crop. The least accurate figures are those for sales of cow products. They start from an estimate of a total of 1,000 milk cows (several thousand cattle) in Chanzeaux around 1964. That total is distributed among Chanzeaux's 111 cow-wheat farms on the basis of the exact size distribution of farms and the general pattern of production on large, medium, and small farms. Sales of calves for raising and of sheep wool are not included.

hand poking precise holes in the ground with a small tool as the other unerringly inserts the plants. Most Chanzeans, however, prefer the planting machine, a simple, often horse-drawn device. Feeding the planter is much like working on an assembly line: one machine sets the pace of the work. The person seated on it must be nimble enough to keep one hand full of seedlings while with the other hand he places them in the rapidly advancing pincers. Each miss means one less plant in the field. As the machine advances, it creates row after row of regularly spaced green dots, imposing a pleasing geometric pattern on the brown expanse of the newly plowed field.

Fodder beets are harvested in November. The cabbage harvest continues throughout the winter. Many older farmers have chilblained ears from their winters of daily trips to the cold cabbage fields. This crop has long been characteristic of the Mauges region, but today fodder beets and cabbages are on the way out, and the incidence of chilblained ears has noticeably decreased.

Once the beets and cabbages have been harvested, it is too late to plant any crop but wheat. Following a traditional rotation pattern, Chanzeaux farmers sow wheat rather than let the land lie fallow. It keeps weeds out without taking many nutrients from the soil. Furthermore, it provides the farmer with straw to bed his cattle and a respectable, reliable secondary income. Now that combines are universally employed, wheat is a crop requiring almost no work. On even the largest farm in the commune, the harvest can easily be finished in one day. But forty years ago the harvest was by far the biggest job of the year. Gangs of men spent weeks making the round of each others' farms, cutting the grain with scythes, tying it in sheaves, and carrying it to the farmyard. The threshing was done with a horse-drawn stoneroller on a huge table of dried manure. The first labor-saving innovation in this tiresome process was the reaper-binder, introduced to Chanzeaux in the thirties. The threshing machine followed close behind it, but the stoneroller persisted among the small farmers for many years. A few were still using it in 1953.

The combine, invented in the Great Plains of North America in the late nineteenth century, made its first appearance in Chanzeaux in 1955. A decade later, it had completely supplanted the thresher. With the thresher went the threshing party — one of the steadily decreasing number of occasions when Chanzeans gather in large numbers. Threshing day was the liveliest day a farm saw all year. Before five o'clock in the morning, twenty to thirty men were shouting and joking over the din of the machine. Ten or twelve men stationed on top of two giant sheaf stacks relayed the sheaves to others who fed them rhythmically into the machine. Still others stacked the straw bales and filled and stored the sacks of grain. At noontime, half a dozen buckets of water were set out so that the men could splash off the morning's dust and chaff before seating themselves throughout the house for the meal that half a dozen women had spent the morning preparing. This scene was repeated for the last time in Chanzeaux on thirteen farms in the summer of 1964. Threshing day has gone the way of card playing on winter evenings and the three-day wedding feast. It has been replaced by the distant drone of the combine, its headlights piercing the darkness long after every other light in the countryside has been extinguished.

The land surface planted in wheat has diminished steadily since the turn of the century. However, fertilizers and new seeds have increased yields so much that total production has probably increased.

In 1910 a farmer with 55 acres might have planted 15 in wheat. Today he would probably plant only 5, but his yield per acre would be three times as great. Ten years ago, wheat was grown exclusively for sale; today farmers keep about 10 percent of their harvest for feed. Most also grow a small amount of barley or oats to be ground into flour and fed to their animals. Flour is not an essential part of a cow's diet, but it provides an additional source of nourishment, useful in fattening animals for slaughter. (See Table 12.)

Wine is the product of which Chanzeaux is the proudest. Almost every farmer keeps at least a small plot of vines. Many bourg residents also own small vineyards. Fully 15 percent of Chanzeaux's cropland is in vineyards, but it is the principal source of income for only ten farmers. These vintners, primarily grouped in wine hamlets, cultivate a third of Chanzeaux's vineyards, most of which are concentrated in the part of the commune bordering on Rablay. The bright green uniformity of the Layon Valley hillsides hides the most fragmented landholding system in Chanzeaux. What appears to be a single field may actually contain rows cultivated by a dozen different farmers. One vintner may even tend rows 8 through 10, 30 through 34, and 41 through 46 in the same field, plus ten other widely scattered parcels in different fields.

The regrouping of winelands presents an even more complex problem than the regrouping of Chanzeaux's other divided land-holdings: no two vintners will ever be convinced that their vines are exactly the same. The slope of the land in relation to the sun, the content and drainage of the soil, the depth at which the rock table is found, all influence the quality of the wine. Some vines are more carefully tended than others. Some differ in age. Since vines produce for fifty or sixty years, the age of a vine is crucial in determining its value. When an old vineyard enters its decline, the vines must be pulled out and the land allowed to lie fallow for at least three years. The planting of new, quality vines, which must be bought from special nurseries, represents a major investment. Once he has replanted, the farmer must wait five years, until the young vines are big enough to yield grapes. Two more years must pass before the vines begin to produce high-quality wine. After the seven-year mark, the quality of the wine increases with each decade. When the vines reach their old age, the quantity produced begins to drop off until it is no longer profitable to keep them.

Table 12. Use of Land

Land	1949	1954	1964
Total surface area (acres)	7512	7512	7512
Total cropland (acres)	3337	3256	3011
Cereals			
Wheat	} 490	650	525
Meteil (wheat and rye)		25	0
Rye	62.5	25	0
Barley	22	25	50
Oats	237	250	100
	811.5	975	675
Tubers			
Potatoes	95	100	37.5
Jerusalem artichokes	15	25	17.5
Fodder beets	550	600	700
Fodder cabbages	387	450	325
Other	572	570	250
	1619	1745	1330
Temporary pasturage	212	312	750
Rotating pasture	187	200	200
Fallow	0	0	0
Miscellaneous			
Tobacco	n.a.	7	12
Camomile	n.a.	} 17	25
Pansy seed	n.a.		5–7
Mint	n.a.		7
Other	n.a.		5
		24	54–56
Permanent pasture	3131	3170	3350
Vines	512	525.5	475
Woods	247	| 247	247
Uncultivable land	177	177	325
Other	108	136.5	104

Source. Chanzeaux mayoralty records. The apparent precision of these figures is illusory: they are simply casual estimates (as converted into acres for this book) made every year by an official representative committee of Chanzeaux farmers.

When many farms had two or three workers, the vines received much more attention than they do today. It was still possible to care for vines on the best slopes — those that were too steep for a horse to plow. On these, continual expeditions were undertaken to recover the soil that had been washed downhill in rainstorms, to roll it back uphill in wheelbarrows, and to redistribute it by hand at the base of the vines. Even today, keeping the vines in condition requires painstaking work. In the winter, the dead wood must be removed and the vines carefully pruned. During the growing season, the rows must be continuously plowed to keep them free of weeds and to facilitate drainage. At least four times during the summer the leaves must be sprayed with a bright-blue sulphate solution that prevents mildew. The farmer with but a few vines to tend will carry the sprayer upon his back, pumping the solution out as, bent almost double, he moves slowly up and down the rows. Whatever free time the vintner may have is devoted to continuous selective pruning.

Weather permitting, the grape harvest is in October. In years when the summer has been cool and wet, however, it may be delayed as late as the middle of November, when the days are short and cold. The whole family gathers the grapes in plastic canisters and carries them to the cart. Depending on the weather, wine varies considerably in quality from year to year. In a good year it sells for approximately twice the price it brings in a bad year. Some producers sell to a wine cooperative, others to merchants, still others to private clients.

The Layon Valley's speciality is a sweet white wine with high alcoholic content, but Chanzeaux also produces a good rosé and an ordinary red table wine. The white and the rosé are destined chiefly for sale, but nearly all of the red is for table consumption. The white is too strong and too valuable to be taken regularly at meals. Nonetheless, whenever one Chanzean finds himself in the home of another, he is sure to be offered "un coup de blanc." It is easy for the very sociable to maintain themselves in a pleasant state of semi-inebriety. In fact, that state is difficult for postmen and traveling merchants to avoid.

In addition to beef, milk, wheat, and wine, many Chanzeaux farmers raise labor-intensive cash crops. Those who would otherwise have too many working hands for their land area can increase their revenue by putting this extra labor to work on such crops, which yield ten to twenty times as much money per acre as wheat and use a nearly insignificant amount of land. Chief among Chanzeaux's cash crops are tobacco and medicinal plants, principally camomile. The cultivation of tobacco requires large inputs of adult male labor. Camomile, on the other hand, is largely work for women and children.

Tobacco production in France is strictly supervised by a government tobacco monopoly, which licenses farmers to raise a certain number of tobacco plants. After careful preparation of the terrain, the seedlings are planted by hand in June. As the plants grow, the buds and the smaller leaves are pinched off so that the remaining leaves will be longer. Then the lower leaves are picked, wrapped in bundles, and strung up to dry. By the time this has been done, the middle leaves are ready to be picked, followed by the upper ones. Great care must be taken not to damage the leaves while handling them: the government's standards are so strict that a broken or blemished leaf is a lost leaf. Once the leaves have been dried, they must be sorted according to size and quality. This is done throughout the winter. All tobacco is sold to the government monopoly, which inspects the farmer's fields and barns to satisfy itself that he is not holding back any tobacco from the market. Delivery takes place on two days designated by the monopoly — one in December, the other in January. If the farmer does not appear on these days, his tobacco will not be bought.

One hectare of tobacco is enough to occupy most of a family's time all year and theoretically to provide most of its annual income. In fact, three Chanzeaux families do derive their principal income from tobacco, and a fourth specializes in a combination of tobacco and medicinal plants. Only three other Chanzeans raise any tobacco at all. Part of the explanation lies in the fact that there is a high element of risk in tobacco culture. Tobacco blights are unpredictable and can be devastating. In addition, tobacco is highly dependent upon the weather. One hailstorm in July or August is sufficient to ruin an entire year's crop. Most effective in discouraging Chanzeans from growing tobacco has been the new government regulation requiring special drying barns, a large investment for any farmer. As a result, only farmers who intend to raise tobacco on a grand scale can afford to raise it at all. In the mid-fifties, when the regulation was instituted, there were at least fifteen tobacco growers. Today there are only seven.

At present, there are 78 camomile patches in Chanzeaux. These yield somewhere between 5 and 10 percent of the camomile produced in all of France. (But camomile is the principal source of income for only one person — an old Belgian woman who came to Chanzeaux as a war refugee.) Women, children, and older people raise the flower in order to provide their families with supplementary income. Camomile is a brilliant white flower that grows on a small tangled plant clinging close to the ground. It is used to brew camomile tea, a drink popular in France for its soothing and healthful properties. Bitter extract of camomile is employed as an ingredient in apéritifs. It is also used to protect women's hair from the harmful effects of dyeing. The flower was first introduced into the southern Maine-et-Loire at the close of the nineteenth century, by a Parisian pharmacist with a country home in nearby Saint-Lambert. From there, it spread to about twelve neighboring communes. At present, 270 of the 280 acres of camomile cultivated in France are located in this area. A half-acre patch of camomile requires the labor of three pickers throughout the summer. Any eight- or nine-year-old Chanzeaux child can flick the flowers off camomile plants with amazing dexterity and speed. Still, their mothers and grandmothers can surpass them.

Gardens and barnyards are standard items on Chanzeaux's farms. Like the camomile patch, they are the woman's domain. Virtually all the fruits and vegetables consumed by the family are normally home-grown, from squash and scallions to peas and peppers. The barnyard is stocked with pigs, chickens, ducks, geese, and rabbits, but these animals are not raised for home consumption alone. On very small farms, the sale of rabbits, angora fur, chickens, and eggs may account for as much as a tenth of total income. An intelligent, efficient farmwife is absolutely essential to the successful operation of a Chanzeaux farm.

What crops a farmer will find it most profitable to raise is determined largely by the character and quantity of land and labor available to him. Just as certain soils are required for certain crops, so certain kinds of labor are required for certain tasks. Haying, harvesting, forking manure, and fixing fences are a man's work. Women, children, and older people do the milking, weed the garden, and pick camomile. On most Chanzeaux farms, the land and labor supplies are fixed by noneconomic forces. The distribution of land is historically determined, as we have seen, the present pattern of landholding dating from at least the eighteenth century. The purchase and rental markets for land are so sluggish that the farmer must be content with what he has. All of Chanzeaux's 124 farms are family farms. Since hired hands are becoming scarcer and costlier daily, the family is the chief supplier of labor. Nor is it possible to banish a brother or father-in-law from the farm simply because it is not economically rational to keep him. The Chanzeaux farmer, then, must decide what to produce given fixed supplies of land and labor with which to work.

In Chanzeaux there exists a division of functions between small farms and large farms. Those under 40 acres tend to put much greater emphasis on milk production, while those over 60 acres emphasize meat. This pattern is not peculiar to Chanzeaux, of course, for it can be observed throughout France. Since the small farmer normally has a large supply of labor relative to his small land surface, he will opt for activities that are labor-intensive. Dairy farming requires much more labor — male and female — than does beef raising. Dairy cattle must be milked in the morning, turned out to graze, and brought back to the barn for the evening milking. The barns must be cleaned daily. Since dairy cattle give birth frequently, there are usually calves to care for. On most farms these duties fall to the women and children. The men concern themselves mainly with producing fodder. Dairy cattle must be fed more generously than beef animals: a milk cow eats between one and a third and one and a half times more. Further, dairy cattle require a different kind of fodder. They pass more time in the barn, and the farmer who emphasizes milk production must stock more hay than the beef raiser does. However, at no time of the year, not even in the summer, will grass or hay alone suffice milk cows. Beets and cabbages are ideal fodder for them, and are also highly labor-intensive.

After he has fully provided for the needs of the cattle his land can support, the small farmer may still have a surplus of expensive labor (that of adult men) and inexpensive labor (that of women, children, and older people). If this remaining labor is to be employed, it must be channeled into activities that are extremely labor-intensive but require very little land: wine, tobacco, medicinal plants. Both wine and tobacco require very large inputs of adult male labor, and no farmer cultivates both. If such inputs are not available, the small farmer will choose to limit his supplementary cash crops to camomile, which absorbs only cheap labor. In fact, almost every small farm in Chanzeaux is brightened by a white camomile patch.

Unlike dairy farming, which guarantees the farmer a regular

monthly income, beef production is speculative. At least two and a half years must elapse between the birth of an animal and its sale. In France, because of the archaic organization of the beef market, it is particularly difficult for the farmer to get an idea of what the supply and demand will be in three years. Variations in prices paid to the farmer for steers are very great. Nor does the trend in these prices accurately reflect the steady upward trend in meat prices paid by the consumer. For the small farmer with a herd of only 15 cattle, speculating in the beef market is simply too risky. The large farmer with 100 acres and a herd of 40 cattle is less dependent on the revenue realized from the sale of any one animal and is, therefore, in a better position to speculate.

More important in determining the large farmer's concentration on meat production are his land and labor resources. Only on a very few farms larger than 60 acres does the farmer work alone. Usually he is assisted by another full-time worker, perhaps his brother or his son, or at least by a part-time hired hand. Still, were he to attempt to cultivate his land as intensely as the small farmer does, he would soon exhaust his supply of adult male labor. For him, dairy farming would be a wasteful use of resources. Meat production offers him a way of economizing on adult male labor. Beef animals require comparatively little care; since they spend almost the entire year grazing in the fields, they need only small quantities of such produced fodder as hay, cabbages, and beets. Sheep, kept by twelve large Chanzeaux farmers, require even less. François Challain, with 50 acres, leaves only 25 percent of it in pasture. Eugène Bourdelle, with 85 acres, leaves over half of his land in pasture. Gérard Bellanger, with 100 acres, leaves approximately 60 percent in pasture.

Adult male labor is the factor in short supply on a large farm in Chanzeaux. Cheap labor is as plentiful as on smaller farms, though it is not as thoroughly utilized. Like the mistresses of small farms, women on large farms milk, tend the garden, and supervise the barnyard. But they are much less likely to work picking, drying, and sorting tobacco, or to be burdened with camomile patches. Less pressed for income, families on large farms need not work their women, children, and old people quite so hard.

On Chanzeaux's farms, the land and the labor are givens. They determine the kind of crops the farmer can produce. But the value of his crops, and ultimately the success of his farm, is determined by a market he cannot control. Because demand in markets for agricultural products is not keeping pace with the growth of the rest of the French economy, many of Chanzeaux's smaller farms are becoming unprofitable, and Chanzeans are being forced to think about radical changes in size of the farms and the farm population.

6

The Farm Problem

THE ANNUAL income of an urban French family is about 17,500 francs. The average Chanzeaux farm family, even taking into account the produce it grows for its own consumption, lives on no more than 7,500 francs per year.[1] More mobile, more widely traveled, better read than their parents, the younger members of Chanzeaux's farm community have become sharply aware of the disparity between their standard of living and that of the citydweller. Like the new generation of farmers throughout France, they aspire to a greater share in the fruits of the postwar economic expansion.

This aspiration expresses itself first in profound dissatisfaction with the present limitations on housing and educational opportunities. The housing problem is acute. Some families of six or seven live in two or three rooms, and many young couples are unable to find space at all. The situation arouses great indignation in the commune. A survey made in 1958 concluded that housing was Chanzeaux's chief problem and described the status quo as "shocking." Sixty-five percent of Chanzeaux's houses were built before 1871; only 4 percent after 1932. Houses are very small, rarely exceeding three or four rooms; and often they are inhabited by families spanning three generations. There are severe limitations on educational opportunity, caused primarily by the difficulty of providing economically for a child's extended schooling. Most young couples had to leave school themselves at the age of fourteen and are apprehensive about the future of their children, who may have to do the same. Indeed, many are determined to see to it that their children will be at least able to complete a secondary-school education. Aspiration toward a higher standard of living is expressed to an even greater extent in the eagerness with which Chanzeaux's younger families seek to acquire the consumer goods and enjoy the leisure time typical of city life. Cars have been a standard item on Chanzeaux farms for the past decade, but in the last five years vintage models have been replaced by newer, shinier ones. (Chanzeaux still has not experienced the phenomenon of the two-car family.) The last five years have also seen the proliferation of washing machines from a handful, owned mostly as luxury items by bourg dwellers, to enough to supply over half the farms in Chanzeaux. The first television set appeared five years ago. At present there are sixty sets in the commune, forty on farms. Chanzeaux's children, nonetheless, have displayed a remarkable immunity to the tube's hypnotic effect.

The younger farmers show a new interest in and desire for leisure time. Claude Chaillou, who works at least twelve hours a day, is a strong partisan of leisure: "In my father's time it was work, work, nothing but work. You need a little rest, a little fun." In recent years the Chaillous and a few other young, prospering couples have begun to take vacations of unprecedented length — a week or more. Many others would like to follow suit but feel that such vacations would be much too costly. They point with envy to the paid vacations enjoyed by factory workers.

With their present incomes, the younger farmers have little hope of satisfying their desire for a more comfortable life. Nor is the outlook for the future bright. The demand and supply conditions that determine the farmer's revenue are not apt to change in a manner favorable to him. The prospects are most promising for Chanzeaux's beef raisers. Almost two thirds of the beef produced in the Maine-et-Loire is exported to Paris to supply national markets (see Table

Table 13. Markets for Agricultural Production, Maine-et-Loire
(Average Year, Mid-1950's)

Products	Average production	Average local consumption	Surplus	Principal outlets
Meat (tons)	28,500	10,700	17,800	Paris, southeast, Midi
Milk (hectoliters)	2,000,000	1,500,000	500,000	Paris, Lyons, Midi, southwest
Grain (quintals)	1,650,000	675,000	825,000	Mouth of Loire and Bordeaux regions, for export
Wine (hectoliters)	1,000,000	—	—	—
Good	350,000	—	—	—
Ordinary	650,000	—	—	—

Source. Institut National des Statistiques et des Etudes Economiques (INSEE), survey.

13). France, like her partners in the Common Market, was suffering in 1965 from a beef shortage. Although demand was growing rapidly, supply has remained relatively constant. Increased demand at the consumer level had allowed intermediaries with monopoly power to widen their margins. Prices paid to the farmer for cattle had been only slightly influenced by the growth in demand. Still, from 1949 to 1963, the index of prices paid to beef producers for their animals rose more rapidly than the price index of industrial goods or the index of the cost of agricultural inputs (see Table 14).[2]

Table 14. Percentage Increase in Various Price Indices, 1949–1963

Index	%
Prices to the farmer	
Beef	156
Veal	196
Pork	115
Milk	60
Wheat	71
Chickens, rabbits	49
Prices of purchased inputs to agriculture	76
Wholesale prices for all industrial products	98

Sources. INSEE, *Annuaire statistique, 1957* and *1964*, sections on prices.

There remains good possibility for improvement. Reduction of the power of intermediaries and in the size of their margins would benefit the farmer greatly.

Small farmers who rely on dairy products for most of their revenue are in a much grimmer position than beef producers (see Table 15). Neither domestic demand conditions nor the demand conditions in the other Common Market countries are encouraging. The French milk producer can expect no real benefits from the integration of European markets for dairy products. As the domestic consumer's income rises, he spends an increasingly small percentage of it on dairy products. A 10 percent increase in income normally generates approximately a 5 percent increase in expenditures on beef, while the increase in spending on milk products is generally much smaller. It produces no additional expenditure on milk for drinking. Because of slow growth in demand, from 1949 to 1963 the price of milk fell relative to indices of the price of industrial products and the cost of inputs into agriculture. If milk producers in France are to raise their standard of living, each must capture a larger share of the market. This requires a continued decrease in the agricultural population.

Table 15. Income Elasticities of Demand, 1956

Product	% increase in amount purchased[a]
Beef	5.1
Veal	5.6
Fresh pork	4.1
Ham	7.2
Fresh and powdered milk	−0.03
Cheese	5.9
Butter	3.1
Bread	−1.2
Chickens, rabbits, venison	13.9
Tobacco, matches	10.1

Source. G. Rottier, "L'Analyse des budgets familiaux," *Consommation* (July–September 1959), pp. 36–39. The estimates are drawn from a cross-section study based on questionnaires. The income elasticity figures given assume a base income of 3,330 francs in 1956.

[a] The percentage increase in expenditures on various items is associated with a 10% increase in the income of an average French household, in 1956.

The French agricultural population as a whole has been steadily decreasing for at least the past century, a trend common to all industrialized countries. In the postwar period the pace of this development has accelerated, partly because of rapid technological advances. The grain sector is the portion of French agriculture that has experienced the most dramatic technological change. Yield per acre has risen from an average of 37 quintals in the period 1935–1939 to an average of 68 quintals in 1958–1962. In 1963 the average yield in Seine-et-Oise, a department with a high concentration of large, efficient wheat farms, was 95 quintals per acre.[3] With demand highly static, large farms capable of realizing such yields are rapidly driving less efficient producers from the wheat market. Although they make up only 3 percent of the wheat growers in France, the farmers of the Paris basin account for 30 percent of the crop. Specialized, highly efficient producers are presently capturing the national markets for chicken, eggs, and pork as well as wheat. Although these products have never been crucial sources of income for Chanzeaux, the loss of the supplementary income they represented has hurt Chanzean farmers. Technical improvement and specialization are continually reducing the range of products that unspecialized farmers can produce profitably.

Beef and milk production have not yet undergone this kind of technological advance. The majority of France's meat and dairy products are supplied by small, mixed farming establishments similar to Chanzeaux's cow-wheat farms. Beef producers are not yet under intense competitive pressure. So far, it is the psychological dimension of the problem that is crucial in Chanzeaux: aspirations have outstripped income. There is evidence, however, that French beef and milk production stands on the eve of technological revolution. Although the number of breeds vying for importance has been drastically reduced since World War II, French farmers have not taken full advantage of artificial insemination and controlled breeding practices. Herds remain dual-purpose. In addition, farmers continue to produce their own fodder. They still feed their cattle grass in place of grain. The introduction of grain feeding, widely utilized in the United States, is being delayed by France's artificially high wheat prices and artificially low beef prices. In all probability, beef and milk production will undergo rapid modernization within the next few decades. Dramatic increases in productivity will result in increased supply and, ultimately, lower prices. The number of families that the beef and milk sector can support will drop.

The French government, itself responsible for creating much of the present crisis atmosphere, clearly anticipates such a development. Thirty years ago the government was still distributing the Mérite Agricole (agricultural equivalent of the Legion of Honor) to families that had lived three generations on the same farm, and was praising the peasant for his "sturdy way of life." All this has changed. The de Gaulle government's main concern has been to force the French farmer to confront the realities of his economic situation. On December 15, 1962, Edgar Pisani, the minister of agriculture, described the government's vision of the future with characteristic bluntness: "Given present economic conditions, the fifty-acre polycultural farm cannot be saved. If evolution is to follow its natural course, there will be in France, in a few decades, 500,000 large farms. The present policy of the government is to preserve about one million viable farms. But for us to say, or to allow others to say, that we can save 1,500,000 farms would be to lie." [4] This is the primary reality with which Chanzeaux must cope.

Market Reform

One consequence of the new awareness Chanzeaux farmers have of their economic situation has been an increased participation in cooperatives and producers' groups designed to improve market position. Cooperatives are not new in France. The largest one presently operating in Chanzeaux, the Coopérative Agricole de Thouarcé, was founded in 1891; it extended its activities to wheat in 1934. During the depression, cooperatives like the Thouarcé one were expanded throughout France. By providing the extensive stocking facilities essential to the success of support policy, they were instrumental in stabilizing the depressed wheat market. Equipped with a fleet of twenty trucks, the Thouarcé cooperative is today one of the largest wheat-marketing concerns in western France, possessing the power to influence the regional, if not the national, market. Although in theory run by the farmers themselves, the Thouarcé cooperative is continually plagued by a disappointing amount of member participation, an inevitable consequence of its size.

The Thouarcé cooperative currently markets over 60 percent of the wheat shipped out of Chanzeaux. Another 30 percent is marketed by other cooperatives. In the past decade, the cooperatives have increased their share of the Chanzeaux market, and the trend may well continue. Most of the farmers who still sell to private grain merchants are older men who do so largely for friendship's sake. Their successors will probably opt for a cooperative. However, given the stability of wheat prices, the economic advantages involved in belonging to one are not too great. The cooperatives usually do offer a few more centimes per quintal than the private dealers who service Chanzeaux. In addition, they are bound by law to accept and market all the grain delivered by their members, provided of course that it meets the standards set by the government.

The structural defects in the wheat-marketing system have for the most part been corrected. The Chanzeaux wheat producer's basic problem is increasing his efficiency in order to compete with the huge farms of the Paris basin and the north. For producers of medicinal plants the situation is quite different. Consider the case of camomile, which is the most important of these plants for Chanzeaux. Highly sensitive to quality, camomile prices show great fluctuation. They normally observe a six-year cycle, involving three poor years followed by three good years. Under these conditions stocking can be highly advantageous. In 1961 first-grade camomile sold for 5 francs per kilogram; in 1962, for 17.5 francs per kilogram. The producer who had stocked his quality camomile in 1961 and waited until 1962 to sell it would have more than tripled his revenues. Very few farmers possess the financial resources to undertake such a maneuver. Most sell their camomile at the prevailing prices to private dealers, two of whom live in Chanzeaux, who then stock and follow the market. They transmit price fluctuations very inefficiently, exaggerating downward movements in the price paid by consumers and minimizing upward movements.

In 1960, thirty-odd growers of medicinal plants from the southern Maine-et-Loire formed the Regional Medicinal Plants Cooperative. Since its founding, the cooperative has grown to include over a hundred producers scattered throughout the department, among them ten from Chanzeaux. Despite its rapid growth, it still retains its original crusading spirit. Unlike the Thouarcé cooperative, with which it is loosely associated, it is run by participant members who take direct responsibility for its actions. In order to become a member, the farmer must not only pay a membership fee but also agree to invest in the cooperative a percentage of the value of his transactions with it. In addition, he must undertake to deliver his entire production of medicinal plants. The cooperative pays the farmer a portion of the value of his plants within a week of receiving them and the remainder when they are finally sold.

The marketing of the plants delivered to the cooperative is directed by the elected administrative council. The council sets base prices below which the cooperative will stock rather than sell. At present, the cooperative has three years of mint production on hand. When the prevailing price is sufficiently high, the administrative council, taking into account prospective developments in the market, decides what quantities to offer for sale. The cooperative executed its most brilliant coup to date in 1964. Throughout 1963, second-grade camomile sold for approximately 7 francs per kilogram. Confronted with this exceptionally low price, the cooperative's directors astutely decided that it would be wiser to stock than to sell. The following year the cooperative was able to sell the second-grade camomile for 15 francs per kilogram, over twice what it would have brought the preceeding year. The medicinal plants cooperative is a dynamic operation that sensibly improves the producer's economic position. Its membership almost certainly will continue to grow.

Milk and meat are Chanzeaux's principal products. It is by organizing to improve their position in markets for these goods that Chanzeaux farmers stand to gain the most. The milk producer's fundamental problem is neutralizing the economic power of the dairy with which he deals. The individual producer cannot hope to bargain in equal terms with a large dairy. Two solutions offer themselves: either an advance up the processing ladder or a grouping of suppliers. Thirteen Chanzeaux farmers belong to the cooperative dairies, ten to the cooperative of Vihiers and three to that of Ancenis. Since Ancenis consistently pays prices that are among the highest in the Maine-et-Loire, the farmers who deal with it are satisfied with their position. However, Vihiers is a small, young cooperative. Not as efficient as the giant Ancenis, it offers prices that are consistently lower than those paid out by the commercial dairies. To survive, Vihiers must increase its efficiency. Over 60 percent of Chanzeaux's dairy produce is sold to two large commercial dairies, Avrilla and Maugeais. Within the past decade, Avrilla's suppliers have formed a producers' organization in order to effect a balance in bargaining power with the dairy. Although not the most active group in the Maine-et-Loire, it has succeeded in wresting substantial price and premium increases from Avrilla. The organization is now demanding that the dairy match the end-of-year rebates paid by the cooperatives. At present the FDSEA (the departmental branch of France's most important farmers' union) is making a concerted effort to organize a grouping of the Maugeais suppliers. In Chanzeaux the initiative is being taken by Eugène Bourdelle. The organization is slated to begin functioning after the spring of 1966. Since Maugeais pays low prices, the proposed grouping can be of real significance to the Maugeais suppliers in Chanzeaux.

The meat-marketing structures prevailing in most of France are archaic and highly inefficient. Privileged intermediaries employ their economic power to make excessive profits at the expense of both consumer and producer. For the latter especially, structural reform of the beef market is a matter of urgent concern. Almost all cattle raised in Chanzeaux are sold at the Thursday meat market in Chemillé. Chemillé, which has been a market town since the times of Roman Gaul, is located roughly 5 miles from the bourg of Chanzeaux. As late as 1958, some Chanzeans were still walking their cattle to market, leaving their farms at one or two in the morning in order to reach Chemillé between five and six o'clock. Supposedly, the long nocturnal trek firmed up the cows' muscles, making them more attractive to prospective buyers. But sometimes cattle used to collapse before reaching their destination. Once in Chemillé, the farmer had completed the largest part of his task. Usually he entrusted the job of selling his cattle to a professional cattle dealer. Quite often, the dealer's father had, in his time, sold cattle for the farmer's father.

Cattle selling was and is a rite in which only men participate: the women sell barnyard produce at a discrete distance from the men in one of Chemillé's smaller squares. After 7:00 in the morning, the spacious main square in Chemillé is brown with bellowing cattle. Buyers, dressed in the characteristic blue smock, mill through the market, adroitly poking the cattle to determine the quality of the meat. If a buyer is interested in a particular animal, he demonstrates his interest by making the seller a ridiculously low offer. The seller angrily retorts that he could never consider such a price. The buyer and seller begin to bargain in earnest, and a rapid-fire negotiation in earthy slang well spiced with insults ensues. Most of the dispute revolves around the animal's weight. Although there is a public scale in the square, the cow is never placed on it. When a bargain is finally made, the two hagglers strike their right hands together with great gusto: often they are personal friends. The buyer, usually a middleman who will then sell to another middleman, then clips his initials into the animal's hair and moves on to begin the entire process again. By 9:30 the cattle have been loaded into tightly packed trucks that will convey them to the slaughterhouse. Leaving a manure-covered square behind them, the men retire to nearby cafés to spend the remainder of the morning joking and drinking wine.

Four or five years ago, farmers took their own animals to market, but now most of them allow cattle dealers to transport their animals, paying a percentage commission in each sale. The basic characteristics of the marketing structure remain unaltered, however. Since the slaughterhouses in the Maine-et-Loire are very small, beef must be shipped out on the hoof. This adds considerably to the number of middlemen involved, each of whom cuts into the farmer's revenue. The buyer normally ships his cattle to the slaughtering center of La Villette, located near Paris. There he hires an agent (*commissionnaire*) to take responsibility for selling the animals, paying him a fixed commission per head. At La Villette there are only 43 such agents, but they have the power to influence prices throughout France. The law does not prohibit their doubling as merchants, buying and selling for their own accounts. These 43 agents sell to 233 slaughtering concerns (*chevillards*). The slaughterhouses in turn sell to butchers who put the processed meat on the market. Between the farmer and the consumer there are at least five intermediaries.[5]

The demand for beef is increasing swiftly in France and in Europe as a whole. But the quantity of beef produced in France in 1965 was about equal to the quantity produced in 1961. The structure of the beef market is largely responsible for this disturbing phenomenon. Rises in price resulting from increased demand are absorbed by powerful middlemen, particularly those at La Villette, rather than transmitted to the farmer, who has no real incentive to expand his production. Today, the French consumer pays more for meat than consumers in any of the other nations of the Economic Community, while French farmers receive less for their cattle than farmers in any other country of the Community. Dutch farmers receive four fifths of the revenues their cattle ultimately yield; German farmers, seven tenths. The French farmer receives barely three fifths of these revenues. Legitimate cause for complaint clearly exists.

In the near future, Chanzeaux farmers will participate in an effort to restructure their sector of the beef market. Since beef is Chanzeaux's most important product, the move can be a profitable one. Ten years ago, hoping to eliminate the numerous middlemen between the farmer and the consumer, a small group of beef producers founded a cooperative slaughterhouse in Chemillé. Incompetently managed, the experiment failed miserably. But the municipality of Chemillé has recently taken up a new project for constructing a slaughterhouse. This time it will be equipped with extensive freezing facilities. The plan is as follows: farmer members will deliver their cattle to the slaughterhouse when they have succeeded in fattening them sufficiently; the meat will then be stored in the freezer until it can be sold at an acceptable price. This advance up the processing ladder offers the farmers many advantages. The quality and amount of meat yielded by a given animal will be known. The farmer will be sure that he is being paid for all the meat his cattle yielded. The stocking facilities provided by the freezer unit will enable him to hold his beef off the market until it can be sold at an attractive price. Previously the producer was at the mercy of price fluctuations, since he could not afford the fodder necessary to keep his animals alive while he waited for prices to rise.

Eventually the greatest boon to the farmer will be the elimination of middlemen between farm and slaughterhouse and the bypassing of La Villette. Profits previously kept by these middlemen will revert to the farmer. The most important of these profits are of course those arrogated to themselves by the most powerful intermediaries, those at La Villette. In the long run, by selling graded carcasses to meat wholesalers, the users of the Chemillé slaughterhouses may help to bring prices paid by the consumer and those received by the farmer into a direct relation, something the French government has been unsuccessfully attempting for over a decade. The breaking of La Villette's power and the rationalization of the beef market could mean a revenue increase of as much as 15 percent for beef producers. Unfortunately, such thoroughgoing reform is at least a decade away. For the present, most Chanzeaux farmers are guardedly optimistic about the opening of Chemillé's slaughterhouse, an important first step toward necessary reform. Claude Chaillou, a Chanzean cattle dealer, is decidedly apprehensive about this event, scheduled for 1966. So is his mother-in-law, the village butcher and caterer, who will no longer be permitted to have animals slaughtered in her backyard.

Certainly, the efforts that Chanzeaux farmers have exerted and are exerting to improve their market position have yielded them important extra revenues. What is doubtful, however, is that this income will be enough to satisfy the aspirations of the new generation of farmers. The measures that Chanzeaux farmers have taken in this area are useful, even necessary ones, but they are only stopgaps. If the new generation of farmers is to fulfill its expectations, a radical restructuring of Chanzeaux's farms is required.

Mechanization

Chanzeaux's population has declined steadily since the mid-nineteenth century, but in the past decade emigration has accelerated dramatically. Between 1958 and 1964, 192 more people moved away from Chanzeaux than came into it. Foremost among the emigrants are farmers' sons in their early twenties or late teens who found blue-collar jobs in nearby towns. There are only half as many boys aged fifteen to nineteen in the commune's countryside as there were ten years ago. Also, an increasing number of farmers' sons are commuting from the farm to jobs in Chanzeaux or neighboring communes. Consequently, the agricultural work force has diminished by 10 percent in ten years.[6] (See Tables 16 and 17 and age-distribution graph.)

Table 16. Farm Labor Supply in Chanzeaux

No. and age	1926	1954	1964
Boys, 15–19	—	47	24
Agricultural workers	132	23	15
Men, 15–59	—	240	214

Table 17. Status of Sons, Aged 15–19, of Farmers and Agricultural Workers Living in Chanzeaux, 1964

Sons living in Chanzeaux		Sons living away from Chanzeaux	
Parent's farm	14	Nonfarm workers, apprentices	9
Someone else's farm	5	Military service	4
Nonfarming jobs in Chanzeaux	6	Secondary school	5
Nonfarming jobs in neighboring		Trade school	1
communes	3	Occupation unknown	4
	28		23

Note. Formerly, those Chanzeans who left for jobs in the cities came almost exclusively from the bourg (see Chapter 8). Farmers' sons left mainly for jobs as farmers or farmhands. Movement directly from a Chanzeaux farm to the city was extremely rare. Almost no farm children pursued their schooling beyond the normal Chanzeaux course. Clearly, the pattern has changed. The two brothers in construction work as apprentices in Cholet, and the one boy in the shoe industry in Jallais are all working in occupations new to Chanzeaux farmers' sons.

Before the Second World War, male farm labor was much more plentiful than it is today. Claude Chaillou's father employed four workers to assist him on his 100 acre farm. This was not exceptional. Any farm larger than 60 acres required the labor of four or five men. Today Chaillou employs only one worker. Only one of the largest farms in Chanzeaux has five men working on it. Since the war, farmers have been replacing increasingly scarce and expensive labor with machines. Mechanization can be both a cause of and a response to a decreasing agricultural labor force but in Chanzeaux the labor shortage appears to have been crucial.

In order to pay for itself, a machine must receive a certain number

AGE OF MEN ON FARMS

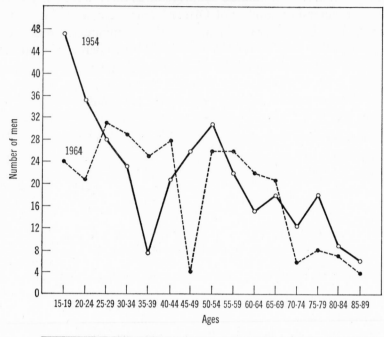

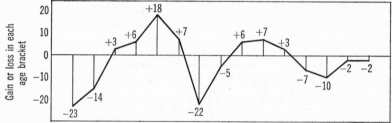

of hours of use: the larger the farm, the more feasible mechanization is. In Chanzeaux, the large farmers have formed the vanguard of each successive wave of mechanization. In the 1930s it was they who first invested in expensive harvesting machinery. Although the small farmers are much more dependent on milk sales, it is the large farmers whose herds are big enough to justify milking machines. Thirteen of the first fourteen farmers to buy milking machines after the war worked large farms. Two thirds of the tractors bought by Chanzeans before 1961 were purchased by farmers with more than 75 acres.[7] Only one fifth of the farms larger than 75 acres remain without tractors today (see Table 18).

Psychological factors played an important part in a second wave of tractor purchases that took place from 1961 to 1965. The tractor has become the symbol of the progressive farmer.[8] In 1961, there were 56 farms larger than 30 acres that were not equipped with tractors. Be-

Table 18. Farm Size and Tractor Purchase

	Farm		
Purchase	12–30 acres (5–12 hec.)	31–74 acres (13–29 hec.)	Over 75 acres (30 hec.)
Tractor bought before 1961	2	9	18
Bought 1961–65	0	17	4
None	39	28	6
	41	54	28

tween 1961 and 1965 the men running 21 of these farms invested in tractors. In 6 cases, the farmer was a young man who had just taken over his lands. In 8 more cases there was a young man over twenty-one about to take over the management of the farm. However, on almost two thirds of the farms that remained without tractors, there were no young men. When asked why the number of tractors in Chanzeaux had doubled between 1961 and 1965, Jean Delaunay replied that many sons had threatened to leave their farms if their fathers did not buy tractors. Some of these purchases certainly were economically irrational. The government estimates that in the region surrounding Chanzeaux at least 50 acres are required to justify investment in a tractor. By this standard, 10 of the purchases made by Chanzeaux farmers before July 1965 were errors. Still, the irrational motive should not be exaggerated. Between 1961 and 1965, no farmer with less than 30 acres bought a tractor.

Those most committed to mechanization are young farmers with large farms. Not only do they dispose of the necessary land surface, but they are free of their elders' crippling fear of credit. Since World War II they have begun to borrow the large sums necessary to buy machinery (see Table 19). It is these farmers who have been the most creative in their response to the problems posed by the need to mechanize. In 1962, eight men with farms in and near the village of Plessis formed the Association d'Entr'aide du Plessis to facilitate and regu-

Table 19. Loans Outstanding from the Crédit Agricole to Chanzeaux Farmers, May 1965

Type of loan	Total amount of debt (francs)	No. of debtors of each type
Short-term (up to 18 mos. at 6%)	57,800	13
Medium-term, equipment (up to 15 yrs. at 6%)	143,389	31
Jeunes Agriculteurs (up to 20 yrs. at 2%)ᵃ	156,480	27
Medium-term, construction (up to 15 yrs. at 6%)	107,811	11
Long-term, land purchase (up to 30 yrs. at 3%)ᵇ	159,945	25

Source. Angers branch of the Crédit Agricole. A number of farmers had several kinds of loans outstanding. Thus the total number of loans is greater than the total number of debtors in Chanzeaux. The number of debtors, May 1965, was 67, of which 49, born before 1930, were liable for 408,400.8 francs and 18, born after 1930, for 217,024.1 francs. (All francs in these tables are new francs.)

ᵃ Special loan for men starting a farming career; ceiling of 12,000 francs per person.
ᵇ Ceiling of 20,000 francs per person.

larize the sharing of labor and machinery. Chanzeaux farmers had previously exchanged both labor and machinery, but never on a regular basis. Five of the eight founders had recently lost labor. Six were younger than thirty-five. Seven of the founders worked farms of more than 60 acres (see Table 20).

Table 20. Founding Members of the Association d'Entr'aide du Plessis

Name	Age in 1962	Size of farm (acres)	Form of tenure
Jacques Pinier	34	102	fermier
André Blond	31	92	fermier
Henri Amelin	29	72	fermier
François Challain	37	62	fermier
Pierre Brichet	31	62	proprietor
Jean Mercier	46	62	proprietor
Joseph Saudreau	34	85	fermier
Michel Fruchaud	32	20	proprietor

The association was born in the minds of Pierre Brichet, Jacques Pinier, and Henri Amelin. Brichet and Pinier practice the most advanced form of cooperation in Chanzeaux. They have merged the operation of their contiguous farms. With their workers they do the day's work without regard to boundaries. Amelin is Chanzeaux's leading agricultural innovator. He is continually experimenting with new techniques. All three are ardent Catholics. In 1961, Pinier and Brichet were weighing the possibility of buying a fork lift to attach to one of their tractors. They decided that between them they could not account for enough use to make the purchase worthwhile. They then asked Amelin if he would consider joining them in making the investment. Amelin replied by asking them if they would be interested in using the powerful but expensive diesel tractor that he was contemplating buying. All three were interested in a regular form of cooperation. They then invited a number of their neighbors to join them; five accepted. In 1962, both the mechanical fork and the diesel tractor were purchased, and the association began to function.

Most of the machines used by the association are individually owned. These include a diesel tractor, heavy plowing equipment, a haybaler, a mechanical fork, a manure spreader, and several fertilizer spreaders. Two cooperatively owned silage machines are exceptions to this rule. By far the largest stock of machinery belongs to Henri Amelin, whose diesel tractor powers many of the other members' machines. The members of the association agree on rental rates for the different pieces of machinery and on a rate of exchange between machinery and labor. Under the section of the Complementary Law of 1962 defining the status of entr'aide contracts, these agreements as well as the charter of the association are legally binding. Throughout the year, running accounts of members' transactions are kept. At the end of the year, these accounts are settled. In practice, since Amelin owns such a preponderant share of the machinery, the other members accumulate debts to him. From time to time they pay them off, sometimes in cash, but normally by forming a day-long work gang to do some large job on Amelin's 70-acre farm. Last July, when eleven men gathered at Amelin's to bring in all his hay in a single day, there was an exuberant feeling of historic accomplishment; everyone agreed that a snapshot should be taken.

Amelin has been criticized for using the association as a means of renting his machines without paying the license fee required by the government. The criticism seems unfair. Amelin probably is not being paid very highly for taking the large amount of risk that he does take — largely because no one else is willing to. Recently, the association's members agreed that a haybaler was needed. Eventually Amelin took both the initiative and the risk involved in buying it.

During the summer of 1965, the members of the association were quite pessimistic about its future. It has grown to include thirteen members and, in the process, has become slightly unwieldy. Some members grumble that renting machines outright would provide a better solution to the problem of mechanization. In addition, the group is split by the kind of petty quarrels that can be found in any tiny settlement. But the basic difficulty is that there is no consensus within the group about its future. Although tireless Henri Amelin and a few other cooperators would like to push on toward the ultimate goal of cooperative operation of the farms, the majority of the members remain more conservative. They point to the present diversity in types of farming to underline the difficulty of more complete coordination. If Chanzeaux farmers were less jealous of their independence, this obstacle would not be insuperable. Despite their justified fears about its future, the members of the association are quick to admit that they have benefited from its existence.

On small farms, too, there is less adult male labor available than formerly. Where there used to be three men, there is now generally one. Many farmers with less than 40 acres work their farms alone. For most of the year these men can manage their tasks by themselves. But there are some jobs that simply cannot be done by a single person. Bringing in the hay, for instance, requires at least two men: one to load the cart, one to fork the hay up to him. Small farmers solve this problem by sharing work with a neighbor on a purely informal basis. Most of the farmers who exchange chiefly labor work farms smaller than 60 acres.[9] Such sharing is usually confined to jobs that neither party could manage alone: the spirit of individualism remains strong.

The small farmer cannot afford to buy machines for his operation. If he wishes to mechanize, he must find another way of doing so. For some, the Association d'Entr'aide du Plessis has provided this alternative. None of the five farmers who have joined it since its founding in 1961 operates a large farm. One acute Chanzean observer of the agricultural scene predicts that three of these will abandon their farms by 1970. Essentially, the association offers these men the opportunity of selling their labor without lowering themselves to the status of salaried agricultural laborers. By involving both large and small farmers in a cooperative mechanization effort, the association minimizes the conflict that might develop if only the large farmers were able to mechanize. In a sense, this means that the influence of this radical experiment in social organization is a conservative influence.

Most small farmers gain access to machines by renting them from entrepreneurs who assemble the necessary hours of use by making a business of operating machinery. When a new innovation appears, normally a new entrepreneur swiftly emerges to take advantage of it. Sometimes this allows small farmers to adopt the innovation before large farmers do. Artificial insemination of livestock is a case in point. In 1956, an artificial-insemination cooperative was organized near Angers. Large farmers, most of whom owned bulls that they rented to small farmers, were not eager to join, particularly since stud fees represented a lucrative source of additional income. The small farmers, anxious to free themselves of dependence on neighbors with bulls, did join. Artificial insemination offered them new flexibility in breeding their stock. Most attractive was the possibility of increasing beef production without detracting from milk production: Charolais bulls, good meat producers, could be crossed with Maine-Anjou cows, excellent milk producers, to yield offspring that give quality veal and beef. Since its introduction, this breeding technique alone has increased Chanzeaux's veal and beef production by approximately 7 percent. Today, the vast majority of Chanzeaux farmers employ artificial insemination, simply because it is so effective in increasing yields.

The combine has a similar history. Having invested heavily in harvesting machinery, the larger farmers were reluctant to adopt the combine. Using the traditional thresher was easier for them than for the small farmers, since they alone had been able to afford sheaf binders. The small farmers had to tie each sheaf by hand in the fields. Since it saved them an enormous amount of labor, the small farmers welcomed the introduction of the combine in 1955. Most of the thirteen farmers who last used the thresher in 1964 worked large farms. In 1965, when they finally switched to the combine, there was much muttering about the inhuman pace of the work. The efficiency of the combine is so much greater than that of the thresher that they could no longer realistically refuse to adopt it. In both cases, artificial insemination and the combine, the services of entrepreneurs eventually benefited large farmers as well as small ones. There is some machinery that no one Chanzeaux farmer can afford to buy.

The new wave of mechanization has produced a new generation of entrepreneurs. Ex-Mayor Courcault and René Lusson of La Hutte were the main suppliers of threshing services. Courcault and Lusson have not made the heavy investment that would have been necessary to buy a combine. The biggest machinery-rental business in Chanzeaux today is that of the Allaire family, tenants of the 120-acre farm of la Rimbaudière. The father René, age fifty-eight, continues to run the farm; his three sons operate the business. Beside two combines, he offers a haybaler, a tractor with plowing equipment, a bulldozer, a feeder, a buzzsaw, and a hedgecutter. The other Chanzean offering machines as expensive as the combine is Louis Barbat. Henri Tarreau, a camomile merchant, and Paul Asseray, a farmer with too little land to support himself adequately, also rent machines.

Entrepreneurs compete with entr'aide. They are most essential to the small farmers. Like the Association du Plessis, the entrepreneurs are a conservative force in that they help to preserve the small farmer and thus to maintain the agricultural population at its present level. Without a rural exodus, farmers will not be able to raise their incomes sufficiently to allow them to meet their new expectations.

Two Farmers

If a farmer cannot enlarge the land area he cultivates, he can still increase his income by raising yields on the land he already works. Were all farmers to increase their yields equally, none would benefit. The eventual result would be a glut in the market. Nonetheless, some farmers manage to augment their incomes by adopting new methods ahead of their competitors. Jean Arrial is such a farmer. To what extent can a small farmer raise his revenues by increasing fodder yields per acre and concentrating in labor-intensive cash crops? A comparison of Arrial's farming operation with that of Serge Menget, a traditional farmer, will reveal the answer to this crucial question. (See Tables 21-25.)

Arrial was born in Chanzeaux in 1928. One of the first Chanzeaux farmers to purchase a reaper-binder, his father was the tenant of a large fertile farm. But he disliked and distrusted his landlady. Desiring economic independence, M. Arrial let his lease to le Verger lapse when Jean was still a young boy. In 1938, he bought a smaller farm near a large hamlet. When M. Arrial died unexpectedly in 1953, Jean found himself master of 27 scattered acres. He still regrets his father's "stupidity" for having renounced his lease on one of the largest farms in the commune. According to his own wry account, Jean's first year alone was trying. He had to learn, among other things, when deep plowing was required, which fields were too damp for cabbages, how much fertilizer to apply and how much grain to sow in a hectare of land. Most important, he had to acquire the ability that each farmer must have to keep in mind all phases of his operation so that he knows what to do each day. Deficiency in this particular skill can result in economic disaster.

Arrial learned quickly. With a mother and a growing family to support, he applied himself to getting the maximum revenue possible from his 27 acres. He expanded the small tobacco patch left by his father and then decided to specialize in the crop. In 1956 and again in

Table 21. Arrial Farm, 1964, Technical Description

Crops[a]	Acres	Livestock	No.
Wheat	5	Milch cows	8
Barley	1	Beef cattle	12
Oats	1	Horses	2
Winter barley	.5	Pigs	2
		Chickens	615
Fodder beets	2	Rabbits	80
Fodder cabbages	2		
Artificial pasture	12		
Permanent pasture	6		
Vines	0.3		
Tobacco	2.5		
Mint, camomile	0.2		
Garden	0.8		
Other	1		
	34.3		

Rotation system	Equipment
Arrial is experimenting with a new rotation system: fodder cabbages or fodder beets followed by fodder beets, wheat, and spring barley planted simultaneously with artificial pasture.	Tractor-drawn plowing equipment, reaper, sheaf-binder, rake, tedder, mower, incubator, stove for drying camomile, milking machine, electric motor, carts; owns shares in planter, 2 sowing machines, fertilizer spreader, combine; in 1965 bought tractor and joined groups owning haybaler and silage machine

[a] In 1965, Arrial added 7 acres. Consequently he now has five more acres of natural pasture, one half acre more fodder cabbages and one and a half acres more fodder beets. At the same time, he bought a tractor and sold one of his two horses.

1962 he took out loans to build drying barns. The Arrials now have 2.5 acres of tobacco. This single crop accounts for more income than all of Arrial's other crops combined, but also requires most of his family's time. His exceptionally hard-working wife Catherine labors full-

Table 22. Arrial Farm, 1964 Budget (francs)

Expenses			Receipts	
Fertilizers, seed, weed killers		5,000	Wheat, cereals	2,000
Feed, other animal expenses			Veal, beef	8,000
Chickens	13,000		Milk	14,000
Cows	2,000	15,000	Chickens	3,000
Operating expenses of own			Eggs	8,000
machinery			Other barnyard	200
Repairs	1,300		Tobacco	17,550
Electricity	300	1,600	Medicinal plants	1,200
Overhead on own machinery				
Interest	790			53,950
Depreciation	790	1,580		
Machinery rentals (incl. those				
rented from Association				
du Plessis)		1,000		
Insurance for worker, farm				
buildings, equipment		1,756		
Tax		450		
Rent		1,500		
Yearly payment to mother				
on farm goods[a]		2,500		
Yearly payment on drying-				
barn loan		550		
		30,936		

Receipts	53,950
Expenses	−30,936
Net income of Arrial plus worker	23,014
Worker's salary [b]	−3,600
Arrial's net income [c]	19,414

[a] Most of Arrial's land is owned by his mother, who inherited it from his father. Arrial pays rent to her and makes annual payments toward the purchase of the farm equipment, which she also inherited. Even though the older Mme. Arrial lives in the same house, this money is not "all in the family" because Arrial is not an only child and will presumably not be the only heir to his mother's estate.

[b] The worker's salary is not included in the expenses column because Menget has a son instead of a hired hand, and we wanted to make the two budgets comparable. In order to compare the profitablity of the two farms, Menget's net income should be compared to the aggregate net income of Arrial and his worker (23,014).

[c] In 1965, Arrial acquired 7.5 acres, bringing the size of his farm up to 45 and increasing his potential income. At the same time, he bought a tractor costing 16,000 francs and committing himself to make annual payments of 4,200 francs for four years. This burden will be made somewhat lighter by the fact that this year's farm-goods payment to his mother will be his tenth and last.

Table 23. Arrial Farm, 1964 Analysis by Sectors (francs)

Expenses		Receipts	
Veal-Beef-Milk-Wheat[a]			
Fertilizers	5,000	Wheat, cereals	2,000
Feed	2,000	Veal, beef	8,000
Machinery operating expenses	1,600	Milk	14,000
Machinery overhead	1,580		
Machinery rental	1,000		24,000
Insurance	527		
Tax	423		
Rent	1,410		
Payment on goods	2,500		
	16,040		
		Receipts	24,000
		Expenses	−16,040
		Net income	7,960
Tobacco and Medicinal Plants			
Insurance	1,124	Tobacco	17,550
Tax	27	Medicinal plants	1,200
Rent	90		
Interest	550		18,750
	1,791		
		Receipts	18,750
		Expenses	−1,791
		Net income	16,959
Chickens (and Other Barnyard)			
Insurance	105	Chickens	3,000
Feed	13,000	Eggs	8,000
		Other barnyard	200
	13,105		
			11,200
		Expenses	13,105
		Receipts	−11,200
		Net loss[b]	1,905

Note. Arrial does not calculate the income of each sector of his operation. In breaking his budget down into sectors, all machine and fertilizer expenses were attributed to the cow-wheat sector; tax and rent were divided in proportion to the land surface used by each sector; and insurance was divided in proportion to the income of each sector in a normal year.

[a] Meat, milk, and wheat production are interrelated.

[b] Arrial's loss in the chicken sector in 1964 was due to a chicken disease in that year.

Table 24. Menget Farm, 1964, Technical Description

Crops	Acres	Livestock	No.
Wheat	7	Milch cows	10
Barley, oats	10	Beef cattle, calves	25
Fodder beets	3	Horses	5
Fodder cabbages	6	Sheep	47
Turnips	0.5	Pigs	1
Artificial pasture	6	Chickens	35
Permanent pasture	52	Rabbits	15
Garden	0.7		
Other	1		
	86.2		

Rotation system	Equipment
Menget uses two systems simultaneously: (1) fodder cabbages followed by fodder beets, and wheat; (2) fodder cabbages followed by fodder beets, wheat, clover, and wheat again.	Horse-drawn plowing equipment, reaper-binder, rake, tedder, mower, carts, planter, fertilizer spreader

Table 25. Menget Farm, 1964 Budget (francs)

Expenses		Receipts	
Fertilizers	3,000	Wheat, cereals	2,700
Feed, other animal expenses	1,000	Veal, beef	24,000
Electricity	200	Sheep	5,200
Machinery rentals	1,000	Milk	8,200
Haybaler 300		Rabbits, chickens	200
Combine 700			40,300
Insurance	1,300		
Tax	1,400		
Rent	4,000		
	11,900		
		Receipts	40,300
		Expenses	−11,900
		Net income	28,400

time throughout the summer. Some days she joins the men picking in the fields; often she goes to the barns to string the leaves up to dry.

In 1961, Arrial increased the labor intensity of his operation by constructing chicken coops capable of housing approximately 600 birds. He gets up regularly at 4:30 in the morning to see to his chickens and returns to check the coop immediately before going to bed in the evening. His wife also helps to care for them. Their eggs and meat now account for about one fifth of the family's receipts. One year later, in 1962, Arrial planted camomile for the first time and left its harvesting to his mother and his wife. Now that his eldest son Jeannot is eight, he too can start to accustom his eyes and fingers to picking camomile flowers.

Since the death of his father, Arrial has acquired, bit by bit, 14 additional acres, increasing the total surface of his farm to 41 acres. Even by Chanzeaux standards this is a small farm. Nonetheless, Jean makes such intensive use of his land that he finds it profitable to hire a full-time worker as well as two part-time workers during the tobacco season. His part-time helpers are a farmgirl from a neighboring commune, who also lives with the Arrials, and Auguste Ballu, the seventeen-year-old son of the *cantonnier*, who each night spends a couple of hours between work and dinner earning extra pocket money at the Arrials. Paul Cautin, the full-time worker, receives 300 francs ($60) a month. The family allocation paid to his young wife averages more than that. The most expensive personal possession that he can afford is a motorbike. Yet, despite his low standard of living, Cautin cherishes no desire to change his status. Asked if he would like to trade places with Arrial, he replied, "Not at all. That would be too much responsibility."

Even though the labor-intensive sector of Arrial's farm provides nearly two thirds of his receipts and demands most of his working time, he, like other Chanzeaux farmers, utilizes almost all of his land to feed cattle. He has eight milk cows and twelve beef cattle. Not content with the extra income that he has earned from tobacco, camomile, and chickens, Arrial is constantly seeking new methods to increase the productivity of his cattle and grazing lands. Unlike many farmers, he attaches great importance to the breeding of his cattle, particularly his dairy cows. Artificial insemination allows him to breed rationally. He is presently converting his dairy herd to the Frisonne race, which is the best-paying dairy breed that he has tried.

Although the quantity of chemical fertilizers that Chanzeaux farmers apply to their land has grown enormously in recent years, Jean Arrial still uses more than the average farmer. Most farmers put chemical fertilizers on all their fields. Not all of them fertilize every year, however, and even fewer apply the quantities Arrial does. He estimates that chemical fertilizers allow him to double the number of cattle that his grazing lands can support. The amount of grass yielded by each acre can be nearly doubled again by preparing artificial pasture — that is, by plowing pastures and sowing special varieties of grass. The resulting pastures last about four years before natural grass begins to replace it. Like natural pasture, artificial pasture can be cut for hay or used as grazing land. Nearly all Chanzeaux farmers have some land in artificial pasture, but Jean Arrial keeps nearly all his pasture in this form.

This year he started cutting part of his artificial pasture for silage. This method of fodder production, though familiar to farmers in some parts of the world, is very new to Chanzeaux. Instead of leaving his grass to dry, Arrial brings his grass in as soon as it is cut, which preserves the nutrients. Unlike hay, silage can replace beets and cabbages as winter fodder. Since it requires much less work, it will probably render these traditional crops obsolete. Another advantage of silage is that it allows the farmer, who need not be deterred by May dampness, to cut his pastures one more time than he could if he were making hay. Only nine Chanzeaux farmers now make silage. All of them belong to groups that share silage machinery. Arrial has just become part owner of a silage machine that several members of the Association d'Entr'aide du Plessis purchased in common a few years ago. His entire operation is thoroughly mechanized. Membership in the association has aided him in gaining access to expensive machines. Not only does he have a share in the silage machine, but he is also one of the twelve owners of the hayloader that the association bought this year. For several years he has been a member of the combine cooperative of Joué-Etiau. In common with his neighbors, he owns several less costly machines — a planter, a fertilizer distributor, a potato planter, and so on. Of all the Chanzeaux farmers who own milking machines, he is the one with the smallest land surface. This year, Arrial took the very important step of buying a tractor, on credit.

Arrial is unusually heavily in debt. The tractor is costing him 4,200 francs a year. In addition he is paying his mother in ten yearly installments for the farm buildings and equipment that she inherited from his father. Finally, a portion of the sale price of his tobacco is deducted each year and applied to repaying the government loans he took out to build his drying barns. Arrial's payments for 1965 will be as follows:

	Amount (francs)	Period of repayment
Tractor	4,200	1965–1968
Farm goods and buildings (to his mother)	2,500	1956–1966
Tobacco-drying barns and heated camomile drying shed	550	1962–1968
	7,250	

This represents almost one third of his total income the year before. (A complete 1964 budget is given in Table 21.) Still, $4,000 a year is enough to allow the Arrial family a comfortable standard of living. They have a new car and a new refrigerator and plan to purchase a television set in the near future. When Jeannot is older, they may well be able to finance any education he desires beyond Chanzeaux's two-room boys' school. However, the Arrials are by no means satisfied with their house, which is becoming crowded as the family grows. Nor is Jean satisfied with his level of income. He does not plan to encourage his son to remain on the farm, feeling that Jeannot would do better to seek a new occupation. Arrial even speaks occasionally of abandoning the farm himself, although he is the first to admit that this is idle talk. His heavy debts commit him irrevocably to farming. He can only hope that, as the rural exodus continues, he will be able to accumulate enough land to maintain the comfort his family now enjoys.

Jean Arrial considers himself a progressive farmer. A comparison of his farming methods with those of a traditional farmer justifies his claim. Serge Menget still runs his farm largely as he ran it in 1936. In that year he and his Chanzeaux-born wife left a smaller farm in a neighboring commune to become tenants of the 86-acre farm of la Bretonnière. Partly because of the size of the farm, Menget became one of Chanzeaux's most respected citizens. After the war, he was elected to the town council and served on it until 1965. Menget is probably Chanzeaux's best-read farmer. Most households subscribe to a newspaper and two or three magazines, but very few Chanzeans feel that they have the time to read a book. Menget is an exception; his shelves contain Malraux and Hemingway, de Gaulle, Proust. He is a strong advocate of education. One of his sons has become a school-teacher and another recently won a scholarship to study at a Catholic boarding school in Angers.

Menget's farm specializes in beef. He has 25 beef cattle and 10 dairy cows. He also keeps some 40 sheep as a secondary source of income. Well over 50 percent of his land is alloted to natural and artificial pasture. Menget's farm is not fragmented like Arrial's: his fields sur-round the farm buildings. Like all farmers, Menget has been forced to adapt to the increasing labor shortage. Before the war, he hired two workers. After the war, his eldest son replaced one of them, but Menget also had to let the other go because farm labor had become too expensive. This loss of manpower obliged him to feed his cattle in new laborsaving ways. Like other farmers, Menget started growing fewer fodder beets and cabbages and made less hay. He learned that he could without disadvantage put his cattle out to pasture more often, even in the winter. The labor shortage also eventually forced Menget to change harvesting techniques. He used the thresher for as many years as he could. But, for the 1965 harvest, when no one was able to round up enough farmers to make a threshing party, Menget became one of the last thirteen Chanzeans to switch over to the combine.

On other counts Menget is even more traditional. He does not own a tractor, though he could easily afford one and though horse plow-ing takes four times as long as tractor plowing. Menget has four horses and a colt; Arrial sold one of his two horses when he bought a tractor. Menget does not make silage, has almost no artificial pasture, and uses much less fertilizer than Arrial does. He spreads about 3,000 francs worth over his 86 acres, while Arrial spends half again as much to fertilize four tenths as much land. (He applies an average of 145 francs per acre for all crops.) Arrial estimates that an amount of fer-tilizer equal to one tenth the price of a cow, spread over one hectare (2.5 acres) of grass, will enable that hectare to nourish two cows in-stead of one. Menget too could take advantage of this high return, but he is not interested. He still relies on the traditional rule of thumb, "One cow per hectare."

Similarly, Menget is not very interested in modern breeding prac-tices. He does not concern himself much with breeds, and his herd is a mixture. Consequently, his cows give lower-quality milk and bring in less money than Arrial's: Arrial realizes 1,750 francs a year per cow milked, Menget only 820 francs. The two men contrast most sharply in their attitudes toward credit. Arrial has saddled himself with a debt nearly equal to his annual income. Menget would never borrow a penny. He thinks French farmers are too deeply in debt and that millions of them will be dispossessed in a second great depression. "In ten years, there will be no more than 300 people in Chanzeaux. It will be like *The Grapes of Wrath*."

The fundamental difference between Arrial and Menget, as men, is in their attitudes about work. To Arrial, labor is a resource to be allocated as efficiently as possible. He once even tried to count the number of hours he spent during each phase in the process of growing and drying tobacco. Menget, on the other hand, works for the sake of working: he *likes* to work. He spent two months one spring removing a long hedge from one of his fields, when he could easily have hired a bulldozer and, for a small fee, had the hedge out in one afternoon. Menget subscribes to the old-fashioned view that work fulfills the spirit. Yet, ironically, he has less of it to do than Arrial. Arrial is always on the run — from the chicken house to the tobacco field, from the pasture to the barn. He rides his tractor, his bicycle, or his car to even his nearest fields. Menget walks. He has the time to lean on his hoe and chat for half an hour with a passing friend.

Moreover, Menget does not share Arrial's desire for consumer goods. He has neither refrigerator nor car, and of television, the Arrials' next planned acquisition, he says, "In the city it may be necessary to keep children indoors so they don't get into trouble, but country children should play in the fields." Menget is satisfied with his income and does not go out of his way to increase the productivity of his land. It is clear that if Menget adopted Arrial's methods, he could nearly double his herd without having to work any harder. He could buy a tractor and, with the time thus saved, prepare four times as much artificial pasture as he now has. He could make silage and grow fewer beets and cabbages. And, with very little extra labor, he could spread four times as much fertilizer on his pasturelands — an investment that would pay off about threefold in one year.

The surprising fact is that, without taking any of these steps, Menget nevertheless makes more money than Arrial. In 1964 his net income was almost a quarter again as much as Arrial's, and he does not have Arrial's three young children to support. Arrial squeezes almost twice as much revenue out of each acre, but Menget simply has more than twice as many acres. The size of their farms is much more important than the difference between their personalities. Menget, on a large farm, supports himself to his own satisfaction using inefficient methods. Arrial, on a small one, does everything he can to make more money and still wishes he had left the farm when he was younger.

The additional revenue that an individual small farmer can reap from innovation is limited. The problem is even more serious for small farmers as a group. If all small farmers increase their yields as Arrial has done, their goods will flood the market. Prices will fall, and their revenues will not rise. The essence of the farm problem is that there are too many farmers on a fixed amount of land.

*   *   *

Some French economists estimate that two men could successfully operate a 350-acre farm by specializing in beef production and making hay and silage for winter fodder. This 350 acres is seven times larger than the present average farm size in Chanzeaux, but it is not the limit imposed by technology. If a farmer possessed enough land, he would stop making artificial pasture and allow his herd to roam Texas-style across the commune. No Chanzeaux farm will approach this size in the foreseeable future. However, if all Chanzeaux's farmers are to realize their ambitions for a higher standard of living, the average number of acres per farming family will have to rise. A continued decline in the agricultural population is both necessary and inevitable.

So far, the agricultural population has declined more rapidly than the number of farms. The number of farms has remained relatively stable; the number of men per farm has dropped. In each generation, more of the young people who once would have remained on the land have left. Recently they have been leaving faster than ever before. In fact, for what is probably the first time in the village's history, today there are actually fewer farm males in the fifteen-to-nineteen age bracket than in any other five-year age bracket under sixty (if one ignores the war years). This exodus has become so great that in several cases old farmers about to retire have been left without successors. Thus, also for the first time in Chanzeaux's history, the number of farms itself has begun to drop. The land left behind by old men retiring from small farms has been absorbed. One farm disappeared in 1960; four in 1964 (see Table 26).

Table 26. Farm Closures, 1960–1964

Year of closure	Location of farm	Size, acres	Details
1960	Les Fraponnières	N.A.	
1961	bourg	15	Retired, Brichet works land now
1961	Les Humeaux	31	Retired, sold all but 5 acres to neighbors
1962	bourg	12	Died, Claude Chaillou has land now
1963	Le Plessis Lambert	8	Became a farm worker elsewhere, brother-in-law now has land
1963	Les Noyers	20	Died, niece (heir) sold land
1963	Le Plessis	17	FASASA, rented land to neighbors
1963	bourg	22	Father retired, son quit, land sold to several
1964	Les Touches Botereaux	7	FASASA, land to neighbors
1964	L'Espérance	21	Died, brother-in-law took over land
1964	Leseau	19	FASASA, rented to several
1964	Le Pin	42	FASASA, land not yet sold

The acceleration in this new trend is due in part to the creation in 1962 of a government pension plan explicitly designed to expedite the painless disappearance of small farms. The plan, financed by FA-SASA (Fonds d'Action Sociale pour l'Aménagement des Structures Agricoles) benefited three of the four men who gave up their farms in 1964. So far, these lands are being absorbed about as fast as the farmers reach retirement age. Chanzeaux now has thirteen farmers over sixty-five, and eleven under sixty-five with no apparent successors. These farms will almost certainly disappear within the next fifteen years. But since they are few and small, their absorption will only raise the average farm size from 53 acres to 61 acres. Many Chanzeans fear that farms will have to be abandoned at an even faster rate. They anticipate the grim beginning of a more painful process of bankruptcy and failure in which young men in their prime will be forced off the land. This will, in turn, bring economic hardship to the bourg. At present the village of three hundred people — with church, townhall, and shops — depends on the farm population for its living. Already families are driving to Chemillé and Angers to do much of their shopping; and the trucks of the traveling food merchants make their rounds through the countryside daily. Some of the tradesmen of the bourg say that their business has fallen off by as much as 20 percent in the past five years.

Understandably, thoughtful Chanzeans are concerned about the town's future. There is much discussion of numerous schemes to preserve the community's population at its present level. Two of these deserve mention. Some town councilors feel that the best solution would be to encourage an industrial firm to locate in Chanzeaux, providing work for those the countryside can no longer support in agriculture. Unfortunately, Chanzeaux has few advantages to offer an industrial concern. Moreover, if a large firm were to establish a plant in Chanzeaux, its economic power would be preponderant. Chanzeans fear that new capitalistic paternalism would take the place of the old paternalism of the nobles. More imaginative proposals for industrializing the countryside near Chanzeaux have been advanced. A federation of, say, six neighboring communes in the region could invite a company to situate a plant in one of its areas. The company would draw its labor from all six and pay taxes to the federation. The federation would constitute a strong enough center of power to prevent the resurgence of paternalism in any form. Setting up the federation, however, is a task that would require more energetic leadership than Chanzeaux and its neighbors have shown up to the present.

The second scheme for preserving population also involves initiative on the commune's part. Chanzeaux could provide housing for workers commuting daily to jobs in Angers, which is only 17 miles away. Rural Chanzeaux may well undergo transformation into a suburb of Angers. The determining factor will be Angers' rate of growth in the next few decades. But if Chanzeaux succeeds in preserving its present population level in these ways, there will be other results as well. Today Chanzeaux is a remarkably homogeneous village. Three quarters of the people live on farms; the remaining quarter depends for its livelihood on the commerce provided by the agricultural population. Population and homogeneity cannot be preserved simultaneously. Factory workers and, to a greater degree, commuters working in Angers or Cholet would constitute social groups radically different from those now found in Chanzeaux, and their addition will generate great changes in the community and, perhaps, new problems to face.

Part Three

POPULATION

Before looking at Chanzeaux's community life, it is useful to have a detailed picture of the residential distribution of the inhabitants — of Chanzeaux's social geography. The place of residence, whether bourg, campagne, hamlet, or farm, is perhaps the first way one Chanzean identifies another. Stemming largely from the history of land tenure, Chanzeaux's residential pattern orders and channels all of its social relationships. As such it provides an essential introduction to later discussion of the way Chanzeans participate in their institutions.

The chapter on migration is a further step in presenting the population, indeed, in identifying it. The complicated and changing composition of the village is like a building from which one is continually removing and adding bricks: Chanzeaux is composed not only of people with differing ages, but also of people with differing times of arrival in the village who are distributed throughout the residential sectors and the occupational categories of the commune. Initially concerned with the tabulation of Chanzeaux's demographic exchanges with the surrounding regions, the chapter ends with an assessment of the influence of these exchanges upon Chanzeaux itself. Most readers may be surprised at the great amount of mobility there is and always has been into, out of, and through Chanzeaux, a "conservative" village. The composition and direction of migration are both crucial in maintaining continuity in Chanzeaux's traditions and character. The patterns of residence in the commune and the history of migration, like many of the economic factors discussed in the previous section, are the given points from which a discussion of social structure must stem.

7

Residence Patterns

IF YOU are a newcomer to Chanzeaux, your choice of residence will be an important factor in determining whom you meet and whom you do not meet — which of Chanzeaux's many sides you see. Living in Doua, a small wine village in the northeast corner of the commune, you would see little of the rest of Chanzeaux at all. Living in the bourg, you would have little chance to meet the transient farm laborers, the people in wine villages, or many of the hamlet dwellers. Living on an isolated farm, you would probably see the bourg and little else; the irreligious[1] people and the clans of the smaller villages would tend to escape you. In this chapter we shall discuss the settlement patterns of Chanzeaux and generalize wherever possible concerning the people living in the different kinds of settlements.

The Bourg

The first question, if one wanted to know where a Chanzean lived, would be whether it was in the bourg or in the campagne. The life of the bourg dweller is different from that in any other part of the commune. The bourg, or town center, is by far the largest settlement in the commune. Its 276 inhabitants comprise 25 percent of the total population of the commune. Its population pyramid shows a high proportion of elderly adults, often unmarried or widowed, and a very small number of married people between the ages of twenty and sixty. The reason for this is clear. Many farm people return to the bourg to live out their old age or widowhood. There is more community life; the church is near at hand; and there are some places for single women as shopkeepers — like Mlle. Bernadette, who runs an épicerie, and Vve. Priou, who is a successful butcher. To a certain extent, then, the bourg is a large group of elderly people without families. Many of them find a usefulness there that they could not match in any other part of the commune. The relative scarcity of younger adults can be explained by a corresponding lack of occupational opportunity for

[140]

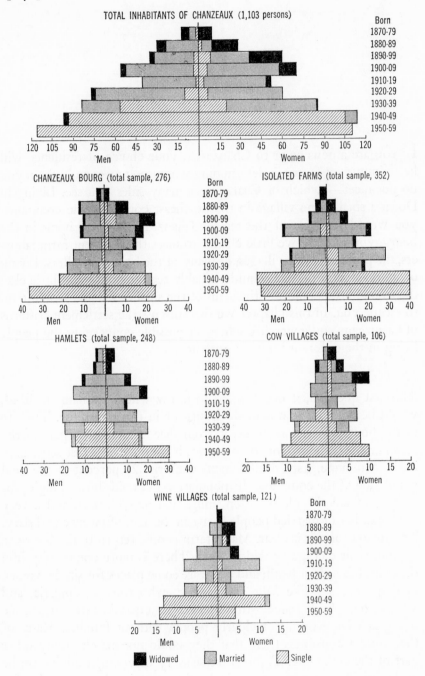

TOTAL INHABITANTS OF CHANZEAUX (1,103 persons)

Born
1870-79
1880-89
1890-99
1900-09
1910-19
1920-29
1930-39
1940-49
1950-59

120 105 90 75 60 45 30 15   15 30 45 60 75 90 105 120
Men   Women

CHANZEAUX BOURG (total sample, 276)

Born
1870-79
1880-89
1890-99
1900-09
1910-19
1920-29
1930-39
1940-49
1950-59

40 30 20 10   10 20 30 40
Men   Women

ISOLATED FARMS (total sample, 352)

40 30 20 10   10 20 30 40
Men   Women

HAMLETS (total sample, 248)

1870-79
1880-89
1890-99
1900-09
1910-19
1920-29
1930-39
1940-49
1950-59

40 30 20 10   10 20 30 40
Men   Women

COW VILLAGES (total sample, 106)

20 15 10 5   5 10 15 20
Men   Women

WINE VILLAGES (total sample, 121)

Born
1870-79
1880-89
1890-99
1900-09
1910-19
1920-29
1930-39
1940-49
1950-59

20 15 10 5   5 10 15 20
Men   Women

■ Widowed   ▨ Married   ▨ Single

this age group in the bourg. Because the bourg is not well situated to be a center of agricultural activity, there are few farmers who live there and commute to their work. Most of the jobs for bourg dwellers are thus in services as artisans, functionaries, and tradesmen.

There is a significantly high proportion of children in the bourg. The bourg dwellers are wealthier than the rest of the inhabitants of Chanzeaux, and significantly more of them attend church. In Chanzeaux it is the religious, well-to-do, educated families that have the highest number of children. Two families in the bourg typify this situation. Mayor Jean-Pierre Gardais, who holds a high position in the lay movement of the Catholic Church, has had eleven children throughout the last fifteen years. Jean-Baptiste Courcault, the former mayor and owner of the town's only industry, the small basket factory, comes from a very devout family, as does his wife. They have eight children, most of whom are now married and have numerous children of their own. Of course, all of the bourg dwellers are not devout, but 63 of the 81 persons who take communion every Sunday are from the bourg. A survey showed that 78 percent of the bourg's adults had visited Lourdes, compared to 64 percent of the country people.

One notices a curious division in the bourg among the tradesmen (*commerçants*), which seems to be set up along lines of religion and length of stay in the community. The two bakers typify this division. One comes from an old, religious Chanzeaux family; his parents were bakers in Chanzeaux before him. The other baker, a Poujadist, immigrated recently into the town, taking the place of another baker who in turn had taken the place of another. His daughter married the postal clerk and will soon move away. He himself has few ties to Chanzeaux. The same division exists between the cafés. The one the town council patronizes is run by Joseph Brée, who comes of an old and religious Chanzeaux family. The other café is run by Georges Lambert. Although he too comes from an old Chanzeaux family, he takes pleasure in assuming a role of skepticism and worldliness. Lambert's café has a juke box and a pinball machine, which the Brée café does not. The irreligious come there for a drink during Mass, and Chanzeaux's militant Catholics feel ill at ease there. The same division exists between the proprietors of the two grocery stores. Bernadette Lebreton is the last of a long line of Lebretons in Chanzeaux. She takes communion every Sunday. The Renous, next door to the Lambert café, are recent immigrants and do not have an established place in the Chanzeaux community. Their daughter and son commute to work and probably will not stay in Chanzeaux.

There are also two garages — the Bertrand garage is run by an ex-blacksmith whose father was blacksmith before him and who is closely linked with the religious families in the bourg; the Davy garage, on a hill outside the bourg, is run by a professed communist from out of town. His wife wears slacks and bleaches her hair, and they employ workers from out of town. It almost seems that, because they are performing the same function, the two sets of tradesmen must have different images to help people choose between them. The fact that both types survive commercially — the deeply traditionalist Chanzean and the nonconformist immigrant — probably testifies that the commune they serve has similar divisions.

What makes the bourg people distinctive is all part of the important role that the bourg plays, not just for its own inhabitants but for the commune as a whole. As the role of the bourg changes, its inhabitants and their occupations change. As an economic center, the bourg is on the decline. In the nineteenth century the bourg could supply many services not available now. At that time there were a doctor, a veterinary, two notaries, and two midwives. Available to serve a population only half again as large as that of today were twice as many men employed as merchants and artisans.

Among the merchants, the shift in recent years from men to women is remarkable. Before the development of modern transportation, when Chanzeaux was still a fairly independent economic unit, a substantial number of men earned their living by supplying needed goods to the Chanzeans. Either they brought such goods from the city, or they bought and sold the produce of the commune. Now middlemen do the purchasing, and marketing is largely out of the hands of the Chanzeans. Shopkeeping is limited to retail sales and delegated to the women, while their husbands take other jobs to support the family — either as artisans, civil servants, or farm laborers.

Most of the artisans have been supplanted because of technological change. The few that remain today are those who have adapted to it: Emile Bertrand converted his smithy into a bicycle shop, and now he spends most of his time selling and repairing motorbikes and operating a filling station. Joseph Davy learned enough about auto-mechanics to convert his smithy into a garage, where he repairs most of the cars and tractors of the countryside around the bourg of Chanzeaux. The farmers near the Route Nationale go for their work to another converted smithy operated by M. Asseray in the hamlet of Espérance. The sons of these artisans are able to learn more about their craft and are following their parents as mechanics and electricians. These men are prosperous and have a great advantage over those who have not adjusted to new demands.

Commercially, except for a few strategic trades and stores, the bourg is losing out to the larger towns and cities. The bourg is still, however, the educational center of the commune. The Catholic schools (*écoles libres*) are, the government school (*école laïque*) was, located there. This is still the place where almost all of the children of the commune meet every day. Yet here too its role is somewhat on the wane, for there has been established within the church system an additional *cours complémentaire* (now called *collège d'enseignement général*), and several children commute by bus to Chemillé. Further, the number of children going on for higher education in Angers and even Paris is constantly increasing.

Even if they are not so religious as the bourg dwellers, most Chanzeans come to the bourg on Sunday. Before, after, and even during Mass the men get together at the Société de la Rue Bourgeoise for a game of boules, or at the Lambert café for a drink and a game of cards. Mme. Lambert must go to the early Mass, for later in the morning she has full responsibility for running the café while her husband is busy cutting hair in the barbershop. Usually after Mass the farm women stand around in the square and pass on their news for the week. Elections are likely to be on Sundays, as are meetings of voluntary associations such as the farmers' union. Jean Delaunay, town clerk, keeps the office open, and most of the stores do more business than on all other days of the week combined. For those citizens who do not come to the bourg on Sunday, whether or not they attend church, Chanzeaux can have little meaning as a community. As the social and religious center of the commune, the bourg has not declined.

The bourg is also the administrative center of Chanzeaux. As such it funnels tax money out of the town and channels national money — in the form of *allocations familiales*, pensions, and support for the schools — into the commune. It is where citizens come to report births, marriages, and deaths, to vote, to make their *déclarations de vin*, to make complaints, or to have a friendly talk with Delaunay or Asseray, the *garde champêtre*.

What is the effect of the bourg's central position on the attitudes of the inhabitants? The bourg dweller is in daily contact with the outside world, since he acts as an economic, administrative, or religious proxy for the rest of the commune. His travels are more extensive and sophisticated than those of the average country dweller. A questionnaire administered in 1963 showed that bourg people travel more often to cities and that a small elite of younger bourg people have been able to take long trips on vacations to all corners of France. Some 66 percent of the bourg dwellers had been to Paris, compared with 46 percent of the country people; seven of the eight women who had traveled abroad (total sample, 72 women) were from the bourg. Furthermore, when bourg dwellers migrate, they tend to go to the cities more frequently than people of the country do. Of bourg emigrants now living, 26 percent live in cities, compared with only 10 percent of country emigrants. No doubt the travel and migration reinforce each other. Much of the travel is to see relatives who have migrated, but the travel itself brings exposure to migration opportunities.

As a result, bourg dwellers are identified with cities by their occupations (which entail habitual contact with cities or citydwellers), by their travels, and by kinship. And for all of Chanzeaux the cities represent the source of the culture and civilization which they know exist outside their village and *pays*. The bourg dweller's exposure to the outside gives him a kind of social leverage over the people of the countryside, whom he usually regards as *moins évolué*. The difference shows up in the pattern of marriage in Chanzeaux and the surrounding region. Although bourg boys sometimes marry country girls, it is rare for any bourg girl to marry a country boy (see Table 27).

The figures underline the nearly complete difference in way of life between bourg and campagne. Besides a kind of snobbishness that inhibits marriage between bourg girls and farm boys, a bourg girl is usually unqualified to take over the highly skilled position of *patronne* of a farm. It is only the most well-off isolated farmers who can marry girls from the bourg, partly because they are the only ones who can support the loss in farm labor that such a marriage must mean

Table 27. Residence of Parents at Time of Child's Marriage,
One Partner from Chanzeaux, 1950–1960

	Residence of boy's parents		
Residence of girl's parents	Bourg	Farm	Total
Bourg	16[a]	7	23
Farm	9	66	75
	25	73	98

[a] On a chance basis, if there were random intermarriage between bourg and farm, the number expected would be 5.

(see Table 28). When Daniel Guitière, the son of a prosperous farmer, married Marie Cottenceau, the daughter of a bourg mason, it was the equivalent of carrying off a princess. The proud father of the groom constructed a modern "annex" to his house and furnished it with the latest goods from Angers, making quite a contrast with the more utilitarian style of the rest of the farm. As a finishing touch to the ceremony, Guitière obtained a special blessing from the Pope for the couple.

Table 28. Residence of Parents at Time of Child's Marriage,
Both Partners from Chanzeaux, 1950–1960

	Residence of boy's parents					
Residence of girl's parents	Bourg	Isolated farm	Hamlet	Farming village	Wine village	Total
Bourg	16	4	—	—	1	21
Isolated farm	3	2	2	—	—	7
Hamlet	—	3	2	1	1	7
Farming village	2	2	1	—	1	6
Wine village	3	—	—	—	—	3
	24	11	5	1	3	44

Whereas to the bourg dweller the chief distinction worth making is that between bourg and campagne, to the rural Chanzean there are significant differences among the four major residence types: the isolated farms, usually containing one two-generation family; the hamlets, smaller settlements of two to eight families; the farming villages, of traditional importance as small community centers, with an adult population of twenty to twenty-five people; and the three villages of vintners in the northeast corner of the commune. (See general plan of commune at front of book.)

Isolated Farms

With 350 inhabitants, the isolated farms comprise one third of the commune. Each farm usually has five or six people living on it — one two-generation family with an occasional grandparent or in-law. Unmarried women and men seldom stay on the farm. Indeed, the isolated farm tends to be an operation limited mainly to the immediate family of the farmer himself. Most of the younger sons will take up farming elsewhere, and daughters, if they pass the age of marriage, find more usefulness in the bourg or migrate outside of Chanzeaux.

Paradoxically, it is the isolated farmers who seem to have the most in common with the bourg inhabitants, mainly because of their favored economic position. An isolated farmhouse is usually surrounded by an integral tract of land, for such farms were formerly owned by the chatelain and worked by his tenants. Thus while the land owned by farmers in the hamlets and villages is usually in small fragmented plots scattered throughout the commune, the land farmed from the isolated farms is likely to be large and intact. It is, moreover, often the best land in the commune. Of the thirty-five farmers who farm plots of land larger than 65 acres, twenty-three, or 65 percent, live on isolated farms.

The isolated farmers have a further advantage in that they are predominantly fermiers, while the hamlet dwellers are more likely to be proprietors (see Table 29). The exact opposite is true of the

Table 29. Residence by Type of Farmer and Average Acreage per Farmer

Farmer	Bourg	Isolated farm	Hamlet	Farming village	Wine village	Total
Fermier[a]	—	27	12	3	4	46
Proprietor[a]	5	9	18	9	5	46
Aver. acreage per farmer	36	63	41	20	30[b]	—

[a] Over half of farm rented or owned.
[b] Wineland is worth two to three times as much as other land.

village and hamlet dwellers: 64 percent are proprietors. Because of his legally protected position as a fermier and his large and undivided farm, the isolated farmer has prospered in Chanzeaux even while the agrarian economy on the whole has been on the decline. The percentage of children under twenty-one (45 percent) is the highest of any residence type, and far above the town average (37 percent). The high birthrate seems to be a reflection of the prosperity of the fermiers and of their special position. The low birthrate in the hamlets (29 percent), far below the town average, is the other side of the same coin. Farmers who own their land seem to have fewer children because of the necessity of dividing the land among sons; the isolated farmers have no such problem because their land cannot be divided. According to the Statut de Fermage, the land must be handed on to only one son.

The isolated farm also has the lowest percentage of persons over the age of sixty (7 percent). Parents can stay on a farm only if they live in the same house as the farmer because, by statute, the fermier cannot build on the land he rents. Thus many of the parents retire to the bourg when they are too old to farm the land. The presence of these elderly ex-fermiers provides another link between the isolated farmers and the bourg dwellers.

It is not surprising that the dynamism of the isolated farms is also reflected in other spheres. Whereas the bourg is the residence center for most of the religious activists in the town, the isolated farm supplies the commune with leaders for many of its secular activities. This is only natural since most of the secular organizations — the CGA (Confederation Générale des Agriculteurs), the Caisse Rurale (Rural Credit Association), the Thouarcé cooperative — center on farming and its problems.

As an example of a successful isolated farmer, Chanzeans are likely to point to Paul Guitière. His landlord, or *rentier*, is a Parisian doctor who is continually returning to Chanzeaux to consider improvements on the farm, making it a model in the commune. Guitière is popular as well as prosperous. He has been a leading member of the town council for many years and president of the school board, and he holds positions of high trust on the tax committee and in the CGA.

Our generalization that the isolated farmer is both economically and socially successful must, of course, be qualified. There are some isolated farmers who own little, and others with large holdings who are not at all prosperous. One fermier, who has 100 acres of what is reputedly the best land in the commune, because of lack of interest and energy barely makes enough money to pay his rent to his landlord. He cannot be removed, however, because so long as he has paid his rent the Statut de Fermage protects him. His son, equally inept, will become the fermier when his father dies.

Yet without a doubt the effective forces for change and evolution in Chanzeaux — partly as measured by participation in voluntary associations — are to be found in the two types of settlement just mentioned, the bourg and the isolated farms.

Hamlets

The hamlets, by way of contrast, are the type of settlement that seems most on the decline in Chanzeaux; indeed, the shape of its population pyramid is characteristic of that of a waning community. The percentage of children in the hamlets (29 percent) is the lowest of any type of settlement in the commune. The hamlets have been losing population steadily since 1870.

Here the cause must be economic. In the agricultural decline of the commune, the hamlets were the hardest hit since their farmers had relatively small and scattered holdings which could not profit by advances in mechanization. Whereas the size of the average holding on isolated farms is well over 65 acres, that of the hamlet farmer averages only 40 acres. Because they live in hamlets, their holdings are not compactly distributed around the farmhouse but scattered over a wide area.

One finds a more withdrawn and socially self-enclosed atmosphere in the hamlet than either on the isolated farms or in the bourg. In contrast to the isolated farmers, the hamlet dwellers have little contact with the bourg. Hamlet people even do much of their shopping from the traveling vegetable man, butcher, or baker, which saves them the trouble of going into town. While it is not uncommon for a girl from an isolated farm to marry a bourg boy, any intermarriage between hamlet and bourg is very uncommon. A network of marriages is set up among the hamlets themselves, and one hamlet often has a whole set of kin in another.

Life in a hamlet seems to have a complication not shared by the isolated farmers or the bourg dwellers: crowding. It is hard to avoid one's neighbors in all the crossing back and forth between separated fields, and people get in each other's way in doing such chores as driving the cows to pasture. In such situations of everyday irritation, it is not uncommon for hamlet dwellers to become *brouillés* ("on the outs") with their neighbors. The normal solution to a *brouille* — avoidance — is not open to the hamlet dweller. As a result, in recent years there have been several cases of families leaving the commune as a result of quarrels with hamlet neighbors. A charged and sometimes disagreeable atmosphere is found also in the villages, which are in many ways merely large hamlets. But it does not seem to be found to any great extent in the bourg. There is more opportunity for competition and conflict between two neighbors who are both farmers than between, say, a plumber and a shopkeeper. In the bourg, where almost everyone is doing something a little different, there is not enough overlap of occupation to cause antagonism. Besides, the bourg has a sufficiently large variety of people so that one can choose one's friends and more gracefully avoid one's enemies.

Farming Villages

The farming (cow-wheat) villages are three settlements of thirty to forty inhabitants each: Le Plessis, to the east; Saint-Ambroise, to the south; and Espérance, to the west on the Route Nationale. Economically the farmers in the farming villages are the worst off in Chanzeaux. Of the villagers who farm, 75 percent are proprietors; their lands are fragmented even more than those of the hamlet dwellers; and the average holding is 20 acres. The average holding for hamlets is twice as large, that for isolated farms almost four times larger. In short, the amount of land a farmer tills is in inverse proportion to the size of his settlement.

All of the farming villages date back to medieval times, when they were the centers of small fiefs. Saint-Ambroise reputedly used to be the center of a town, and both Plessis and Saint-Ambroise had their own churches. But from the Middle Ages on, these villages have steadily lost to the bourg. The churches fell into disuse, and their memory is preserved only in the names of farmhouses on their sites. (Although the chapel at Saint-Ambroise was repaired recently, it is not used.) Even in the nineteenth century these villages were far larger and more autonomous economically than they are today. Now, with the depopulation of rural Chanzeaux and the new mobility of the farmer, the villages have lost most of their former role as minor bourgs. As retail centers they have retained only épiciers and scattered artisans. The isolated farmers and hamlet dwellers who used to be within their orbit now go to the bourg for goods and services or buy from traveling merchants.

The fairly high proportion of elderly people (21 percent) in the farming villages testifies to the fact that, as settlement types grow in size, the proportion of the aged increases. One fact difficult to explain is the relatively high birthrate. Considering the straitened economic circumstances of the villages, it is probable that a high proportion of the village children born between 1940 and 1960 will not remain there. Indeed, one quarter of the population of these villages has left the commune since 1954, and, unlike the situation in the other residence types, this emigration has not been even partially counteracted by a corresponding immigration. No one has moved into the farming villages since 1954.

The political manifestation of the low economic and social status of the farming villages has been the prevalence of communism. The communist Chauvin-Davy clan lives in Saint-Ambroise, and people refer to Plessis as "plutôt communiste." A large percentage of non-religious Chanzeans live in these villages. The cow-wheat villages provide no town-council members. In fact, the only leader in any community activity is Bernard Chauvin, who used to be head of the school board for the public school before it closed.

What distinguishes the farming villages from the hamlets is not only size, but also a lower economic and social standing and the occasional presence of certain nonagricultural occupations.

Wine Villages

The wine villages are three settlements of from thirty to fifty persons each, in the northeast corner of the commune: Doua, on the Rablay border, La Brosse, and La Jutière. Together they comprise, like the cow villages, about 10 percent of the commune population. Although the wine villages exhibit few demographic irregularities (the percentage of children is close to the average of the commune, as is that of older people), the population pyramid does reveal a curious variation between 1910 and 1930. Whereas in the commune as a whole there is a gap in people born between 1910 and 1920, a result of World War I, in the wine village those ten years have a higher proportion of births than the years before or after. And whereas in the commune as a whole there was a marked increase in births in the postwar generation of 1920–1930, in the wine village there is a gap in these years. More than likely these variations are due to fluctuations of the wine economy, which would provoke or inhibit migration at periods different from those in the rest of the commune.

There is great variation in wealth within the villages. Although the average holding is only about 30 acres, wineland is estimated to be two to three times more valuable than the other land in the commune. On the other hand, a good number of the wine villagers have no farms at all, and not all the land that is held is wineland.

The village seems to be the standard type of residence for French wine farmers. To the north, in Saint-Lambert where the economy is directed almost uniquely to wine, there are no isolated farms. The growing and harvesting of grapes seem to require community effort, not merely the help of kin, as is usually the case with wheat harvests. There have been, nevertheless, examples of feuding in the wine villages. The most notable case was that of Mme. Bonneau of La Jutière; she was apparently angry with her stepson over a land transaction. The older couple eventually left the commune, but in the meantime the whole village took sides for or against the two households.

Like the cow-wheat villages, the wine villages are of medieval origin. At Doua there used to be a manor house and a monastery. But whereas the power of the farming villages has been absorbed by the Chanzeaux bourg, that of the wine villages has gone to bourgs outside of Chanzeaux: Saint-Lambert, Beaulieu, or Rablay.

Because of the difference in occupation and the proximity to these other communes, the wine villagers do not participate in many Chanzeaux activities. They send one town councilor, Louis Ditière of La Jutière. He is exceptional in that he owns 75 acres of land and has kinship ties with the cow-wheat community. The only other resident active in Chanzeaux circles is a farmer of La Brosse, who is also linked by kinship to the rest of the community. Indeed, perhaps the factor that most differentiates the wine-village people as a whole from the rest of the commune is their lack of kinship ties with it.

When the vintners sell their wine, it is largely through individual deals, and each may have several regular customers. The buyers, however, unlike the cooperative markets for cattle, wheat, and medicinal plants, are scattered throughout the department. Thus in the course of their business the vintners are exposed to a much larger community than most Chanzeaux farmers are. As a result, the attitude of the wine villagers toward the rest of Chanzeaux is similar to that of the bourg dwellers toward the campagne; the wine community regards itself as more "à la page." There is an element of sophistication in the wine villages that is lacking in the rest of rural Chanzeaux.

The community life of these people is also quite different from that of other Chanzeans. They participate in a larger community composed of three surrounding wine communes — Saint-Lambert, Beaulieu, and Rablay — and the children of La Brosse, La Jutière, and a neighboring hamlet without exception attend school in Saint-Lambert. But whereas in Chanzeaux less than 1 percent of the children attended the public school, about half the children of La Brosse and La Jutière attend the public school in Saint-Lambert. This is another similarity that places La Brosse and La Jutière ideologically closer to the more radical religious tradition of Saint-Lambert than to the strictly *bien pensant* attitude of Chanzeaux. In point of fact it is known that there are families in both villages who vote communist. Of those adults who do attend church from La Brosse and La Jutière, all but two families attend church in Saint-Lambert.

The people of Doua, the third wine village, are more closely associated with Rablay. Doua was an important seigneurie in the medieval period, and a large village grew up around a priory and a small chateau. But when the boundaries of the parish were drawn, half of Doua was in Rablay and the other half in Chanzeaux. Considerably smaller now, the village still remains divided, although it is much closer to the Rablay bourg than to that of Chanzeaux. This proximity, added to the fact that the villagers share a common occupation with the people of Rablay, has naturally kept the Chanzeaux half of Doua affiliated socially with Rablay. Several times in the nineteenth century the Doua farmers appealed to the Chanzeaux town council, with the seconding of the Rablay council, to be allowed to join Rablay. The Chanzeaux council, however, fearing a loss of taxes and perhaps also revealing some lack of understanding for the vintners to the north, consistently rejected their pleas. Today the problem persists, and, like La Brosse and La Jutière, Doua has divided allegiances. Two Doua adults attend church in Chanzeaux, two go down to Le Champ, two go nowhere at all, and the rest go to Rablay. Doua participation in Rablay affairs even extends to voting there, although this would seem to be legally impossible. Maurice Prestreau, who came to Doua from Rablay in 1948, still votes in Rablay; he says he "hasn't got around" to changing his name on the voting list.

Whereas Chanzeaux as a whole is definitely a Mauges town, the wine sector of the commune has a significantly lower percentage of immigration from the Mauges area to the south and west. In the wine communities the distinctive source of immigrants is the Layon region to the north and east.

	% of immigrants to wine sector	*% of immigrants to cow-wheat sector*
From Layon (north, east)	35	19
From Mauges (south, west)	40	68

All of the differences that distinguish the wine communes of the north and east from Chanzeaux and the Mauges distinguish the wine villagers of Chanzeaux from the rest of the commune's inhabitants. They vote significantly less than anyone else, and their voting is noted for leftist or radical tendencies. They form a left wing of non-believers in a very church-minded town. A higher percentage of their children go on to secondary school (see map, p. 154).

These, then, are the main residence patterns in the commune and the influences that color the life of the inhabitant of Chanzeaux. He lives either in the bourg or in the campagne; this fact already tells much about his occupation, his attitudes, and his habits. Each of the settlement types in the campagne — the isolated farm, the hamlet, the farming village, the wine village — adds still another dimension. Certain factors determine the range of people who are likely to move into a given type of residence; such factors are usually economic and intimately linked with the history of land tenure. Other factors affect the people once they have moved into a given settlement, sometimes even determining whether or not they will stay in Chanzeaux. Both sets of determinants combine to make certain residence types the centers of stability in the town, and others the centers of change. (See Table 30 for the population figures.)

Chanzeaux has witnessed a transformation of the function of its

Table 30. Residence Types, Basic Facts

Residence	Population, 1962	% of commune	% born pre-1900	% born post-1940	% decline since 1870
Bourg	276	25%	22%	36%	33%
Isolated farm	352	32	9	45	5
Hamlet[a]	248	22	16	29	33[a]
Farming village	106	10	21	35	50
Wine village	121	11	11	42	30
Commune	1,103	100%	15%	37%	21%

Note. These 1962 population figures differ from official census figures in that they do not include students away at school and young men doing military service.
[a] With the exception of two-farm hamlets.

settlements. Before the era of automobile and motor bike, the farming and wine villages were, in effect, sub-bourgs with shopkeepers and craftsmen. Some of them even had their own chapels. They served as bourgs for the circle of farmers in their sector of the commune. Farmers on the commune border, in some cases, would be tied to Chanzeaux life because it was easier to go to the nearby village than to the bourg of the neighboring commune.

With the introduction of improved transportation and the paving

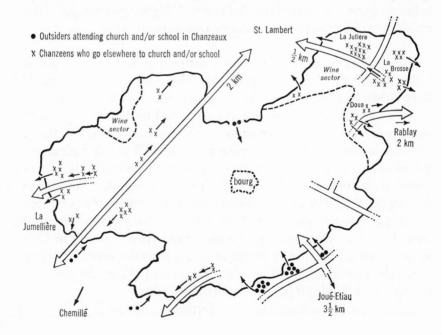

of Chanzeaux's roads (mostly since 1930), the little sub-bourgs lost any hope of competing with the large town center, which could provide more specialized services in a central location. Especially important was the ability of the bourg grocers and bakers to reach out to the farms by delivering their goods in trucks. Hence the artisans have moved away from the villages into the Chanzeaux bourg, and the remaining shopkeepers are disappearing. The border people, who previously had been linked to Chanzeaux through their local village, were lost to the neighboring communes for church and school attendance as well as for commercial trade (see map).

The villages lapsed into mere residences with greatly reduced populations. The neighborhood tie between the isolated farmer and his village was broken, and a new tie was set up between the isolated farmer and the bourg. Now the same process is going on on a larger scale. The bourg of Chanzeaux is giving way as a social and economic center to the larger towns to the north and south. Again, better transportation can be seen as the major cause. Chanzeaux is becoming part of a larger urban network for more and more goods and services.

As the nonagricultural sector of Chanzeaux's villages disappears, Chanzeaux's bourg will decline as a place to work. Already the bourg is the dwelling place of most Chanzeans who commute to non-agricultural jobs outside the commune. It is precisely the nonagricultural people in the bourg who are being squeezed out by the competition from larger towns. Just as Emile Bertrand moved his smithy to the bourg from La Brosse, so Roger Girault, the other blacksmith, is closing down his shop in the bourg, and his son is taking a factory job in Cholet.

The bourg occupations are the hardest hit; there the result has been commuting or emigration. For the rest of the residence types, multiple adaptations, albeit less drastic ones, may be observed. More individual Chanzeans are going to the larger towns, not only to buy and sell at the markets but to shop, to go to church, or to see a movie. Friendships are growing up on a regional basis rather than strictly on the communal level. All Chanzeans are becoming residents of a larger community.

8

Migration

In CENTURIES past the French cherished the myth of a static, peaceful countryside supporting the glories of France upon its sturdy, peasant shoulders. Today the France of de Gaulle and the Common Market is concerned with economic stagnation in the provinces. Thus, whether in praise or in condemnation, generations past and present have seen the countryside as unchanging and rigid. But in Chanzeaux, at least, the time-honored archetype of the traditional farmer rooted to a single spot is false.

The majority of the inhabitants of Chanzeaux today have migrated or will migrate.[1] Consider these statistics on the people of Chanzeaux who are of voting age:

Born elsewhere, living in Chanzeaux	297
Born in Chanzeaux, living in Chanzeaux	398
Born in Chanzeaux, living elsewhere	508
Born elsewhere, lived in Chanzeaux, living elsewhere (est.)	1,250

Some of this information is shown in Table 31 and the voting-age diagrams. Only slightly more than half of the residents of Chanzeaux in 1962 were born there. Only one out of every two born in Chanzeaux still lives there. Only a small minority will die there.

We have studied migration in Chanzeaux from three different points of view. One was to analyze in detail the characteristics of the population in 1954 and again in 1962. Another approach was to look at all the voters still alive in 1962 who were born in Chanzeaux and to compare those who left with those who stayed. A third approach was to focus on the flow of arrivals and departures between 1954 and 1962.

Most of Chanzeaux's population movement is made up of people who come from other towns, stay awhile, and then move on. These we shall call the flowthroughs. Of all the people who left Chanzeaux

Table 31. Chanzeaux Population Change from Migration, 1954–1962

1954 Voting-age population	
Born in Chanzeaux, stayed to 1962	273
Born in Chanzeaux, left 1954–1962	43
Immigrants, stayed to 1962	233
Immigrants, left 1954–1962 (flowthroughs)	95
Died 1955–1962	69
	713
1962 Voting-age population	
Stay-ons	
Born in Chanzeaux	273
Immigrants	233
Arrived 1955–1962	
Immigrants	47
Turned 21 in 1955–1962	
Born in Chanzeaux	125
Immigrants	25
	703
1955–1962 Flowthroughs	31

between 1955 and 1962, 154, or 65 percent, were born elsewhere. In other words, flowthroughs accounted for two thirds of the migration through Chanzeaux. For these people, leaving Chanzeaux was at least the second displacement in their lives. The statistics below reveal, moreover, that over half of them stayed in Chanzeaux less than five years (see Table 32). The largest element of the migration through

Table 32. Flowthroughs, 1955–1962

Length of stay in Chanzeaux	%	No.[a]
1–5 years	61%	(55)
5–20 years	21	(19)
20 years and more	18	(16)
	100%	(90)

[a] Information was not available on 36 of the 126 adult flowthroughs in this period.

Chanzeaux is thus surprisingly transient. Imagine a family — grandparents, parents, and children — sitting down at a dinner table in Chanzeaux. If the family is at all typical, the grandparents will have

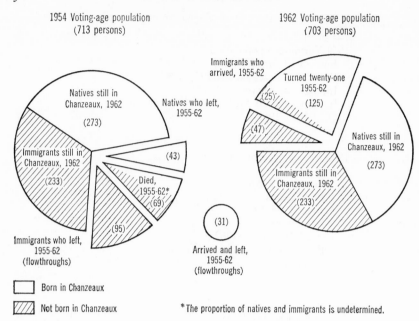

1954 Voting-age population
(713 persons)

1962 Voting-age population
(703 persons)

Natives still in
Chanzeaux, 1962
(273)

Natives who left,
1955-62

Immigrants still in
Chanzeaux, 1962
(233)

(43)

Died,
1955-62*
(69)

(95)

Immigrants who left,
1955-62
(flowthroughs)

Immigrants who
arrived, 1955-62

(25)

Turned twenty-one
1955-62
(125)

(47)

(31)

Arrived and left,
1955-62
(flowthroughs)

Natives still in
Chanzeaux, 1962
(273)

Immigrants still in
Chanzeaux, 1962
(233)

☐ Born in Chanzeaux

▨ Not born in Chanzeaux

*The proportion of natives and immigrants is undetermined.

lived much of their lives outside of Chanzeaux, and the children will, when they grow up, take root in still another community. Some moves, whether of emigrants, immigrants, or flowthroughs, have greater significance than others. Some 30 percent of the emigrants and 37 percent of the immigrants migrate to or from a contiguous commune. A move to a large city or a different region of the Maine-et-Loire often means a far more important change. But, in any case, even a move to a neighboring commune has profound effects on the migrant's social relations, since much of his activities are organized on the basis of commune and parish.

Clearly, the measure of Chanzeaux's population today understates the number of "Chanzeans" alive in France. We have seen that only 677 of Chanzeaux's adults are living in Chanzeaux today. Adding native-born emigrants and past flowthroughs to that number gives us an estimate of about 2,400 "Chanzean" adults scattered throughout France.

Age and Sex of Migrants

The people leaving Chanzeaux who were born there leave when young. The average age of the 88 native-born Chanzeans who left between 1955 and 1962 was twenty-four.[2] The exodus definitely slowed down among people who were married. Several of the people who left will return to Chanzeaux in their old age. But young people make up the main stream of migration. Men tend to leave before marriage, women at marriage, as Table 33 shows. For men, the decision

Table 33. Stage of Life at Which Native-Born Chanzeans Leave the Commune, 1962

Stage	Men	Women	Total
From birth to 13 years	53	50	103
From 13 years to marriage (or age 30)	33	22	55
At marriage	29	55	84
After marriage (or 30 years) to fifty	18	21	39
After fifty	2	5	7
Unknown	103	117	220
	238	270	508

Note. Figures from a 1962 list of voters born in Chanzeaux but living elsewhere.

to leave generally involves looking for a job; for women, it means marriage. The marriage customs of Chanzeaux are at the root of this situation. Table 34, listing all the marriages between 1954 and 1961

Table 34. Marriage Choices of Chanzeaux Residents, 1954-1961

Choice	Men	Women	Total
Married another Chanzean	18	18	36
Married an outsider and left Chanzeaux	7	27	34
Married an outsider and brought him (her) to Chanzeaux	15	2	17
	40	47	87

Note. The extent of exogamy in these 87 marriages was even higher then the figures indicate (51/87). In this table we consider anyone who was already living in Chanzeaux at the time of marriage to be a native Chanzean; clearly a number of them were residents born elsewhere. This table is compounded from information on file in the townhall about residents of Chanzeaux in 1962 and from the town secretary's personal knowledge of people who married out of Chanzeaux during the 1954–1962 period.

that involve at least one Chanzeaux resident, is revealing. Many Chanzeans, about 60 percent, marry outsiders, and this is true of men and women to almost exactly the same degree. After that, the similarity between the sexes ends. Over three quarters of the men (33 out of 40) stayed in Chanzeaux. Those young men who intended to leave

Chanzeaux had left before marriage time. By contrast, more than half of the women left Chanzeaux at marriage. Those women who married Chanzeaux husbands were almost the only ones to stay. A mere 2 out of 47 women brought their husbands to them from the outside. The reason for the departure of the woman, of course, is that it is traditionally the man who takes over the family property.

One must not conclude from this, however, that all Chanzeaux girls stay at home until the day they are married. In 1962, 43 of Chanzeaux's 89 working girls held jobs outside of the commune. Eleven of these still lived at home, but the rest came back at most only once a week. Juliette Bordereau, the baker's daughter, went to Paris in the mid-1950s and became a waitress in a pastry shop. Her case is a rare one, since most girls do not go so far from home before marriage; but that of the two Brochet girls is less exceptional. Both have had secretarial training. One of them lives in Angers; the other works in Saint-Lambert for a wine exporter and lives at home. Their father used to own one of the two cafés in Chanzeaux but sold it to Lambert because he knew that neither of his daughters wanted to stay in the village. The mother of the Brochet girls was also an independent woman in her time. She left her home town in Brittany as a young girl in 1917 and came to Chanzeaux two years later as a cook at the chateau. She married Charles Brochet (whose family had been in Chanzeaux for generations) when he returned from the First World War.

The women who leave Chanzeaux at marriage often travel farther than the men. Though it is the boys and the men who go about on motorbikes, to the movies or to the café, they are also tied to their jobs and, if they are farmers, to the countryside. The world of women, on the other hand, is family and church; they have less stake in the community life of Chanzeaux. Because the life of a farm girl is especially hard, to many girls marriage brings a possibility of escape. Hence, compared with men, the women have both greater freedom and greater desire to leave.

Occupation and Residence of Immigrants and Flowthroughs

Most of the immigrants who are farmers live on the prosperous tenant farms. The relatively poorer farms in the wheat villages and larger hamlets do not turn over nearly so fast. Two thirds of Chanzeaux's immigrant farmers are fermiers, and almost none of the recently arrived farmers owns land. Immigrants, in fact, lease many of the most desirable of the isolated farms. Eugène Bourdelle, for example, came to Chanzeaux from La Jumellière as a young hired hand before World War II. He married a Chanzeaux girl and took over the lease on the large farm her father tenanted. Bourdelle has been on the town council and is a leader of the school committee and the agricultural union.

The reason that most migrant farmers settle on isolated farms becomes clear when one considers the plight of the relatively smaller number who have moved into the cow and wheat villages and hamlets. To accumulate land in a village a farmer has to buy it, parcel by parcel, over many years. The farmers who were born in Chanzeaux and have always lived there have an advantage. One local grain merchant, who knows Chanzeaux's farms well, rated the economic status of each farmer in the commune. On the basis of these ratings we can construct a table which makes it clear that immigrants on the isolated farms are richer than natives, in the villages much poorer (see Table 35).

Table 35. Economic Status of Farmers

Rating	Bourg, villages, and hamlets		Isolated farms and two-house hamlets	
	Native-born	Immigrants	Native-born	Immigrants
Very good or good	10	3	14	16
Average	12	3	11	6
Not good or farm will disappear in 10 years	23	16	10	6
	45	22	35	28

The marginal farms in the wheat villages, which do not attract immigrants, are rapidly disappearing as the older farmers retire or die and their land is taken over by people already in Chanzeaux. In the three villages of Saint-Ambroise, Le Plessis, and Espérance, only two new people settled in the eight years from 1954 to 1962. Many of the people who leave these villages stay within the commune, finding jobs in its more prosperous areas. Although there is just as much flux in the bourg of Chanzeaux as in the countryside, the bourg has a stable core of inhabitants that the campagne lacks. Whereas very few farm families have been in Chanzeaux for more than three generations, in the bourg there are several families that have been in Chanzeaux, and even in the same trade, for eight or nine generations. François Devanne, the carpenter and sacristan, descends from the nephew of the sacristan who died in the burning of the church tower in the Vendée Rebellion. His family have been sacristans in Chanzeaux since long before the Revolution.

The bourg is one of the settlements of Chanzeaux that have a high proportion of native adult residents (59 percent — see Table 36).

Table 36. Origin and Location of Residents and Native-Born, 1962

| Residents | Origin of residents | | | | | | |
	Bourg	Wine village	Farm village	Hamlet	Farm	Un-known	Total No.
Immigrants	41%	49%	35%	48%	51%	13%	297
Native-born	59%	51%	66%	52%	49%	87%	359
Total No.	159	61	58	174	189	15	656

| Native-born | Location of native-born (living adults) | | | | | | |
	Bourg	Wine village	Farm village	Hamlet	Farm	Un-known	Total No.
Living in Chanzeaux	34%	35%	50%	40%	43%	48%	359
Living outside Chanzeaux	66%	66%	50%	60%	58%	52%	510
Total No.	173	87	165	189	193	62	869

Most of these natives are artisans; some are tradesmen. Among them are Girault the blacksmith; Lambert and Brée, the café owners; Bernadette Lebreton the grocer; and Bordereau the baker. The particular traditions of Chanzeaux have been perpetuated in the shops and professions, not on the farms. Still, it takes only one child to run a family bakery or blacksmith shop; the other children leave Chanzeaux to find work. Compared to other areas of the commune, the bourg has a high emigration rate — two out of every three people born in the bourg leave. Almost none of the people born in the bourg move to other parts of the commune. If they move, they move out of the commune altogether. We can see the pattern at work in the Bertrand family. Emile, the electrician, is taking over and transforming his father's mechanic shop in the bourg. But Raymond works in a soft-drink factory in nearby Rablay, and Georges is away at boarding school. Neither will return to Chanzeaux.

The bourg's higher share of wealthy people is another cause of its higher emigration rate. Children of the chatelain, for example, have never stayed in Chanzeaux. When there were a doctor and a notary in the commune, their children did not remain Chanzeans. Mme. Priou, the well-to-do butcher's widow who owns Chanzeaux's banquet hall, recently married her daughter to a man whom she proudly describes as having "une grosse affaire à Saumur."

In our comparison of the mobile and stable parts of the commune, the contrast has been between people who stay two generations and those who stay two centuries. Both groups are very different from people who stay for only ten years or ten months. Yet it is the latter who are the real transients, accounting for over half of the population movement that Chanzeaux experiences. Every year about twenty people come to Chanzeaux who will move on again in a few years. We have used the word "flowthrough" to describe someone who has come to Chanzeaux and left again. The flowthroughs are so different from the other migrants that we can consider them as a distinct class.

The turnover of flowthroughs is so rapid that there are never very many of them in Chanzeaux at any one time; indeed, there is a danger of overlooking them in a static analysis of the community. The typical flowthrough stays five years, though the average length of stay is nine and a half years. Two thirds of those who arrived in Chanzeaux between 1955 and 1962 had moved at least once before in their lives. (See Table 37.) Perhaps the single most telling difference between the flowthroughs and other migrants is that most of the flowthroughs move in family groups. The great bulk of native emigrants, moving for the first time, leave before or at marriage (see Table 33). For a whole family to pick up and leave town is quite a different matter from the departure of a single person or a newly married couple.

The job that most flowthroughs have held and hold now is the least prestigious job in Chanzeaux, that of hired hand. Farm work is almost exclusively a flowthrough occupation in Chanzeaux. Almost

Table 37. Residence of Flowthroughs Who Left in 1955–1962

	Bourg	Wine village	Farm village	Hamlet	Farm	Un-known	Total
Flowthroughs	29%	7%	8%	11%	43%	3%	100% (150)
Total population, 1962	24%	9%	9%	26%	29%	2%	100 (656)%

twice as many flowthrough agricultural workers left Chanzeaux between 1955 and 1962 as were actually living there in 1962. The next largest group of flowthroughs in this eight-year period were farmers. Most of these, however, unlike the hired hands, had stayed in Chanzeaux quite a few years before leaving. The agricultural workers stayed an average of only four and a half years, whereas the flowthrough farmers stayed sixteen years on the average. The flow-through farmers made up a large, slow stream, the agricultural workers a small but rapid one.

In the campagne, the most disruptive element between 1955 and 1962 appears to have been the decision on the part of the owners of la Berthelottière, les Chauvellières, and Plaisance to manage them directly. Four farm families had to leave because the owners of their land chose to take it back at the end of the lease. Three families of hired hands who had been working on these same farms were forced to move at the same time.

In the bourg, most of the flowthroughs were shopkeepers or arti-sans — such as Chanzeaux's last shoemaker, who left in the late 1950s because business was bad. Paradoxically the flowthrough shopkeepers were often in the same trades as the most stable elements in the bourg. Chanzeaux's two bakers are examples: Bordereau is from an old family; Chevrier is an immigrant whose bakery has changed hands four times in the last ten years. The other flowthroughs in the bourg were primarily functionaries. André and Gabrielle Baignon, post-office officials, came to Chanzeaux in 1955 from outside the Maine-et-Loire, managed the postoffice for four years, and then left in 1959 to take over a bigger postoffice in Saint-Lô, in the department of Manche. All the local employees of national institutions live in the bourg. This includes the postal clerks, the schoolteachers, the curé and his assist-

ants, and the nuns in the girls' school — all the intermediaries necessary for a small community within a modern nation. Between 1955
and 1961, each of the officials just named left and was replaced.

The flowthroughs taken as a whole have tended to be either very
high or very low in social standing. Of the unfortunate ones, some
are people having trouble making ends meet. Some are in the anticlerical minority. Some are just "pauvres types," who can barely
make a living. Those at the top of the social scale are the people who
are bigger than Chanzeaux, those for whom Chanzeaux is merely a
stopping place.

Origins and Destinations

Leaving town is almost the only way for a Chanzean to change his
occupation. Those who stay behind are very largely the children of
farmers and artisans who choose to remain in their parents' occupations. Those who leave usually change their occupations and often
move "up" the social ladder (see Tables 38 and 39). This process

Table 38. Occupational Mobility of Native-Born, 1962

Occupation of father (at son's birth)	Adult Chanzeaux males						
	Civil servant, profes- sional, mer- chant	Artisan	Salaried non- farm worker	Farmer	Farm worker	Un- known, retired, unem- ployed	Total
Civil servant, professional, merchant	2	2	—	2	—	1	7
Artisan	—	16	1	—	—	4	21
Salaried nonfarm worker[a]	—	—	—	—	—	—	—
Farmer	5	6	2	97	1	42[b]	153
Farm worker	—	—	2	—	1	1	4
Unknown, retired, unemployed	1	1	—	2	—	2	6
	8	25	5	101	2	50	191

[a] None of these (apprentices, shop employees, etc.) stayed in Chanzeaux long enough for their sons to reach the age of 21 and thus be included in this sample.
[b] These are mostly young people and retired farmers.

Table 39. Occupational Mobility of Native-Born Emigrants

Occupation of father (at son's birth)	Civil servant, profes- sional, mer- chant	Artisan	Salaried non- farm worker	Farmer	Farm worker	Un- known, retired, unem- ployed	Total
Adult male emigrants							
Civil servant, professional, merchant	7	3	4	1	—	2	17
Artisan	17	5	4	3	1	2	32
Salaried nonfarm worker	2	2	—	6	0	2	12
Farmer	21	17	9	76	6	14	143
Farm worker	4	4	5	8	1	2	24
Unknown, retired, unemployed	1	—	1	2	1	2	7
	52	31	23	96	9	24	235

reflects the phenomenon occurring in all industrial countries: the agricultural population is diminishing while the number of people in the services and professions is increasing. About three times as many emigrants moved up on our occupational scale as moved down. (Our ranking of occupations is admittedly arbitrary, but it corresponds to the opinions of most young people in Chanzeaux.) Virtually none of the children of agricultural workers (an occupation at the bottom of the scale) followed in their fathers' footsteps. Farm hands are rapidly disappearing; there are scarcely half as many of them in Chanzeaux today as there were ten years ago. Today younger agricultural workers are Chanzeaux farm boys who are earning a little extra money for the family before they move away to urban jobs.

Although 41 percent of the emigrant farmers and farmers' sons left farming, very few are working in city jobs — either factory or professional. This pattern may well change in the next few years, as the farmer's horizon broadens to include the city, but so far it is the emigrants from the bourg who have been the most upwardly mobile. For instance, almost all the teachers and priests that Chanzeaux has produced in recent years have come from the bourg. This fact also illustrates the economic difference between the bourg and the campagne. Not many farm families can afford to send their children away to school. Furthermore, when a farmer's son does go off to the city and train to be a teacher or a priest, this represents both a sacrifice and a risk for his parents. Not only is he being taken from the farm at an age when he can contribute a man's share of work but, should he fail to become a priest or a teacher, there would be nothing else for him to do. He would by then have lost the taste for farm work.

In this matter of mobility, it is interesting to note that native-born women are more likely than native-born men to emigrate to the cities, as the following figures show:

	Men	*Women*
In cities	16% (34)	21% (57)
Other	84% (204)	78% (213)
	100% (238)	100% (270)

As a general rule, emigration from Chanzeaux follows a predictable pattern. It varies directly with the size of the place of destination, and inversely with the distance of the destination from Chanzeaux.[3] (See maps of birthplace, residence, and destination.) But there are differences and exceptions to this rule, which must be explained in terms of the dynamics of the region and by sociological considerations.

Half of the immigrants come from neighboring communes; more than a quarter of the emigrants move to neighboring communes. The majority of the displacements, as a matter of fact, take place within a well-defined region south of Angers and ten miles on both sides of Chanzeaux. Much of this migration must be considered normal movement within a larger economic community or between overlapping social communities (see Table 40).

In a general sense, this pattern of close-to-home migration is the result of the different orientations of Chanzeaux's three main regional groups: the bourg dwellers, the farmers, and the wine growers. Each of these groups is not only well defined within Chanzeaux, but is also culturally allied to similar groups outside the town. Thus many vintners emigrate to those neighboring communes where there are more wine villages, to Saint Lambert, Beaulieu, and Rablay, for example (see Table 41). Farmers are responsible for most of the close

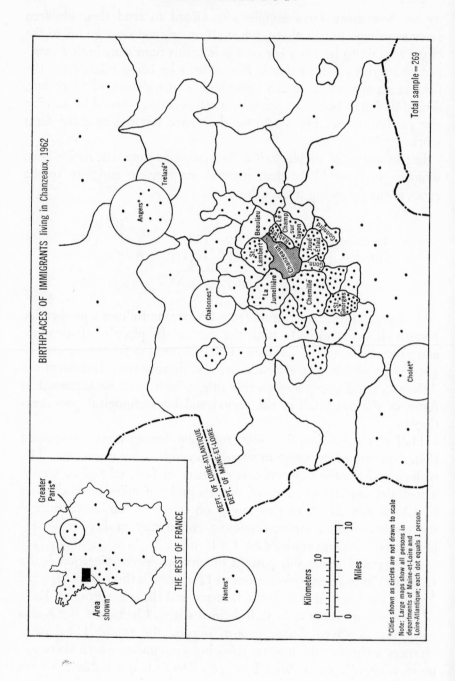

BIRTHPLACES OF IMMIGRANTS living in Chanzeaux, 1962

Total sample = 269

Angers*
Trelazé*
Beaulieu
Le Champ sur layon
Chanzeaux
St. Lambert
Rablay
Joué Étiau
Gonnord
Gonn
Chalonnes*
La Jumellière
Chemillé
St. Georges
Cholet*

Greater Paris*

THE REST OF FRANCE

DEPT. OF LOIRE-ATLANTIQUE
DEPT. OF MAINE-ET-LOIRE

Area shown

Nantes*

Kilometers
10   0
Miles
10   0

*Cities shown as circles are not drawn to scale

Note: Large maps show all persons in departments of Maine-et-Loire and Loire-Atlantique; each dot equals 1 person.

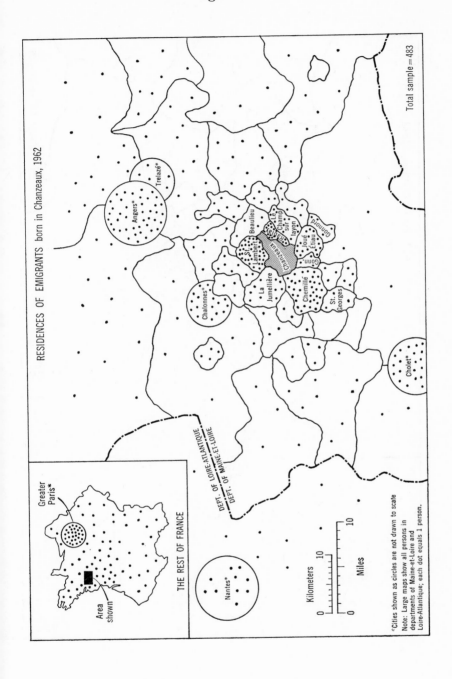

RESIDENCES OF EMIGRANTS born in Chanzeaux, 1962

Total sample = 483

Greater Paris*

Area shown

THE REST OF FRANCE

DEPT. OF LOIRE-ATLANTIQUE
DEPT. OF MAINE-ET-LOIRE

Nantes*

Kilometers

Miles

*Cities shown as circles are not drawn to scale

Note: Large maps show all persons in departments of Maine-et-Loire and Loire-Atlantique; each dot equals 1 person.

Angers*

Trelazé*

Beaulieu

Le Champ sur Layon

Chanzeaux

St. Lambert

Gonnord

Joué Étiau

Bonn

Chalonnes

La Jumellière

Chemillé

St. Georges

Cholet*

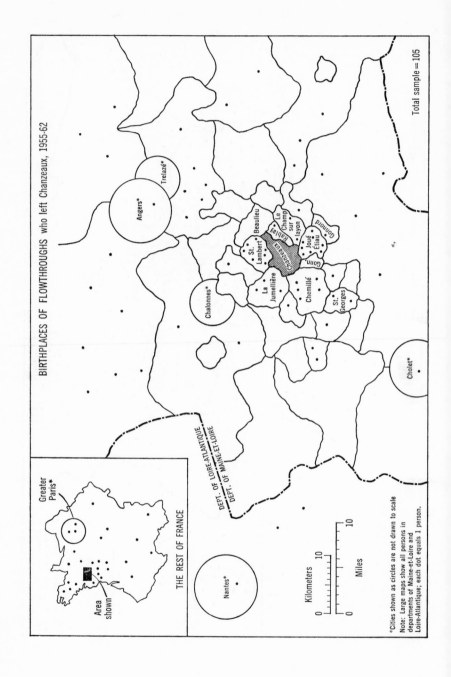

BIRTHPLACES OF FLOWTHROUGHS who left Chanzeaux, 1955-62

Total sample = 105

Trelazé*

Angers*

Beaulieu

St. Lambert

Le Champ sur layon

Gonnord

Joué Étiau

Chanzeaux

Tablay

Gonn

Chalonnes*

La Jumellière

Chemillé

St. Georges

Cholet*

DEPT. OF LOIRE-ATLANTIQUE

DEPT. OF MAINE-ET-LOIRE

Greater Paris*

THE REST OF FRANCE

Area shown

Nantes*

Kilometers   10   10

0   Miles   10

*Cities shown as circles are not drawn to scale

Note: Large maps show all persons in departments of Maine-et-Loire and Loire-Atlantique; each dot equals 1 person.

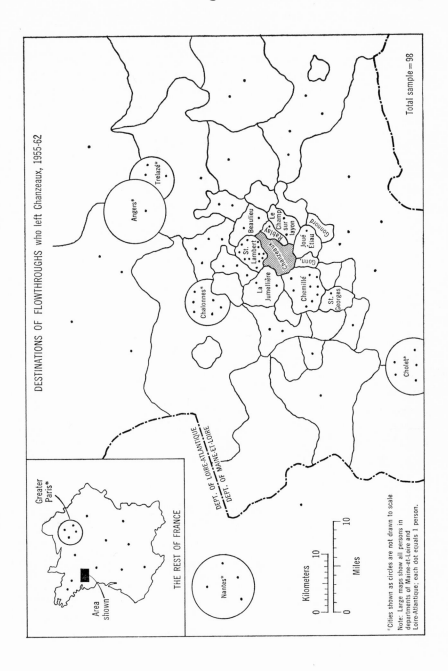

DESTINATIONS OF FLOWTHROUGHS who left Chanzeaux, 1955-62

Total sample = 98

Greater Paris*

THE REST OF FRANCE

Area shown

DEPT. OF LOIRE-ATLANTIQUE
DEPT. OF MAINE-ET-LOIRE

Nantes*

Angers*

Trelazé*

Chalonnes*

Beaulieu
Le Champ sur layon
St. Lambert
Chanzeaux
Rablay
Joué Étiau
Gonnord
Gonn.
La Jumellière
Chemillé
St. Georges

Cholet*

Kilometers
10
10
0
0
Miles

*Cities shown as circles are not drawn to scale
Note: Large maps show all persons in departments of Maine-et-Loire and Loire-Atlantique; each dot equals 1 person.

Table 40. Origin and Destination of Chanzeaux Migrants

	Contiguous communes	Other Mauges, Layon, Saumurois	Other Maine-et-Loire	Other departments and unknown	Total no.
Destination of emigrants (1962 residence)	30% (152)	34% (169)	15% (73)	21% (124)	508
Origin of immigrants (birthplace)	37% (109)	38% (112)	7.5% (22)	17.5% (54)	297
Destination of flowthroughs (residence after Chanzeaux)	26% (33)	29% (37)	13% (16)	32% (40)	126
Origin of flowthroughs (residence before Chanzeaux)	30% (38)	13% (16)	17% (22)	40% (50)	126

Table 41. Emigration to Contiguous Communes

	Residence in Chanzeaux[a]					
Destination	Bourg	Wine village	Farm village	Hamlet	Farm	Total no.
Emigrated to contiguous commune	9%	37%	36%	40%	34%	145
Emigrated beyond contiguous commune	91%	63%	64%	60%	66%	336
Total no.	114	57	83	116	111	481

[a] Residence is that of parents at emigrant's birth.

regional migration. Most, like Jean Arrial, have little economic dependence upon the Chanzeaux bourg because they sell their produce through either regional farmers' cooperatives or city-based firms. In addition, some farmers, because they reside closer to a bourg other than that of Chanzeaux, are more likely to participate in its social activities. The Chanzeaux farmers belong to a community engaged in agriculture, and they need only to stay somewhere within the region. The bourg, on the other hand, is not an important source of the nearby migration. This is because the bourg residents are allied by occupation to residents of a wide network of more distant bourgs and larger towns.

Despite the predominance of close regional migration, trends in migratory movement are evident. The migration through Chanzeaux has a definite direction to it: from southwest to northeast (see Table 42). The stream of immigrants entering the town comes primarily

Table 42. Direction of Origin or Destination within the Maine-et-Loire

	NE	NW	SW	SE	Total no.
Immigrant origin	22%	12%	45%	21%	241
Emigrant destination	47	17	22	14	389
Flowthrough birthplace, 1954–1962[a]	26	20	23	31	71
Flowthrough destination	34	24	30	12	86

[a] Figures are for those flowthroughs whose birthplace and destination are known.

from the conservative, religious area of the Mauges. Those who emigrate from Chanzeaux almost exclusively move toward the more progressive area along the Loire River, nearer Angers. Chanzeaux is thus a relay station on an economic and cultural route of migration, as well as on a geographical one. Many of the immigrants come not only from the southwest but also from communes smaller than, or only equal in size to, Chanzeaux. By the same token, among the emigrants there is an appreciable movement toward larger, more modern towns.

In the nineteenth century the industrial centers of Angers and Chalonnes were the poles of attraction of Chanzeaux's emigrants. Since then, Cholet, to the southeast of Chanzeaux, has grown into an important urban center, the most rapid growth occurring after the 1950s. The result is that the time-worn pattern of southwest-northeast migration has been somewhat altered: while the origins of the immigrants remain nearly constant, an increasing number of emigrants are turning southward. The destinations of Chanzean emigrants (whose date of departure is known) who left the area before 1940 and after 1940 are revealing:

	NE	NW	SE	SW	Total no.
Before 1940	50%	18%	9%	23%	72
After 1940	39%	19%	12%	30%	174

It is clear that the breakdown of Chanzeaux into three primary areas helps to explain far-flung migration as well as movement to nearby regions. Chanzeaux bourg sends many emigrants to the city. A steady contact with the outside world and a lack of need for fresh manpower contribute to increased movement toward the city. A good example of the tendency of bourg families to scatter is the Bordereau family. Louis Bordereau, for years the baker of Chanzeaux, finally handed his trade over to his eldest son, also Louis. But the other children dispersed: Juliette works in a pastry shop in Paris; Henri now drives a truck in Cholet; Jeanne lives in Trelazé, near Angers; Emile is now a priest in Constantine, Algeria. Wine growers, the second of our three groups, generally move to wine towns even when they move far away. Thus, when a vintner does not emigrate to a neighboring wine commune or to one of the Layon wine towns, he generally moves to the east, toward the Saumur region of the Maine-et-Loire, one of France's major wine-growing areas. Finally, the pattern holds true for the third group, the farmers. The most active group in local migration, the farmers, are least likely to move far afield. Table 43 shows the tendency of each of the three groups to

Table 43. Destination of Emigrants by Residence in Chanzeaux

| Destination | Residence[a] | | | |
	Bourg	Wine sector	Rural Chanzeaux	Unknown
Cities	29%	17%	15%	—
Layon	4%	41%	23%	—
Mauges	15%	14%	25%	—
Other	52%	29%	37%	—
Total no.	113	108	259	28

[a] Residence is that of parents at emigrant's birth.

emigrate according to its type of residence in Chanzeaux.

The story is repeated in the pattern of immigration into Chanzeaux (see Table 44). Each of the three areas under discussion is, on the whole, replenished from corresponding areas. While a sizable number of immigrants to the Chanzeaux bourg come from outside the Maine-et-Loire, almost all of the incoming farmers come from the Mauges. A large number of Chanzeaux wine-area residents come

Table 44. Origin of Immigrants by Residence in Chanzeaux

	Residence		
Origin	Bourg	Wine sector	Rural Chanzeaux
Cities	8%	7%	3%
Layon	15%	35%	19%
Mauges	46%	40%	68%
Other Maine-et-Loire	10%	9%	6%
Outside Maine-et-Loire	21%	9%	4%
Total no.	61	55	161

from the Layon wine towns. Only a small percentage of Chanzeaux farmers come from the city.

Within the trends and generalizations of migration through Chanzeaux lie personal histories or idiosyncrasies that can affect the general picture. One such personal factor is kinship. A Chanzean is more likely to cut across economic and cultural lines if a relative has already done so, thus making more readily available some familiarity with a new mode of life; but kinship can also reinforce existing traditional patterns of migration. The role of Emile Abellard in influencing migration from Saint-Georges du Puy de la Garde is a case in point. Saint-Georges, which lies to the southwest, is a very traditionalist, rural commune, smaller than Chanzeaux. Of all the communes of the Mauges it is the one that has sent the greatest number of migrants to Chanzeaux, and Emile Abellard was the first of the modern wave to come. He arrived in Chanzeaux in the early 1900s. The majority of the immigrants from Saint-Georges since then are related to him. The presumption is that his cousins, nephews, and nieces made contact with Chanzeaux through him, on visits or at family reunions.

Migration in the Past and Urbanization Today

That the large-scale migration we have described is not a phenomenon of recent years is evident from a glance at the figures in Table 45. In the 1840s Chanzeaux saw even more population turnover than it does today. The turmoil of the period can be partly explained by the fact that then there were many more agricultural workers. In 1841, indeed, there were more farm hands than farmers (owners or tenants). By 1962, there were only a dozen. Table 46 shows that, then as now, agricultural workers moved a great deal. But it also

Table 45. Migration in the Past

Period	Adult departures[a]	Adult arrivals[b]	Adult population[c]
1841–1851	409 (39%)	342 (33%)	1,054
1954–1962	138 (19%)	47 (7%)	713

[a] An "adult" in 1841–1851 is defined as anyone who was not a dependent child; in 1954–1962 an "adult" was anyone 21 or older. In the earlier period we list as a departure: anyone who was an "adult" on the 1841 census and was neither listed on the 1851 census nor listed on the *état civil* as having died; anyone who was a dependent child in 1841 and, by similar reasoning, was presumed to have left independently of his parents before 1851. In the later period we list as a departure anyone who resided in Chanzeaux, left between 1954 and 1962, and was over 21 in 1962.

[b] These figures do not include persons who came and left again before the end year of the period (i.e., before 1851 or 1962).

[c] In 1841 and 1954.

Table 46. Migration of Agricultural Workers

Period[a]	Departures of adult men	Total no. in adult population	Arrivals of adult men
1841–1851			
Agricultural workers	92	179	99
Others	103	345	88
1954–1962			
Agricultural workers	14	27	7
Others	56	362	13

[a] For 1841–1851 emigrants, we consider the occupation in 1841 or, if the individual was a dependent child in 1841, his father's occupation in 1841; for 1954–1962 emigrants, occupation at leaving; for immigrants, occupation in 1851 or 1962.

shows that, even discounting these transients, Chanzeaux had a higher rate of turnover in the 1840s.

Nevertheless, the general migration pattern was similar to what it is today. If we compile a list of the boys living in Chanzeaux in 1841 who stayed in Chanzeaux and were working by 1851, we see that there was a stable core of farmers and artisans, just as there is now:

Sons of farmers who remained farmers	41		
Sons of farmers who were working on family farm	18	70	62%
Sons of artisans who remained artisans	11		
Other sons who continued in father's occupation		13	12%
Sons who changed occupation		29	26%
		112	100%

These figures show us that about three quarters of the men who remained in Chanzeaux when they reached adulthood continued in their fathers' occupations. In recent times, leaving Chanzeaux has been a way to move up the occupational scale, but we have no way of knowing what happened to those who left in the 1840s. Then, too, most of the migrants were young. In fact, more than half of the adults who came to Chanzeaux between 1841 and 1851 were still single in 1851. There were also migrants in all occupational groups. In the twentieth century, it appears that the same kinds of people have been leaving Chanzeaux in about the same proportions (though not in the same total numbers) for quite some time. This is not surprising, of course, since we know that the people who stay behind are mainly the children of farmers and artisans.

Over the last hundred years, the countryside of France has been losing population to the cities. But, if Chanzeaux is representative, the flow from rural areas to the cities is by no means regular. In times of national prosperity, Chanzeaux's loss through migration has been large; in times of depression, it has usually been small. In the 1840s, although the total movement was substantial, most of the people who left Chanzeaux were replaced by new arrivals. This was a depression period, when there were few new jobs in the cities. Consequently, people who left small towns like Chanzeaux had no place to go but to other small towns. In the modern postwar period, on the other hand, the French economy has been booming. Some of the people who leave Chanzeaux every year can take urban jobs in larger towns. Similarly, some of the people who leave other small towns can go to larger towns. As a result, Chanzeaux's immigration rate in recent years has been much lower than its emigration rate. In the past five years, its population loss through migration has been greater than at any other time in this century.

By counting births and deaths between every two censuses, we can calculate Chanzeaux's net emigration (total departure minus total arrivals) as far back as 1835. In almost every period, more people have left Chanzeaux than have come into it. But in times of prosperity emigration has been much greater than in times of economic stagnation. The graph below shows how net migration in Chanzeaux closely follows the long-run French business cycle. From a peak in the 1870s and early 1880s, France fell into a depression that lasted almost until the turn of the century. Net emigration also fell during this period. Starting in 1896, the French economy grew rapidly until 1920, staggered a little, then continued to boom until 1930. Net emigration increased during this period. After 1930, during the

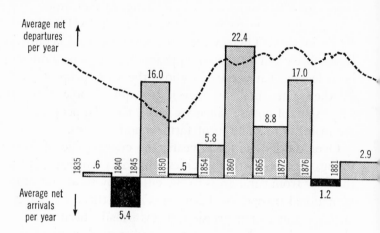

Great Depression, it fell, reaching a low point during the German occupation in the 1940s. Since the end of the war, net emigration has been very high. In the past six years, an average of thirty-two more people per year have left Chanzeaux than have come into it. This high rate is unprecedented.[4]

Few people go directly to the cities from Chanzeaux. Still, we know that in France small towns like Chanzeaux are getting smaller and big towns are getting bigger. The movement toward urban areas takes place in small, discrete steps, according to the process described by L. M. Goreux.[5] Growing cities draw workers from the surrounding countryside. Since this leaves a sparser farm population behind, with more land per person, farming becomes more lucrative in these areas; as a result, new farmers and agricultural workers move in. Thus there is also a nonurban migration toward cities. The same argument would presumably apply to persons in small-town urban occupations. A city would draw people from the bourgs of small nearby towns, and these bourg people would then be replaced by immigrants from towns farther away from the city.

Chanzeaux seems to fit the pattern. People come to Chanzeaux from towns slightly smaller and leave it for towns slightly larger. People from these larger towns, in turn, move to still larger ones. Here are the figures for adults in 1962:

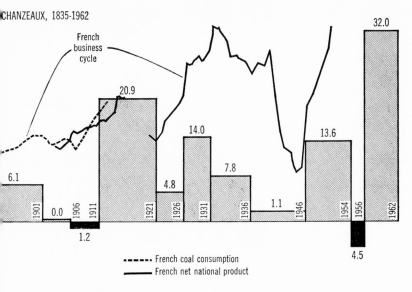

CHANZEAUX, 1835-1962

French business cycle

French coal consumption
French net national product

	Smaller than Chanzeaux	Same size as Chanzeaux (1,000–2,000)	Bigger than Chanzeaux
Size of birthplace, immigrants	42%	31%	27%
Size of residence, emigrants	26%	28%	46%

Furthermore, individual people often move several times — each time to a larger town. In general, the flowthroughs who also moved through Chanzeaux went to larger towns than they had come from:

	Smaller than Chanzeaux	Same size as Chanzeaux	Bigger than Chanzeaux
Size of birthplace, flowthroughs	37%	37%	36%
Size of destination, flowthroughs	12%	35%	53%

In the figures just above, we are comparing the birthplaces and destinations of the *same* group of people. Another indication that people tend to move to larger towns each time they change residence is the fact that those emigrants who left Chanzeaux several decades ago now live in larger towns than those who left more recently:

1950–62	1940s	1930s	1920s	Before 1920	Date of departure unknown
35%	43%	48%	58%	63%	(60%: 301 out of 517 in sample)

A higher proportion of the people who came several decades ago were born in smaller towns, a fact further suggesting that people who come from towns the same size as, or larger than, Chanzeaux tend to move on to bigger towns:

1950–62	1940s	1930s	1920s	Before 1920	Date of arrival unknown
37%	45%	33%	53%	69%	(24%: 74 out of 304 in sample)

The Effects of Migration

Migration in and out of Chanzeaux has systematic variations. Certain types of people have been shown to be more likely to migrate than others. There is a direction to the migration. Areas of origin and destination are related to areas of residence within Chanzeaux. Fluctuations in net migration reflect national economic fluctuations. Systematic differences have been analyzed between men and women, families and individuals, and the distance and size of the commune of origin or destination.

Our studies of occupation and residence indicate that the people who stay in Chanzeaux are those who are fairly well off or hold the type of job which is more or less fixed and often hereditary — those who are tied to a shop or to an owned piece of land. This places the centers of stability in the bourg and in the villages. The people who leave are those whose jobs are mobile or transitory, whether they are at the top or the bottom of the social structure — the *ouvriers agricoles* as well as the government and church employees in the bourg and the children who are better educated. The studies of religious and political behavior in this book indicate that secular and religious deviants or nonparticipants (which often adds up to the same thing) are quite likely to leave the commune. In a large city or even in another type of village, this might not be true. There, those who were on the outside of most of the established social life might form a minority that would oppose the prevailing traditions, beliefs, and behavior. Chanzeaux, however, offers a limited variety of ecological niches for people to occupy, and migration provides an easy outlet for those who do not fit in.

The factors determining whether someone will leave Chanzeaux ultimately ensure Chanzeaux's homogeneity in political and religious behavior and the maintenance of its traditional and conservative tone. Time and time again, the lament is repeated that the best part of Chanzeaux is leaving it. One doubts, however, that the present differs much from the past. There is no place in Chanzeaux for Chanzeaux's best, if what is meant by "best" is "most educated." In the first place, those students who earn higher qualification would waste it working on a parent's farm or at a parent's trade. In the second place, the better-qualified student is not the kind who would choose to stay in Chanzeaux. André Blond discussed the effect of this type of migration upon local politics. Of his *classe* (military-service group), he said, only three out of eighteen remain, and the most intelligent and the most active have not stayed. He pointed out the resulting lack of political quality in the younger generation of Chanzeaux today and the preponderance of older voters, which ensures a more cautious town council and a more conservative outlook on national affairs.

In terms of personality, a factor often overlooked in this area, migration is probably of the utmost importance as a selection process. Extreme deviants in personality may literally be hounded out of town. One old man and his wife, a sour and bitter couple, were accused of being sorcerers and departed after their house was surrounded by barbed wire and all sorts of curses and hexes were called down upon them. Every year one hears of families who leave Chanzeaux, especially from the hamlets and villages, because of neighborhood disputes. This also seems to be a potent source of emigrants within families. Indeed, when we began interviewing Chanzeans about emigration, we were told that we would have trouble getting information because people often left for personal reasons. The girl who feels stifled by the village's sexual mores finds a more congenial atmosphere elsewhere. Young people who are ambitious do not want to stay in Chanzeaux. Emigration thus also maintains a certain level of homogeneity or at least equilibrium in the village network of personalities. The result, in short, is a set of people who are more or less satisfied with Chanzeaux and more or less happy there.

Migration also affects Chanzeaux through the place of origin of immigrants and through the destination of emigrants. The southwesterly origin of Chanzeaux's immigrants strongly reinforces Chanzeaux's religious and political traditions. The immigrants tend to come from smaller towns, and towns in the Mauges, where the rate of religious practice is high and the political orientation is very similar to that of Chanzeaux. Although Chanzeaux is only at the border of the Mauges, it shares the Mauges outlook. The fact that many of Chanzeaux's inhabitants come from this area, and from villages like Chanzeaux, must be a key factor in the perpetuation of this outlook. This can be seen most clearly in terms of the religious practice of immigrants: those coming from the Mauges are more likely to be very religious and less likely to be irreligious than those born in the Layon, Saumurois, or Angers areas (see Table 47). The traditionalist, rural origins of Chan-

Table 47. Area of Birth and Religious Practice of Immigrants

Degree of religious practice[a]	Area of birth		Total no.
	Mauges	Layon, etc.	
Devout and intermediate	35%	18%	69
Normal	30%	33%	71
Irregular and irreligious	15%	27%	42
Unknown	20%	22%	49
			231

[a] See Chapter 13 for definition of categories.

zeaux's immigrants help to maintain the traditionalist and rural aspects of present-day Chanzeaux.

Conversely, the destination of Chanzeaux's emigrants — the more radical northeast, larger towns and cities — is a force for change in Chanzeaux itself. Since most people migrate to the north, move up the occupational ladder, and live in more and more agglomerated settlement patterns, these factors have become an ideal for much of Chanzeaux's youth. Many of the expectations of adolescents (see Chapter 16), which seem so incongruous if taken purely within the context of Chanzeaux, are more understandable if Chanzeaux's emigrants are considered a possible frame of reference for these young people. It should be remembered that virtually everyone in Chanzeaux has relatives, close friends, neighbors, or landlords who are emigrants. Increasingly large sections of Chanzeaux's population are looking toward the city for hints on behavior. It has become fashionable, for instance, for a certain group of people to skimp on church attendance as an exhibition of sophistication. Georges Lambert's brother lives in Paris, but he comes back with his wife in the summer to visit for a while. They wear elegant clothes, drive a new car, and talk of life in the city. Claude Drouais, son of a mason, is now an engineer in Nantes but, when he brings his children back to Chanzeaux for a month in the summer, he also brings back a part of his new way of life. The emigrants from Chanzeaux seem to have an important, although relatively indirect, effect upon Chanzeaux — their behavior conditions the expectations of the community for change. It is often through them that Chanzeaux gains intimate and personal contact with the "New France," which in many other respects has bypassed the small villages.

Migration in and out of Chanzeaux involves a greater number of people than most Chanzeans themselves might have suspected. This is surprising not only because Chanzeaux is a rural community, which is generally supposed to be a stable center of population, but also because Chanzeaux is a part of what is supposed to be one of the most stable and traditional parts of France. Unlike the Midi, the Maine-et-Loire is known for its conservatism, its faithfulness to the church, and its relative rural prosperity, and it has long been assumed that all of these factors are tied with a general population stability. But we have seen that, despite an indirect influence toward change, migration is one of the key factors in Chanzeaux's maintenance of its traditions; far from being a sign of instability, its effect is just the reverse. Migration actually works to ensure village homogeneity and stability.

Part Four

SOCIAL ORGANIZATION

So far we have considered the various ways that people in Chanzeaux identify one another. Chanzeans consciously separate themselves into groups according to occupation and wealth, according to place of residence and the regional affiliation it implies, and according to length of residence in the community. This section is an analysis of Chanzeaux's system of social relationships, a system ordered to a large extent on the basis of membership in these groups. The chapter on kinship describes the relationships that are the most permanent and the most important to people in Chanzeaux. Membership in a larger network of families in turn leads to another way in which Chanzeans classify one another. In the remaining chapters we attempt to determine how kinship as well as occupation, residence, and family origins are related to participation in community life.

Our second concern in this part is the nature of community life itself. What do Chanzeans consider matters of common interest? What are their common aspirations, what kinds of institutions have they organized to fulfill them, and what kinds of leaders have they chosen? We find that in this respect, as in so many others, the experience of the past no longer suffices in Chanzeaux today, and that the social organization of the community is also undergoing rapid change.

9

Kinship

THE KINSHIP system of Chanzeaux appears at first sight to be identical to that in the United States, and anthropologists would define both systems as bilateral and cognatic. These terms simply mean that a Chanzean, like an American, is expected to behave in the same way toward his mother's and his father's sides of the family, and that he thinks of his kinship network as branching outward from himself rather than from some other person, such as an ancient or mystical head of a clan. Yet, despite this apparent similarity, kinship plays a much larger role in Chanzeaux than it does in urban, middle-class America. In work, in social activities, in political life, in religion and education, Chanzeans emphasize kinship ties, and for many reasons.

First, Chanzeaux is a rural community in an agricultural region. Contacts in this setting, unlike those in large cities, normally take place between people who have known each other for a long time. Contact with strangers is rare, since a Chanzean, especially if he lives outside the bourg, has little time and few resources to travel beyond the commune's borders. Trips outside are made for well-defined purposes: to shop for clothes or machinery, to see the doctor, to take in a movie. But in his daily life, the Chanzean usually sees only the familiar faces of his family and nearby neighbors. Given these conditions, it is hardly surprising that about 50 percent of the people in Chanzeaux marry within the commune. Of the Chanzeaux residents who were born outside Chanzeaux, over 80 percent come from within a forty-mile radius. This tendency to marry close to home means that most of the people have relatives close by. In Chanzeaux, each adult has an average of two adult relatives (first cousin or closer) in the commune — a number that would be even higher if contiguous communes were included in the figure.

Emphasis on kinship in Chanzeaux also reflects traditional French cultural patterns, the sanctity of the *foyer* or family group. Americans in France often notice how difficult it is to penetrate into the "inner circle" of a French family, to be accepted as more than a casual acquaintance. The family is the all-important social unit, and relationships within it are expected to be intense and enduring. When questionnaires were sent to the teenagers in Chanzeaux to discover how their attitudes differed from those of American adolescents, one of the clearest findings was that the young people stressed good relationships with their parents and the needs of the family much more than their own desires or ambitions. In the Chanzean family, the authority of the *pater familias* is by no means dead; nor is that of his wife, who rules her brood with a loving but strict hand.

Roman Catholic ideology, which occupies an important place in the thinking of most Chanzeans, also encourages strong kinship ties. As the social encyclicals of the last hundred years have stressed, the family is the focus of lay organizations within the church, as a builder of moral and spiritual values. As Catholics, Chanzeans are encouraged to produce large families, and families in Chanzeaux are in fact larger than those in less religious areas of France. The normal Chanzean family has three to five children, but larger families are not uncommon. Three families in the commune each have thirteen children. Unlike certain less religious areas of France, where family size seems inversely proportional to religious devotion, a large family in Chanzeaux is usually a good index of religious fervor.

Although kinship ties affect every Chanzean, their strength and content vary. For example, the vintners in the northeast section of the commune have significantly fewer relatives in the commune than do people who live elsewhere in Chanzeaux. Instead of drawing them into Chanzeaux, the vintners' relatives, who presumably live in the wine-producing communes to the north and east, pull them away, helping to emphasize the social distance between the vintners and the other farmers. While town leaders normally have a superabundance of relatives within the commune, political and religious deviants also, like the vintners, have fewer kin than the average Chanzean. Often the deviants have moved into the commune from distant areas; moreover, they tend to choose their husbands or wives from within the deviant group, further decreasing their chances for building up extensive ties within the community.

Often kinship relations are complemented by other ties, such as *classe* affiliations. Class is determined by year of birth, all people born in the same year belonging to the same class. Boys are drafted according to their class, and class affiliations become most important to them during the year before their induction. During this year, they meet as often as possible to drink together, to attend a dance, or to go to the movies — and to spend evenings visiting the homes of the girls in their class. They are expected to enjoy themselves as much as possible before settling down to the serious work of being a soldier. They become like brothers, a relationship that often continues during later life.

Kinship affects the working life as well as the social life of the community. People draw on their relatives for help in all phases of their work. They will borrow machinery and, if necessary, money from relatives; they also borrow personnel. Borrowing may be done on a long-term basis, as when a young nephew comes to live with his uncle's family for a year or two, supplementing the manpower that may have been lost as the uncle's children married and moved away. At present, over half of Chanzeaux's *ouvriers agricoles,* the nonproprietied farm workers, are working for relatives. Short-term borrowing also occurs, usually during harvest season, when the crop must be gathered quickly. At one *battage* (threshing), for instance, a farmer had adequate assistance in the fields, but called on his married daughter and a young niece to keep the men supplied with refreshments during the day and to help his wife prepare the meal following the work. Students on vacation during the summer often travel around to different relatives, helping to pick camomile or to plant the cabbages. The *vendanges,* or grape harvest, may also demand the services of relatives, who in this case are eager to help, for it is a lively social occasion. It not only provides a rare opportunity for men and women to work together, but sometimes serves as a meeting place for future husbands and wives.

Relatives also help one another through patronage. In the bourg, the mayor patronizes the bakery most distant from his home because the owner is his daughter-in-law's brother. The American students who lived in Chanzeaux found repeatedly that, if they needed something done and the person asked could not do it, he would produce a relative who could, even if slowly or badly. A "pseudo-kinship" relationship may also develop out of working arrangements. The Malinge and Faligand families provide an excellent example. The Malinges are a childless couple in their sixties who have no relatives in the commune. The Faligands, a middle-aged couple with several children, are their tenant farmers, the fermiers who work M. Malinge's land. Although the Faligands have some distant cousins in the commune, they too lack close kin ties. Starting from their economic bonds, the two families have developed behavioral patterns that usually occur only between blood relatives. The Malinges act like parents to the Faligands and, more important, like grandparents to the Faligand children, babysitting for them and bringing them treats. The two families also gather together after church, just as close relatives do.

Through work and social activities, kinship also affects patterns of immigration and emigration in the commune. There are numerous examples of people who entered the commune to work for a relative and later settled there, increasing the kinship networks of particular families. Perhaps more interesting are the cases of repeated intermarriage between two parts of the commune, or between Chanzeaux and another commune. Since people visit relatives in nearby areas so frequently, when the times does come for a young person to marry, he can choose not only from among his near neighbors but also from among the people he knows in these other areas. This phenomenon is best illustrated by the frequency of marriages between Chanzeaux and Saint-Georges du Puy de la Garde, a commune of similar size some twelve miles southwest of Chanzeaux. This is relatively far for a Chanzean to go to seek out a marriage partner, yet the chances of his marrying a person from Saint-Georges are as great as those for communes much closer to Chanzeaux. The phenomenon dates back several generations at least, to a time at the beginning of the century when Chanzeaux became a desirable new location for Saint-Georgians. Today the immigration pattern is perpetuated through the activities of kinship groups.

Kinship also affects politics. Town councilors have significantly more adult relatives in the community than the average Chanzean. At an average age of about fifty-five, they stand in the center of their kinship networks, with adult relatives in both ascending and descending generations, as well as brothers, sisters, and cousins in their own generation. The former mayor provides an outstanding example of the strength of such kinship ties. He has five adult children living in Chanzeaux, four of whom are married and all of whom are active in commune life. He also gains in prestige by having two children in religious orders. Although he has no brothers or sisters in the commune, his wife's brother, the bicycle repairman, has several grown children with whom the mayor maintains close relations. The mayor's aged mother-in-law is also living. Through these relatives and in-laws, the mayor is related to a great number of Chanzeans. The town councilors' wives usually belong to even more extensive kinship networks than their husbands do.

Kinship has a bearing on religion as well, and in ways other than its influence on the birthrate. Religious holidays and various *rites de passage* invoke a gathering of the kin group more readily than any secular occasions. Whereas during christenings or weddings relatives assume formal roles in the ceremony, religious holidays, requiring nothing specific from relatives, draw them in equally great numbers. For instance, the entire family of the bicycle repairman gathered together one Christmas, coming from distances of sixty or seventy miles, a long way by Chanzean standards. This reunion spanned four generations, from an aged priest, the repairman's uncle, to his small grandchild. Another religious occasion that draws the family together is the annual *kermesse* (folklore festival), held each August to raise money for the Catholic schools. This is an especially good time for priests to return home, since they can spur their relatives to make large contributions. At a recent festival, six priests from Chanzeaux were present, one on leave from Algeria.

There is a significant correlation too between the size of one's kin group and the frequency of church attendance. About 85 percent of the adults in the community attend Mass regularly — and these people have more relatives in the commune than those who do not come to church. This correlation may reflect the fact that people who lack relatives in the commune often come from far away, where Catholic influence is not so strong and church attendance is less expected. But it may also indicate that people without relatives do not attend church because they feel socially as well as ideologically isolated; they cannot be a part of the family groupings that appear each Sunday. By staying home, they are denied the main social occasion of the week, for after church people jam the cafés and stores as at no other time of the week, picking up both groceries and gossip. Even the townhall is open.

Religion and kinship interact in yet another way. Chanzeaux sends a relatively large number of its sons and daughters into religious orders. At present, there are eleven priests and twenty-five nuns active in the world who come originally from Chanzeaux. One sixth of the adults in the commune have a relative in a religious order. These nuns and priests, however, come from fewer than thirty-six families; while most Chanzeaux families produce no nuns or priests, some produce two or three. An extreme case was the family of a woman known as "la Sainte" Pinier, whose children and grandchildren during the later nineteenth century included no less than five priests and four nuns — about a third of the total number for Chanzeaux during that period. Today, two families (one is that of the former mayor) can claim five relatives each in religious orders, while four families claim two each. According to one mother who has children in orders, these relatives give the family a *don de grâce,* a sense of spiritual protection and enrichment. In this way, religion and kinship act and react on one another, for a devout family is almost certain to include one child who will become a priest or nun. Once committed, the child provides the example and incentive for the family to become even more devout and to encourage other members to take religious vows.

Religious fervor is not the only quality that seems the exclusive property of certain families in Chanzeaux. Many of the Chanzeaux "clans" are tagged with particular traits, both good and bad. Sometimes these are based on tangible proof, such as involvement in religious orders or in higher education, but often they have less definite origins: one family may be considered high-spirited (this is attributed to people from Brittany), another immoral, a third miserly. People in the commune are always anxious to know who one's relatives are, to place a person as quickly as possible within a certain framework of traits. A family may have more than one image, of course, since black sheep will always exist, but the majority of relatives usually fall under a single rubric. Chanzeans are very suspicious of one family, for example, because "they're all crazy." One aunt was the town laughingstock for years, owing to her strange behavior; she was finally sent to a mental hospital. A son became mentally disturbed as a young man and later committed suicide. His father and mother act normally, but the Chanzeans still treat them with fear and suspicion. A Saint-Lambert clan with the same name must explain continually that they are not related to the Chanzeaux family; none of *them* is crazy. The only relative who has escaped antagonism is a daughter who married into a "good family" and who is highly respected in the community for her piety.

Another quality appearing in some families is a stress on education. Although such an emphasis is of course related to many factors —

intelligence, income, number of children — nonetheless at least two families in the commune seem to have a tradition of sending their children to college and of producing schoolteachers. Within the bicycle repairman's group, for example, there are no less than eight teachers, with a ninth in training. The town clerk, who holds the only white-collar job besides teaching available in the commune, also comes from a family that prizes education.

A newcomer to Chanzeaux may be aided by these family stereotypes, but he must be wary of two pitfalls: first, does the community recognize exceptions to the stereotype, and, second, to exactly which family does the stereotype apply? Does a stereotype of the Duval family, for instance, apply to the Duvals of Le Plessis or the Duvals of les Bordages? Or are they all related somehow? To a native, this is no problem. Anyone who lives in the commune for a considerable length of time and becomes involved himself in the kinship network inevitably acquires a detailed knowledge of these relationships, which form the basis of a large part of his dealings with other people in the commune. Because Chanzeans rely on kinship ties so extensively, it is the binding force in all community life. For those who have few relatives in the town, the town can have little meaning. Conversely, the people at the center of community activities are those with many relatives in the commune.

As time goes on, many of the elaborate manifestations of kinship behavior in Chanzeaux may disappear, for they can flourish only in a community that is relatively self-contained. As more and more people take jobs outside the commune, and as the influence of the city grows, it will become increasingly difficult to escape the impersonality of urban life. Already Saint-Lambert, just north of Chanzeaux, sends practically all its young people into Angers each day to work. In their friendships and business contacts there, kinship can mean little, since they must deal with people who are unfamiliar with the peculiarities of the Saint-Lambert kinship network. Although Chanzeans have not left in such numbers, the seeds of change are present. The line dividing city and country, which can now be drawn very easily, will in time become more and more obscure. As the population and industries of Angers continue to impinge upon Chanzeaux, Chanzeans will be less able to retain the sense of identity that kinship provides.

10

Traditional Organizations

THE TRADITIONAL structure of the community is based in the main on two institutions: the family and the church. In the past, the family was usually a functioning economic as well as a social unit. Less dependent on the exigencies of an external market, the Chanzean family nevertheless did not enjoy full autonomy, for the system of land tenure made most farmers dependent on the good will of a few landlords for their living. Perhaps because of this common situation, independence from one's fellow townspeople came to be highly prized. The family carried out the enterprise of the farm or trade with as little outside help as possible. In times of need, people turned to their relatives for help.

The only strong socially unifying institution in Chanzeaux was the church. As one of the very few expressions of community solidarity, religious participation acquired extreme symbolic importance; no one who did not attend church regularly could be a true Chanzean. But while the church brought people together in a common ceremony, it did not require them to cooperate in other ways; it, too, respected the independence of the family. The church was in turn the model for all traditional organizations. These associations were characterized by the autocratic style of their leadership, the community-wide but occasional participation they required, the limited scope of their activities, and their ceremonial or protective functions. Because most people in Chanzeaux lacked familiarity with the world outside the village, the few intermediaries between the village and the outside — the curé and the town bourgeois before the Revolution, the curé and the seigneur after it — were endowed with great prestige. To these leaders Chanzeans willingly delegated the power to run what few affairs they had in common, as long as the leaders in turn exercised their authority with a minimum of interference in the daily life of the individual.

As we have already seen, in the eighteenth century virtually the whole organization of the community was carried out through the church and directed by one man, the priest. The role of the priest was strengthened in Chanzeaux by the fact that for generation after generation the curés of the parish remained in office during most of their careers. From 1703 to 1955 Chanzeaux had only six priests — each of them remaining in office for an average of forty-two years. Several had already lived in Chanzeaux for some years as vicaires, when they succeeded their superior on his death. In a community where the church was already important, this long tenure increased the general identification of the religious life of the community with the person of the priest himself.

In the eighteenth century, when the church was also in effect the town government, the curé was assisted by an advisory body of laymen, which he appointed. This was the *fabrique* (vestry). In the nineteenth and twentieth centuries, however, as the church lost more and more of its civil functions, the fabrique was largely supplanted by the town council. On matters concerning the running of the church itself, the priest apparently had little use for the advice of a group of laymen, and the minutes of the fabrique throughout the nineteenth century are bleak and sporadic. By 1960, the fabrique consisted of two devout men representing two very old traditions in the community. One was M. Delbosc, the chateau owner who carries on a greatly diminished gentry tradition; the other was M. Bertrand, the representative of the older generations for whom religious duty consists largely of periodic devotional practices. Neither of these men was a leader in the community, and the priest rarely consulted them. Most of the business of the church was his responsibility alone.

Although the Revolution officially put an end to the one-man rule of the curé, he retained a great deal of his authority over the parish. Until World War II the chatelain and the curé were the two poles of power in the commune. Even if they interfered with each other at times, nevertheless they exerted a tremendous influence over the population. Curé Cailleaux, who was Chanzeaux's priest until after the war, never hesitated to bring the full moral authority of his position to bear on anyone whose conduct violated Chanzeaux's social standards. Chanzeans still remember the harshness of his sermons and his explicit references to those who did not attend church.

Today, Curé Raimbault finds it prudent not to make such references. He no longer has the power over his congregation that his predecessors could exercise. At the same time that the authority of his position has diminished, the amount of work it demands has increased. A hundred years ago, the curé Pelletier had two vicaires to help him with his tasks. Father Raimbault has none. The drop in the French birthrate twenty years ago means that there is a smaller supply of vicaires in France today, and the drop in the size of religious orders has further diminished the supply of priests, so that every priest must work harder today to accomplish the same tasks his predecessor performed. The shortage has occurred, moreover, at a time when the need for priests has increased, for the activities of the church are expanding into new areas. With the growth in extradevotional activities of laymen, the need for church leaders in Catholic Action programs, the increased burden of administrative detail in all aspects of life, the deepened awareness of the complexity of man and his religious needs — with all of these, the priest's functions have multiplied as the relative number of priests has diminished.

Ceremonial Activities and Devotional Associations

The primary task of the priest is of course the celebration of religious rites. In this, the aid of laymen has always been required. Chanzeans assist in the rituals of the church as sacristan, altar boy, cantor, organist, gravedigger, and pallbearer. The nuns of the girls' school are also present at all religious services, but except for their responsibility in arranging flowers on the altar they have no special role in the ceremonies.

To translate the French *sacristain* properly into English, one must use two words: *sexton* and *sacristan*. In this country the sexton serves as janitor, rings the bells, and even digs graves, whereas the sacristan cares for the sacred material stored in the sacristy. The French sacristain has the responsibility for all of these jobs, although he may delegate part of the work to others. In Chanzeaux the sacristain, M. Devanne, is assisted by Mme. Gaudin and Mme. Forget, who serve as cleaning women for the church, and by M. Frémondière, who digs the graves and is in charge of the cemetery.

Tradition has made the office of sacristain especially important in Chanzeaux because it has been passed down in the Devanne family from father to son since the seventeenth century. M. Devanne likes to repeat that "my family has been ringing the bells for three hundred years." Ten minutes before each Mass and before each religious service in the church, the Devannes, *père et fils*, pull all the ropes dangling at the base of the belltower. The sound reaches five miles to the farthest corner of the parish. In other parts of France the churchbell, perhaps rung by the priest himself, may bring only a handful of people to the church. In Chanzeaux the Devannes dominate the community with the sound of their bells.

The altar boys (*enfants de choeur*) are the most active aides of the priest after the sacristain. Not only must they be on hand at one of the Masses on Sunday, but they take turns assisting the priest at daily Masses and at all special ceremonies. There used to be six of them, all between the ages of ten and fourteen, but in accordance with the new church policy of getting more and more parishioners involved in the functioning of the church, the number has been increased to nineteen, although the whole group serves together only on very important occasions or for public processions. At High Mass there are from six to ten boys attending the priest; at lesser ceremonies there may be only one and rarely more than four. The oldest boy in the group, called the *cérémoniaire*, serves as captain of the boys, initiating neophytes into the mysteries of their functions and carrying out the main role in the ceremonies. The other boys may be *servants*, *acolytes*, or *thuriféraires*. When a boy has reached the age of fourteen and stopped going to school, he automatically stops being a choir boy. Since this occurs in June, every year the priest recruits a number of six-year-olds to replace them, taking advantage of summer vacation to call them to the rectory several times a week to teach them their new duties.

Although it might be better to choose the altar boys from over the whole parish, there is a practical consideration that forces the priest to concentrate on boys living in the bourg or near it. Farm boys have a difficult time getting into the bourg for the early Masses and for the special occasions, unless they are already in the village at school. It is likely that this is one of the main reasons that so few farmers' sons become priests and that so large a percentage of priests come from village artisan and merchant families. Serving as altar boy is often an informal apprenticeship for the priesthood. Not only does the child learn some of the technical skills of the priest — the details of the Mass, the Latin used at Mass, and so on — but also, and more important, the priest gets a chance to detect among the children of the village those boys with the qualities considered essential for the priesthood.

In spite of the difficulties involved in serving as altar boy, most boys like to serve, and the men who have done so look back on this period with nostalgia. Although the boys may be irked by their responsibilities, they actually find many compensations. The most obvious is that they are paid. At the end of the year they receive a gratuity from the priest — twelve francs for the older boys and ten for the younger ones. But the most valued privilege is participation in the Holy Week egg collection. During the whole week the boys are excused from school and visit every farm requesting eggs. For many it is the only time they see the whole commune. Free from adult supervision, the boys are treated to wine and learn to smoke. This is what makes the older men look back fondly on their experience as altar boys.

Since only a few people can participate in the ritual of the church in these special capacities, the church has always found other ways of involving large numbers of people in religious observances. One traditional method is through devotional associations organized for giving greater emphasis to certain aspects of religious practice. The oldest association of this type in Chanzeaux is the Confrérie de St. Fiacre. Chanzeaux has for centuries been a center of veneration for this saint, the patron saint of gardeners and of people suffering from stomach ailments. Perhaps in Chanzeaux where good drinking water is rare and where liver infections are endemic, there is special reason to appeal to St. Fiacre. At any rate, St. Fiacre's feast, on August 30, used to be an important occasion in Chanzeaux. The Confrérie de St. Fiacre had the task of securing hospitality for hundreds (some histories say thousands) of pilgrims who came to ask help from St. Fiacre on his feast day.

The Confrérie de St. Fiacre still exists, but largely in the memory of the older people and in the sparse records of the sacristan, François Devanne, père. Theoretically most of the people in the parish belong and should pay their annual dues of about a quarter apiece to cover the cost of the Masses. In practice, however, most people have forgotten about the organization and have no idea that they should be paying dues to M. Devanne. His records, not brought up to date for several years, list only a score or so people who until recent years had paid their dues. No one is even aware of the special privileges granted to members of Chanzeaux's Confrérie de St. Fiacre by Pope Pius IX. On April 8, 1862, he granted in perpetuity a long list of indulgences of different degrees to those who made special prayers at St. Fiacre's altar. Sixty days' indulgence was given for participating in St. Fiacre's procession. The same indulgence was given "for attendance at services in Chanzeaux in the Saint's honor, for accompanying the holy sacrament in processions or when it is brought to the sick, or, if this is not possible, for saying one Pater Noster and one Ave Maria at the sound of the bell that announces the sacrament." Apparently the need for such privileges has all but disappeared; there is at least no public display made to earn them. The feast day of St. Fiacre is celebrated, but it is no longer an important festival.

A stronger tradition exists in Chanzeaux for devotion to the Rosary. Before the Vendée rebels went into battle, they knelt and said their rosary together, and republicans reported that the republican prisoners were forced to say their Aves and Paters before the Vendée captors executed them. In the nineteenth century the cult was represented less violently by organizations that sponsored special devotional practices for the Virgin Mary. Most Chanzeans are still listed as members of the Associés du Rosaire, but the membership now plays a small role in their lives. They are supposed to pay twenty centimes a year as membership dues and to say private prayers for each other, especially at funerals. It would be hard to know whether this practice is carried out, for one never hears anyone mention the organization or its activities.

In May or in October (months especially devoted to Mary) another sort of Marian organization is activated, the Rosaire Vivant. At the time of the Mission of 1960–61, the curé organized two sets of Rosaires Vivants for the boys and two more for the girls. Fifteen children were included in each set, and each child assumed the responsibility for saying a *dizaine* (decade), that is, a Pater Noster followed by ten Ave Marias and concluded by a Gloria Patri. Day after day the members took their turn saying their *dizaine de chapelet*, and when all fifteen had had their day the rosary was completed. So each member not only participates, but he represents a bead, a human bead, in the rosary. In order to heighten the meaning of the procedure the priest gave each child a pamphlet explaining the fifteen mysteries associated with the Rosary and suggesting a meditation for each decade. A *responsable* named by the priest had charge of keeping the members of the Living Rosary in contact with each other and with the church authorities who sponsor Marian activities in the diocese. A Dominican father in Angers is in charge of the regional office of the Rosary.

Although there is no lessening of devotion to Mary in Chanzeaux, the fact is that Marian activities, like all the devotional programs of the church, no longer play the vital role in the community they once did. The energy of the most active people is directed toward other aspects of church life — toward intensifying liturgical participation, maintaining the church educational system, and activating movements intended to inject religious ideals into the search for solutions to the practical problems of life. Although all of these areas have always been concerns of the church, they received little emphasis in the past. Until well into the twentieth century, the decennial reports of Chanzeaux priests to the bishop were almost exclusively limited to an inventory of church property and a detailed description of the physical condition of the buildings and ceremonial materials. The state of the schools, the living conditions of the villagers, and even the religious practice of the community received little attention.

The traditional church united the community through common participation in ritual. It did not directly involve its parishioners in the day-to-day business of the commune. But as the focus for community life, it served as a model for lesser communal activities, whether or not they were organized under church auspices. In their strong leadership, in the limited extent of their activities, and in their ceremonial function, all these organizations resembled the church.

Leisure Organizations

The church has traditionally sponsored organized recreation. For many years the center of leisure activities was the parish house, the *salle de patronage*, which in Chanzeaux was built around the turn of the century on land donated by the gentry and largely with money contributed by them. It consists of a large building with a theater, containing a stage and three hundred seats, a billiard table and several card tables, gymnastic equipment, pinball machines, and a bowling alley (*jeu de boules de fort*).

In recent years, however, Chanzeans have neglected the parish house. The older men prefer to get in their new cars and go visiting on Sunday afternoon. The younger men also have less interest in

Woman at a window in the bourg

Farmer and son

Playing ball

Children in a barn

Bourg children "twisting"

Boys with racing bikes

Boys and girls

How styles change

Family portrait in a hamlet of Chanzeaux

Blond and his son

Pruning the tobacco

Hoisting tobacco into the barn

Picking camomile

Two farmers pause while plowing a field

Guiding a horse-drawn plow

Loading sacks of wheat

Planting fodder beets

*Farm machinery:
the traditional harvester
in 1958 (above);
the combine in 1965*

Bonnerot the harnessmaker

La Société de la Rue Bourgeoise

Water cart in front of the church

Church mural commemorating
the Vendée Rebellion

The churchtower in Chanzeaux

The chateau of Chanzeaux and its owner

Mme. Voisin pitching hay

Pierre Brichet's farm

The cattle market in Chemillé

Procession for the Feast of Corpus Christi

A class of seven-year-olds

Procession on All Souls' Day

A wedding

drinking at the parish, for they have developed a great enthusiasm for basketball. A new basketball court was black-topped behind the parish house in the winter of 1958, and the interest in it has grown tremendously, not only in Chanzeaux but throughout the region. The first year there were only two teams in Chanzeaux — the young men and the boys. By 1962 there were two more, and three new teams were formed in 1963. There is practically no formal organization for the activity. The groups interested in playing simply appoint a *responsable* to keep them informed of games, secure transportation, and so on. Diocesan leagues are organized by the chaplain for all Catholic youth activities in the region, including the Scouts and the Guides de France.

Once a year the boys and young men put on a play to help make money for their activities, and for this function they take the name of Groupe Théâtral de la Société Jeanne d'Arc. The boys who are known to be interested in helping are called together by their *responsable* after Mass, usually at the prompting of the vicar in charge of youth activities. A play is chosen in Richer's bookstore in Angers, from the special shelf where one finds plays written expressly to be put on without girls. There is another shelf with plays for girls only, for there cannot be mixed performances put on by unmarried young people in Catholic organizations. The vicar and the boy recognized as the best director assign the roles and start rehearsals. Other boys are chosen to take care of staging the play, selling tickets, and so forth. The play is usually given on two successive Sunday evenings in December and normally the attendance is high, for the people of Chanzeaux have always had a fondness for dramatic productions.

Activities for girls and young women are even more loosely organized than those for the boys. Theoretically there is a parish group for the girls (the Patronage Ste. Cecile), whose quarters are in the girls' school and under the direction of the nuns. Formerly on every Thursday afternoon, when there was no school, and every Sunday afternoon, activities were organized by the Sisters — games, singing, reading. Once a year the girls also produced a play. Usually the story was laid in a convent, for in that way it was simpler to produce a play with roles for fifteen or twenty girls and no males. Now, however, with the change in personnel in the girls' school, all activities except for the annual play have been dropped. The Mother Superior says that there is no need for Thursday and Sunday afternoon activi-

ties: the girls are too occupied with other interests to be attracted by
any activities that could be arranged in the school. Some of the more
active parishioners criticize the Mother Superior for her defeatist
attitude. They say that activities *should* be organized for the young
people, who would then be less inclined to go off driving with their
parents, ride their scooters over to Saint-Aubin to the movies (and for
clandestine meetings with boys they have met there), or simply roam
the streets of Chanzeaux in a group that vaguely flirts with an
equivalent group of boys — the two groups sometimes even mingling.

In recent years a constructive effort has been made to organize the
young people in such a way that they might be together (according
to the new mores) but still participate in activities more virtuous
than movies, flirtations, and neighborhood dances. Two folk-dancing
groups were organized according to the techniques of the militant
Catholics — that is, a vaguely defined group who agree without much
discussion on putting someone in charge of getting things done. There
was one group of young people from the bourg and the right bank
of the Hyrôme who called themselves the Compagnons du Val
d'Hyrôme. Up along the Route Nationale, a slightly "faster" group
of young people formed the Quadrille Angevin.

Often on Sunday afternoon there is a folk festival somewhere in
the region, and both groups take part in the competition. Their most
important local appearance is at the Chanzeaux school committee's
festival. One year Yvette Bourdelle, Eugène's daughter, won a
regional competition and was crowned "Duchesse d'Anjou" for her
beauty and for the loveliness of her Angevin costume. After the
school committee's August festival, the most important single amusement of the year is the play performed on three successive Sundays
in January or February by the Groupe Théâtral Mixte du Comité
des Ecoles Libres. As chairman of the school committee, Paul Guitière
also manages this theatrical performance, and, like everything he
manages, it is a success. The parish hall is usually filled for each of
the three performances. It is a relief to see a play with men, women,
and children in it, rather than the sexually segregated plays produced
by the boys' and girls' groups.

Although the church has always played an important part in promoting organized leisure activity, it has never held a monopoly.
Several formal and informal groups have developed around the
national institutions of war and conscription. Chanzeaux has an

organization of *anciens combattants* (veterans) and *anciens combattants prisonniers de guerre* (ex-prisoners). About fifty Chanzeans owe their membership in this group to World War II. The veterans get together to talk over common experiences and organize outings for themselves and their families. In a recent year they hired a bus to go to Mont Saint-Michel for a day. Since the men in this organization are linked by common experiences outside the commune, membership cuts across the basic community divisions.

Another informal organization that draws its members from the whole community is the *classe,* the group of young men (usually aged nineteen) who receive their draft notices during any given year. Prior to entering the service, they meet frequently on Saturday night, Sunday afternoon, or weekends at different houses throughout the commune to "raise the roof" and enjoy their precious moments of freedom. The class allegiance endures even after military service is over through a yearly banquet, honoring all the people born in years ending in the same number as the current year. The class is a factor that draws the commune together. The only ties, for example, that link Joseph Catrou, a farmer living near the La Jumellière border, to Chanzeaux are his trips to vote, to register his wine, and to reunite with his class. He attends church and sends his children to school in nearby La Jumellière. In answer to a questionnaire enquiring about the farms personally known to bourg dwellers, the men who had had their class in Chanzeaux revealed that they had visited every farm in the commune; those who had had their class elsewhere did not know where some of the farms mentioned were. Again, as in the case of the veterans, the class operates regardless of the social, economic, or political standing of its members. It is perhaps the last of the "leveling" associations in the life of the Chanzean. Participation in organizations later in the individual's life depends upon occupation, political inclination, religiousness, or economic standing.

The largest leisure organization existing outside the church is a venerable club of 140 years known as the Société de la Rue Bourgeoise (showing its antiquity even in the name, since street names disappeared in Chanzeaux about a hundred years ago). The society might be termed a "drinking cooperative," for its chief purpose is to provide wine to its members at lower rates than those charged by the local cafés. Over half of the adult men in the commune belong to the society (no women allowed). They own their own building, which has facilities for playing cards. Apart from providing wine and sport, the society has two serious functions. First, all members are required to attend the funerals of departed members, and the pallbearers are normally drawn from its ranks. After the funeral is over, the members return to their meetinghouse, where a roll is taken. Absent members are fined. They also assemble each year on Veterans' Day to read off the names of members who died in the two world wars. Through these activities the society perpetuates the spirit of fraternity which is first sparked by the meetings of the classes of conscripts.

The membership of the society is heavily weighted toward the older generation. Most of the retired men in the bourg belong, and they can be glimpsed at a table in a back corner playing cards, with their old black suits and black hats, their canes propped against the wall. One man described them as "the people of the First World War." The officers are not only the oldest men in the bourg, but are probably the most inactive men in the commune. In 1963 the executive committee included three elderly town councilors. Ten of the thirteen old town councilors belong to the society. Few of the young and energetic men of the commune and none of the Catholic activists belong. The cafés have largely taken over the functions of this venerable but slowly dying association, which now subsists for the most part on ritual.

Protective Organizations

Chanzeaux's two fire-protection associations, which number among the oldest organizations in the commune, also provide occasional recreation for their members. The Sapeurs-Pompiers, or volunteer firemen, were first organized by Quatrebarbes, who apparently had grander things in mind for them (see Chapter 2). Today the firemen are rarely called — perhaps once or twice a year — but they stand ready in case of emergency. Their annual banquet in December, to which wives are invited, is the only event of its kind in Chanzeaux. When a member of the group marries, the others appear at the *vin d'honneur* in full uniform. In 1963, they organized a two-day excursion for members and their families.

Most farmers in Chanzeaux belong to the communal fire-insurance association, the Société des Agriculteurs, which also dates from the time of Quatrebarbes. In the event of a barn fire, an outside expert is called in to estimate the damage, and all members contribute to make up the sum. The president of the association, Auguste Hérault, is a retired farmer in his eighties. Although more modern insurance companies have begun to supplant the Société des Agriculteurs, its annual meeting in February is still something of a social event. The society represents the traditional limit of economic cooperation. The organizations that go beyond this point are almost all the product of the last twenty years. Previously, barring a disaster such as fire, a farmer was generally expected to rely on his own savings and his own family and to be independent of his neighbors.

Political cooperation, similarly, has traditionally been limited. The functions of the Conseil Municipal, which has been the town government since the Revolution, have in the past been restricted to a few basic tasks, the most important being the upkeep of roads and tax collection. Throughout much of its history, the town council has met only one time a year to approve the budget that the mayor presents. Membership on the council has come to be considered a kind of honorary office granted to respectable elders of the community.

The only strong traditional organizations outside the family have been those which, like the church, served to unite the community symbolically, through ritual. The hierarchical structure of the church demanded wide but passive participation. Its leaders were absolute in their sphere of activity, but this sphere rarely extended beyond the ceremonial. Lay institutions like the town council also resembled the church in their forms of organization and leadership. Chanzeans gladly delegated all functions of communal government to their town councilors, because the extent of the council's activity was always minimal and the type of leaders elected were conventional, serious, prosperous men who would do their jobs without consulting anyone but also without interfering in other people's lives.

Until quite recently, most Chanzeans preferred this style of leadership. The present curé is more popular than his predecessor because "he leaves people alone." It is generally admitted, however, that he has not quite kept pace with the changes of the times. For since the Second World War, Chanzeaux has witnessed the growth of a multitude of new organizations, which differ from the old in almost all basic respects. To these developments we shall turn in the next chapter.

11

New Organizations

THE NEW associations of Chanzeaux owe their existence in part to recent demographic changes that have accompanied the breakdown of the family as a self-sufficient enterprise, in part to the economic and technological evolution that has made agricultural modernization imperative. Whereas the traditional organizations limited their activity to what was beyond the competence of the family, the new associations extend their activity into the life of the family itself. Whereas the old organizations served mainly to reinforce the existing structure of the community and thus to unify it, the new organizations seek to change it and thus provide an occasion for divisions. Often the new leaders feel called upon to interfere in what most Chanzeans regard as their private affairs, the way they run their households or their farms, for instance. These attempted intrusions are resented by the older members of the community, who remain unaware of the needs that provoke them.

In the old system, the people were accustomed to abdicate authority to a leader, on the condition that the leaders were not to intervene in their lives. The town council used to accept Mayor Courcault's budget without discussion every year, but only because there was nothing in the budget. The mayor's solution to the economic crisis in Chanzeaux was "each man for himself," and the majority of the people voted for him, knowing that the town council under his leadership would leave them alone. In the style of participation and leadership, as well as in the scope of their activities, the new organizations are the antithesis of the old. Because of the challenges they are facing, they have recognized the necessity for collateral action, involving group discussion and cooperation to solve a problem. Typical of modern Catholic Action organizations, this is also seen in the interminably long meetings of the Syndicat d'Initiative and the Groupe d'Entr'aide.

The new methods, however, have aroused the fear and skepticism of people who would do things the old way. It is true that the old town council and the more traditional farmers see these new formations and their leaders as a challenge to the power they possess. But, more basically, many people in Chanzeaux react almost automatically against a way of action for which all their upbringing, all their organizational experience, and all their communal traditions have left them unprepared. Thus the new leaders had two barriers to break down at the start. The immediate one was the power of those in authority. But more important was the dogged spirit of independence that lay behind it. Many Chanzeans still avoid all associations except those involving recreation or minimal protection. The leaders of the new organizations, however, believe that the resistance they face at present will eventually be overcome. Joseph Brée, one of the most philosophic of the new leaders, puts it, "The world evolves, little by little. People always go too far, first in one direction, then in the other, always correcting the mistakes of the past. Progress comes slowly, but it comes."

Church Organizations

Under the auspices of the church itself, several new lay organizations have sprung up in recent years. Partly they owe their origin to the church's chronic shortage of manpower and partly to a conscious policy directed toward increasing the sense of involvement among laymen.

In 1955 Curé Cailleaux, the last of Chanzeaux's long-tenure curés, retired and was replaced by Curé Alleaume, an energetic man with an obvious talent for administration. (He was soon promoted to the office of a dean — "He was too talented to stay in a little town like this," remarked one woman wistfully.) Feeling the need for a number of advisers on parish business, Alleaume unofficially brought together a group of men which he called the Union Paroissiale. It was obvious who these men should be: Jean Delaunay, the town clerk; Jean-Pierre Gardais, town councilor and secretary of the Mouvement Familial Rural for the department; Paul Guitière, Eugène Bourdelle, and Joseph Brée. Jules Fruchaud, a farmer from the hamlet of Les Humeaux, was also invited, to represent the more traditional religious forces in the community. Since this group had no official existence and since it had the effect of replacing the ineffectual and moribund fabrique, its existence was not made public. In fact, even the members were not aware that in the mind of the curé they formed an organization with a name. They considered themselves an informal group simply called together by the priest whenever he needed them. When we asked them about the Union Paroissiale, they did not know what we were talking about, but it was the curé himself who gave us the name of the group and its membership.

Apparently the situation in Chanzeaux was general throughout the diocese: the old fabriques no longer were serving their purpose, and new councils of laymen were needed. During his brief term as Bishop of Angers, Monseigneur Veuillot instituted a new parish organization and stipulated that the synodal statutes be modified to read as follows:

1. In every parish, the curé is assisted by a Parish Council in the administration of the property of the parish.
2. The Council is composed of competent persons of different social backgrounds and belonging insofar as possible to organizations of the Catholic Action.
3. The Parish Council is legally under the presidence of the curé. It includes, furthermore, three, six, or nine lay members. When the curé finds it useful he may invite the vicaires to participate in the deliberations of the Parish Council.

He ordered each parish to reorganize its administration according to these directives by October 1, 1961.

Curé Raimbault, who succeeded Alleaume in 1960, effected a compromise between his predecessor's unofficial Union Paroissiale and the old fabrique by combining the two. From the fabrique he appointed both Delbosc and Bertrand to the new Conseil Paroissial, making Bertrand president of the new group. Three members of Alleaume's Union Paroissiale were named: Delaunay, Gardais, and Bourdelle. Four new members were then added to complete the group: Jean-Baptiste Courcault, son of the mayor; François Devanne, the sacristan; Charles Ditière, a representative of the wine-growing northern corner of the parish; and Guy Roulleau, blacksmith and garageman representing the more self-consciously citified part of the parish lying on the Route Nationale. Instead of picking the most active members of the church and of the Catholic Action movements, as Alleaume had done for his council and as the bishop had suggested in his directive, Curé Raimbault chose a group representing the different social, economic, and geographic areas of the parish. Yet, under this curé, the activity of the parish council has slackened considerably, for Raimbault apparently prefers to solve problems himself, without consultation. It is generally felt, however, that Raimbault represents a temporary reversion to the traditional style of operation of the church and that, although Alleaume was ahead of his time, the organization he set up is more in keeping with the modern trend.

The celebration of religious ceremonies has always required the involvement of laymen, in such time-honored roles as sexton and altar boy, but in this area, too, lay participation has increased. A few years ago, the priest appointed a group of young, devoted men to lead the congregation in participation in the Mass. They read the scriptures in French over the loud-speaker as the priest reads them in Latin at the altar; they read some of the announcements. When they are not on duty in the choir of the church but sitting with their families, they take the lead in following the Mass closely, singing hymns, giving responses, taking communion every Sunday, and generally setting an example for the rest of the congregation. Officially named the Equipe Liturgique, the team has little formal organization. Two men were named *responsables* for distributing the work among the whole group — François Courcault (the son of the former mayor) and his brother-in-law Pierre Brichet. Both men have brothers who are priests. The other members of the group are precisely the individuals one would expect to be named: members of the parish council, members of devout families, participants in Catholic Action movements. They are Louis and Jean-Paul Brichet (Pierre's two brothers), René Courcault, Joseph Brée, Serge Clément (teacher in the Catholic boys' school), Jean-Pierre Gardais (who also serves as cantor), and Henri Amelin. It should be pointed out that, while the members of this group set an example for the rest of the congregation, the other people of the broader parish do not express the same enthusiasm. Some of them sharply resent this institution which establishes a group of individuals as models for their peers.

The new involvement of laymen in the work of the church has been accompanied by a general change in the type of activities that receive emphasis. The declining devotional organizations, like the Confrérie de St. Fiacre, represent the traditional extent of the church's role in community organization. These ceremonial functions were perhaps well adapted to the needs of a relatively stable and isolated community. In recent years, however, the church has become sensitive to new parish needs, which have grown as the economic integrity of the commune has declined. One response to the prospect of accelerated decline of rural communities has been the formation of new lay organizations that seek to influence the material as well as the spiritual life of the commune. In Chanzeaux, the Catholic militants have been leaders in groups devoted to family welfare, education, and agricultural cooperation.

Catholic Action

The Catholic Action movement, as it is generally known, is officially embodied in two organizations. One is a general association of Catholic laymen brought together at the parish level to foster church activities and to carry the aims of the church into all aspects of community life. The other is the specialized organization that cuts across parish lines to center on professional and family communities. If the goals of these two movements were actually achieved in Chanzeaux, every adult Catholic in the parish would belong to at least two organizations — the general Catholic Action group of the parish and his own professional Catholic group. Both sorts of organization do exist in Chanzeaux, but, since there are so few very active Catholics in the community, people do not have time or energy to divide their activities between the two. Consequently the Chanzeans involved are only nominally members of the general Catholic Action movement, but they devote themselves wholeheartedly to the specialized groups, which are divided according to age and sex. For the boys and girls there are the clubs Fripounet and Marisette, mainly recreational. For the older children, again divided by sex, there are the Coeurs Vaillants and the Ames Vaillantes. For the young married people there are the different branches of the Mouvement Rural de Jeunesse Catholique. For adults there is the Mouvement de la Famille Rurale.

All of these are parts of national organizations with offices in Paris, although they are of course under the legal authority of the bishop. In fact, however, the bishop rarely interferes with the movement. He appoints diocesan chaplains (*aumôniers*) who have offices in Angers, where they receive directives from Paris and exercise them within the diocese. The diocese is divided into zones, consisting of three or four cantons. Within the cantons there are sections, made up of three or four parishes. Within each section a parish priest or vicar is made the local chaplain to oversee the activities of his group.

When the children finish school at the age of fourteen, they automatically graduate from the children's movements to the youth movements. For a rural community like Chanzeaux there are only two real groups of importance in the youth movements: Jeunesse Agricole Chrétienne for the boys and Jeunesse Agricole Chrétienne Féminine for the girls. Although there are more complicated categories for artisans and shopkeepers, the whole group is generally subsumed under the title, Jacistes. The number of Jacistes in Chanzeaux varies considerably from year to year, but the type of young person active in the movement has certain characteristics. He usually lives in the bourg, has a close relative who is a priest or nun, and is progressive in his ambitions for the village and for his own economic and professional interests. Usually he would like to remain home and participate in the parish life rather than move away.

The active Jaciste veterans of Chanzeaux have now graduated to the ranks of young married couples and have enlisted in the specialized Catholic Action movement for rural adults — the Mouvement de la Famille Rurale (MFR). This is the logical culmination of all the Catholic youth movements, which are designed to prepare young people to bring into adult institutions the spirit of the social doctrine of the church. In the MFR there are no membership lists, no dues to pay, no executive committee at the local level, and no regular meetings. There are, however, irregular sessions planned by the *responsables* from time to time to discuss problems of general interest, to prepare projects (*enquêtes*), and to arrange for action to be taken. About thirty couples can be counted on in the whole sector to attend such sessions. Often this is enough, however, to determine the adoption of a policy for the whole community, for the militants who participate in the sessions are usually leaders who play a substantial role in other organizations. It is these leaders whom the youth movements have sought to form as vanguards of the church.

The list of MFR militants in Chanzeaux could be anticipated from what we know of the most committed participants in other activities of the church, for they are the same people: Jean-Pierre and Louise Gardais, Joseph and Claire Brée, Henri and Monique Amelin, Serge and Jeanne Clément, Jean and Marie-Noëlle Delaunay, François and Marthe Courcault, François and Geneviève Devanne. This is a list not of members but of the most militant participants. Other couples join them from time to time — the Forgets, the Viauds, the younger Bertrands. It is their function to utilize their positions in the community to instill Christian ideals into every aspect of the life of the people. In 1963 the essential goal of the MFR was defined as: "the inspiration of Christians engaged in the temporal institutions of the rural world. Our object is not to transform temporal institutions into Christian ones, but rather to put these temporal institutions more perfectly at the service of all." This program may sound vague, but it is implemented by practical means. Each year the national office, composed of lay officers and priests, institutes a campaign. A problem is proposed and members of the group all over France attack it, following the old slogan of the Catholic Workers' Movement (JOC): *Voir, Juger, Agir*. The MFR activists then set about studying the problem in the manner they learned as Jacistes: setting up study groups, gathering information, making and filling out questionnaires, comparing notes with militants of other sectors, writing reports to suggest practical methods of attack. The results in Chanzeaux are impressive. The militants have supported the formation of organizations which do not depend directly on them but which probably would not have been formed and could not continue to exist if the militants were not actively behind them.

Family Associations

The organizations most closely associated with the Catholic activist group in Chanzeaux are those concerned with education and family matters. At present, Chanzeaux has branches of two "family-aid" organizations, the Association Familiale (AF) and the Association de l'Aide Familiale. Such groups have grown rapidly in many parts of France in recent years, and the impetus for their formation has apparently been at the local level. Although the local chapters of the organization have preserved a great deal of autonomy in their operations, they have grown to such proportions that they have formed departmental and national federations which have semipublic status and receive a government subsidy.

Of the twelve-member governing council of the AF, eight belong to the small minority of the population of Chanzeaux who take communion every week. Most of the young families that are active in other religious organizations are represented on the council: the president is Joseph Brée; the secretary is Jean-Pierre Gardais; and the other members include Mmes. Marthe Courcault, Monique Amelin, and Jeanne Clément. A conscious attempt is made, however, to stress the lay nature of the organization, in order both to minimize religious differences as a source of friction and to prevent the association from being branded as an exclusive clique. Although the attempt is only partially successful, two members of the council are in fact young, progressive farmers who are generally recognized as good men but who have the reputation of "not being interested in religion" and who rarely go to church.

Residents of the bourg seem to take a more active interest in the AF than farm people do. Over half of the twenty-five families that have enrolled as members and pay the annual dues of 6 francs live in the bourg, as do eight of the twelve members of the council. There are no members from the wine-growing sector of Chanzeaux; since parents living in this neighborhood send their children to school in Saint-Lambert, it is natural for those who are interested in the AF to join the Saint-Lambert chapter. The AF provides many material services to the parents and children of Chanzeaux. In past years they have organized a washing-machine service, a *ruche enfantine* (summer nursery) for little children, and a series of sessions of *vulgarisation ménagère*, a kind of home-economics course that meets once a month. The association also enables Chanzeans to utilize services that are organized among several communes, such as the rest home at Saint-Georges du Puy de la Garde and the *centre aéré* (summer day-camp) near Chemillé. In the summer of 1963, about ten boys of grade-school age traveled by bus each morning to the camp, along with their *moniteurs* Luc Monnier and Georges Bertrand, two students from Chanzeaux who were spending their vacation at home.

The budget of the AF is not firmly set, and each project is financed in a slightly different way. Virtually all of the money from dues goes to the departmental federation of the AFs, so that Chanzeaux can benefit from services operating on a wider scale, such as the day camp. In order to provide a salary for the *monitrices* of the nursery, who were also students at home for the summer, the AF charged a certain fee for each child. For the largest portion of its budget, however, the association relies on subsidies from the commune. In this they are fortunate to have Town Councilor Gardais on their governing board. For 1964 he managed to obtain an appropriation of 700 francs for the AF and 150 francs for the Association de l'Aide Familiale (and it was apparently no mean achievement to persuade the town council to appropriate money for anything at all).

Although the activities of the AF are directed to concrete and practical services, its president, Joseph Brée, considers its primary purpose moral and educational. The ultimate goal of the organization is to protect and strengthen the family and community life. In order to counteract the trend of migration to cities, which is seen as a major threat to rural families, the AF attempts to improve and modernize the conditions of farm life — especially for women, who are currently leaving rural areas at twice the rate of men. Community participation in these improvements, however, is as important to the leaders as the improvements themselves. "People are too passive," explains Brée. "They expect everything to descend from the top. We try to encourage as many people as possible to take the responsibility for their own welfare, but that does not always make us popular."

An example of the educational approach of the AF is the mimeographed newsletter sent to members and parents of the boys in the day camp. One main article was entitled: "Why Is It a Good Idea to Send Children to Camp?" Several "typical" responses were presented:

La maman fatiguée: "The children are unmanageable in the summer with nothing to do. At camp, they will at least be off my hands for the day."

La maman   "With the *bonnes soeurs* we know that they will
"bien pensante":   be in good hands, won't meet the wrong kind of playmates or get into mischief."

The article then explains that neither motive is a good one, since both reveal an abdication of parental responsibility and a distrustful attitude toward children. The best reason for sending children to camp, the article concludes, is that it is natural and healthy for children to play outdoors in the summertime with a group their own age.

Much of the effort of the AF is directed toward developing a wider sense of community in Chanzeaux. Two summers ago, when the day nursery was organized, two public-school children were enrolled. They belonged to one of the poorest families in Chanzeaux, one recognized by the state as incompetent to handle its own relief money (the family is *sous tutelle*, which means that the mother receives her monthly *allocations familiales* in the form of coupons for bread and other staples so that she cannot spend the money for anything else). When it was determined that the government would pay the fee for the two Cordier girls, they were accepted in the nursery.

Every time the Brées spoke to the *monitrices* of the nursery, they made a special point of asking how the little Cordier children were getting along with the others, admonishing the girls to be sure to treat them just like everyone else. The *monitrices* passed on this warning to the children, who occasionally needed to be restrained from teasing the Cordier girls. For most of the summer the two sisters, aged six and four, played only with each other and with the children of one neighboring family in similar economic straits; but in the last weeks of the summer, the other girls began to admit them to their games. With the end of the summer and the day nursery, the situation returned to normal, of course, and nothing had been permanently changed for the Cordier children; but the AF had made its gesture. In the future, this group is likely to continue its efforts to counteract social ostracism.

Although the Association de l'Aide Familiale is officially a distinct organization from the AF, the animating power behind it is the same. Jean-Pierre Gardais is the president, Mme. Brée is the *responsable du travail*, and six of the seven members of its council are also on the council of the AF. This organization provides only one service, but an extremely important one: it maintains in Chanzeaux an *aide-familiale*, a young woman who combines the duties of social worker and mother's helper. Aides-familiales go through a year of training to qualify for their jobs and are licensed by the state. They are competent to take over the temporary management of a household. The aide-familiale is most in demand when there is a new baby in a family or if the mother becomes ill, and families in these circumstances have first claim on her services; but many mothers welcome an occasional day's visit from the aide-familiale as a respite from the less dramatic burden of overwork. The association charges a certain fee for each visit, although it can waive the charge in cases of real need. With the money it collects, and with subsidies from the town council, it provides a house and a monthly salary for the aide-familiale.

In spite of the valuable services that the family associations have provided, they have not gone uncriticized in Chanzeaux. The general resentment against the Catholic militants is directed especially against these two organizations, which they dominate in fact and in spirit. It is said maliciously that the AF is a clique of a few families who are interested only in benefiting themselves and who use the money of the town to do it. It is true that most of the services of the AF, like providing bus service to the *cours complémentaires* and the bourg nursery, cannot by nature have an extremely wide appeal.

It is the Association de l'Aide Familiale, however, which comes in for the most severe criticism, because everyone would like to have the help of the aide-familiale occasionally. On Sunday mornings, as many as seven or eight women may stop at the Brée café to ask Mme. Brée to send Mlle. Christine over in the coming week. "It's rather a delicate situation," confesses Mme. Brée, "when two families ask for the aide-familiale the same day. We have to use our own judgment in deciding who really needs her most." The Brées are not generally suspected of favoritism, but the president of the association, Gardais, has been accused of using his influence to prevent the aide-familiale from visiting families whose religious practice does not meet with his approval. It is certainly true, also, that Mme. Brée is reluctant to expose the aid-familiale too often to families she considers depraved, like the Cordiers. "After all," she says, "Mlle. Christine is only twenty-one years old, and we ought to be careful." For whatever reason, it is clear that Christine does not visit every home in Chanzeaux and that she spends a great deal of her time with a few families. When we talked to her about her work in the summer of 1963, she had already been in Chanzeaux for five months, but she had never been outside a mile radius of the bourg. She had never been to the wine villages near Saint-Lambert, the village of Saint-Ambroise and the surrounding farms, or the farms across the national highway toward La Jumellière.

Thus although the family organizations are officially secular, and even try to emphasize their secular nature, they have become the preserve of the Catholic Action militants, most of whom are not farm people. As a result, these organizations have acquired a religious and intellectual atmosphere that is the source of both their effectiveness and their limitations.

The School Committee

Whatever resentment the majority of Chanzeans may feel against the militants, they recognize their authority and competence in matters of education and consistently elect militants to serve on the parents' board of the Catholic schools. The real working organization of the church school system is the Comité des Ecoles Libres (CEL).

Membership on this committee is no sinecure, for it must find means to finance both schools. Until the Second World War there was no real problem, for up to that time the schools were largely supported by the local gentry. The heirs of these former lords of the chateaux, however, received only a small portion of the total inheritance, which was divided among several children. Thus the present owners have comparatively little land beyond their chateaux; and since they come to Chanzeaux for only a few days or weeks during vacations, they have little interest in the town and little money to devote to its life other than what they are obliged to put into the upkeep of the chateaux themselves. The people of the parish must finance the education of their children themselves if they want to continue to have them educated in independent Catholic schools. Now that the government pays the teachers' salaries, the greatest financial problem has been solved. But for the time being the situation is still serious because the government has insisted that several thousand dollars' worth of repairs and improvements be made in the schools to bring them up to government standards. The committee is kept very busy raising money. The tuition paid by the children is minimal — only a few cents a month. Most of the money comes from other sources, the traditional sources that committees everywhere use to seek money for worthy causes: cake sales, collections, and entertainments. Each winter the committee sponsors a play, and each summer it organizes a festival, the kermesse, for the benefit of the schools.

Since membership on the school committee entails such heavy responsibilities, the election every two years is taken very seriously by the parents of the schoolchildren. The method of election is simple. The electors simply write down a list of ten men and ten women they would like to see on the committee, and their vote is weighted by the number of children each has in school. Each family gets one vote, plus one vote for every schoolchild in the family. The results have shown a remarkable consensus among the voters. Although the votes may be distributed among twenty-five or thirty men and the same number of women, the first ten places are filled by people who get an absolute majority of the votes. The gap between the tenth and eleventh positions is great. In 1961 the ten highest-ranking men received from 222 to 147 votes apiece; the eleventh man received only 47. The ten highest-ranking women received from 224 to 122 votes;

the eleventh woman received 51. The twenty members elected to the committee form the council, which meets after Mass once a month, but their bureau, the executive committee, meets more often: President Paul Guitière, Vice-President Jean-Pierre Gardais, Vice-President Mme. Chaillou *mère,* Secretary Mme. Lacroix of Vignaud, and Treasurer Jean Delaunay. There are also two important committees appointed to deal with the two most difficult problems, the care of school property and the organization of the annual kermesse.

It used to be that when the educational facilities of the parish were taken care of, that was the end of the responsibilities of the people of Chanzeaux. The children who wanted to go on to school after the age of fourteen went off to live in a boarding school over which the parish of Chanzeaux had no control. This situation began to change after the Second World War, when an extra year of technical education was required of all children fifteen years old if their families wished to continue to receive government allocations for them. Now parents and students alike have come to realize that young people have no chance to get ahead unless they acquire more knowledge and skill. There is also a growing feeling that the schools of Chanzeaux do not offer a good enough program — either general or technical — to satisfy modern demands. Parents have therefore begun to take advantage of educational facilities in nearby towns, especially in Chemillé.

In order to compete with the public-school system, the Catholic schools have had to develop their own *cours complémentaires.* Inevitably the question of finding money to build more schoolrooms and facilities has been the main problem, and to solve it the diocese organized regional committees. Chanzeaux was included in the region centered on Chemillé, along with seventeen other nearby communes. Two representatives were appointed from Chanzeaux, the first being the president of the Chanzeaux school committee, Paul Guitière. The second was Jean-Baptiste Courcault *fils,* father of two boys who have left the Chanzeaux school to continue their education in Chemillé. The school-expansion program was largely financed by loans from people in the area. Thanks to the good efforts of Guitière, Chanzeaux was one of the most important contributors to the school campaign. At present, the school board is considering more ambitious schemes to consolidate the schools of several communes, so that neighborhood facilities for secondary education can continue to expand.

Agricultural Organizations

The rise of new organizations has come in response to new needs that only an organized effort can meet. Perhaps the greatest challenge to postwar Chanzeaux has been the decline of agriculture, and many organizations have been formed to face the necessity of cooperation in marketing, mechanization, work sharing, and uniting for political pressure. As in other areas, the formation and methods of some of the new groups have made explicit the differing attitudes of the older and younger generations, as well as the more progressive and the more conservative Chanzeans. Many of the leaders of these new movements, not surprisingly, are militants who are active leaders in the religious or social-welfare organizations.

A growing number of Chanzeaux farmers have been putting Jaciste ideals into practice by sharing work or buying machines in common with their neighbors. Whether this new cooperation is directly inspired by Catholic Action ideas is difficult to determine, but clearly both the cooperation and the ideas are a response to economic change. Although teaming up with a neighbor in order to make hay or to run the combine is not far in spirit from the help French peasants have always given each other in times of need, some Chanzean farmers have made formal commitments that are more of a departure from tradition.

The Groupe d'Entr'aide was formed in 1962 for the sharing of machines and labor. Since then, five more men have joined, bringing the total membership to thirteen. Most of the members live in or near the farming village of Le Plessis. The complex network of cooperative relationships in and around this village far surpasses anything else in Chanzeaux and even extends into neighboring Rablay. Every one of the six active farmers in Le Plessis belongs to the Groupe, and most of them own shares in at least one piece of machinery. The kind of organized commitment represented by buying a machine in common, or by working regularly in a group, entails a greater surrender of personal sovereignty than do the less formal kinds of cooperation. According to the charter of the association, one of its members is to be elected each year for a one-year term to fill the office of *organisateur*. This official, who collects requests for machinery and labor and who coordinates and synchronizes their use, is paid for his work. The hourly rates on machine rental and labor are determined by a two-thirds majority vote of all the members. The results, however, are kept secret; the rental and wage rates determined within the association are not revealed to farmers who are not members. Whenever one man works for another or lends a machine to another, a bill is written up in two copies. The user keeps his copy as a receipt, and the lender takes the other copy to the organizer, who debits and credits the appropriate accounts of the two members on the books of the association. All outstanding debts are settled once a year, under the supervision of the organizer. The charter also establishes a system for settling disputes. If at any time the owner of a machine feels that the renter has not cared for it "en bon père de famille," he may appeal to two experts elected from among the members (on three-year terms) or eventually call for a vote by all the members. A simple majority settles the issue. So far there have been no disputes, and the provision has not been required.

Membership in the Groupe d'Entr'aide also requires a willingness to be conspicuous. Jacques Pinier tells how he came in for a good deal of criticism when he went in with Amelin and Brichet to buy machinery. Two or three years later, when machinery owned in common was more usual and therefore more acceptable, he was again criticized — this time for his work arrangement with Brichet. For these reasons, it is a special type of person who enters into organized entr'aide. For one thing, the "cooperators" are young:

	Under age 45	45 or over
Cooperators	15	4
All other farmers interviewed	8	23

Like the leaders of the activist organizations, the cooperators tend to make themselves conspicuous in another way — many of them take communion every Sunday:

	Church infrequently or never	Church every Sun., communion on holy days	Church every Sun., communion nearly every Sun.
Cooperators	2	9	6
All other farmers interviewed	5	22	1

The foremost organizers of agricultural cooperation are also the leaders of the militant organizations. Most take communion regularly, most were born in Chanzeaux, and all have a more collectivist view of the community than do the majority of their fellow townsmen. The Chanzeaux representative of the oldest regional cooperative is also a militant. Joseph Brée, the owner of the café, school committeeman, and president of the Association Familiale, is also the *dépositaire* of the cooperative of Thouarcé.

Although many Chanzean farmers sell their produce to the cooperatives, few engage in their organizational activities. Only a half dozen, at most, serve on the administrative boards of the cooperatives. These men complain that most farmers put too little faith in the cooperative system, which seeks to obtain a higher price for farm products by regulating supply. Although the farmers are suspicious of the cooperatives' "taking over," and give only lukewarm support to such innovations as cooperative retailing of farm machinery, Chanzeans active in the cooperative movement are not discouraged and even predict that expansion will continue.

In contrast to the cooperative organizations, the farmers' union attracts widespread participation and represents virtually all the farmers of the commune. The Féderation Départementale des Syndicats des Exploitants Agricoles (FDSEA) is the farmers' pressure group vis-à-vis the government. Their national organization, the FNSEA, claims membership of about one third of all the farmers in France. (The FNSEA is in turn part of the CGA, Confédération Générale des Agriculteurs, which includes farm laborers.) The FNSEA is the group that organized the farm riots and road blocks of 1961. Farmers in Chanzeaux seem to think that the FNSEA has helped them in some ways — for instance, in helping to ensure fair prices for farm products. The FNSEA is doubled with a young farmers' organization, the Cercle des Jeunes Agriculteurs, offering a lay parallel to the Jaciste movement that has attracted the more devout Chanzeans. The Jeunes Agriculteurs support more direct economic action and pressure than the Jacistes. The Jeunes Agriculteurs are also considered more radical, and, since they lack church backing, they have gained few members in Chanzeaux. Nevertheless, this group has provided the opportunity for one Chanzean farmer, André Blond, to exhibit his talents. An extremely capable organizer, he quickly rose to the position of departmental president of the Jeunes Agriculteurs.

Membership in the various agricultural organizations varies with their functions — from the protection of farming interests to the introduction of new techniques. Practically all the farmers belong to the pressure groups; extremely few participate in the entr'aide and Jaciste programs; the cooperatives, which act as both protectors and innovators, attract many but still far from all the farmers in Chanzeaux. This situation reflects not only the protectionist, conservative outlook of the farmers, but also the kinds of commitment these organizations demand. The FNSEA demands mainly a monetary commitment; aside from the few officers, most members simply pay dues once a year and attend the social functions. No continuing labor for the organization is necessary, since even demonstrations are one-shot affairs. The cooperatives demand more of the farmer's time, just to arrange the mechanics of selling. Few Chanzeans are willing to involve themselves in the administrative work of the cooperatives or actively to recruit other farmers to the joint cause. With the Jacistes and the Groupe d'Entr'aide, commitment is tied to religion in the case of the former and to a progressive outlook toward farming in the case of both. The nature of the commitment — action to change the status quo — gains few adherents in the community. No Jaciste can sit back and merely pay his dues once a year; he must go forth, organize, and proselytize in a relatively unaccepted cause. Few Chanzeans are willing to spend their leisure moments in this manner.

The variety and complexity of agricultural organizations in Chanzeaux are matched by those of the mutual-aid and credit societies. These are primarily local chapters of groups existing at departmental and national levels, whose main goal is to protect the physical well-being of the farmer's family and stock and to expedite replacement and improvement of his equipment. Three of the mutual-aid societies are part of a departmental organization, the Mutualité Sociale de Maine-et-Loire, which in turn is part of the Fedération Nationale de la Mutualité, du Credit, et de la Coopération Agricole. The most important branch of this organization in Chanzeaux is the medical program, similar to Blue Cross–Blue Shield, which enrolls 450 members. A second program of fire and accident insurance also attracts many people. In 1961 a third branch, the equestrian mutual-aid group, began to provide services to farmers owning horses. Although much of the working capital of the departmental and national organizations comes from the government, they operate independently of government control. Eugène Bourdelle, head of the communal and cantonal FDSEA chapter, also leads the equestrian group. The success of these organizations in Chanzeaux attests to a considerable evolution in outlook since the days when insurance barely extended beyond the communal fire protection of the Société des Agriculteurs.

Syndicat d'Initiative

In addition to the organizations devoted to the improvement of farm and family life, a new association has sprung up that combines economic and recreational functions and aims at the development of the commune as a whole. The Syndicat d'Initiative, or Tourist Bureau, was formed at the suggestion of Jean Delaunay, Chanzeaux's imaginative town clerk, in 1962. In its first three years it has taken over the secular festivals of the commune, organized receptions for various groups, and instituted yearly elections for a Chanzeaux beauty queen to receive distinguished guests to the town. In spite of the opposition of the former mayor, who is said to disapprove of dancing, it has sponsored dances that attract young people from neighboring communes; those teenagers who are allowed to attend enjoy them much more than the folk dancing organized by the Catholic Action group. It has set up a camping site for summer visitors and prepared a publicity folder extolling the virtues of Chanzeaux's scenery, historic monuments, and wines.

The Syndicat d'Initiative is the first organization to bring together representatives of almost all the activist groups. Most of its members live in the bourg, for the businessmen clearly have more to gain than the farmers from an organization that will publicize the commune. Several men, the most vocal and politically active shopkeepers, were members from the start. Leaders of other organizations were founding members: Jean-Pierre Gardais, Paul Guitière, André Blond, Joseph Brée, and Eugène Bourdelle. It has two of the most progressive town councilors on its council, Gardais and Guitière. Thus it unites in one organization forward-looking men from all areas — social welfare, the church, the cooperative movement, union organizations, the school committee — and at the same time provides an association in which tradesmen can have their say and achieve organizational status. The group received only grudging support from the former town council, which granted it a small budget ($100) on which to finance its activities.

The Syndicat d'Initiative is perhaps the only new organization that does not go beyond the commune's boundaries. The Catholic

Action groups and the mutual-aid societies are organized from above, and the Chanzeaux members are part of a "sector" of several communes. The establishment of the Catholic *cours complémentaires* is also necessarily carried out on a regional level, like the consolidated rural highschool in the United States. The entr'aide group is branching out into Rablay; the cooperatives are all located outside Chanzeaux and serve a wide area. Such a regional orientation is another feature distinguishing new organizations and new leaders from the old. The traditional organizations are based explicitly within the parish or within the commune. For more effective regional promotion, even the Syndicat d'Initiative will eventually have to join with others nearby.

One reason that the former town councilors took such a dim view of the Syndicat is that they suspected Blond and the others of political ambitions beyond the avowed purposes of the organization. The suspicion was entirely justified. The Syndicat was only the latest in a series of alliances of the leaders of Chanzeaux's most progressive organizations. Twice in the past, these leaders had drawn together in an attempt to gain control of the town council, and, although they failed, most people acknowledged that time was on their side. In the spring of 1965 their third attempt was successful (see Chapter 12).

The chief concern of almost all the new leaders is for Chanzeaux's future. Realizing the seriousness of the economic problems that the community will face in the next twenty years, they know that the organizations they control are inadequate to cope with them. The town council alone has the potential to unite Chanzeaux in achieving significant progress for the whole of the commune. Under the previous regime, the power that the younger leaders see in the council went unrealized, for the former councillors were unwilling to expand the scope of the council's activities beyond traditional limits. Their resistance to change was supported by a large proportion of the Chanzeaux electorate, which twice returned their slate to office against the challenge of the progressive group. Thus the town council has become the focus for all the problems raised by the new economic and social circumstances in which the community finds itself.

12

The Town Council

THE town council (Conseil Municipal) receives the highest degree of respect accorded any group by the commune's population. As such, the nature of the town council and the mayor has faithfully reflected the mood of the commune, far more than the voluntary associations with their limited memberships. In the past, the town council was the prototype of the traditional organization. The first sign of impending change came in 1959, when the town councilors were challenged in elections by a group of younger contenders. In the succeeding years, the membership split over proposals for communal improvement. The process of change culminated in the elections of March 1965, when new members and a new mayor were chosen. Under their regime, the town council has assumed a role radically different from that of the traditional organization; it is closer in spirit to the voluntary associations of the last decade.

The town council consists of thirteen members elected each six years by the adults of the commune. At election time, thirteen candidates organize one slate, different slates representing various political beliefs and plans for community improvement. An effort is usually made to have each geographical area or *quartier* of the commune represented. Although the candidates usually run on slates, they are elected as individuals. The thirteen people with the highest number of votes win. Often a run-off election must be held, since candidates must win by a majority of votes cast, and thirteen candidates can rarely obtain a majority in a first election. The mayor is not elected directly but is chosen by the town councilors after their election.

The town council is the smallest unit in France's centralized governmental system. Though it has power to decide on communal matters, its decisions are subject to review by the prefecture, which is its legal guardian. The town council is also linked to national politics by the electoral system, which specifies that senators shall be chosen by an electoral college of delegates from each town council in France.

Every town council must fulfill certain obligations. It must set aside maintenance monies for public buildings, cemeteries, and roads, and guarantee funds for salaries of communal employees. It must also provide for public assistance and educational expenses. Questions of sanitation, lighting, and other improvements, however, are left to the discretion of each commune.

The Old Town Council

Jean-Baptiste Courcault was elected mayor in 1945, when his predecessor and the deputy mayor were removed by the prefecture because of alleged collaboration with the occupying Germans. Courcault owns the town's only industry, the basket factory, which employs from twenty to twenty-five persons. Although he has risen in the world, and enjoys the full prestige of his position as factory patron, the old man retains the simplicity of the days when he was just another artisan. As mayor he could often be found in the townhall in working clothes. Not a brilliant speaker, he had none of the flair of his political opponents. He is unpretentious, and his simplicity is a quality much admired in Chanzeaux. Still other advantages suited M. Courcault for his position as mayor. His wealth and four grown sons who direct the operation of the factory allowed him the time necessary for the duties of this position. Moreover, living in the bourg he was readily available in case of emergency. Coming from a large family himself, he had eight children, most of whom have married into other prominent Chanzeaux families, so that he has a large number of kin in the town. His family is known for its devoutness — one of his sons is a priest — but he did not seem to discriminate against the small minority of unbelievers in the town.

M. Courcault exercised his powers as mayor in the traditional style to which Chanzeans were accustomed. It was he who made most of the policy decisions in the communal government, and the councilors themselves had little actual say in the town council's policies. Although there were subcommittees — roads, finance, farms, municipal buildings, future planning — they met rarely if at all. An insider's description of a council meeting as it used to be runs as follows: "The mayor comes in, calls the meeting to order, and reads off what he proposes to do. Everybody talks for a while, then votes to do what the mayor suggests." There were no open meetings and no communal newssheet, as in some progressive communes. As one councilor said of Mayor

Courcault, "He is for as little change as possible, the kind who wants to do very little and do it secretly. He keeps everything to himself; the councilors are there mainly to approve." Most people seemed to feel secure in leaving communal affairs in the hands of "le père Courcault," just as they still leave national affairs to "le père de Gaulle."

The former town councilors themselves were a choice group of the most conservative elements of the population. Although there were four members from the bourg, they represented only the older citizens of the bourg and drew much support from the country. (As a local official said, "It may be surprising, but the mayor gets most of his votes from the countryside.") The four consisted of the local chatelain (a staunch royalist), a wealthy retired vintner, the mayor, and a retired army officer who is regarded by the people as a "monsieur" and who associates with the chatelain when he can. Outside prestige played a large part in the election of these men. Except for M. Courcault, they did not in fact represent the interests of the bourg; none of them was an artisan or a tradesman, as are about 50 percent of the bourg's population. Rather they were what one present town councilor characterizes as the "grosse ou petite bourgeoisie." The rest of the thirteen councilors were farmers or vintners with large landholdings. Uniformly well-off, they represented the success of the economic system which has been coming to an end over the last years. (Their methods of farming are traditional, and they do not participate in entr'aide.) They are the people one would expect to be chosen by an electorate that is in the main elderly and traditionalist.

The average age of the former town councilors was sixty-five years. They were the oldest working age group in the community, and the age group with the largest number of kin, both younger and older. The old town councilors, Jean-Pierre Gardais excluded, had few children under the age of twenty. Almost all of their sons and daughters were settled and established economically. The Courcault brothers are provided for by the factory. Old Eugène Faye's son, Marcel, has run his farm for years. The Manceau, Lusson, Ditière, Guitière, and Plancheneau boys will take over their fathers' farms. Most of the daughters have been married off. These men have few worries for the future of their children. Age was the main factor in determining the political attitudes of these councilors. As one younger citizen put it, "They are people of the eighteenth century; they don't realize that things are becoming modern. Events have passed them by." Most of them were trained in the old school of frugality and have been untouched by the revolution in credit that has swept over rural France in the past ten years. They were reluctant to utilize new sources of capital for the benefit of the commune.

Besides age and wealth, one of the key factors in the election of a town councilor (and a key component of prestige in general throughout the commune) used to be the amount of contact he had with the outside world; as long as the travels of Chanzeaux citizens remained limited, this qualification carried great weight. In 1945 a group of repatriated prisoners was elected to the council, in spite of their youthfulness. When their special status wore off, they were not re-elected. The chatelain has always owed part of his prestige to his connection with the wider community of noblemen. In the last council, Charles Couilleau (the retired army officer), the chatelain Delbosc (who works in Paris), and Gardais (who commutes daily to Angers) all belonged to a larger community and were respected for the degree of sophistication their associations reflected. The Chanzeans obviously felt that the prestige of these people was in turn conferred upon the town by their being on the council. In this respect, Chanzeans seemed sensitive to their backwardness and rural isolation from the rest of France. Throughout the nation, outside prestige used to be one of the factors responsible for keeping rural town councils in the hands of older men. Local men who returned to their communes to retire were acquainted with the world and were consequently elected.

For those not endowed with outside prestige, having an open, "sympathique," and unassuming personality was essential for election. In November 1962, we visited Chanzeaux at the time of the national elections and stayed in the townhall while the people came to vote. One of the few public functions of the town councilors is to monitor elections; they work in shifts of four and then all reassemble for the vote count in the evening. They engaged in a remarkable amount of politicking when the voters came in. During the intervals when no voters were present, they would all be silent, would discuss their war experiences (the retired army officer and the chatelain), or make conversation with us about America; but as soon as a voter came in, they would turn on a smile, inquire about the farm or the baby, or make a personalized friendly joke. For some of them, this behavior was obviously unnatural, for usually when they were in town they would stay with men of their own age or temperament and fraternize very little with the population as a whole. In this case they were acting in their formal roles as councilors and making a great effort to "receive" the people in a conspicuously informal way — in short, at this moment they were acting like politicians everywhere. Apparently there was (and is) little overt campaigning except in the few days immediately preceding the elections for town council. The most conspicuous feature of the campaigning consisted in treating the boys in the café to a round of drinks. One predatory voter related how he had been treated to ten rounds of drinks by the same man and then had voted against him.

Another factor helpful, though not essential, to becoming a town councilor was to come from or have married into a well-established Chanzean family. Because kinship plays an important role in Chanzeaux, those with the most relatives in the town, other things being equal, have a political advantage. Some families have had a tradition of leadership in the town. The first person one used to think of to fill a vacant office was usually the holder's son. But except in rare cases, like that of the chatelain, this process was limited to two or three generations, depending on the state of a family's wealth and the emigration of politically eligible sons.

The main point to be made about the former town councilors, then, was that their chief qualifications were not their ideas, dynamism, or interest in the welfare of the commune; their seats on the council were the rewards for their economic success and social conformity. In some degree they were merely a herarchy of reputable men with leisure time. They were elected not because they wanted to get things done or because they had something to do. One younger shopkeeper described the typical councilor as "le vieux bonhomme qui ne vexe personne." Another said, "Ils sont surtout des gens qui symbolisent." Indeed the only feature common to all the councilors was that they were good fellows who would avoid doing anything to alienate them from any part of the population.

Note that in the past those who were energetic were quickly weeded out by the voters. Eugène Bourdelle was not re-elected to the council in 1953, although he was certainly a most able member. Three young artisans with a program of communal improvement were elected in 1947 but defeated in 1953. According to one cynical ex-candidate, there were two ways to get elected: either to have no ideas or, if you had ideas, not to let anyone know about them. A young farmer involved in union organizations said this: "If you want to be elected to the town council, it is better not to get involved in an active organization because, as soon as you start anything, you're bound to get in somebody's way." These criteria might have been suitable for the election of men to a council that served only a symbolic function, as long as there was a mayor who had a program and the prestige to put it through. But this type of council is inadequate to meet the present needs of Chanzeaux.

The Challengers

In 1953 an attempt to elect three young men to the council was defeated. In 1959 another challenge took place, and four of the most liberal heads of organizations ran for the council. Before that election the Chanzeaux men got together and decided that it might be time for the older political leaders to step down. The strategy decided upon was not to have any candidates announce that they were running and thus to let the voters decide at election time. As many men in the younger group now admit, this was a tactical error. The voters, confronted with no candidates at all, were far more likely to vote for the existing councilors than to try to imagine anyone new in office. The results were predictable. On the first round nine of the old councilors were re-elected. The young activist group quickly organized to form a list of candidates for the four remaining seats in the run-off elections. The three leaders of this group were Eugène Bourdelle, Jean-Pierre Gardais, and André Blond. Henri Amelin would have been a candidate except that, having previously been asked by his landlord, the chatelain, to run and having refused, he could not now be a candidate with the progressive group without compromising himself. Joseph Brée tried to set up a so-called Christian Action ticket with Gardais, but somehow ended up on the sidelines. Louis Faligand was asked by Gardais to run, but said he would wait for the next election since he was preoccupied with his family and farm. Finally a ticket of Gardais, Bourdelle, Blond, and Jean Arrial was formed. Against them were running four elderly councilors. Of the progressive ticket, Gardais alone was elected.

Of this slate, the most widely acknowledged of the younger leaders is Jean-Pierre Gardais. Gardais is the only citizen of Chanzeaux who commutes every day to a job in Angers. Because of his position as departmental secretary of the Mouvement Familial Rural, he is given credit for legal, governmental, and social welfare know-how. Within Chanzeaux he has been a leader of welfare and church groups. A member of Curé Raimbault's Union Paroissiale and the Equipe Liturgique, he is vice-president of the Comité des Ecoles Libres, secretary of the Association Familiale, and president of the Association pour l'Aide Familiale. He takes communion every Sunday. His preoccupation with family associations is no coincidence: at the age of forty-four, he has eleven children and lives in one of the four modern homes in Chanzeaux, just outside the bourg.

The second most important leader is Eugène Bourdelle, head of the farmers' union, not only for Chanzeaux but also for the canton. The oldest member (fifty-two) of the younger group, he held a position on the council from 1945 until 1953.

A third leader and unsuccessful candidate in the 1959 election was André Blond. At twenty-eight he is the former president of the Jeunes Agriculteurs for the whole department and is looked on as the head of the lay union movement in Chanzeaux. As such he draws his political support from a different group — a younger, more volatile group of farmers and shopkeepers — than Bourdelle and Gardais do. Whereas Bourdelle has been deeply involved in church activities, Blond has not been attracted to them — a fact that has helped to make him suspect in Chanzeaux. Endowed with energy and new ideas, he is recognized in Angers as the best union organizer in the department. In 1963 he was elected president of the Syndicat d'Initiative and has made it far more useful and effective than it has been in the past. He has organized a department-wide union of camomile growers, of which he is the president, and is a key figure in hunting and fishing organizations in Chanzeaux. He is living proof, however, that abundant organizational activity can be harmful to a political career; of the four candidates in 1959, he received the smallest number of votes. The town council distrusted him; and the town as a whole considered him to be motivated only by personal ambition. For this reason he has received the nickname of "Robespierre."

The fourth candidate, Jean Arrial, is involved in almost everything in Chanzeaux. While he is not the head of any organization, he holds secondary positions in practically all of them. He is vice-president of the farmers' union, a member of the school committee, a member of the council of the Syndicat d'Initiative, and the communal distributor of

supplies for the tobacco cooperative. At thirty-seven he has five children and comes from a respected family. Two of his uncles are former
town councilors, and he has relatives all over the commune.

What do these four candidates and the three more (Amelin, Brée,
Faligand) considered as possible candidates in 1959 have in common,
and how do they differ from the former town councilors? First, and
most obviously, they are much younger. In amount of land farmed,
there is little difference; they are also wealthy men by the town's standards. They have more children than the old councilors and are far less
sure of their children's future. Arrial says of his son, now age seven,
"Perhaps I will be able to stick it out here in Chanzeaux, but for my
son it is finished. He will have to go to the city." Bourdelle predicts
that his son also will leave Chanzeaux if the agricultural decline continues. And like the present councilors, and perhaps to an even greater
degree, they all come from old Chanzeaux families. (See Table 48.)

It is interesting to note, furthermore, that this younger group is
linked together by a combination of kinship, organizational, and occupational ties, to a far greater extent than the present councilors. Henri
Amelin and Jean Arrial are cousins. Joseph Brée is Arrial's brother-in-
law. Because of this, the Brée children come out to the Arrial farm to
play, and Arrial harvests Brée's grainfields. Blond, Amelin, and Arrial
help each other in the Groupe d'Entr'aide. Bourdelle, Arrial, and
Amelin are all officers of the FNSEA, and Louis Faligand is an active
member. Blond has been deeply involved in union activities. Amelin,
Gardais, and Brée are all active members in the Mouvement Familial
Rural. Bourdelle, Brée, and Gardais are on the council of the school
committee and are active, as is Amelin, in the Catholic Action. Blond,
Arrial, and Bourdelle are officers of the Syndicat d'Initiative, and
Gardais is a member of the bureau. These seven men hold more organ-
izational offices than all twelve of the former councilors did.

All are characterized — with the exception of Gardais, who is really
a "town" man — by a deep interest in the economic future of Chanzeaux and in a search for solutions to its farm problems. Bourdelle has
tried to encourage farmers to consolidate their holdings by property
exchanges. Faligand experiments with new types of wheat, Blond with
new types of camomile. Amelin was the first in the commune to raise
chickens on a large scale, and now Arrial has taken it up. The whole
group, especially Brée, were pioneers of the cooperative movement.
Arrial alone is involved in milk, harvesting, tobacco, and grain coop-

Table 48. Old Councilors, Challengers, and New Councilors

	Councilors re-elected, 1959	Challengers, 1959	Councillors elected, 1965
Aver. age	63	38	46
Age range	52–75	28–52	29–63
Aver. no. of children	3.2	4.4	3.2
Aver. no. of children still in Chanzeaux	1.8	4.2	3.2
No. of offices held in organizations	14 (12 men)	21 (7 men)	28 (13 men)
Aver. size of farm (acres)	60	72	87
	Jean-Baptiste Courcault	Jean-Pierre Gardais[b]	Jean-Pierre Gardais
	Emile Abellard	Eugène Bourdelle	Eugène Bourdelle
	Paul Guitère[a]	Louis Faligand	Louis Faligand
	Charles Couilleau	Jean Arrial	Claude Chaillou
	Joseph Arrial	Joseph Brée	Paul Amelin
	Georges Brée	Henri Amelin	Gérard Bellanger
	Ferdinand Delbosc	André Blond	Jean-Baptiste Courcault *fils*
	Eugène Faye		François Challain
	André Plancheneau		René Allaire *fils*
	Paul Manceau[a]		Paul Guitière
	René Lusson[a]		Paul Manceau
	Louis Ditière[a]		René Lusson
			Louis Ditière

[a] Re-elected, 1965.
[b] Elected.

eratives. All of this group reacted enthusiastically to a study made of Chanzeaux's agriculture made by a student in the Ecole Supérieure d'Agriculture in Angers. All are more than willing to discuss their farm problems with American students.

Most of these younger men have taken advantage of the enormous expansion of credit that has taken place in France in the last ten years. For example, Jean Arrial has built his three tobacco barns on ten-year loans. He has also purchased an automobile and a tractor, and set up his chickenhouse on low-interest cooperative credit. Twenty years ago such installment financing would have been unthinkable. The younger farmers are naturally eager to see the town council make use of the new sources of capital, such as they have used on their farms, for long-overdue communal improvements. All of their proposals were rejected by the old council because of a financial conservatism that the younger candidates considered outdated.

As long as the challengers and the generation they represent were barred from the town council, the voluntary associations of Chanzeaux expressed the basic conflict of interest and values between the older and younger generations. The older group was firmly entrenched in the oldest organizations of Chanzeaux. In particular because they controlled the town council, they could claim to be the true representatives of the commune. The organizations they controlled were not oriented toward the future or toward change, and they did not rely upon cooperative activity. In the case of the town council itself, restriction of power was a matter of deliberate policy, and delegation of authority to the mayor a matter of long-established custom.

The exclusion from power of the younger generation diverted their energies into the multitude of new organizations, which, in contrast to the old, aim for improvement, appeal to the spirit of cooperation, and require a new kind of active leadership. All of these organizations were viewed, by members and nonmembers alike, as steppingstones to the town council. Until 1965 the Syndicat d'Initiative represented the most advanced stage of coalition between the farm, commercial, and religious factions within the younger group. Out of this coalition emerged a challenging slate in the town council elections of 1965. It was widely expected that the old council would withdraw, but the final decision, which was made in February 1965, may have been precipitated by an event of the previous year. The Syndicat d'Initiative, spearheaded by André Blond, decided to set up a tourist camping ground on the banks of the Hyrôme. They hoped by this device to revive business and bolster the town's economy. The mayor and most of his councilors were quite opposed to this plan.

Nonetheless, the Young Turks managed, through a bizarre parliamentary maneuver, to obtain a municipal appropriation for the project. The proposal was brought before the council in the form of a request for a grant larger than that normally given the Syndicat d'Initiative. A majority of the councilors opposed granting the larger sum; but the procedure in such a case is to take the average of the amounts proposed by each councilor. Three or four councilors who favored the plan managed to pull the average up to a high enough level to make the project feasible. The mayor threatened to resign when he thought that one councilor planned to break the tacit rules of procedure by naming an astronomical figure. It was quickly discovered that the misunderstanding was nothing more than a confusion between new and old francs, but this incident indicates how tense relations between the generations had become. In an unprecedented gesture, the Syndicat d'Initiative turned out in force — on a Sunday morning — to construct Chanzeaux's new tourist Mecca. Since M. le Maire was conspicuously absent from the dedication ceremony, Blond took advantage of the situation to proclaim that this magnificent achievement would benefit all the people of Chanzeaux, and that it had been made possible only by the generous and enthusiastic support of the town council.

The New Town Council

In the weeks preceding the election of March 14, 1965, the mayor and the six oldest councilors announced that they would not run for re-election. Eight new councilors were elected, and Jean-Pierre Gardais was selected mayor. The complexion of the council was entirely changed. The new group is in many ways a middle way between the two extremes presented to the voters. On the one hand, all of the oldest candidates who presented themselves were elected; on the other hand, the candidates who received the most votes were those in their early forties. There were only a limited number of such men available, however, for this is the generation of people born right after World War I. Therefore, the voters did elect some young people (René Allaire *fils* at twenty-nine is probably the youngest town councilor ever elected), but the young men elected were not the most radical. Of the seven men who considered forming an opposition ticket in 1959, only the three oldest and least radical, Bourdelle, Gardais, and Faligand, were elected. Blond and Arrial were again defeated; Amelin and Brée were not candidates.

The eight new councilors have certain similarities to their older predecessors: five of them have virtually no organizational offices; and probably belong to that class of people who have simply minded their own business and concentrated on building up a good farm. Like their predecessors, they are uniformly well-off; in fact, their farms are even larger. Like the old town councilors, they are representatives of economic achievement in Chanzeaux. Four out of eight new councilmen are related to the former town councilors; they symbolize the success of many families that have extended over generations. Claude Chaillou was elected deputy mayor (*premier adjoint*) in March 1965; his father was deputy under Courcault. Jean-Baptiste Courcault *fils* himself missed being deputy mayor by only one vote. Paul Amelin, related to two former councilors, is the son-in-law of Emile Abellard, who was deputy after Chaillou *père* died. François Chaillain of Le Plessis is related to another councilor, Paul Manceau, through his wife. The new councilors hold the same place in the social structure as their predecessors did twenty years before, in terms of family and economic position.

Yet the new councilors are strikingly different in many respects from the group they succeed. The most obvious is the age drop of twenty years. These are men of another generation, with a different outlook. They use new farming methods and modern sources of credit. One member participates in the Groupe d'Entr'aide, another (Bourdelle) is the head of the FNSEA and on the board of the Thouarcé cooperative. René Allaire runs an extensive machine-rental system in the commune and owns two harvesters. The council is notable also in the absence of authority figures. The chatelain, M. Delbosc, was not re-elected. He was the only incumbent councilor in the running who was defeated, and the only older man on a list of twenty-five who was defeated. The dominant place of the chatelain in Chanzeaux politics was, in effect, lost many years ago, but the defeat of Delbosc closes a chapter in Chanzeaux's history. This defeat also symbolizes the end of the automatic delegation of authority to outsiders. Today, since most of the young Chanzeaux people have traveled much more than the older generation, the mystique of outside contacts has lost some of its potency.

Perhaps the most practical difference between the new councilors and their predecessors is that they will support the new mayor, Jean-Pierre Gardais, whereas he was in a small minority on the previous council. Gardais himself typifies in a multitude of ways the new directions that Chanzeaux is taking in the 1960s. The new councilors' support of Gardais is all that is necessary for a dramatic change in council policy. Both in his Angers contacts and in his leadership of Chanzeaux's associations, Gardais is outstanding. Perhaps equally important is his total commitment to "collateral" modes of organizational procedure, which he learned in the Catholic Action. He has said in interviews that he will not accept any authority-figure status. Rather, he will ask each town councilor for his list of necessary communal projects and then draw up a budget that contains those projects most often listed. As a member of the bureau of the Syndicat d'Initiative, he will presumably support their work in the future, as he has done in the past. Another point Gardais stresses is the necessity for cooperation with town councils of surrounding towns for regional development. Gardais' ideas of regional cooperation go beyond the grouping necessary for Chanzeaux's long-awaited public water supply and include an association for the development of the Hyrôme valley as a natural attraction. Such an orientation is to be expected from a man who participates in so many associations with regional ties.

Jean-Baptiste Courcault for twenty years represented a communal consensus for protection of the family cell and a laissez-faire attitude toward economic and regional planning. Gardais represents a change in attitude not only in his belief that something should be done, but also in his conviction that something can be done. Similar to its predecessor in many ways, the new council is nonetheless a response to basic changes in the way of life of Chanzeaux. It is a change that was reflected in the last election throughout the area. In all of the surrounding communes, dramatically younger town councils were elected. The men elected in Chanzeaux were a younger generation of farmers with children who will grow up in Chanzeaux, who recognize the need for collateral action and the need for regional action. In a way this mild communal revolution is a delayed reaction to the nation's broader problems of the 1950s. With elections every six years, communal government has lagged behind the national government since 1952. The Fifth Republic, the offspring of political instability, was nourished by an economic boom unparalleled in the postwar years. This national transformation has posed new problems to farmers with which all levels of government, including at last the communal level, have had to come to terms.

Part Five

RELIGION AND POLITICS

This part is a study of the way Chanzeans react to the series of political and religious options put to them from the outside. There has been very little discussion so far of the beliefs of the inhabitants of Chanzeaux. Yet it is the Chanzeans' beliefs and the way that these are expressed in religious and political terms which most obviously set Chanzeaux apart from the rest of France. By comparing the differing choices of Chanzeaux's electors throughout the last one hundred years, and seeing which electors tend to vote for which party, a line of continuity can be traced that we believe to be the essence of Chanzeaux's political conservatism. In a similar way, although the information is not available for a detailed historical perspective, the first section of the chapter on religious behavior is concerned with the spectrum of religious belief and observance within the commune.

One is naturally interested in the extent to which expression of political choice and degree of religious observance are related to a Chanzean's place in communal society. Our speculations on the mechanisms that ensure the continuity of Chanzeaux's political conservatism and religious faithfulness arise out of the analysis of the commune's social structure, more especially in terms of kinship networks, land tenure, patterns of migration, and traditions of leadership. Hence an attempt is made to isolate the social and economic characteristics of people in the various political and religious categories.

Following as it does a detailed discussion of village institutions and organizations, this section also provides an opportunity to discuss the whole question of participation in community life. The traditional organizations, the newer movements, and the town council are the organizing agencies for community action and thereby provide the community with a corps of leaders. But many Chanzeaux men, and many more women, are active members of the community, even though they do not do the organizing. Voting and church attendance are better indexes if one wishes to separate out meaningfully the nonparticipants from the rest of the population. By isolating the abstainers in these two key areas, we have a good chance of studying the characteristics of those residents of the commune who fall outside village life, having either no reason to share in the general beliefs or no reason to express them. Abstention in voting and poor church attendance are found to be prime evidence for a lack of integration into other aspects of village life.

1 3

Religious Behavior

IF ONE were to choose the single feature that best distinguishes Chanzeaux from the average village in France, it would be the great importance of Chanzeaux's religion. While only a quarter of France's
population are practicing Catholics, 85 percent of Chanzeaux's adults
attend church every Sunday. Another figure is equally striking: three
quarters of the adults in Chanzeaux have made the pilgrimage to
Lourdes, several hundred miles away in the Pyrenees.

For the Chanzeaux child, the church is the main point of contact
outside of the family. Virtually all of the children attend church
schools and go to the curé for catechism until their confirmation at
age twelve. The church sponsors most of the youth organizations.
Bright children who go on to secondary schools usually go to the
Catholic girls' school at La Pommeraye, to the college in Combrée,
or to a Catholic college in Angers. Finally a good number enter religious orders or the priesthood, with the boys preparing at the seminary
in Beaupréau. One sixth of Chanzeaux's population are closely related
to at least one priest or nun. The church also provides a focus for the
social life of the commune. For farmers, and especially for their wives,
the Sunday trip into town has great importance as a social occasion.
The shopkeepers do more business in the hour after Mass than at any
other time in the week. The many lay organizations that the church
sponsors affect every area of Chanzeaux life, as we have seen. Devout
Chanzeans vote in a Catholic framework, generally supporting the
MRP or the UNR, the Catholic-oriented parties. Because of the great
importance that religion plays in Chanzeaux, gradations of religious
behavior tend to reflect other gradations, economic and social, within
the community.

Our figures for church attendance in Chanzeaux were obtained
from the curé (with the understanding that they were to be used for
statistical purposes only).[1] He is required by his superiors to keep a
record of the religious practice of the town's citizens. The curé rated

each Chanzean on two counts: how regularly he attends Mass (every Sunday, irregularly, never), and how often he takes communion. From his ratings five distinct gradations of church attendance emerged, which are defined below:

1. Devout — Those who attend Mass every Sunday and take communion every Sunday; 16 percent of the people rated (81 persons).
2. Intermediate — Those who attend Mass every Sunday and take communion on most of the Holy Days; 23 percent of the people rated (116 persons).
3. Normal — Those who attend Mass regularly but receive communion only on major Holy Days (Easter, Assumption, Toussaint, and Christmas). This group is the largest: 46 percent of the people rated (229 persons).
4. Irregular — Those who attend Mass irregularly but take communion on major Holy Days; 8 percent of the people rated (39 persons).
5. Irreligious — Those who never attend Mass and never take communion; 7 percent of the people rated (37 persons).

(Because of the small numbers involved, the irregular and the irreligious were often combined for statistical purposes in this chapter.) As a general summary, five sixths of the adults rated attend Mass every Sunday; 93 percent of the people rated are officially Catholics and receive Easter communion. The number of persons who take communion every Sunday and the number who do not regularly attend Mass are equally small. These two groups form two distinctive minorities.

How clear are these categories to Chanzeans themselves? Those who receive communion every Sunday are well known, although they are sometimes linked in people's minds with the intermediate group. At any rate, the Chanzeans regard the intermediate group as being more like the devout than like the "normal" attenders. In everybody's mind, attending Mass every Sunday but receiving communion only on major feast days is the norm. Those who receive communion more often are quite as aware of their nonconformism as are those who do not attend church regularly. The irregularly religious distinguish themselves from the bottom group, but few other people do. To the outsider, however, each of these categories appears to have distinctive characteristics.

The first three categories of church attendance differ in the frequency of receiving communion. The people who take communion less often should not necessarily be considered less devout. The Catholic church in France has always been divided by two points of view on the desirable frequency of communion. There is a traditional, deeply ingrained practice of taking communion only three or four times a year; often the people who subscribe to this view consider themselves unworthy to commune more often. This tradition has been periodically challenged by reform movements that have emphasized more frequent communion in order to make church and the service more meaningful. In Chanzeaux both points of view exist, but the traditional is the more common. Of the adult population, 46 percent receive communion only three or four times a year.

Those Chanzeans who take communion every Sunday are thus in a conspicuous minority. These people must go through a veritable ritual of nonconformity each week; while everyone in the church is looking and waiting, they must go out of their pews to receive communion at the altar rail. Their distinctiveness is emphasized throughout the service as well, since they usually sit at the very front of the church, and there is always a gap of several pews between them and the rest of the congregation. During the service they tend to participate actively in the worship, singing along with the priest. Unlike the irreligious people, whose nonconformity is only in their absence from church, the people who take communion every Sunday are constantly reaffirming their distinctiveness in public.

What are the differences between this clearly defined group of people and the rest of the population? In the first place, three fourths of them come from the bourg. The bourg dwellers, of course, have the advantage of the closeness of the church, which makes it easier for them to go to confession on Friday evenings. Added to this fact is the high percentage in the bourg of elderly women who are more devout in their old age. Indeed, the large number of very religious people in the bourg makes for a tension there that is not found elsewhere. In the past the presence of the curé and the Catholic schoolteachers have increased this tension. Towndwellers who do not attend Mass are made to feel very conscious of their deviance and therefore talk about it more freely with strangers. The cafetier will loudly proclaim that church does not mean anything to him. Because all religious ceremonies, processions, and celebrations take place in the bourg, those residents who are not churchgoers feel that much more left out than do their country counterparts.

Some 83 percent of the very religious are female, and many are unmarried or widowed. The preponderance of females in this category is a sign of tradition. In Chanzeaux it is considered far more scandalous for a woman not to attend Mass than for a man. The devout are different in another respect. They are twice as likely to be related to a priest or a nun than other Chanzeans are (see Table 49). For most of

Table 49. Church Attendance and Relation to Priests or Nuns

Category	% related to at least one priest or nun	Total no. in each group
Devout	33%	76
Intermediate	20	111
Normal	15	213
Irregular	6	35
Irreligious	0	31
All Chanzeaux	18	466

the devout families, there is a tradition of religious behavior passed on from generation to generation.

The group of very religious people in Chanzeaux can easily be divided into two categories: the younger militants and the older women living in the bourg, known as "les bonnes femmes." This division can be seen most graphically by considering the population pyramids shown in this chapter. The group born before 1900 is strikingly different from that born since 1910, because of the increase in the number of men in the later years. The militants, as we have seen, are a group of younger people prominent in Catholic Action. One of the first men in this reform group said of his experience: "I was always noticed and criticized. Things were very difficult for me. I assure you, it wasn't easy to go up and take communion before everybody." Most of the militants are tied together in a network of kinship. They tend to be cliquish and to identify themselves as a group separate from the rest of the population. One couple active in the movement in fact asserted, "We are not Chanzeans; we are militants." When we asked them whether their reform movement had village-wide support, they answered, "No, it was a group, a cell — of militants." The militants are quick to attack what they consider the hypocrisy of much of the village. "Just because everyone goes to church in this region doesn't mean that the faith is stronger here than anywhere else," says one of these militants (the descendant of a Vendée hero). "They just come because they're afraid people will talk about them if they don't. Those who sit in the back of the church and talk business — well, they might just as well not come at all." Since to the American observer, at least, the militant men appear to be the most energetic, active, and modern men in the commune, one is not surprised to find them in positions of leadership. Of 31 leaders in secular organizations, 6 may be classified as devout (19 percent), 7 intermediate (23 percent), 17 normal (55 percent), and only 1 irreligious (3 percent). Of the 29 leaders in religious organizations, 16 are devout, 13 intermediate and normal, and

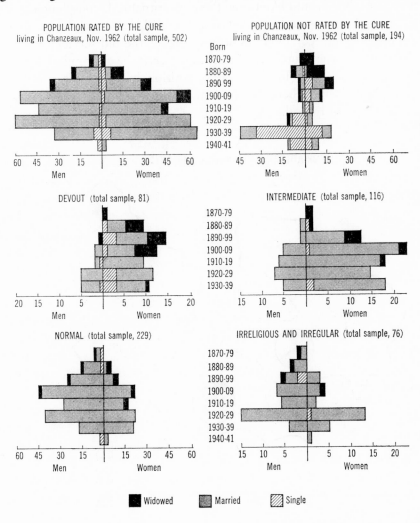

POPULATION RATED BY THE CURE
living in Chanzeaux, Nov. 1962 (total sample, 502)

POPULATION NOT RATED BY THE CURE
living in Chanzeaux, Nov. 1962 (total sample, 194)

Born
1870-79
1880-89
1890-99
1900-09
1910-19
1920-29
1930-39
1940-41

60 45 30 15 | 15 30 45 60
Men   Women

45 30 15 | 15 30 45 60
Men   Women

DEVOUT (total sample, 81)

INTERMEDIATE (total sample, 116)

1870-79
1880-89
1890-99
1900-09
1910-19
1920-29
1930-39

20 15 10 5 | 5 10 15 20
Men   Women

15 10 5 | 5 10 15 20
Men   Women

NORMAL (total sample, 229)

IRRELIGIOUS AND IRREGULAR (total sample, 76)

1870-79
1880-89
1890-99
1900-09
1910-19
1920-29
1930-39
1940-41

60 45 30 15 | 15 30 45 60
Men   Women

15 10 5 | 5 10 15 20
Men   Women

■ Widowed   ▒ Married   ▨ Single

none irreligious; the religious practice of the ordinary members of these organizations, by way of contrast, shows 65 devout, 331 intermediate and normal, and 76 irreligious.

The other category of the devout, the older bourg women, often attend church on weekdays, at the 7:00 Mass and Vespers. Some play the part of "dévotes" as found in the plays of Molière. According to a farm worker who does not attend Mass, the only resentment caused by his absence is on the part of "quelques bonnes femmes du bourg." The old women of the town, as one would predict, have been a force against the *renouveau liturgique* that took place in Chanzeaux. For their part they would like to see the more ritualized, conspicuous features of church attendance restored — the old processions and fetes, the more stately ceremonious atmosphere of the old service. Thus it is that among the people who kneel together at the altar rail each Sunday there are two groups in severe opposition, in the matter of church policy as in many other attitudes toward life — the most conservative versus the most radical.

CHURCH ATTENDANCE IN CHANZEAUX BY DIFFERENT SECTORS

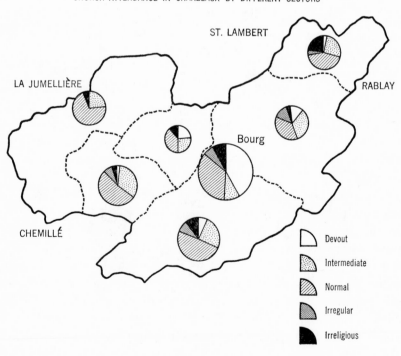

The intermediate group between the devout and the normal consists of the same type of person as the devout, except that they are predominantly farm people. Compared with 74 percent of the devout, only 15 percent of these people live in the bourg. As can be seen in the accompanying church-attendance map, in the farm areas around the bourg the intermediate segment increases as the devout decreases.

Most of the religious elite of the countryside fall into the intermediate category. Again, a split can be observed between those who are in favor of change and those who are in favor of tradition. Among the latter are the bourg husbands of the devout women and the religious women of the countryside. On the other hand, the younger couples found in this category are usually liberal, militant farmers, equivalent to their militant bourg counterparts in the devout category. These men are the leaders of farm organizations. The way the two different groups, progressive and traditional, overlap in the different categories of church attendance is shown in Table 50. Thus in the older, more

Table 50. Religious Chanzeaux Couples and Communion

Category	Traditional pattern		Militant pattern
Devout	Bourg wife	—	Bourg wife and bourg husband
Intermediate	Bourg husband	Farm wife	Farm wife and farm husband
Normal	—	Farm husband	—

traditional category, the husband takes communion less frequently than the wife. The traditional behavior implies not that men are decidedly less religious than women, but rather that there are two norms, one for men and one for women. In the more modern, younger generation, the wife and husband receive communion with the same frequency.

The people who attend Mass every Sunday, but who take communion only on Assumption, Christmas, Toussaint, and Easter, comprise the largest proportion of the town, the normal group. The population pyramid shows that these people are largely married men. Many of the old town councilors are in this group, as are the great majority of well-to-do farmers. The close relationship between economic position of the farmer and his church attendance is shown in Table 51. Indeed, if an observer were given one factor on which to establish a "lower class" in Chanzeaux, it would be the factor of reli-

Table 51. Religious Practice of Farmers and Economic Situation

Category	Farm viable	Farm will disappear soon
Devout	3 (100%)	0 (0%)
Intermediate	14 (77%)	4 (23%)
Normal	58 (69%)	26 (31%)
Irregular	8 (50%)	8 (50%)
Irreligious	2 (25%)	6 (75%)

gious behavior. Attendance at church in Chanzeaux is so universal that those who do not attend are bound to be outside the community in other ways. For instance, only 40 percent of the irreligious category were born in Chanzeaux, compared with 61 percent of the town as a whole. Twenty-seven percent of the irreligious people migrated to Chanzeaux after their marriage, compared to only 10 percent for

Table 52. Religious Practice of Native-Born Compared with Immigrants

Category	Native-born	Immigrating before marriage	Immigrating after marriage	Total no.
Devout	18%	19%	4%	70
Intermediate	22%	29%	18%	101
Normal	51%	36%	47%	199
Irregular and irreligious	9%	16%	31%	60
Total no.[a]	254	121	55	430

[a] Those with birthplace or time of immigration unknown are omitted.

Table 53. Religious Practice and Number of Adult Kin in the Commune

Kin	Devout	Inter-mediate	Normal	Irregular and irreligious	Total no.
Few (0–2)	53%	49%	55%	78%	216
Many (3 or more)	47%	51%	45%	22%	163
Total no.	58	90	173	58	379

the town as a whole (see Table 52). These figures are related to the irreligious group's evident lack of kin in Chanzeaux. Those migrating after marriage cannot perforce be integrated by means of marriage into the social structure of Chanzeaux, as is the case with most immigrants. Thus only 22 percent of the irreligious group have more than two adult relatives in Chanzeaux, as against 44 percent of the town as a whole (see Table 53).

Economically, the irreligious as a group are at the bottom of the heap. The most notoriously ill-kept farms and households in the commune all belong in this group. Only 9 percent of the irreligious farmers hold farms larger than 62 acres, in contrast to 25 percent of the farmers in the commune as a whole. Fourteen out of twenty-four of the farmers in this group have been predicted to lose their farms within the next ten years (see Table 51). There are virtually no leaders of organizations, religious or secular, in this group.

Of those members of this group who live in the countryside, a high proportion live in the farming and wine villages. A large number live on the fringe of the community, in places where it would be natural for them to be part not of Chanzeaux but of the neighboring community. The fact that there is a high rate of irreligiosity on the fringes of the commune points to the unique freedom of these people to choose between two communities or to choose no community at all. For most of the people in Chanzeaux, church attendance is not only a moral but a social obligation, enforced by the pressures of seeing everyone else going to church and of their seeing and disapproving if one does not. This is especially true in the bourg, where there is a real sense that "the curé is watching you." But the people of Chanzeaux do not expect the wine villagers to come to church in Chanzeaux, since for them Saint-Lambert is much closer. When Eugène Bourdelle was asked where certain persons in the wine villages attended church, he said Saint-Lambert — but in reality those people do not attend church at all. A similar situation exists in Saint-Lambert and Rablay; if people do not come there to church from the nearby border villages in Chanzeaux, their absence is not noticed. As the schoolmaster said, referring to a family on the Chemillé border, "They're supposed to be going to church in Chemillé, but no one really knows; they can play on both teams (ils jouent sur les deux tableaux)." The result for the fringe people seems to be a freedom from pressure to participate in community life. Drawn in two opposite ways, the solution of many is not to move at all.

Of all the irreligious people in Chanzeaux, the Americans became best acquainted with those in the bourg. These people, form a small clique, set up their own social sphere apart from that of most Chanzeans. They seem to substitute hunting and fishing for church attendance, and it is they who run the hunting and fishing clubs. On Sundays Armand Coulon, who works a lathe in the basket factory, and Emile Boutin, who commutes to nearby Beaulieu and also works in a factory, get up long before the six o'clock Mass and go fishing along a quiet stretch of the Hyrôme. Far in the distance they can hear the Chanzeaux churchbells. At noon their wives and children join them for a picnic lunch. As Coulon explained, "When you're fishing, you don't get in anyone's way."

Another group of irreligious people in and around the bourg are the town pariahs. There are two supposedly immoral and irresponsible families — one rather heterogeneous ménage made up of drunkards and ragpickers, who have a suspiciously high rate of turnover of wives; and an old man who is lame, lives alone, and is called funny names by the children. Sometimes the irreligious people help each other out, whereas they are ignored or scorned by the town as a whole. We were talking to the Emile Boutins when the old man, whom people regarded as witless, stopped in. "We give him something to eat every night," Mme. Boutin explained, "He doesn't have any friends and he's some company for us."

If one combines the top three religious categories, one comes out with a very distinct group, quite separate from the other two. They are people largely born in Chanzeaux, with a large number of adult kin there, who have the largest and most prosperous farms and who are leaders of Chanzeaux's organizations. As a general principle, the more involved a Chanzean is in the community, and the more deeply rooted he is in the town, the more likely he is to attend church regularly. Other towns have been studied where the more isolated people — either people coming in from the outside or people cut off from the community on the inside — were the churchgoers, and the standard was not to attend church. Such was largely the case of Roussillon, the village in the Vaucluse. In Chanzeaux, the opposite is true: when people are cut off from the community in other ways — by their habits, because they are newcomers, because they live on the fringes of the

commune or on a farm that is equally close to another community —
they tend not to attend church. This is especially true for men. For
women, Roussillon and Chanzeaux are more similar. When women,
especially those who are single or widowed, no longer have any value
to the community or to the family, they turn to religion as a home
and the church becomes their family. Whereas the "peculiar old men"
of Chanzeaux never attend church, the "queer" or neurotic women always do (see the church-attendance graph below).

Chanzeaux's traditional patterns in church attendance are radically
changing. On the one hand, the old practice of men and women taking
separate communion is breaking down and couples take communion
together, with men participating as often as women. On the other
hand, fewer people are attending church. The present curé recognizes
the trend. Whereas the old Curé Cailleaux used to militate against nonchurchgoers and Curé Alleaume used to ignore them, the present curé
recognizes them as residents of his parish and freely talks to them. He
makes no great effort to bring them back to the church, because
there is no real chance of doing so. Their behavior is becoming more
and more accepted. Our hypothesis for why this is so is based upon
the foregoing analysis of church attendance in Chanzeaux as a social
function calling for conformity. Because of increased mobility, not
only in migration but in transportation within the region, Chanzeans
are able to escape from the social order of their community with in-

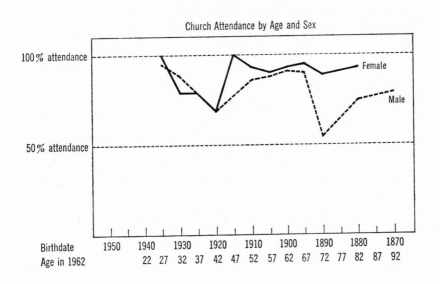

Church Attendance by Age and Sex

creased agility and frequency. And when they are able to do this, they are able to escape from its norms of religious behavior.

An analogy can be drawn between the effect of modern transportation and the behavior of the fringe people described above. The fringe people play their two communities off against each other and thus gain a large degree of personal freedom from the social norms of both. This phenomenon is probably a very old one. What constitutes a new factor is the presence of automobiles and motorbicycles, which enable other Chanzeans to take trips every Sunday. A recent census shows that there are over one hundred and fifty cars in Chanzeaux, or about one car for every three families. Whereas in the horse-and-buggy days Sunday afternoon used to be the time for visiting from family to family within the commune, now it is a time of mass exodus to the banks of the Loire, to see relatives in the Vendée, or to the ocean. Many families leave early in the morning in order to have more time at their destination. In theory they plan to attend church along the way; in practice many do not. Here is a clear case of abandoning a habit when society is no longer watching. When we asked one girl (who was a recent immigrant with her family to the town and who had an automobile) whether she would be going to Mass on Sunday, she said, "Oh, I'll be going to church elsewhere," and winked. That wink is the difference between the theory and the practice of Sundays away from town.

Church attendance in Chanzeaux is closely linked to Chanzeaux as a particular community, with its particular kinship network, its particular priest, and its particular organizations. No matter how much nearby towns are like Chanzeaux in percentage of church attendance (and they are quite similar), the less a person becomes a Chanzean — even if he is only becoming a firmer member of the community next door — the less likely he is to attend church, even next door, until he becomes fully integrated into the new community. This is crucial for the large numbers of young people who are now commuting to work in neighboring communes. Commuting is a recent change that only increases the extent to which the Chanzean is becoming the citizen of a region rather than a commune. The amount of travel of today's young Chanzeans has a similar effect. The average young couple today has seen roughly twice as much of France as their parents have. Moreover, France comes to Chanzeaux: the empty houses in the Chanzeaux bourg are now filled in the summer with vacationing city dwellers from Nantes and Paris, and tourists from all over France camp on the new camp ground.

Since Chanzeaux, compared with the rest of France, has a very high percentage of church attendance, as Chanzeans become exposed to more of France, the church has a harder struggle to maintain its high attendance rate. In fact, the 1960 revision of the conduct of the service was a partial abandonment of this struggle. No longer was direct pressure brought to bear upon nonchurchgoers. No longer were schoolchildren marched to school under the watchful eyes of their teachers and made to sit together in the balcony. The very devout younger Jacistes, along with the curé, agreed that it was unhealthy to have so many people in church who did not really care about the Mass. The habit of many of the men who would come and sit in the back of the church to whisper business during the sermon was particularly annoying to the devout. And so emphasis was placed upon having a meaningful service, even if it meant a less populated attendance. As the curé said, referring to those who come to church merely to conform, "It would be better if they didn't come at all."

When discussing religion the first thing that most people, including the curé, mentioned was that simply going to church does not make a good man and that nonchurchgoers are no more likely to be bad men. Chanzeans are currently very much aware of the difference between conforming to a social norm and true devotion, the leading of a good life. Their awareness stems not only from the current conflict between the militants and the traditionalists, but also from the increasing number of acquaintances who do not attend church and yet are their friends and neighbors. The trend in church attendance in Chanzeaux is a slow movement toward the extremes, toward the devout groups, which remain at the heart of Chanzeaux community life, and toward the irreligious groups, which grow larger as Chanzeans become more integrated into the national community.

14

Political Behavior

W HEN the polls have closed on election day in Chanzeaux and the totals are tallied, people are rarely surprised at the results. In the village, there is no serious betting on the outcome, for the best-informed men can all predict the returns to within 4 or 5 percent. In the *circonscription* (electoral district), the candidates of the left-wing parties go through the motions of a campaign, but they convince no one, not even themselves. "I can't be disappointed," the socialist candidate in the last elections confessed. "I know the results in advance." Since the institution of universal suffrage more than a century ago, the region has consistently returned right-wing candidates to the Chamber of Deputies. The issues involved in the elections have changed, but the pattern of the vote has retained a certain continuity. Although most of the voters of Chanzeaux are unaware of it, when they go to the polls on election day a tradition of a century informs and guides their choice.

Observers who are aware of this historical continuity like to trace its origins back to the Vendée Rebellion. In the political stereotype, the people of western France, unreconciled to the twentieth century and to the rest of the nation, still vote, as one reporter put it not long ago, "soixante-dix pour Chouan." [1] Yet no one in Chanzeaux today explains the vote in terms of the commune's history. In spite of all the visible monuments to their heroic ancestors, people in Chanzeaux, by general consensus, "are not interested in that sort of thing any more." But the tradition of the counterrevolution has in fact remained alive in Chanzeaux, not so much in the minds of its citizens as in the political organization of the region. To a large extent it was the Vendée war which prevented the breakdown of noble property in the west and which, early in the nineteenth century, permitted aristocrats like Quatrebarbes to return to their estates and to establish political control of their territories. The advent of universal suffrage in 1848 did not seriously affect their political hegemony, for, as we saw in Chapter 2, the people of Chanzeaux accepted Quatrebarbes' leadership even though they did not share his opinions. And so it was, wherever the great estates prevailed.

In the last decades of the nineteenth century, at the time of the founding of the Third Republic, the rural nobility of the west remained unreconciled to the republic and determined to retain what political power they had. As the republican parties developed political machines, the nobility fought to consolidate their own decentralized and territorially based form of political organization. Throughout the west, the election results divided on lines that corresponded roughly to the structure of land tenure. Wherever the nobility had preserved their estates, their candidates were elected. Most of the electoral districts in the Maine-et-Loire became the political fiefs of single families. For twenty years without interruption, the electoral district of Cholet (Beaupréau) returned M. de Maillé, the seigneur of La Jumellière, to the Chamber of Deputies, while the district of Saumur became the preserve of the de Grandmaison family and remained part of its patrimony until World War II. Chanzeaux itself, as part of the second electoral district of Angers, was represented continuously from 1875 to 1898 by M. de Soland, mayor of Thouarcé. Often, indeed, the elections in these districts were uncontested, for the republicans found it close to impossible to recruit candidates locally. When opposition candidates did run in these districts, they were almost always party regulars from outside the region.

Until the turn of the century, the local political barons were avowed royalists. As late as 1910, the prefect of the Maine-et-Loire reported that "The main issue is the very principle on which the regime is founded, and current questions play only a secondary role." [2] Later, as the restoration of monarchy became a patent impossibility, the emphasis shifted to the defense of the upper-class establishment: the Army and the Church or, as they might have preferred to phrase it, the Nation and Religion. The success of the nobility at the polls, however, was due more to their personal reputation, their social position, their familiarity with the people, and their claim to "know the region" than to their avowed convictions. As in Quatrebarbes' day, the vote remained a kind of acquiescence in the social ascendency of the nobility rather than a vote of opinion. The royalist newspapers of the day were fond of quoting the testimonials of peasants in favor of their noble deputies, and, apocryphal as these quotations are, they reveal something of the attitude that the vote must have expressed: "As deputy we have M. de Maillé of La Jumellière, and that's fine for us. He is *un brave et bon monsieur* whom everyone knows and who helps all those needing help." [3] In fact, when the elections were seriously contested, the controversy tended to focus more on the style of representation than on ideological questions, although of course the two were related. In 1893, when a republican candidate ran against M. de Soland (in the second electoral district of Angers), the campaign was fought mainly on the challenger's claim to know the region. Soland, in his declaration of principles, drew attention to his Angevin ancestry, his years of service as mayor and *conseiller général* as well as deputy, and to the benefits he had obtained for the region. He denounced his opponent as an outsider, "a Parisian who comes here, his pockets stuffed with government money, to buy your votes." The republican candidate, on his side, although he made a valiant attempt to establish a connection with an "old Anjou family" and offered the same program of protection of regional interests, high tariffs, and low taxes, could not escape the stigma of being an outsider and a city man.

Although the republicans could not carry districts outside of the city of Angers, they were able to obtain appreciable minorities in years of so-called détente (1893, 1898, 1910), when issues of church and state were not critical. In the campaign of 1893, M. de Soland, in spite of his Angevin ancestry and his distinguished service, preserved his seat by a relatively narrow margin of 1500 votes (9 percent of the registered voters). In Chanzeaux itself, the republican candidate was able to obtain 130 votes, about 30 percent of the total. From the results of elections in other years, it appears that about half of these, or 15 percent of the registered voters, were "hard-core" republicans, men who would abstain on principle if there were no republican candidate. In this period in Chanzeaux's history, the eminent position that Quatrebarbes had occupied for so long lay vacant. The old man had died without heirs, and the estate had passed into the hands of a distant relative. In the absence of strong leadership from the chateau, the village twice elected republican mayors. Though the republicans were never more than a minority in Chanzeaux, they included some of the town's most respected and best-educated citizens, similar perhaps to the minority of bourgeois republicans in Chanzeaux at the time of the French Revolution. (See Chapter 3.)

By the end of the First World War, the spectrum of political issues and parties had evolved to such an extent that the old extreme right, though still firmly entrenched in some parts of the west, no longer found any place in national politics. In the period between the two wars, the Maine-et-Loire witnessed the extinction of the royalists and the formation of a new right wing, events that had occurred some-what earlier in France as a whole. In the second electoral district of Angers, however, the gradual evolution of the right had little effect on the institution of political fiefs, and the people of the district soon became accustomed to voting for the same man under new sobriquets. In 1898, when M. de Soland retired after a long career, he was replaced by one Ferdinand Bougère, the nephew of a powerful Angers banker who himself controlled the district of Segré. At the time, the nobility of the region considered him something of an upstart, but (as the prefect reported) they found it prudent to support him, since many of them were considerably in debt to the Banque Bougère.[4] At first, the new deputy was little known and less admired in the region, but after two or three terms he managed to invest himself with the dignity of a long-term incumbent, and he continued to represent the second district of Angers until 1932 (see Table 54). Before the

Table 54. Legislative Elections in Chanzeaux, 1914–1936

Party	% of vote					
	1914	1919	1924	1928[a]	1932[a]	1936
Royalist or conservative	60	39	58	49	21	0
Independent republican	⎰ 27	37	26	23	44	67
Radical, radical-socialist[b]	⎱			16	20	13
Abstentions, blank ballots	13	24	16	13	15	16
No. of registered voters	459	423	388	391	393	400

[a] First-ballot results.
[b] Socialist and communist vote never exceeded 4%.

First World War, Bougère ran as an avowed royalist. In 1919 and 1924, he ran as a "conservative." Finally, in his last term, he made the great concession to changing times and let himself be known as a "républicain conservateur."

The scramble for Bougère's vacated place in 1932 revealed that the faithful old-time conservative vote had fallen to about 20 percent.

The majority of the vote was divided among three republican candidates: M. Cointreau, "indépendant," an industrialist who had made a rather good showing against Bougère four years earlier; M. Rosin, a political newcomer who ran as an "anti-cartelliste" and who emphasized regional issues in his campaign; and M. Boutin, a radical-socialist who had practically made a career of running against Bougère. The most important general issue of the campaign was the division between the "cartel des gauches" (the radical-socialists allied with the socialist party, the SFIO) and the conservative parties. This division became evident on the second ballot, as the conservatives transferred their decisive support to Cointreau in his contest with Boutin (see diagrams below for the 1928 and 1932 elections).

Cointreau as deputy soon learned to adopt the traditional style of the representative of the second district of Angers. Running for re-

Voting in Chanzeaux, 1928 and 1932

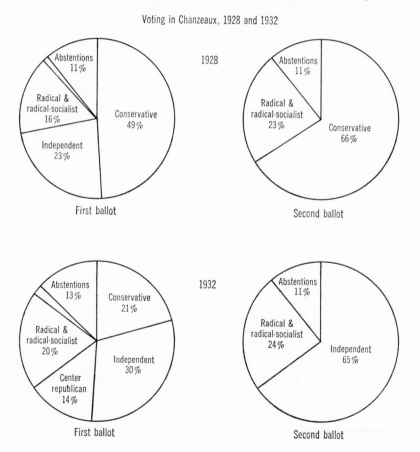

election in 1936, he emphasized the time-honored program of fiscal responsibility (meaning low taxes), agricultural protection, "amélioration du sort des travailleurs," and much attention to regional problems. He assured his constituents that he was opposed to revolution and would do anything possible to avoid war. On this platform, he defeated his radical-socialist opponent on the first ballot by a margin of two to one. Chanzeaux's election returns, almost identical on the second ballot in 1928 and 1932, reveal the significance of the split between radical-socialist and conservative republicans in the village. Independents and conservatives in each case combined their votes in support of a single candidate. Between these groups and the radical-socialists no such compromise was possible. Although the minority vote in Chanzeaux was still sizable, it had clearly diminished since the years before the war, when republicans could muster as much as a third of the electorate; and it was continuing to decline. In the year of the nation-wide victory of the popular front, Chanzeaux's total left-wing vote fell to 15 percent (see Table 54).

During this period, Chanzeaux once more had a chatelain who took seriously his role as lord of the village. Soon after the First World War, M. de Kerdouec became mayor of the commune, and he dominated village life until the outbreak of the Second War. "He was very imposing and reactionary," recollects Joseph Brée whose grandfather was a town councilor at the time. "He insisted on running everything his way. Well, my grandfather didn't like to take orders. He himself was (naturally) fairly conservative, but even so he didn't last long on the council." M. de Kerdouec found a worthy second in Curé Cailleaux, a thunderer whom the present generation remember from their childhood. "M. de Kerdouec paid for everything in the church and the schools," according to Brée, "and so naturally the church became involved in politics." Once again the "histoires de guerre de Vendée" were revived, and the people of Chanzeaux were reminded of their ancestors in every sermon and at every religious festival. There were few outright challenges to the leadership of these two formidable patriarchs. At one point, apparently, a radical-socialist did manage to gain a seat on the town council, but he, like Joseph Brée's grandfather, found little support in the village for his quarrels with the chatelain and was never re-elected. It was difficult to be a respectable political dissenter in the days of M. de Kerdouec and Curé Cailleaux.

Since World War II, the traditional pattern of the vote, in Chanzeaux as in the entire Maine-et-Loire, has undergone some modification. There is still no sign of a left-wing vote; in the last twenty years the combined strength of the radical, socialist, and communist parties has never risen above 10 percent of the vote in Chanzeaux. On the other hand, the support for the traditional right has gradually dwindled. The old elitists, who now run under the label of "independent," still present themselves to the electorate in the same style and spirit as their predecessors under the Third Republic, but their political fiefs have disappeared along with the social system that gave rise to them. Discredited after the war, they have been unable to effect a comeback. In 1958, the scion of the de Grandmaison family attempted without success to reclaim his old territory of the Saumurois. (The electoral districts had in the meantime been redrawn so that Chanzeaux was now included in the district of Saumur.) In Chanzeaux, even on the first ballot, he trailed considerably behind the Gaullist candidate, Hauret (see Table 55). In other districts, even in Cholet,

Table 55. Legislative Elections in Chanzeaux, 1946–1962

	% of vote					
Party	Nov. 1946	June 1951	May 1954[a]	June 1956	Nov. 1958[a]	Nov. 1962
Independent (traditional right)	8	15	20	19	19	6
Poujadist	—	—	—	21	16	4
Gaullist (RPF in 1951, UNR since 1958)	4	36	2	10	29	52
MRP	60	22	37	22	12	—
Radical, SFIO and PC (traditional left)	9	9	6	7	3	3
Other	3	—	—	—	3	3
Blank ballots	1	2	5	5	3	5
Abstentions	15	16	30	16	15	27
No. of registered voters	736	711	713	728	722	721

[a] First-ballot results.

the heart of the Mauges, the old notables have not fared any better; the people no longer look to them for leadership. "In the past it was all very well," explains Joseph Brée. "They played an important role because they alone had the education and the means to do it and they did render important services — though not without an eye to their own advantage, of course. But now they can't adjust to new conditions; they don't treat us as equals. It offends one's dignity, and these days people are capable of running their affairs themselves." The maximum vote for the traditional right in Chanzeaux has fallen to 20 percent.

In the place of the old parties, Chanzeaux, like the department generally, has supported a succession of parties that express a basic opposition to the politics of the Fourth Republic. Each has come into being as a third force, against the traditional divisions and the institutional machinery of the old parliamentary system, and each, until now, has lost credit as the deputies elected under its aegis have been forced back into the old political alignments. In the first years after the war, the Mouvement Républicain Populaire (MRP) filled this role. Later, in 1956, it was Poujade. But Poujade, too, went the way of politicians before him. "He got involved in politics," explains Paul Guitière, "and maybe this is what defeated him." Finally, de Gaulle emerged as the magician who would liberate France from its own internal divisions.

In general, this discontent with traditional politics does not reflect profound social or economic discontent. Only in the crisis years of the Fourth Republic did a large number of Chanzeans give their support to anything that could be termed a radical protest movement; and even in this case, it is not clear that Poujade's extremism was appreciated at the time. Now that the Fourth Republic is a thing of the past, the majority of people in Chanzeaux vote for the party that represents de Gaulle's precarious position. In the 1962 elections, the only serious issue was the choice between de Gaulle's party, the Union Nationale Républicaine (UNR), and the *vieux partis,* which bore the stigma of participation in the old system. The word politician itself was anathema, and almost all the candidates who ran in opposition to de Gaulle attempted to disclaim their connection to the old parties. "De Gaulle made our deputies look ridiculous," observed Jean Delaunay. "Otherwise they'd all have taken him for their patron." The result of the election was entirely forseeable. The Gaullist candidate, the incumbent Hauret, took the election easily on the first ballot. A little over half (52 percent) of the registered voters in Chanzeaux voted UNR. In previous years, about the same percentage have divided their votes between candidates of similar antiparty parties. The frequent changes of name have not disguised the fundamental consistency of political attitudes since the war. (See Table 55 and the voting diagrams for 1946–1962.)

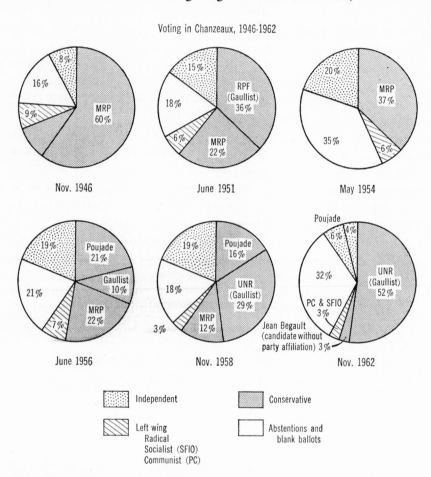

Voting in Chanzeaux, 1946-1962

Nov. 1946 — MRP 60%, 16%, 9%, 8%

June 1951 — RPF (Gaullist) 36%, MRP 22%, 15%, 18%, 6%

May 1954 — MRP 37%, 20%, 35%, 6%

June 1956 — Poujade 21%, Gaullist 10%, MRP 22%, 19%, 21%, 7%

Nov. 1958 — Poujade 16%, UNR (Gaullist) 29%, MRP 12%, 19%, 18%, 3%

Nov. 1962 — Poujade 4%, UNR (Gaullist) 52%, PC & SFIO 3%, 6%, 32%, Jean Begault (candidate without party affiliation) 3%

Independent

Conservative

Left wing Radical Socialist (SFIO) Communist (PC)

Abstentions and blank ballots

The Ideological Content of the Vote

Outside its own borders, the Maine-et-Loire is considered an extremely conservative department, for the Gaullist or MRP vote is still vested with right-wing connotations. To outsiders, villages like Chanzeaux have not yet shaken off the Vendean stereotype; to the mind of one Angers storekeeper, "They are Chouans, true and pure." Chanzeans, however, certainly do not put the same interpretation on their own votes, for they like to consider themselves fairly progressive.

Yet the party labels are not meaningless: each party and name have an ideological significance that is well understood in Chanzeaux. But it is a significance that must be understood in local and to some extent historical terms.

Part of the confusion surrounding the use of the tag "right wing" stems from the fact that the term itself has undergone evolution, and a certain fragmentation. Until as late as the Second World War, it should be recalled, the dominant political class in the west was the rural nobility. Their doctrines on economic, social, and religious as well as political matters defined the extreme right of France's traditional political spectrum. With the decline of this class, the components of the old right-wing ideology have become dissociated, and each has taken up to some extent an independent political life. At present, many of the existing parties share certain points in common with the old right, but very few exhibit all its traditional features. Thus, one may find parties that are economically and socially conservative but anticlerical, or clerical but socially progressive. The right-wing epithet is in general so indiscriminately used that it might be applied in either case.

The main ideological split in Chanzeaux occurs in reference to the religious issue. Regardless of its policies on other issues, a party that supports the Catholic schools and the interests of the church will be branded right-wing, and anticlerical parties will be considered left-wing. The radicals, with conservative economic policies, are considered leftist in Chanzeaux because of their traditional association with freemasonry; on the other hand, while the MRP and the SFIO both favor much more progressive social legislation, the MRP is nationally considered rightist because of its support of the Catholic schools. Even though the practical matters relating to the religious issues have now been settled in the main, the traditional division remains uppermost in the minds of many Chanzeans. "There are only two parties," says Henri Voisin of La Brosse, "right and left; the right fight among themselves, but it is absurd because they are all alike."

The old parties themselves adhere stubbornly to this distinction. In a recent campaign, the socialist candidate Miollet offered privately to desist in favor of another candidate, Galisson, who was running without party affiliation, on the condition that Galisson declare himself to be *laïque*. Galisson's refusal to take a position on the Catholic school issue, which he considered an irrelevant remnant of the past, outraged the good party man, Miollet. "That's a man who doesn't want to come out and say what he is," he told us indignantly, "so that everyone will go along with him — in French we call that *un pêcheur en eaux troubles* [a fisher in troubled waters] — that's not too honest, if you know what I mean." The communists, too, always openly oppose the Catholic schools on principle, though they are well aware that this position is political suicide in the region.

It is this religious division which maintains the historical continuity of the vote in Chanzeaux. As long as the parties of the left maintain their anticlerical stance, they remain outside the pale of respectability in a village where the church is still the symbol of community and the ultimate source of legitimacy in all aspects of life. A left-wing vote in Chanzeaux is a vote against the church, and therefore an antisocial vote. Because the left is excluded from politics in Chanzeaux and in the region, often a new political movement that has very little to do with the religious issue will take on two parallel forms, one within the right-wing tradition and one within the framework of the left. In 1956, there were two protest movements of national importance, one associated with Pierre Poujade and one with Pierre Mendès-France. Although in many ways Mendès-France's policies might have better suited the needs and aspirations of the people of Chanzeaux, there was no question of his developing a following in the region, for he was a radical. Poujade, on the other hand, came out in favor of the Catholic schools and so became acceptable to the people of Chanzeaux.

Even de Gaulle, who claims to be above ideology as he is above class, is forced to work within the framework of the left-right split. His support for the Catholic schools has identified him with the right elsewhere in France; in Chanzeaux, it has simply earned him political respectability. He is not considered particularly right-wing in Chanzeaux because people recognize that his accommodation with the church is based entirely on practical considerations. The Catholic school settlement is an institutional arrangement intended to put an end to the old ideological split by making it irrelevant. For this reason, certain of the militants in Chanzeaux are a bit disappointed with de Gaulle; they feel that he has not supported the *écoles libres* strongly enough. ("De Gaulle," reflects Jean-Pierre Gardais, "is a Christian, but we don't know to what degree.") Yet the alternative to his solution, it is generally admitted, would be no solution at all, and everyone is relieved to have a compromise that works, whatever its failings. As a campaign issue, the school question was dead in the elections of 1962.

The central issue of the 1962 campaign was in a sense even more basic than the religious controversy. De Gaulle had given the country peace, and with it a certain degree of prosperity. Now he presented himself and his party, the UNR, as the only assurance of continuing stability, the only force against a return to the "quarrels of the past" that had threatened the country with civil war. The people of Chanzeaux certainly understood the campaign in these terms. "First, we have to think of the essentials," said Gardais, "the unity of the country, its autonomy, financial stability." The vote in Chanzeaux was a vote against all internal threats to the existing stability. The communists, of course, were widely considered such a threat, and many Chanzeans defended their vote for de Gaulle as a vote against the communists, but many people were also concerned about the threat from the "extrèmes conservateurs" and voted for de Gaulle in opposition to them. This was in particular Jean-Pierre Gardais' interpretation of the elections. "I believe that the Gaullist majorities we have seen in the last few years can be attributed to the great scare we had on a certain May 13. We have been obliged to admit that de Gaulle saved the country a second time when he resisted those who brought him to power." Certainly, then, the Gaullist vote in Chanzeaux is not indicative of general right-wing sentiment in any but the religious sense.

The extent to which the old symbols of right and left continue to provide the context for politics in Chanzeaux depends on factors quite outside the control of the community. In great degree it depends on the future of the traditional parties after de Gaulle. If de Gaulle is at all successful in creating a permanent alternative to the system of the *vieux partis*, the erosion of the old political symbols, already begun, will undoubtedly continue. If he is unsuccessful, the traditional stance of the parties on the religious issue may continue to shape the pattern of the vote in Chanzeaux.

The Social Meaning of the Vote

Even on the village level, some parties that participate in Chanzeaux's elections can easily be identified with particular interest groups. For instance, people who vote independent in Chanzeaux, according to Paul Guitière, are "people with traditionalist ideas who vote — no, I wouldn't say against the republic, no, it's not that, but who are nevertheless opposed to republican principles — people who would be ready to throw over the Independents if they could find anything further to the right." From its aristocratic antecedents, the independent party has inherited an upper-class identification and is generally known as the *parti des capitalistes*. Its nineteenth-century liberal program and the way in which it is presented do not appeal to the mass of Chanzeaux's voters. The campaign style is elegant, educated, and refined — too refined. "He spoke too well," was Jean Delaunay's comment on the independent candidate in the last election. People who vote independent in Chanzeaux are those who feel themselves in a superior class to the majority. Guitière says, "We know who they are. I don't want to name any names; it's not worth the trouble. They're grosse or petite bourgeoisie, *voilà!*"

The MRP, of widespread appeal in Chanzeaux upon its entry into politics in 1945, has lost most of its support to the UNR and in so doing has been increasingly identified with the Catholic Action movements in town. It has the support of the young, militant element in Chanzeaux. Guitière estimates that, if an MRP candidate had run in the last election, he would have collected "a certain number of votes — representing, for example, the clergy, the family associations, certain of the more religious people who remain attached to the principles of religion." Just as in the case of an independent, a person's classification as MRP implies a whole syndrome of political and social attitudes.

The overwhelming choice of Chanzeaux in the 1962 election was the UNR, and the high percentage of votes shows that its appeal was not limited to any single interest group. In village and countryside, most of those without gravely pressing economic problems were voting UNR for the stability and continuity that the government of de Gaulle represented. Because the UNR was the village choice, and everyone knew it, the conspicuous nonconformers both in the bourg and in the campagne did not vote Gaullist; some turned in blank ballots, many abstained, some voted for unknown candidates, some voted for parties that served as local protests — Poujadist and communist.

When he first entered politics in 1956, Pierre Poujade received a percentage of Chanzeaux vote (21 percent) which represented a fair cross-section of Chanzeaux's population. But like the MRP, the Poujadists in the town gained a particularist identification when the majority of the supporters of the movement switched to other parties (notably the UNR), leaving a hard core of shopkeepers. Most others regard Poujade now as an extreme conservative, so extreme in fact that some consider him antisocial.

A small group of Chanzeans (numbering from twelve to sixteen) regularly vote communist: included are a dealer in medicinal plants whose father "caught on" in the First World War; a garage man from out of town; and several farmers. These communists form a clan of families all intermarried, all anticlerical, all militant nonconformists. Sitting ostentatiously at a table in the "modern" café during High Mass on Sunday, Pierre Socheleau, the town leader of the group, says, "I'm not like the others — I can't pretend." Communism in Chanzeaux represents an extreme stand against the church, not merely away from it. As a rule of thumb, those people who never attend church, yet who vote regularly, vote communist.

The communist and Poujadist vote in Chanzeaux is an active vote against the system. It is a vote of people who are in some cases quite well-off. The Poujadists object to control of the economic system by government and big business. The communists in Chanzeaux are against the religious establishment. Both the Poujadists and the communists are actively involved in town life. They are part of the system and are reacting within it. Their protest seems a natural and necessary part of it. The abstention vote, often larger than these two votes combined, is a vote of people passively against the system — of the Chanzeaux inhabitants who do not even participate in the system. For those who find all the possible choices equally distasteful, one alternative is always open: to vote for none of them. Even in this final form of protest, there is room for individual style. One can simply use a blank ballot, or one can display one's contempt for the system even more obviously by marking the ballots or tearing them up so that they will be disqualified. When M. Guérin the postman came to vote in the last election, he left no doubts in anyone's mind as to his opinion of the whole business. He had torn up all the ballots and crumpled them before putting them into the envelope, so that the envelope could hardly fit into the ballot box.

But the people who are most disaffected do not dramatize their discontent; they simply do not come to the polls. In every election, at least a hundred people out of the seven hundred or so eligible voters abstain. Although some of course are people who do vote regularly but who happen to be sick or out of town on election day, many more are those who make a habit of abstention. The hard core of this group is made up of about fifty people who have abstained three times or more in the last seven elections and referenda and who were not prevented from voting for incidental reasons such as health. The great majority of the habitual abstainers are women, for politics is, traditionally, part of the man's world. It is only since the war that women have been eligible to vote. Most of the women who do not vote are already over sixty; they are accustomed to being excluded from politics and see no reason to change their habits now. Among the younger women, there are many fewer chronic abstainers, but it is still quite unconventional for a woman to display an active interest in politics. She is rather expected to vote the way her husband or her family does. "Girls aren't *allowed* to be interested in politics," complains Odile Brichet. (See the population pyramids for voters below.)

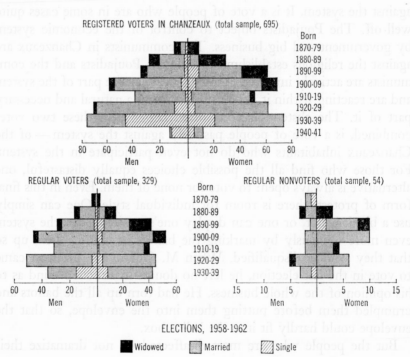

REGISTERED VOTERS IN CHANZEAUX (total sample, 695)

Born
1870-79
1880-89
1890-99
1900-09
1910-19
1920-29
1930-39
1940-41

80   60   40   20   20   40   60   80
Men   Women

REGULAR VOTERS (total sample, 329)

Born
1870-79
1880-89
1890-99
1900-09
1910-19
1920-29
1930-39

60   40   20   20   40   60
Men   Women

REGULAR NONVOTERS (total sample, 54)

15   10   5   5   10   15
Men   Women

ELECTIONS, 1958-1962

■ Widowed   ▨ Married   ▨ Single

It is more than age and sex, however, which sets off the chronic abstainers as a group from the rest of Chanzeaux. The regular non-voters are people who live on the fringes of the community, literally and figuratively. The farther one travels from the bourg in any district, the higher the proportion of chronic abstainers (see Table 56). The highest concentration of all may be found in the wine-

Table 56. Abstentions and Distance from Bourg of Residence

Distance from bourg (km.)	Voting performance[a]	
	Regular and intermediate voters	Abstainers
0–0.5	203	7
0.5–1.5	166	19
1.5–2.5	61	6
2.5–3.5	49	20
3.5–5.0	6	2

Distance	% of regular voters
0–0.5	96.7%
0.5–2.5	90.1%
2.5–5.0	70.1%

[a] Definitions of voting-performance categories: regular voters — voting every time in 7 elections, 1958–1962; intermediate — missing once or twice in 7 elections; abstainers — missing three or more times in 7 elections. *Chi Square Test:* 2.5–5.0, abstainers, vs. 0–2.5, regular and intermediate voters. Significant at the 0.01 level (i.e., if there were no relation between abstention and distance of residence, a community by chance alone would show results as extreme as those above less than one time in 100).

Table 57. Abstentions and Number of Adult Kin in Commune

Kin	Voting performance[a]			Total no.
	Regular voters	Intermediate	Abstainers	
Few (0–2)	60%	63%	85%	352
Many (3 or more)	40%	37%	15%	192
Total no.	315	145	84	544

[a] *Chi Square Test:* regular, many kin, vs. abstainers, few kin; significant at 0.01 level.

growing quarter, which we have already found to be the area in many respects least integrated into the life of the commune. These people seem impervious both to the attractions of community social life and to the strong pressures for conformity. The bourg, center of commerce, neighborly watchfulness, and gossip, is far away — farther, for many, than the bourgs of Saint-Lambert or Rablay. They have few relatives in the commune, proportionally many fewer than the regular voters have (see Table 57). This means again less contact within the community, and less motivation to seek it. In time, too, as in space, the abstainers are precariously tied to the community. Many were born outside the limits of the commune (see Table 58), and many more live on such marginal farms that it is predicted they will leave them within the next ten years (see Table 59).

The proof and symbol of the tenuousness of their attachment to the village is the degree of their religious practice. Among the old

Table 58. Voting and Birthplace (Voters on Isolated Farms)

	Voting performance[a]	
Birthplace	Regular voters	Abstainers
Chanzeaux	52%	28%
Elsewhere	48%	72%
Total no.	88	21

[a] *Chi Square Test:* significant at 0.05 level.

Table 59. Voting and Economic Status of Farmers

	Economic status of farmers[a]		
Voting performance of farmer	Viable	Marginal	Total
Regular voters	64	22	86
Intermediate	19	13	32
Abstainers	2	9	11
	85	44	129

Voting type, abstentions	% on marginal farms
Regular voters	25.6%
Intermediate	40.9%
Abstainers	81.8%
Average	34.1%

[a] Economic status as rated by *dépositaire* of the cooperative of Thouarcé in Chanzeaux. A marginal farm is one predicted to disappear within the next 10 years.

women, a great number attend church erratically or not at all. Even when only country people are considered in comparison, in order to eliminate the effect of the bourg-campagne differential in religious practice, the difference in church attendance between abstainers and regular voters remains extreme (see Table 60). The church, of course, exerts pressure against abstention, which it condemns as a neglect of civic duty. But the connection between religious practice and voting in Chanzeaux can also be understood at a less overt level. Integration into the community is expressed ceremonially through conformity in church attendance, and social and economic divisions within the village are expressed through differences in religious practice. Since voting habits follow so closely the pattern of religious practice, one can conclude that the same kind of symbolism is attached to voting. Coming to the polls on election day is not simply a sign of interest in national politics; it is also, perhaps primarily, an expression of involvement in the community.

Table 60. Religious Practice and Voting

| Voting performance | Degree of religious practice[a] | | | |
	Devout and intermediate	Normal	Irregular and irreligious	Total
Regular voters	133	134	19	286
Intermediate	46	48	23	117
Abstainers	3	19	26	48
	182	201	68	451

[a] For definition of categories, see Chapter 13.

This is why one would not expect a man like Jean Delaunay to abstain willfully in an election, no matter what his private misgivings on the issues; he is too good a Chanzean. Even Guérin, who tore up his ballot, or Lambert, who turned in a blank, made the gesture of voting. They are not the town's most respected citizens; both have personal faults that elicit much gossip and criticism; still, they are respectable, and one of the tokens of their respectability is the fact that they do vote, even if they have nothing to vote for. The people who do not vote at all are far more ill-favored. Among them one finds the "pauvres types," the public-school parents, the queer old women and suspicious old men. They are the few really discontented people in Chanzeaux. If they voted at all, they might express their grievances against the commune or against life in general by voting communist, but instead, as though aware of the futility of such a gesture, they remain for the most part sullenly silent.

Perpetuation of a Tradition

The left, then, is still excluded from politics in Chanzeaux, as it has been for a hundred years. In this sense, Chanzeaux's historical tradition is very much alive. But the forces that keep it going now are not the same as those of the past. Until the Second World War, politics was controlled by a well-defined elite. The kernel of their ideology was the defense of their own class interest, but from this grew a complex of symbols to which the people of the region could respond: the idea of a territory and a faith to defend. The domination of the landed gentleman over the people he claimed to represent was to be forgotten in the common solidarity against an external threat: regional solidarity, against the political invasion from the cities, and religious solidarity, against the attacks of virulent unbelievers. In fact, of course, it was never entirely possible to disguise the narrow class basis of right-wing ideology, and the rallying cries of the landed gentry, phrased though they were in supernatural terms, excited little popular enthusiasm.

Still, the aristocrats ran unopposed in the rural districts of the Maine-et-Loire, and in the villages the people continued to vote for them. For the potential sources of real opposition were not, as we saw in the case of Chanzeaux in the 1840s, the local pillars of the community: not the relatively prosperous tenant farmers, the few proprietors, or the handful of rentiers of bourgeois pretentions, like the Forests of Chanzeaux, who could be found in every small commune. The nobility, accustomed to an active role in local affairs, was prepared to cooperate, as Quatrebarbes did, with the village notables, and they in turn were pleased enough to accept the advantages of patronage. The one potential source of opposition was the rural lower class, the displaced textile workers, the impoverished day laborers, and perhaps by the 1890s the smallest of the small proprietors. But these were precisely the people who were most likely to leave the village for the cities. As long as the rural exodus continued, as it continues today, no serious challenge to the political control of the aristocracy could develop within the region, for the class basis of such a challenge would be constantly undermined by emigration.

When, by the end of the Second World War, the great estates of the nobility had collapsed in bankruptcy, the traditional right all but collapsed with them, and its lack of a popular base became evident. But this decline brought with it no compensating growth of the left. Instead there emerged, in abrupt succession, the various parties of opposition to the old political system, all of which, because of their support for the church, have been considered right-wing in France as a whole. To this extent, the right-wing tradition in villages like Chanzeaux has been maintained, and it is largely the church that has been responsible. In Chanzeaux, the overt involvement of the church in politics is minimal. The Catholic activists are proud to point out that the old days, when the curé instructed his parishioners how to vote, are gone. But as a symbol of community, as the single most important criterion of respectability, the church continues to control the vote indirectly. The men who are in a position to influence the opinion of the village are those who are most respected: the leaders of secular organizations, the former town councilors, the heads of some of the largest family clans. These are the people who feel most deeply the pressure toward religious conformity. Not all are militants, but all are good churchgoers and would certainly never support a political party that openly attacked the church.

On the other hand, Chanzeans have constantly before them the image of their potential left wing, the poor families who move into town and stay a few years before going on, who do not come to the bourg on Sundays, who do not go to church, who perhaps sent their children to the public school before it closed in 1964 — the one institution in the village that was closely associated with the left. This group of deviants is in reality the nucleus of a more clearly defined lower class, but the group is so small that no one in Chanzeaux would call the difference between them and the majority a class division. They are just "pauvres types." No one stops to reflect on the number of "pauvres types" who have moved into the commune and out of it over the years, for they are little known while they remain there and forgotten when they leave. As in the past, this is the "class" that might challenge the political traditions of the village — it might, that is, if it were a large stable group or a growing group within the commune. But the economic range in Chanzeaux is too narrow to permit this situation to develop. Lower-class people cannot remain in the village and hope to better their position there; they can only move away. As in the past, migration continues to prevent the growth of any real class division and, with it, sharp political division.

Even before they decide to move away in fact, therefore, most of the "pauvres types" withdraw in spirit from the community in which they do not belong; they do not go to church, and they do not vote. Occasionally, in an unusual demonstration of discontent, one will vote communist, but even this display implies a minimal, though negative, bond with the community. The two or three known communists in the village are native and well-entrenched Chanzeans. As long as a few deviants remain in the community, their presence reinforces the identification of the left as an outgroup and thus helps to maintain the political tradition of Chanzeaux. As in the past, the continuation of this tradition, or rather its confinement within certain limits, is built into the economy and the social structure of Chanzeaux.

Part Six

THE INDIVIDUAL AND THE COMMUNITY

To understand how Chanzeans preserve a way of life from one generation to the next, we must describe how a young person is trained for life in Chanzeaux and how an older person lives in the community after his most productive years. The emphasis on family and kinship in raising children, the teaching of religion in the schools, the demands and regulations imposed on adolescents, the respect and security offered to old people, all tend to strengthen and preserve traditional values. But, at the same time, economic changes, migration, and increased exposure to the outside world are disrupting the place in the community traditionally assigned to the young and the old. While Chanzeans are still being trained for a community that is slow-moving and conservative, their lives are being profoundly affected by the nature of the community as a changing organism. This section will explore what happens in the life cycle of an individual within a community that is both fostering traditional values and undergoing transformations.

15

Childhood

THE FAMILY is an organizing institution of the community in social
activities, work, politics, religion, and education. It also plays a
central role in the life of each Chanzean, directing the process of
growing up. All the *rites de passage* in the life of a Chanzean are
family functions. At baptisms, the godmother and godfather are
usually relatives, often the sisters or brothers of the baby's parents.
Chanzean godparents are not expected to give a godchild any substantial financial help as he grows up. They act more like grandparents in American society — friendly adults to whom the child
may turn for small favors and affection. By choosing relatives to be
godparents, Chanzeans further strengthen the kinship network.

At marriages, relatives again play a primary role. They are the
preferred witnesses for the required civil ceremony. If there is a
priest in the family, he will make every effort to return to Chanzeaux
to perform the service. Recently, when the mayor's youngest son
was married, family involvement reached a high point. The young
man's sister was a witness; his father performed the civil ceremony;
then the wedding guests moved next door to the church, where his
brother celebrated the wedding Mass. Since it often happens that
younger brothers and sisters meet future spouses at a wedding party,
which is normally restricted to the families of the married couple,
two Chanzeaux families may often be linked by more than one marriage. These marriages of cousins or of brothers and sisters in different
families strengthen family bonds and turn the kinship network back
upon itself.

A funeral makes even more serious demands on family attendance.
Nothing like the Irish wake occurs to attract the relatives; mourners
gather solely to express their grief at the dead person's passing. Yet
most Chanzeans feel strongly obligated to attend a relative's funeral.
Funerals also exemplify the importance of "ritual relatives" in Chanzeaux. The Société de la Rue Bourgeoise provides pallbearers for

the funeral of members. After the funeral, a roll call is taken, and absent members are fined. The club acts like a second set of relatives, the ritual brothers.

These major events in which relatives play a central part are complemented by many minor occasions. For many families, Sunday afternoon means traveling to see nearby kin, or gathering all the married brothers and sisters with their children at the old family home. This can be done without great difficulty, of course, since most relatives live close by. The departure or return of a young man in the service, the success of a student in his examinations, and the celebration of one of the numerous religious holidays during the year also provide occasions for relatives to get together.

A Chanzean's family surrounds him at every important event in his life. Through his own experience he learns the importance of the family, not only in the workings of the community but also in his own development. For the most part, young couples live in accordance with the accepted and familiar patterns of life in Chanzeaux as their parents knew it; as parents themselves, they feel responsible for carrying on these traditions to the next generation.[1]

From what we know about past and present behavior of families in Chanzeaux, we can make certain inferences about the expectations of young couples. It goes without saying that every couple intends to have children, and to have them soon after marriage. No *foyer* is considered really complete until the first baby arrives. Parents who are articulate on matters concerning the family, especially the Catholic activists, consider the raising of children a kind of service that man and wife dedicate to something greater than themselves, not only to God but also to their country and to humanity in general. These Chanzeans cite the low birthrate of France in the 1930s, the need to stimulate it with *allocations familiales*, and the continuing low birthrate in cities as signs of the growth of materialism and decadence in the nation.

Certain Catholic activist couples like the Brichets, the Gardais', the Courcaults, and the Bellangers have had very large families, and this fact is generally taken as further evidence of their devoutness. Although these families are generally prosperous, supporting such a large number of children is never an easy matter. In the case of the Gardais family, more than financial sacrifices are involved. Although Jean-Pierre Gardais' salary and allocations have allowed the family to live comfortably and to build a new house, they will not be sufficient to provide secondary education for all thirteen of his children. To M. Gardais, whose ambitions for his children's education are much higher than those of most Chanzeans, this is a constant disappointment. Although the Gardais' do not claim that all their children have been "intentional," and they complain about the hardships of having a large family, it is clear that the family is a source of great pride to them.

While the majority of parents in Chanzeaux may not feel obliged to follow the example of these exceptional families, they accord them their respect and admiration, showing that they share at least the same ideal of parenthood. Local political analysts (such as Delaunay) attribute much of M. Gardais' popularity, especially among women, to his distinction as a family man. Sheer size, however, does not automatically entitle a family to respect, for people believe that one ought to be able to provide adequately for the children one has. A very sharp distinction is drawn between those families who have many children as a religious duty and those who "don't know any better" or who simply seem improvident. Some of the "outsider" parents of the community, those who attend church irregularly or not at all and who do not hold steady jobs, have large broods of children. These people are accused by their neighbors of having children simply to get relief money, and the women are suspected of promiscuity at worst and feeblemindedness at best. Mme. Pinier, who lives next door to the Cordiers, the most notorious of the families, complains about the government policy that allots a bonus to women who become pregnant at intervals of less than two years. "Just think," she says, "because we waited a little more than two years between our first child and the second, which I think is only *decent*, I get a smaller allocation while the government encourages people like the Cordiers to live like animals." Mme. Cordier and her counterparts themselves complain they have had too many children and that childbearing has ruined their health, but they seem to consider themselves helpless in the matter and give the impression that their husbands brutalize them. "It's really almost a crime," says Mme. Brée, "for such people to bring children into the world."

These families are much less respected than those of the one or two convinced communists in Chanzeaux, who at least live according to antireligious principle. Joseph Davy and Pierre Socheleau, the communist leader, have kept their families small, probably intentionally. M. Davy, the proprietor of a prosperous and efficient garage, has a special claim to respect because he can afford to send his only son away to continue his education, and he is often cited as an example of a father who has done well by his children — in a material way at least.

In general, three to five children are considered to be a good number to have, and considerably fewer families have six children. Most young couples have their first baby within a year and a half of their marriage. The second baby generally follows in a year or two, and often the third about two or three years later. The birthrate is not uniform in the different parts of the commune, tending to vary directly with the prosperity of the group under consideration. Thus the small families are likely to be found in the hamlets, while a greater number of the large families live in the bourg or on isolated farms.

Once they have decided that they have enough children, many couples must use some sort of birth control, but what methods they use are not known, since people are very reluctant to imply even that "other people" may practice birth control. One indication of the prevalence of "family planning," however, is the present policy of the curé on the subject. We were told that thirty years ago Curé Cailleaux used to ask the men in confession whether they had done their "family duty," but now no curé would take this liberty. Father Alleaume (curé until 1960) confirmed this report, complaining that he had no effective way of controlling the habits of his parishioners in this matter. The most devout people in the village, however, have no need of strict supervision, for they still tend to have larger than average families (about five children per family for the most religious group as compared to two or three children per family for the entire village). These figures imply that only the devout seriously observe the church's ban on all forms of birth control.

It is fair to conclude, then, that the norm is affected by both moral and economic considerations, which often work at cross-purposes. If we consider M. Gardais, a Catholic militant, and M. Davy, a communist, as representative of the opposite extremes in family planning, however, it is unquestionably the former who remains the symbol of Chanzeaux's ideals. But the tendency of material considerations to limit the size of the family is undeniably effective —

except perhaps in the two "nonconformist" groups at the top and bottom of the social scale. In other words, most families try not to have more children than they can afford to support at the moment, but they do not include planning for the child's future among the necessities they must provide.

The birth of a child is always considered an important and joyful event, not only for the family but also for the community. News of the birth is published in the parish bulletin. It used to be that baptisms were held within a week of birth because of the high infant-mortality rate. Now that danger of death before baptism is all but removed, the ceremony is usually postponed until the mother is well enough recovered to attend. The traditional ritual of throwing candy to the village children from the steps of the church is still observed. Everyone, including the communists, has his children baptized. Usually it is the father who presents the child to the community. The father, as the breadwinner, is the public representative of the family; the mother's domain is the home.

Bringing up children is considered primarily the woman's responsibility. She is the first source of comfort and affection and the child's first teacher. Later, as proper social behavior is demanded of the child, she is the main disciplinarian, although the father is nominally the ultimate authority for the dispensation of rewards and (especially) punishments. Because women are considered to have more sensitive and religious natures than men, people also agree that a child should receive his first notions of God from his mother. "The mother is the best person to teach a child anything," said Mme. Bellanger, a very devout farmer's wife and the mother of eight grown children. "She shows him how to make the sign of the cross, tells him about God and the church, takes him to Mass now and then, teaches him his evening prayers. Later, she sees to it that he learns his catechism."

Beginning at a very early age, a distinction is made in the way a child is disciplined according to whether it is a boy or a girl. Since it is believed that boys are naturally willful, more self-assertion is tolerated from them. When four-year-old Camille Brée has temper tantrums on being refused candy or soda, M. Brée exclaims, "Aha! Monsieur Camille is asserting his *volonté d'homme!*" Although this does not mean, of course, that Camille gets his candy, it does mean that he is rarely punished for his fits of temper. If the Brées had a girl, they would probably not accept such displays from her with equal complacency. Girls are generally thought to have gentler natures and more natural self-control than boys. It is believed, for instance, that it is easier to toilet-train girls. Girls are also taught modesty sooner than boys.

As soon as a child is old enough to do chores, he is given tasks appropriate to his sex. Girls stay home with their mothers and learn to help with housework, while boys begin to accompany their fathers to work. This situation widens the difference in the ways that boys and girls are disciplined. Since most men's work is too heavy for small children, the boys have a good deal of freedom to play, with a minimum of supervision, while they are watching their fathers. Moreover, they are allowed to share men's amusements as well as men's work; their fathers will occasionally take them along to the café, for instance. At home, on the other hand, the mothers can generally find enough work to keep their daughters busy, and enough time to keep an eye on them.

The upbringing of children soon ceases to be exclusively a family affair. Between the ages of two and six, the major institutions of the village beyond the family — the church and the schools — enter the lives of all children in Chanzeaux. Through them, children are introduced to the community in which they live. For the most part, the church and the schools reinforce the lessons learned at home; in certain instances, however, they contradict them. In learning to maneuver among home, church, and school, children acquire most of their knowledge of the village's unwritten rules.

School

Almost all children, as we have seen, learn elementary facts about religion from their parents when they are very young. By the time they are ready to go to school, they have learned to say prayers and to recognize statues of Christ and the Virgin, and their families take them to Mass on Sundays. In the *classe des petits,* the children are taught to extend their experience with their own families to include the idea of the Holy Family; each morning they begin the day by kissing their hands in greeting to "maman Marie." They learn, too, that their divine parents expect the same things from them as their own parents, that they reward them the way their parents do, with love, and punish them somewhat more gently than their own parents, by withdrawal of love. These first lessons, which concentrate on the creative and loving aspect of God, attempt to impart to the children a sense of His presence in nature and in all familiar things.

At the age of four, children begin to learn to read, and by six they read rather well. The following year in the Catholic schools the boys and girls go into separate classes. The separation according to sex reinforces the division that the children have already learned from the way their parents behave and from the chores their parents assign them. By the age of seven at the latest, boys and girls no longer play together, except perhaps in their neighborhood at home. During the recess at school, the girls form small cliques, while the boys are encouraged to play in a large group and acquire a sense of comradeship with their whole class.

At some time between the ages of six and eight, when the curé, the child's parents, and the child himself agree that he is ready, his first communion is celebrated privately. "From that moment on," wrote Thérèse Brichet, describing her religious education, "I began to understand what God was, and afterwards I went to Mass and said my prayers voluntarily." Thérèse, who belongs to one of the most devout families in the commune, may have been more impressed by the experience than other children, but the community certainly shares her idea of the efficacy of the Sacrament in one's spiritual progress. With this ceremony, the first stage of religious education comes to an end, and the child is considered ready to receive more formal instruction.

When the boys' and girls' classes separate, schoolwork begins in earnest. Homework is given every day, and included in the assignments, along with French and arithmetic, are lessons in the catechism and biblical history. Often when a teacher gives a test on several subjects at once, he includes a few questions on the catechism along with those on elementary science and history. Here is one such potpourri for twelve-year-olds:

1. What is the great commandment by which Jesus Christ summed up the entire law of love? (2 points)
2. Around what date did the first automobile appear? (1 point)
3. What are the economic and social consequences of this invention? (2 points)
4. To what scientist do we owe the radio? (2 points)
5. Sketch the stomach of a cow. (4 points; 1 point for each of the four stomachs)

Since the catechism is considered a formal school discipline, albeit a rather special one, the stigma attached to a poor performance in this class is not much greater than that attached to poor work in any other subject. One can be a weak student in catechism and a very good Christian. But any sign of laziness or unwillingness to learn is reprehensible, and if a child has too much homework, he would generally be wise to neglect something other than the catechism lesson.

In each of the subjects that he studies, the Chanzeaux child is led by his teachers to discover how small pieces fit into the larger picture, and finally where he himself fits in. To illustrate: one day the *classe des petits* was grouped around Sister Maria discussing occupations. "What does your father do, Camille?" she asks of a four-year-old child. Camille is too shy and merely looks at the floor. Sister Maria turns to the rest of the children. "Can anyone tell me what Camille's father does as a job?" A number of hands wave, and the class gets very excited. She pauses before calling on anyone until they are all quiet again. Then, "Anita, can you tell me what Camille's father does?" "He owns a café." "Good," says Sister Maria, "and, Anita, what does your father do?" "He bakes bread." "Does he have to get up early in the morning?" asks Sister Maria. "Yes, he must get up at three o'clock every morning," replies Anita.

Sister Maria comments, "We should all be very thankful that our fathers take such good care of us, and we should pray to God to ask Him to bless them." Then she continues, "Does anyone know what a carpenter does?" Many hands wave, but she calls on one little boy who does not have his hand up. "Yves, what is a carpenter?" Yves, whose father is a carpenter, does not know and looks at his feet. The class becomes more excited, and hands wave in all directions. There are even a few jeers from some of the six-year-old boys. Sister Maria waits until they are all quiet and have stopped squirming. Then she says, "Can anyone tell me what a carpenter is? Jean?" "A carpenter is a man who makes things out of wood," states Jean definitely. The class applauds his answer. "Good," says Sister Maria. Then she motions the class to repeat with her in chorus: "What-is-a-carpenter? A-carpenter-is-a-man-who-makes-things-out-of-wood." Sister Maria asks, "Henri, what is a carpenter?" "A-carpenter-is-a-man-who-makes-things-out-of-wood." The whole class applauds Henri. Then Sister Maria asks, "Yves, what does your father do?" "A-carpenter-is-a-man-who-makes-things-out-of-wood," replies Yves, still looking at his feet. Sister Maria leads the class in applause for Yves, and a slow smile spreads across his face.

In question-and-answer sessions such as these, the children are never encouraged to ask questions after the final answer is given. For instance, when the ten-year-old boys are given an arithmetic problem to solve, even a fairly complicated one, they are taught that there is only one way of doing the problem, the way the teacher has done it. Even if a boy has arrived at the correct answer by another method, he would never think of raising his hand to ask if that method might be acceptable as well.

The way in which material is presented, like the material itself, is designed not only to make children think logically, but also to accept what is given. One of the most popular ways of teaching grammar, spelling, handwriting, and vocabulary is the *dictée*. The teacher writes a short passage on the board, reads it through with the children, explains the meaning of difficult words, and asks the children to come to the board to underline certain parts of speech or to point out difficult grammatical constructions. After that, the children copy the passage onto their slates; the teacher checks them for mistakes. Next, the children copy the passage into their notebooks, this time using an old-fashioned dip pen which must be managed with care to avoid blotting. The use of this pen is supposed to encourage careful script and neatness. Later in the day the teacher will again dictate the passage to the children for copying. They will receive a scolding from the teacher and ridicule from the class if they make more than one or two mistakes this time.

In the schools, the child must learn to accept verbal punishment from his teacher and ridicule from the rest of the class without showing shame or discomposure. Any sign of weakness only brings on more ridicule. He must learn to take his punishment in silence and with a moderately penitent look on his face. One of the teachers seems to enjoy driving a less intelligent pupil to tears when he cannot read or recite correctly. She taunts him and then encourages the rest of the class to laugh at him until he begins to cry; of course the class only laughs harder.

The social code that the child learns in school teaches him strict forms of politeness to his elders. Officially his elders are always right, and he is not encouraged to question or challenge them, just as he is not encouraged to question the material he learns in school. A child discovers that his position in the world is a lowly one and that, even if he is intelligent or gifted, he is not supposed to be aware of this fact — and by no means, of course, to talk about it. For example, a ceremony is held at the end of each year for the distribution of prizes; the ceremony is arranged so that each child receives a prize as part of a small group. Thus no child is either at the absolute top or bottom of his class. Jean-Gabriel Brée, a very good student, mentioned to his mother that he thought he was at the head of his class because his name was called off in the first group at the prize distribution. His mother assured him that he was mistaken. Later she explained that, if he had gone on believing this, he would have stopped working so hard. In school, Jean-Gabriel was rarely praised for his work, though it was excellent, and if his teacher found anything wrong, he was told he must work harder. At home, as in school, children are not rewarded for every mark of excellence; but they come to know that their parents are proud of them.

From the first day of school, children must learn the proper social behavior, which will be required of them for the rest of their lives. A four-year-old child attending class needs to be tamed. He will soon learn to accept sitting at his desk and playing or working quietly by himself for long periods of time. By the time he enters the boys' or girls' school and begins his regular lessons at the age of six or seven, he is ready to work seriously and to accept rigid discipline. Almost everything the children do in the *classe des petits* is done in a neat, orderly fashion. Twice each morning the children stand by their chairs until all is quiet, file silently into the adjoining room to get their wraps, line up again by the door, and when all are at attention file outside in baby-step fashion to the playground. They follow the Sister as she slowly and carefully places one black-shoed foot in front of the other, her hands held properly behind her back. They tiptoe across the playground in this manner and line up in front of the two outdoor privies. Then all fifty children wait as one by one they are allowed to use the facilities. As each child comes out, he or she goes to the end of the line, and the Sister allows the next one to enter. Only after all the children are finished are they allowed to break the line and run about in the sunshine.

Until 1939, the Catholic schools in Chanzeaux were supported by the chatelain, M. de Kerdouec, who also used his influence to strengthen the links between the church and right-wing politics. In

the forties, the responsibility for maintaining the Catholic schools devolved on the parish. The Chanzeaux school committee charged with
this function raises money by holding bazaars and fairs, such as the
annual kermesse, and by collections in church each month. The tuition charge of sixty cents a month per child also helps in a small way
to finance the schools. But most important for the financing of the
Catholic schools is de Gaulle's educational reform of 1959. According
to the *contract simple*, agreed to by the Chanzeaux school committee,
the Catholic schools must meet certain requirements, and in return the
government pays the teachers. The Catholic schools have thus improved their standards and are for the first time paying their teachers
decent salaries.

Until the fall of 1964 there were three schools in Chanzeaux: the
two Catholic schools and the public one. Since there were only six
children enrolled in the public school, however, and since the Catholic
schools had finally met the state requirements, the school inspector in
Angers decided to close the public school. When the six children arrived at school that September, they found no teacher. The government offered bus transportation to public schools in neighboring
towns, but all the parents decided instead to enroll their children in
Chanzeaux's Catholic schools.

For most families in Chanzeaux, there was never any question about
which school a child would attend. Even parents of the very poor
and very large families in the commune would try to avoid sending
their children to the public school — although the monthly tuition
for the Catholic schools could become a financial burden. In 1962
only seven couples in the commune sent their children to the public
school: these included the avowed communists and the only two families with illegitimate children. Even the public-school teacher was
an outsider in the community. She confided, "Just because I teach
in the public school doesn't mean I'm not a good Catholic." If you ask
parents about their preferences, you get a variety of answers. Some
say that the Catholic schools offer a better education. By this they
mean that the Catholic schools are more strict and give more homework than the public school. Or they say that the other children who
attend the public school are not suitable friends for their children.
The public-school children are considered dirty, ill-mannered, and
stupid. Most Chanzeans, moreover, claim that children should compete with others of their own age and class — which was impossible

in a school with so few pupils. Another compelling reason for attending the Catholic schools was that Chanzeans believe children should receive religious training as part of their education.

People claimed to feel no hostility toward the public school; however in fact they regarded it as an evil influence. "The Cordiers are not crazy but immoral," said Mme. Pinier of her neighbors, "and their children will turn out the same way. I've heard that the oldest boy (nine years old) is a thief, and you may be sure the little ones will be too before long. But what can you expect with parents like that and the education they've had!" Another equally poor family was considered more decent than the Cordiers because they at least sent their children to the Catholic school. Only one family that sent its children to the public school, the Lorseaus, escaped the stigma, and this was because of special circumstances. They were good Catholics, but they rented their farm from the heir of an old republican family in Saint-Lambert which has traditionally required that its fermiers send their children to the public schools. The irony of the situation was that the present owner of the land is quite religious, but could do nothing to invalidate the clause in the contract. The Lorseaus were the only farmers among the public-school parents; the rest were workers or farmhands, usually unemployed.

The insistence of the government on maintaining a public school in Chanzeaux until 1964 is attributed by some Chanzeans to the continued domination of public education by the radical-socialist party, which was believed to be secretly controlled by the freemasons. When the Brées were asked who the freemasons were, they replied that no one knew because they were a conspiracy. "People used to say that they had signed a pact with the devil," said Mme. Brée. "But since we don't believe in the devil any more, we really don't know what they are." As recently as five years ago, M. Clément was still teaching his boys' class that the people who control the public schools celebrated the Black Mass. Thus the continued presence of the public school in Chanzeaux kept alive old political and religious prejudices that had little relevance to the present. The public school was the only institution in the village representing the political left, and, since the distinguishing feature of the public school was its secularization, religion was seen as the basic issue dividing right and left.

Ideological divisions were also reflected in the content of subjects taught in Chanzeaux schools. In purely academic subjects such as

French and arithmetic, the public- and private-school children received equivalent training, since they must all take the same examinations for the Certificat des Etudes Primaires, the diploma a few good students receive at the end of their primary education. The two schools differed, however, in the teaching of religion and history. The public school, in two half-hour sessions per week, taught much the same material on social morality as the Catholic schools — but of course it was without religious applications. In the Catholic schools the religious training is intense, and, in addition to the hour of *morale* taught each week in the classroom, the children attend special classes on Wednesday morning for one and a quarter hours of catechism. Although these sessions are sometimes similar to the *morale* lessons, usually they have more religious content: explanations of holidays and religious terms, meanings of different parts of the Mass, and a few straight question-and-answer pairs from a catechism book.

The Catholic and the public school each taught quite different — even antagonistic — views of history. The children in the public school learned the political traditions of republican France; the private-school children learn the Catholic version of history, which is also the historical tradition of their village. The text used in the Catholic schools emphasizes the role of the church in French history, idealizes the Middle Ages, and is rather complacent about the existence of social inequalities. The public-school text ignores the church whenever it can, idealizes the Enlightenment, and stresses *égalité*. One of the few figures common to both textbooks is Joan of Arc (another is de Gaulle), but one would hardly recognize her as the same person from the two accounts. The public-school text glorifies her as a national heroine, while the Catholic text states quite matter-of-factly that the Archangel Michael appeared to her, entrusting her with the mission to save France, and goes on to describe her martyrdom and canonization. M. Gardais, one of the chairmen of the Catholic school committee, cites this particular difference as an example of the errors of public-school teaching.

Neither version of history admits the existence of the opposing tradition. The Catholic text never explains, for instance, why the republicans were anticlerical during the nineteenth century; and the public text never admits that they were. The following is the entire explanation that the Catholic text offers for a famous incident in the Revolution, the king's flight to Varennes: "The king, who was very pious, protested [against the law requiring the clergy to sign an oath of loyalty to the government]. He was prevented from hearing Mass from a priest of his choice. He decided to flee the country." [2] The public-school text, as one might expect, gives an entirely different interpretation of the same event. The civil constitution of the clergy is not mentioned, and the king's defection is explained as an act of treason: "The king was not willing to cease being the master of France, and to remain the first servant of his country. He conspired with foreign governments and decided to escape." [3]

Because of the part Chanzeaux played in the Vendée Rebellion, the history of that period has a special significance for the village. To determine whether the children now growing up in Chanzeaux make the connection between their own village traditions and politics today, we asked the teachers in the Catholic schools to assign a composition on the events in Chanzeaux during the Vendée war. From the essays it was clear that the children were familiar with the most colorful local incidents in the war and knew that they themselves were on the side of the "whites" (royalists); but it was equally obvious that very few children had a clear idea of who the "blues" (republicans) were or why they were enemies. The story was rarely put in the context of the Revolution, and the explanation commonly given for the war, when any explanation was offered at all, was that the people of Chanzeaux were fighting to save the faith. Most of the children gave the impression that once upon a time some wicked outsiders attacked the village for no particular reason. Twelve-year-old Chantal Bazantay wrote one of the most vivid accounts of the violent events:

One day a troop of men arrived in Chanzeaux. As they passed, they killed all the people they saw. Then they arrived at the Place de l'Eglise. Some people of Chanzeaux had taken refuge in the belltower in order to kill the enemies, and to protect themselves. The men shot at the enemies. The women and children loaded the guns. The enemies set fire to the Church and shot at those who had taken refuge in the tower.

The children cried, wailed, and called for their mothers.

The flames climbed up the tower, which crumbled gently. The skirts of the women burned like torches. Many died from burning; others were killed by bullets from enemy guns.

This war broke out because the Chanzeans wanted to obey only the King and not the other.

So the explicit connection children make between the myth of the Vendée Rebellion in Chanzeaux and present-day politics is, at best, tenuous. The children do learn that Chanzeaux has had enemies in the past, but they identify these enemies very vaguely as "the other" or the "blues," or occasionally as republicans. A similar vagueness exists in the definition that adults give of the present "enemies" of Chanzeaux: "We don't know who they are, but we used to believe that they were in league with the devil." In the course of a Chanzean's education, it seems, an ill-defined association is established between the traditional Vendée enemies and the outside forces considered inimical to religion today.

The only institution in the village that represented this alien tradition was the public school, the harbor for outsiders and nonconformists. Its presence in the community was felt as an intrusion, and its most important effects in Chanzeaux were to define the outcast group and to help preserve the right-wing political attachment of the overwhelming majority. We know little about the way public-school children in Chanzeaux felt, except that they quickly learned to expect to be treated as outcasts. At the other end of Chanzeaux's social scale there is another small group of families, the militants, whose children also receive a somewhat different education. These families place great emphasis on deep religious education with family participation; encourage more progressive pedagogical methods in the schools; and believe in sending their children on to secondary school. Although a small minority, they exercise an influence out of proportion to their numbers. The most important identifying characteristic of this group, we have seen, is religious practice: these parents go to church regularly and receive communion more often than the average Chanzean. Many were Jacistes when they were younger and are now active in community organizations.

Many militant parents feel a personal mission for carrying on the faith and try to transmit this sense of responsibility to their children. Jean-Pierre Gardais awed his two eldest daughters one evening when he told them, quite gravely, that the future of Christianity depended on them and on their generation. These parents are also likely to criticize most Chanzeans for negligence in the religious training of their children. "They think because they send their children to school with the *bonnes soeurs*, they've done their duty and everything will turn out all right," says Joseph Brée, "but the schools are helpless if the parents don't back up by example what is taught there." Thérèse Brichet described religious training in a militant family: "My religious education was in the catechism class, the same as for everyone who was with me in the Catholic school, and in my family; we talked about it every day and said our prayers together in the evening, while in certain families people talk very little or not at all about religion. Another thing which impressed me when I was a child was to see all the adults in the parish come and pray in church. Since my family went to all the religious ceremonies, I saw this often, while certain children are only rarely taken to church. All Christians, you know, are not at the same level."

Militants try to impress children with a sense of family solidarity in religious practice. Following a general trend in the Catholic Action movement, they are attempting to break down the stereotype of religion as the woman's domain. Couples in the militant group attend Mass together whenever possible and sit with their children, rather than splitting into the traditional men's and women's sections. (The old distinctions have not been entirely obliterated, however, and even this group considers it more scandalous for a woman not to attend Mass than for a man to commit the same offense.) The principles of progressive education have also gained a tentative foothold in the Catholic Action movement: the militants are apt to criticize traditional disciplinary measures in general because they believe these methods produce only passivity and deviousness in children. "With the new methods," says Mme. Brée, "what you lose in authority you gain back in trust. The children may not be so obedient, but they are incapable of telling lies." In recent years, progressive ideas have inspired several reforms in the teaching methods in the Catholic schools. Although the initiative for the current liberalization comes from higher up in the educational hierarchy, the new policies have been welcomed by the most influential members of the Chanzeaux school committee, who do their best to encourage them. One of the major reforms has been the change in the teaching of the catechism, first in the Catholic schools and now in the weekly catechism classes of the curé.[4] The object of the new methods is, again, to encourage the children to participate more actively in religious education.

To this end the church and the Catholic schools encourage parents to help children with their catechism at home, for as the priest says, "The parents have more influence on the religion of their children than the schools and the church combined." Each year all parents receive catechism handbooks corresponding to the workbooks their children use in school. These handbooks contain ideas on activities for parents and children and their friends. But bridging the gap between home and school has proved very difficult even in Chanzeaux. Mothers say that they are too busy to take on the extra responsibility. Moreover, the idea of inviting neighboring children into the house is almost unheard of; only children of close relatives play or eat in each other's houses. Besides the handbooks, an instruction sheet is mimeographed by the curé every week for mothers who may be interested in going over the lesson with their children, but only a few militant families have adopted this practice.

Because the militants stress the importance of personal religious commitment as opposed to outward conformity, they are often less harsh in their judgment of Chanzeaux's lower class, the nonchurchgoers. "You can't judge bad faith by the exterior," says Thérèse Brichet's younger sister Odile. "Many people who do go to church are no more religious than those who don't." Certain militant families have special contacts with certain outcast families. The Brichets, for instance, employ Mme. Cordier and Mme. Gaignard as extra hands at harvest time. Relations between the women are cordial and familiar, and the Gaignard children have been known to spend an afternoon at the Brichets'. Militants make an effort to impart a tolerant attitude to their children. "Many parents call their children away and never let them play with *those* children," says Mme. Brée, "but we teach our boys that those children are the same as anybody else, except for being unfortunate." This charitable attitude is limited, however; no parent would allow a close friendship to develop between his child and one of "those children." "They would pick up bad habits," explains Mme. Brée.

The militants are also distinguished from other parents by their attitude toward higher education. All Chanzeans respect learning abstractly, but most parents, especially on the farms, feel it is something entirely out of their reach. Few parents send children to school past the age of fourteen: education is not generally considered an investment as valuable as machinery, livestock, or land.

The prevalence of the militant leadership in education and other community activities has reinforced the social importance of the school in the community. Like the family and the church, the school is expected to train children to respect authority, to follow the rules, and to live in a community where the strongest ties are kinship and religion. But at the age of fourteen children leave the Chanzeaux school and their formal religious training ends. The question is whether these traditional means of early socialization are enough to maintain the Chanzeaux child's respect for the authority of family and religion, through adolescence into adulthood.

16

Adolescence

"Dear parents: Your daughter is fourteen years old; she is leaving school; she is no longer a child; she is entering her life as a young woman. To help her make this passage, we are organizing a day of work orientation for all the girls of her age." This is from a letter that parents in Chanzeaux received from the Jeunesse Agricole Chrétienne informing them that the community was about to hold a *rite de passage*. As indicated, the age of fourteen is a turning point: school has ended, childhood is over, and family and church are ready to help prepare young people for a career and marriage.

At fourteen children must either begin work or enter secondary school. In 1963 there were seventeen boys and ten girls — about 13 percent — of Chanzeaux's adolescent population in secondary schools. Six were commuting daily to *cours complémentaires* at the parochial school in Chemillé, and the rest were living away from home attending *collèges* and technical schools. The complementary courses offer a four-year program after which a student can transfer to a lycée or college. The colleges, official equivalents of the lycées, have a six-year program leading to the baccalaureate. Most of the children who go away to school plan to get their "bacs," and about half of them intend to become teachers. If they live up to their ambitions, they will probably not return to live in Chanzeaux.

The families who send children to secondary school have distinctive characteristics of residence, occupation, and religious practice. Of the twenty-four families with children in secondary school, half live in the bourg, a quarter on isolated farms, and the rest in the villages and hamlets. The high percentage of bourg children in secondary schools is striking: 50 percent of the bourg families who have children of secondary-school age are sending at least one of them away to school, while only 8 percent of the country families who might send a child away to school do so. About half the parents of secondary-school children are nonfarmers, and many of the rest are particularly prosperous farmers like the Brichets and the Bourdelles. On the average, the parents who send children to secondary school have lived in Chanzeaux longer than most families, have more relatives, and are more active in religious organizations.

These students, then, are children of an elite in Chanzeaux, and during adolescence they form their own elite. Every Sunday a small group of teenage boys and girls sits together near the front of the church, following the service attentively. There is little whispering among them and no flirting. The group is depleted in the winter, for it is made up mainly of the secondary-school students who return to their families during the summer. They are not likely to remain in the village, but those of their brothers and sisters who stay will inherit through them a secure position in the community and close family contacts with the educated outside world. They will be the next elite of Chanzeaux.

The majority of fourteen-year-olds — those who do not continue school — begin a career, which is generally determined by their parents' occupation, place of residence, and social standing. For example, there are 17 artisans working in Chanzeaux, discounting those who are retired or unemployed; 16 of their sons became artisans. Similarly, 97 out of 111 sons of farmers became farmers. Many families carry on traditional occupations: the church sexton Devanne is training his son to take his place, just as Devannes have trained their sons since the Vendée war. The bicycle repairman's family traditionally produces teachers — 8 are now teaching and another is on the way. Even the few boys and girls who continue their education have, by the time they are fourteen, a definite career in mind, such as teaching or engineering. Their secondary education is called "la formation": its purpose is not to open opportunities for choosing a vocation, but to train them toward objectives already set up by their parents.

Most of the adolescent girls in Chanzeaux are needed by their parents to work in the home, shop, or farm. Opportunities for other jobs are extremely limited within Chanzeaux. There is the basket factory, but only 15 Chanzeaux girls work there. Some girls have found jobs outside the commune: 19 of them have jobs in factories, 18 work as domestics, 6 work in trades, and 13 in such professions as nursing, teaching, or secretarial work. Most of these jobs outside of Chanzeaux are part-time and the girls live at home. Still, the girls appreciate their relative freedom from their families and the opportunity to make new acquaintances in another commune. For the same reasons, most parents are wary of letting girls work outside; they are afraid that family ties will be weakened and that their daughters will be influenced by people whom the parents do not know.

The necessity of beginning work at the age of fourteen may alleviate the adolescent's problem of what to do next, but it produces other frustrations. As one young Chanzeaux girl said, "Work is imposed by parents; perhaps one girl in Chanzeaux is content with her work." The girls who are students, teachers, or officeworkers outside Chanzeaux are satisfied to remain in these positions. But according to a JAC survey of adolescents in the Maine-et-Loire in 1956, at least one fourth of the girls working on farms wanted to change occupations. They consider farm work difficult, masculine, and unexciting. Dissatisfied farm girls have several ways out: they can train for other vocations, they can marry a nonfarmer, or they can dream. The first two possibilities are rarely realized; the third is the general rule. Thérèse Brichet (an exception) began preparing to be an *aide-familiale* at twenty, when her brothers and sisters had grown old enough not to need her care. After five months of intensive training in hygiene, cooking, and sewing, she was authorized to help families where parents were sick, old, or absent. Another Chanzeaux girl told why she trained to be an aide: "I was twenty-two years old, my parents were farmers, and I didn't want to stay in the occupation of my parents. I wanted a feminine occupation which at the same time would serve a rural milieu."

But very few farm girls are able to find rural jobs other than farming, and very few are trained for any jobs at all in larger towns. Nor are these girls, as we will see later, likely to marry men who do not work on farms. Most just think about work that they will probably never do. We distributed a questionnaire in 1963 asking Chanzeaux girls to rank the occupations they preferred and those they were planning to begin. Their responses showed a striking difference between aspirations and prospects. Some wanted jobs in factories, where they would be free from their families and would meet outsiders, but there are few factory jobs in or near Chanzeaux and many parents will not allow them to fill them. Others would like to become secretaries or teachers, but both jobs require training they neither have nor anticipate. Furthermore, there are only one or two places in Chanzeaux for teachers and none for secretaries. If these girls should get the training, they would have to leave the commune. One of the girls we talked to, Yvette Bourdelle, has worked on her parents' farm since she was fourteen. She hopes to become a secretary or a teacher someday, though she has no training, and she would like to live in the city as the wife of a businessman. How does a girl like Yvette develop such aspirations? For one thing, she has the example of her own family: her father came to Chanzeaux as a hired agricultural worker and is now a prosperous farmer who serves on the town council; and her older sister married an artisan and left the farm. Because friends and relatives of farm girls have married and left their farms, adolescent girls feel that they need not confine their dreams to rural Chanzeaux.

Although the boys have less desire to leave the farm, they too are uncertain about their futures. According to a recent survey of Maine-et-Loire adolescents, 40 percent of the boys who work on farms in the Chanzeaux region think they may have to leave. Adolescents who were born during the population boom of the 1940s and 1950s are beginning to feel the pressure of a rural economy that cannot support them. Between 1954 and 1961 thirty boys from Chanzeaux left their farms to look for land in other communes or to work in factories; only two boys came into Chanzeaux from outside to find work on farms. At first most adolescent boys regret having to leave; but once they have gone, they do not want to return. Other farm boys who have been exposed to the outside world, through military service or motor-scooter trips, look forward to moving away.

A small percentage of young people from farming families go away to school, but most farmers are unwilling or financially unable to send their children away. To them the land represents security. Some farmers say, if their children do not succeed in the city, who knows what will happen to them? They would never return to the farm. M. Lacroix, whose family has had a vineyard for generations, asks himself why he should go on keeping vines when his sons will not take over after him; regretfully he admits that only two of them were able to stay on his farm — one became a doctor and the other a lawyer. This mild defeatism in the face of the possibility of having to leave the farm has immobilized rural adolescents: a fifth of the farm boys who think they will change occupations say they would like to become agricultural technicians; yet they do not take agricultural training courses because they are uncertain about remaining in a rural area. Boys from the bourg have a similar occupational problem. There are so few jobs in the bourg that only one or two members of a family can stay; the rest work in neighboring communes or are sent away to school. Like the farm adolescents, they are not always satisfied with the work their parents have determined for them. For instance, Emile Bertrand was able to remain in the bourg, but his father pays him such a small salary that he wants to find work in a city. And Gabriel Labarre, who was sent to business school in Paris, wants to come back and become a veterinary. Both boys are dissatisfied with their work, but neither will disobey his parents.

Since occupational opportunities for Chanzeaux adolescents are limited, those who are dissatisfied with the jobs they have or those who have to leave the jobs they like may have no alternative but to live with their discontent. Fortunately, by the time they are adolescents they have learned to tolerate dissatisfaction. As children, they were mindful of their own limitations; not expecting too much of themselves, they were less easily disappointed. They have also learned to accept their parents' right to make demands on them: thus, they work at the job their parents have chosen, and many of them turn their salaries over to their families.

Like an adolescent's choice of occupation, the choice of a marriage partner also depends on the parents' preferences, occupation, residence, and social standing. And, like adolescents' attitudes toward careers, aspirations and prospects do not always coincide. A girl can expect to marry a boy from the same occupational group as her father. For example, 77 percent of the girls from farming families who married between 1958 and 1960 married farmers; and 80 percent of the girls from nonfarming families married nonfarmers. But even farm girls say that a farmer would be their last choice as a future husband. Most would be very pleased to marry an officeworker, a teacher, or a professional. In actuality, only one Chanzeaux girl in the last few years has married a teacher, and even she followed her family pattern, for she had eight teachers among her relatives. There are exceptions to the relation between occupation and marriage, but they also have their rationale: two Cottenceau girls, both teachers, married farmers — but their husbands were among the wealthiest, most progressive farmers in the commune. One son of M. Courcault married the daughter of a Chanzeaux artisan who was not wealthy, but he was a member of the religious and political elite of the bourg; another son married a girl who worked in his factory, but her family was prosperous and highly respected and she happened to be the prettiest girl in town.

Marriage choice is also circumscribed by the parents' place of residence. A girl from a bourg family can expect to marry a boy from the bourg of Chanzeaux or another commune. A girl from a farming family is likely to marry a country boy (see Tables 27 and 28, Chapter 7). Yet none of the Chanzeaux country girls who were questioned wanted to marry a farmer; in fact, most of them thought of farmers as the least preferable marriage partners. The marriage aspirations of country boys are more within the range of possibility: few farm boys in the past have married bourg girls, and few in the present want to. They know that a girl not brought up on a farm will not be able to do the work. Girls can afford to pin their marriage hopes high for several reasons. They have friends or relatives who have married Chanzeaux boys and left the farm, and a large number of girls have married men from other communes: 27 of the 47 women who were married between 1954 and 1962 married men from other communes and moved away; only two women brought their husbands back to Chanzeaux. Most of the women who leave upon marriage go to communes of approximately the same size as Chanzeaux, or in the same region; thus marriage does not necessarily mean an improvement of position. But adolescent girls can always envision a change of environment as an improvement. In marriage and career aspirations, adolescent girls have plenty of room to dream, and this allows them to accept the present and the probable. They take no steps toward aspirations they know to be unrealistic.

A group of adolescents at a meeting sponsored by the Jacistes in Le Champ sur Layon spoke of marriage in this way:

Jeanne: We want a husband who is on the lookout for change, not the routine professional who truly would be satisfied with what satisfied our parents — a worker, but also a seeker.

Annette: And we wouldn't refuse to help with outdoor work, but, as a general rule, women aren't made for it. There are girls married to farmers who would have preferred to marry factory workers.

Henri: Those are girls who have too much ambition.

Bernard: Or they just aren't happy in the country.

Annette: But a girl who doesn't marry you because you work on the land — well, I think you haven't lost much.

Henri: Once a boy is married, if he has difficulty living in the country, his wife will push him to work in the city; he doesn't really want to go to the city, but it's she who pushes him.

Annette: He shouldn't change his occupation because of his wife. You see teachers and family aides and such married to boys who work on farms.

Jeanne: Well, it's the parents more than the girl who look at the boy's position.

Parents are indeed concerned with a young man's situation. The way that boys and girls meet reinforces the influence of their families on choice of husband or wife. Adolescents form cliques according to the part of the commune in which they live. In church young people from the bourg, who are considered the most religious, sit together at the front, and people from the hamlets sit at the back. After Mass these groups stay together to talk in the main square or to sit in the café. Boys and girls also get together at weddings, where kinship and residence determine the attendance; country people are rarely invited to bourg weddings — one exception was the case of the baker, who invited his best country customers to his daughter's wedding. The purpose of a wedding is to get as many people married as possible; the unmarried boys and girls — often relatives of the bride or groom — are paired off by the parents to spend the day together. They march to the mayor's office and then to the café. In the evening these couples dance together and then go from house to house looking for the newlyweds; when the young people find the couple, they offer them a gift with a Gallic touch of scatology — a chamberpot of white wine with bits of chocolate floating in it.

After a boy and girl have met, at weddings, dances, work, or school, they are expected to get to know each other for at least a year before becoming engaged. Most adolescent girls think that they should be married by the age of twenty or twenty-one, and that boys should marry between twenty-three and twenty-six. However, in the past few years, the average marriage age for girls has been twenty-four. This means that, between the time girls consider themselves ready for marriage and the time they actually are married, they have to live through a period of waiting. By helping their mothers in the house and taking care of the younger children, they have been preparing for marriage for years; but boys at this age are hard at work or are away in the army. One Chanzeaux girl rationalized this difficult period: "When one is younger, one would like to get married from the age of fifteen, but when one gets older, one sees that marriage cannot be taken lightly, that it takes all one's lucidity to found a *foyer*. That's why I think now: the older one is, the more sensible one is."

Adolescents consider marriage a very serious obligation, which must be approached with maturity and foresight. They have been trained to harbor as few illusions about human nature as possible. As one Chanzeaux husband said, "On s'aime tels qu'on est, quoi" (We love each other as we are). Adolescents consider maturity particularly important since they expect to be independent of their parents after marriage — though they realize that in a small agricultural community one marries not only a person but a whole family. Some young couples try to move to a different community after marriage. In families that have to share a farmhouse, young couples are beginning to build partitions in order to have, as one young husband put it, "un petit bonheur à deux."

Adolescent girls think that the marriage decision should be left up to them, though they agree that a career decision should be left to their parents. They report that parents sometimes object outright to marriages for such reasons as: "the young man is not of the same social rank," "the girl's family has a bad reputation," "the young man is not very serious," or "the mother had another girl in mind for her son."

Parents regulate the social relations between boys and girls throughout adolescence until marriage. Girls are not allowed to go out alone with boys until they are eighteen — and in more conservative families not until twenty-one. Younger girls are allowed to stay at dances only until 9:30, and many are not permitted to go to dances where there will be older boys from other communes. These rules help parents to control their daughters' marriage choices; they are also characteristic of the parental attitude that adolescent girls are not prepared for independence, that without rules or chaperonage they are bound to get into trouble. But the very rigidity of the rules tends to encourage cheating. Even the schoolteacher confides that, though her girls are very obedient, they are basically deceitful. Knowing how to take advantage of "Système D" — the ability to get around regulations — Chanzeaux adolescents are better able to accept what American adolescents often dispute: both the strictness of rules and the principle that parents have the right to make them.

The importance of maintaining a good reputation provides the strongest reason for adolescents to obey social regulations, for their personal standing, their eligibility for marriage and work, and even their family honor depend upon reputation. In public they are careful to be discreet; for instance, when a girl passes a boy on the street, she looks down, except from the corner of her eye. Girls say that, if people saw them flirting in the street, what would they imagine them doing in private? Public displays of affection are limited to horseplay between older girls and younger boys. Since the older boys spend their time with each other or are away in the army, the older girls often play with the younger boys, under the guise of sisterliness. Parents claim that there are no premarital sexual relations among the older adolescents they know; but bourg people have the idea that things are going on in the country, and country people have much the same idea about the bourg. It is difficult to know exactly what does go on among adolescents, for they are reluctant to talk about themselves. But what they say about others is revealing. In a conversation about adolescence, two girls from Catholic militant families avowed that there were girls in Chanzeaux who are free about sex, implying at the same time that well-brought-up girls are not. Sexual behavior, like education, residence, and occupation, provides a way for those who consider themselves the elite to distinguish themselves from the rest. Respectable girls are kept constantly under the surveillance of their respectable parents; furthermore, Chanzeaux is too small to hide anything, and gossip is too destructive to a girl's reputation. This is not to say that nothing ever happens in Chanzeaux: there are cases of sexual relations between unmarried couples and more frequently between engaged couples. But sex is generally kept at a safe distance, outside the commune. Boys disappear into other towns or cities, or they take advantage of their years in the military service. Within the borders of the commune, they are careful to behave well. Couples who want to be alone together arrange to meet in larger towns or out in the country somewhere.

Another control on the relations between boys and girls is the fact that most of the time adolescents associate with their own sex. Groups of girls or boys, who live in the same part of town or work in the same place or are relatives, go everywhere together; on Sundays the girls gather in the square or by the river where the boys, miraculously, have also assembled. They go in separate groups to the movies, and a boy does not usually pay for a girl until they are engaged. At dances girls all sit on one side of the room and often dance with each other.

One of the strongest ties among adolescent boys is their *classe* affiliation. Class is determined by year of birth. Every year all the classes with the same last number (1923, 1933, 1943) hold a celebration. The class group becomes particularly important in the year before induction into military service. During this year adult norms are reversed: boys are expected to get drunk, to visit different girls every weekend, to let go. Every Sunday the class of nineteen-year-old conscripts is entertained by the family of a different girl of their age: the fathers give them wine — they have been known to drink more than a bottle apiece — and the girls make them pouches and tassels. At the end of the year, the conscripts pass a baton to the next class group as a signal for them to begin their year of letting go. Whereas girls are expected to be obedient and moderate (unless they are left alone), boys, it is recognized, will not always be good and the community gives them a time to be bad. Even the year of celebration, which is supposed to compensate them for the end of youth and the beginning of the army, is a sanctioned tradition so that, far from rebelling, the boys are still doing what is expected of them; they are having a good time within the rules, not in defiance of them.

"After all," said one Chanzeaux girl, "one has to have fun when one is young. So many adults seem to claim that. And I think the majority of girls have a horror of boys who aren't done with it during their youth." A Chanzeaux boy added, "You should have a good time up to a certain point, but not too much or you will risk harm to your reputation." Aside from the times when adolescents are encouraged to celebrate, they are expected to be serious; their reputations depend on it. To adolescents in Chanzeaux, being serious means two things: knowing what you want, and behaving in the right way at the right time — particularly in respect to love and work. There is a current Parisian song that says of love: "C'est pas sérieux, mon amour, mais c'est bon, mais c'est bon." Chanzeaux girls expect themselves not to believe this. They are critical (but also envious) of girls working outside the commune who are free to go out with a number of boys. In work also, it is so important to know where one is going that the custom is to decide on a career at the age of fourteen. And in their personal lives adolescents are expected to know what kind of people they should be.

The ideal qualities a woman should possess are clearly defined by parents, school, and religious groups so that girls may develop these qualities during adolescence. The whole educational system, which separates girls and boys at the earliest age, is designed to make girls aware of what women should be. Even a geography book contains such lessons as: "Little girls, patient, charitable, humble, and sweet; never lose your modesty and piety." One recent JAC meeting was devoted to a discussion of the most important qualities of women. The girls emphasized simplicity and sensitivity. When the priest criticized the "femme égoïste," the girls agreed that "a woman who does not receive will still give anyway." Girls do not have to make guesses about the feminine ideal, which Joachim du Bellay called in another context, "la douceur angevine." Fortunately, they can forgive themselves for falling short, having been trained since childhood that ideals are faultless but people are not.

Whether or not adolescents live up to the defined ideals, they are at least expected to behave appropriately for their age. The younger adolescents, from fourteen to eighteen years old, are kept under the surveillance of their parents. They are not allowed to have their own money and are expected to associate only with children of the same sex. Once, when boys and girls of this age were together without parental supervision to plan a folk dance for the kermesse, the necessity of dancing together caused an uproar. Boys did cartwheels, girls smoked, and the session ended in chaos. Nonetheless, adolescents of this age know what is expected of them. When a fifteen-year-old was asked what he thought of de Gaulle, he answered without hesitation, "I'm too young to be interested in politics yet."

The eighteen- and nineteen-year-olds are more independent of their parents and more interested in each other: boys have their year as conscripts, and girls are permitted to go out unchaperoned. At the age of twenty, adolescents experience their first abrupt change since the end of primary school: the boys go off for some sixteen months of military service (the term of service varies considerably), and the girls are left home alone. During this period some girls get jobs outside Chanzeaux and meet boys from other communes. When Chanzeaux boys return from the army, they lead a different life from that of younger adolescents. Although some go back to their former jobs, and the *classe* still goes to dances or the café together, many things have changed. They have what one adolescent called "the liberty after the army." They get new jobs, keep their own salaries, and spend their money on trips to dances and cafés in neighboring communes;

others leave Chanzeaux to find jobs or wives. It is only after military service that the "liberated" think about settling down.

Aside from a sharp break for military service, the path between childhood and adulthood is relatively continuous. The behavior of an adolescent is supposed to show that he has learned well such childhood lessons as obedience to parents and respect for rules; he is to continue believing that parents know what is best for him. In the United States a period of grace between childhood and adulthood is tolerated, if not encouraged, so that the adolescent can "find himself" or "find a direction." In Chanzeaux the adolescent is given a clear idea of what is expected of him: but if he does not live up to expectations, he need not be too upset; after all, someone else set up the standards. Because the expectations for adolescents are more clearly defined in Chanzeaux, one should not infer that adolescence is an easier period there than in America. Even parental decisions about occupations and social life do not necessarily minimize anxiety. Still, the community places little positive value on struggles and insecurity in this stage of life. American adolescents are supposed to act independently and to take the consequences if they become "lost"; if French adolescents are also lost, they are not supposed to show it.

The years between primary school and marriage, then, are not a time for breaking traditions, but for turning childhood lessons into adult habits. For one thing, the habit of association with people of the same sex is carried on without interruption from childhood to old age. Both in family and in school, boys and girls are separated from an early age. In adolescence this separation is reinforced by cliques and *classe* groups, rules that limit dating, and clear definitions of feminine and masculine qualities. Girls begin imitating their mothers as soon as they finish primary school: they clean the house and take care of younger children; when a guest comes, they act as hostesses. Like their mothers, for whom the family comes first, adolescent girls usually do not take their careers seriously; and like their mothers, they are usually devout Catholics and uninterested in politics. Adolescent boys begin taking on the habits of the men of Chanzeaux: they play cards and drink wine at the café, sit in the backroom of the café after Mass, and keep themselves from being tied too strongly to the home. This pattern of associating with one's own sex, so important in childhood and adolescence, continues through adulthood. Married men spend their leisure hours with each other; married women work together, spend Sundays gossiping in each others' houses and shops, and even dance together when they attend a dance.

Religious practices also persist into adulthood. Girls are expected to be very religious as children, and not to swerve from religious devotion throughout life. And in fact women make up 83 percent of Chanzeaux adults who are considered devout. The only change in the religious practice of a girl at adolescence is that she is likely to sit with a group of girl friends midway back in the church, instead of with her mother. It is tacitly understood that this arrangement allows her a bit of leeway for whispering and flirting, and a well-brought-up girl who is never seen speaking with boys in public knows how to speak with her eyes during Mass. As the boys reach adolescence, they drift toward the back of the church to sit (or stand, arms crossed) with their fathers, leaving their mothers with their younger brothers and sisters. (The preference of the few militant households for families to sit together at church is still an exception.) The big break comes at the formally recognized turning point, age fourteen. After this age, boys attend Mass in a group, and occasionally three or four may sneak off to the back room of the café during Mass. The religious behavior of adolescent boys runs contrary to what they were taught as children in church and school, but is in conformity with the example set by the adult men of Chanzeaux. At the point in adolescence where church and community pressures come into conflict, the community, in most cases, wins hands down. The authority of the church, which children first experience primarily through women, comes to be identified with women, and the model of religious behavior held up in the catechism becomes primarily a feminine model; thus a man who is overly devout may be considered effeminate. In order to escape resentment and ridicule, boys have to learn to steer a middle course between the "official" norms of Chanzeaux, those that have religious sanction and are taught early in childhood but are not followed in practice by the majority of the people, and the purely social norms, which are taught informally but strictly observed. Traditional preferences, such as church attendance, are passed on by young adults to their own children because they are taught in pure form by family, school, and church. Since lapses in practice are tolerated, the values themselves remain in unchallenged form for teaching to the next generation.

Because growing up in Chanzeaux is considered part of a continuous process of training in the habits of the older generation, adolescence tends to perpetuate traditional values. There are other reasons for this: for one thing, the family continues to exert a strong influence. It circumscribes adolescents' occupational and marriage choices, regulates their social relations, and persuades them of the importance of kinship ties — a traditional value, par excellence — for the individual and for the life of the community. Chanzeaux adolescents strongly feel this emphasis on the importance of family. Some were asked to fill out a questionnaire in 1962 in which they were to list their major concerns: the majority of respondents indicated that their relations with their parents concerned them more than their relations with their friends or the opposite sex. One reason for the preoccupation with parents is that the force of parental influence over occupations and social regulations produces frustrations, and many adolescents are dissatisfied or uncertain of their futures.

We have seen that adolescent restlessness and discontent with life and work in Chanzeaux is not particularly disruptive for the community. Instead of worrying about making what they have into what they want, adolescents tend to transform discontent into dreams that they know are unlikely to be fulfilled, such as the desire of girls from farming families to marry nonfarmers. Or they count on leaving Chanzeaux to fulfill their aspirations. Thus Chanzeaux as a community benefits little from the potentially constructive force of adolescents' desire for change.

What adolescents are taught explicitly and implicitly by Chanzeaux adults trains them for life in Chanzeaux as it was led by the older generation. But there is a pull on them from another direction that counteracts this training: emigration. Boys from farming families are forced to leave the commune under economic pressure; bourg boys leave to find positions that are not available in the Chanzeaux bourg. Bourg and country girls leave to marry. Other adolescents leave for education and find that they cannot return to a commune with no place for them. Leaving Chanzeaux is probably less upsetting to adolescents themselves than to their parents. In the 1956 election, Poujade and other candidates for the Chanzeaux region were able to use the theme of adolescent emigration to get parents' votes: they told of the plight of the small artisan who works all his life so that his children can be educated; then his children leave for the city and never return. But adolescents know that they can find more opportunities outside Chanzeaux. Nor do they have to fear that they will be isolated in a new community; they have before them the example of Chanzeaux, where some of the adults at the center of political and religious activity were born in other communes and moved to Chanzeaux. Girls make the transition to new communities with a minimum of disruption: they have rarely participated in Chanzeaux political or communal activity, and, like the adolescent boys, they have no particular loyalty to Chanzeaux. Their world is their *foyer*, which they are prepared to establish in any community. Even adolescents who are reluctant to leave, but are forced to for economic reasons, can look forward to getting away from the constrictions of Chanzeaux. As Christine Cady put it, those who are ready to leave have at least the illusion of liberty elsewhere.

The problem for Chanzeaux is that the most talented and ambitious young people have left or will leave. Today there are only three native Chanzeaux adults with secondary education who are still living in the commune. Thirty Chanzeans have recently completed a secondary education, and all have moved away. Girls and boys who leave Chanzeaux move up in the social and occupational scale: for instance, over 40 percent of sons of farmers who emigrated did not become farmers, while only 13 percent of sons of farmers who remained in Chanzeaux left their farms (see Tables 36 and 37, Chapter 8). Stories of improvements of emigrants, and offers of jobs by members of the family who have already left, appeal to Chanzeaux adolescents. The necessity or possibility of emigration means that those with talent and those who seek to improve themselves will probably do so outside Chanzeaux. The community is left with those adolescents who are least committed to change.

The character of adolescence in Chanzeaux tends to keep the community as it was before: childhood lessons are absorbed and adult habits imitated; the family continues to dominate the adolescent's life; those who desire change either accept the impracticability of their aspirations or leave the community. Yet Chanzeaux is changing, and the question is whether young people will grow up to lead lives like their parents' — the lives for which their adolescence was supposed to prepare them.

There are many indications that they will not. Jean Mercier is a farmer who has too many sons to allow them all to stay on the farm. Mme. Devanne was born in the bourg and married an artisan from the bourg; her daughter may well marry someone she meets at school and live in Angers or Paris. Eugène Bourdelle said of his twelve-year-old son: "If he does not know soon what he wants to do with his future, I'll decide for him." But, according to the new education law, his son will not finish school at fourteen but at sixteen. Bourdelle will find it more difficult to make the decisions for an older, better-educated adolescent. Brigitte Renou was considered adventurous for working and living outside of Chanzeaux before she was married. Her younger sister may not give a second thought to living at home or working for her family. The most energetic of the Chanzeaux adolescents cannot and do not want to stay in Chanzeaux; through school, work, and marriage, they are finding ways out. Chanzeaux adolescents have been trained for tradition and exposed to change. The consequence should not be considered disastrous, however. When they are parents, they will train their children according to what they have learned from both sides of their experience.

17

Old Age

As you drive into the bourg by the chateau road, you will see that
the streets are not deserted, but it is mostly old people who are there.
If you should look carefully from your car window, you could even
see huddled figures peering cautiously from doors and windows. In
the first house on the left live the Monnier grandparents, and on the
other side of the alley running straight up the hill to the Renou
grocery store is the tiny wool shop of Mlle. Macé: she sits, seemingly
all day, in the dark interior, knitting. Opposite the entrance of the
road to Chanoiseau, still on the left as you drive into the bourg, old
Mme. Michaud may be taking the sun in her wheelchair, with two or
three dark-veiled nuns hovering over her. Her neighbor Rémy
Bonnerot is sure to be there; though all you may see of him is the
white shock of hair bent closely over the worktable of his harness
shop, his quick, curious glance registering your arrival. The Bonnerot
house is almost on the square, and now you must watch for pedestri-
ans, like old Mme. Forget sweeping the streets with a straw broom as
tall as she is, or her husband, the retired tailor, shuffling up the road
to help his son, the present tailor. Few of these people will fail to note
your arrival, and you will remark that all these people are very old.

In fact, your first impression of the bourg is a true one, for almost
one out of every four inhabitants in the bourg is an old person.[1] Some
of these old people have retired from their farms, like the Monnier
grandparents or Mme. Coulon, who retired to the bourg with her
husband when their oldest son replaced them on their farm. Others
are retired civil servants, like M. Guérin, who used to be one of the
two postmen. But most of the aged people in the bourg are artisans
or storekeepers who have lived there most of their lives. Until 1957,
M. Forget was the tailor in Chanzeaux; then, at the age of seventy-
two, he moved fifty feet down the street and allowed his son to take
over from him. M. Bonnerot across the street has no one to replace
him; when he dies there will no longer be a leather-working shop in

Chanzeaux. And among the aged in the bourg there is a special category of old spinsters, like Mlle. Macé, who run specialized small shops.

The bourg, however, is not typical of the commune as a whole. While the bourg represents only one quarter of the total population of the commune, more than one out of every three inhabitants over sixty lives there. Only the village of Espérance on the national highway has an equally high concentration of old people. Farmers from the western area of the commune retire to Espérance to live beside older artisans who have been there most of their lives.

Distribution of the aged follows roughly the economic status of the different areas in the commune. There are fewer old people on the isolated farms because some, like the Coulons and the Monniers, retire to a larger community. Wine villages also have fewer old people, or rather fewer old men, than is average for the commune. Although one suspects that wine consumption is a factor in the higher deathrate of men, some of the vintners, like Henri Joubert of La Jutière (who at fifty-eight is not dead yet, although he says that his back is so bad he finds working very painful), claim they work harder than either the people of the bourg or the other farmers. Whether this is true or not, hamlets and especially cow villages have almost twice the proportion of old people as the wine villages.

Although old women outnumber old men in the commune as a whole, nowhere is the proportion so dramatic as in the wine villages, where the women over sixty outnumber the men by almost three to one. Only in the hamlets do old men outnumber old women, and the difference there is only slight. The proportion in the bourg is similar to that of the commune as a whole — about four women to three men — but the old women stand out because they are much more active in everyday social activities. The daily round offers unending excuses for gossip — the weekday seven o'clock Mass, lugging water from the town spigots on the church square, buying vegetables or fruit from the traveling merchants. The roly-poly, black-clad figure of grandmother Oliveau crossing the square in the early morning mist after Mass, chirping cheerfully with another widow, is a typical sight on a weekday morning all year around. Widows make up a great part of bourg society. A bride of fifty years ago was likely to be a widow for an average of at least eight years, for she usually married a man four years older than herself and then exceeded his lifespan by four years.[2] Widowers have no such social grouping, and when the older men do gather socially, they sit together in the dark, low-ceilinged room of the Société de la Rue Bourgeoise.

Whether seated at the tables of the Société or by the fireplaces on the farms, the aged give one the impression of a bedrock of stability in Chanzeaux. Yet the older inhabitants of Chanzeaux are much less likely to have been born in the commune than the generation twenty to forty years younger. A rough comparison shows that less than half of the present inhabitants over sixty were born in Chanzeaux, whereas more than half of those between twenty and sixty were born there. For men this tendency is even more exaggerated. Part of this may be the result of an unusual influx of agricultural workers during the decade before the First World War. Grandfather Guitière came to the commune during this period because of his marriage to a local girl. To help him work his farm he hired for three days a week a young worker from Chemillé, M. Tessier, who settled in the nearby village of Les Touches and several years later also married a local girl. Although it is true that in the bourg older people are more likely to have been born in the commune, even there old M. Forget and his wife are exceptional because they were both born in the commune — and M. Forget can trace his ancestry in the bourg back at least as far as the Vendée war.

M. Forget, like most of the old people, enjoys telling of his youth. A favorite story is his description of sitting at the feet of a very old lady — at least a hundred years old — when he himself was a very young child, and of listening to her tell of her own childhood. At the age of three, during the Vendée war, she had been lifted down from the burning church tower in the Chanzeaux bourg. When the republican troops allowed the women and children to escape, she was one of them. For most of the old men, M. Forget included, the First World War stands out as the most important event in their lives, much more noteworthy than the Second World War. M. Fribault served for fifty-two months of active service on all fronts and came through without a scratch — much to his chagrin since he now receives no pension. Auguste Hérault of Le Plessis was not so lucky; he has scars of shrapnel wounds in his right hand and almost died of the fever that followed; he was saved only because his wife traveled to the hospital and fed him the soup of an unknown fruit after the doctors had given up hope. Today he enjoys discussing de Gaulle's *force de frappe* and the American military-service laws. The older women do not speak often of the war, although many had fathers, brothers, or husbands who went to the front. They prefer to reminisce about school experiences. Grandmother Ditière of La Brosse insists that young children today are not taught as well as she was taught seventy years ago; she knew all the place names of the department and her grandchildren do not know even the commune. Or, more often, the old women gossip about everyday incidents.

Although the hardiness of the older generation has become legendary, few of the old would want to return to the conditions of the past.[3] Today they eat better, they have radios and newspapers, they can travel greater distances, and they have better medical care. Sixty years ago, Mme. Ditière explains, black bread was a staple in her family's diet; they were lucky to have meat once or twice a month. Now even a family of moderate means can have meat almost once a day. M. Tessier, who is making up for past abstinence, explains that as an agricultural worker he had wine only on special feast days and was lucky if he drank a bottle a year. Moreover, he worked harder. Fifty years ago it took several workers with small scythes a month to harvest a field by hand; now it takes less than a day with a combine.

While most of the old readily accept these changes, some point out that changes in values have accompanied material gains. The virtual revolution in transportation is a most striking example of changing attitudes. M. Tessier says that he was almost twenty when he had his first bicycle and, because he was one of the first to have one, it was made completely of wood, without even rubber tires. To spend Sunday in the bourg was an all-day expedition for him; once in the bourg he had to do his week's business as well as his socializing. The seven cafés were full all day long with men. M. Forget, who was brought up in the bourg, was also one of the first to have a bicycle, but the roads were so bad and the bicycle so uncomfortable that he rarely left town, let alone the commune. His son had a little more freedom and would often make thirty-mile tours with his friends on a Sunday afternoon. There were, he remembers, even groups of young people in Chanzeaux and neighboring communes who formed drama clubs and took turns putting on various plays. His seventeen-year-old daughter, however, has only a bike and is unhappy. All her friends who work with her at the basket factory have mobylettes and think nothing of making a trip to Chemillé or even Chalonnes.

Besides the motorbikes, there is now a bus to Cholet and Angers which comes into the bourg itself twice a day, not to mention the frequent buses along the national highway that can be flagged down at the Bon René. With such freedom of movement comes independence of spirit. Grandmother Oliveau and her daughter, Mme. Frémondière, both say this change has come only in the last twenty years. Grandmother Oliveau, although born in Chemillé, has lived most of her life in Chanzeaux, and both her daughters married in Chanzeaux. Now Mme. Frémondière's daughter is engaged to a mechanic in Versailles, and her son commutes to work in a neighboring commune. But both grandmother and mother accept the change: what can they do when confronted by such an advance in transportation?

The myth of the Vendée Rebellion and the prerevolutionary values — the veneration of the local priest and the local chateau owner — have little meaning in this new world. M. Forget still speaks of the rebellion, but he cannot explain its causes and talks only of the beautiful murals and the stained-glass windows in the church that commemorate it. For the nobility he has no love — the people were slaves to the chatelain, whose wife would order stale bread from Forget's mother in order to feed her animals and then hand out what was left to the poor of the bourg. These old men know little of the rebellion and care little for the nobility they are acquainted with, but they feel an affinity for a pre-Revolution nobility they never knew. As one astute old man explained, the older generation today is closer to the generation of the Vendée Rebellion than the generation after World War II is to its elders. Traditional values no longer have much meaning, and most of the old accept the change as inevitable.

Among traditional values, however, that of family closeness is still emphasized. The aged expect their children to take care of them when they retire. For farmers this means that their children will help to support them if they retire to the bourg or, as is more common, when they retire to a restricted part of the house. André Blond *père* moved into a separate part of the house when he signed over his lease to his younger son. Even when the family finances are meager, arrangements for the old will be made. The Ditières of La Brosse live with three generations in three rooms, and the grandfather is cared for constantly because he must stay in bed all day long. In the bourg, on the other hand, one or the other generation usually moves into a separate household. Grandfather Forget and his wife moved from their shop when their son and his family moved in as head tailor.

The old usually accept retirement in family as well as business matters without complaint. Occasionally there are instances of bitterness between generations, and the scandal this causes proves the prevalence of peaceful patterns. When Georges Pinier took over his father's farm, for example, he expected to move into the farmhouse with his wife and three young children, but his mother refused to let the young family have more than one room in which to cook, eat, and sleep. The son took his case to court where, despite the letter of the law, it was ruled that the mother should move out. Even faced with the court's ruling, the mother will not move, and the son does not have the heart to force her. As a result he drives out to the farm from the bourg every morning at five, not to return until after ten in the evening (his wife is quite bitter about this). The Pinier case stands out so sharply because the limits of the family bond are usually accepted without question by the old. Grandfather Guitière moved into a separate room when he allowed his son Paul to take over the lease of the farm. Paul, in his turn, has built an addition to the house so that his recently married son will stay on the farm with him. In the meantime grandfather Guitière is free to do as he likes.

Although grandfather Guitière, like many of the old people, is quick to point out that he is free to do as he wishes, he will also admit that he does everything he can to help. On the farm the old men help outside, while the old women help with the housework. André Blond *père* often helps to pitch manure in the barn, and his wife and maiden sister pick camomile during the summer. The sister, who also lives with the Blond family, does most of the cooking. So does grandfather Tessier, who is unable to help outside and who learned to cook in the army. Mme. Ditière, who at eighty can no longer walk about, spends her time knitting for her grandchildren.

If an old person lives alone or has no children, ties with more distant members of the family often develop. Auguste Hérault has lived alone since his wife's death in 1959, but his daughter, who lives a quarter of a mile away, comes every day to wash his dishes and tidy up. Mme. Diard, on the other hand, had no children; and when she and her husband grew older, Madame asked a niece who lived in Chemillé to move in with them, promising that her family would inherit the farm. Since then, M. Diard has died and the nephew has taken over the farm, but Mme. Diard has a privileged place by the fire and is surrounded by family.

Sometimes there is no nephew or niece to call upon, and in this case other relationships replace family ties in old age. The Malinges and the Faligands developed such an arrangement; the Malinges were childless and the owners of the farm that M. Faligand farmed. The Malinges celebrated the Faligand children's feast days, and the two families would often spend Sunday together. A similar relationship grew up between the Bertrands and the Mérits, who also happened to be childless and landlords of the Bertrands. Charles Mérit, sixty years the senior of Georges Bertrand, insists that Georges call him by his first name. One of the Sage brothers, who is deaf and earns something of a living by pedaling a cart to collect rabbitskins and other odds and ends, has no family; so his neighbor, Mme. Emile Boutin, sometimes invites him in for a glass of beer and cookies, talking with him in a special sign language that they have made up, or simply shouting in his ear. A 1963 survey of Chanzeaux by the group Economie et Humanisme shows that no one in the commune of Chanzeaux is alone in his old age; all are in contact with children or neighbors. The results of the survey would not surprise the Chanzeans, for family and quasi-family bonds are expected.

Yet forces are now developing that may break down such bonds, not the least of which is the revolution of transportation in the last twenty years, as the example of the different generations of the Oliveau family has shown. Two other major developments have been old-age homes (*maisons de retraite*) and social-security pensions. Traditionally homes for the aged were confined to larger cities, such as Angers and Cholet, and to communities where there were religious orders to run the establishment, as in Gonnord and Salle de Vihiers. Today, in the vicinity of Chanzeaux, there are old-age homes in Angers, Chemillé, Gonnord, La Jumellière, and Rochefort. Of the homes in Angers and Chemillé, the old people of Chanzeaux know little. The old-age home in Gonnord, however, has a bad reputation because it is a hospital where both the old and the sick are taken. Since there is no longer even a resident doctor, each patient must have a private doctor from a neighboring commune. In La Jumellière each old person has a separate room, and again he must have his own doctor.

The old-age home in Rochefort, on the other hand, may be a sign of the future. Even though the building was not quite finished, the home opened at the end of the summer of 1964 and the first inhabitants were received. The communes of Rochefort, Denée, Beaulieu, and Saint-Aubin joined together in financing the home, although their contributions amounted to less than one fifth of the final cost of 700,000 francs; the *conseil général* of the Maine-et-Loire and social security covered the rest. These four communities share the facilities. The home has accommodations for sixty people, who have the choice between a single room or a double one, if they feel they cannot live alone. Together they share a common room, complete with television and cardtables, and a dining room where they are served specially prepared meals. Social-security funds help to finance the building, and most of the old people living in the home will pay the bulk of their expenses with old-age pensions.

Closer to Chanzeaux is a projected old-age home in the neighboring commune of Saint-Lambert. It is being planned by the Association de Bienfaisance, made up of a dozen men who were worried by the number of old people being forced to leave their families. Plans were proposed in 1956 to build a home for twenty retired people; eight years later they had to be revised on a larger scale, for forty people. Because the plans have to be approved not only by building coordinators at the department level but also by the national committee on old-age homes, much time has gone by, and only recently has the association received permission to start construction. In the meantime, the cost of building has gone up and, because the association is forced by an old anticlerical law to be philanthropic,[4] it lacks funds even to start demolition of the buildings on its property. Several years ago the association offered the municipal council of Saint-Lambert the opportunity to underwrite the operation, but the proposal, presented by the elderly and wealthy mayor who did not understand the need for the home, was turned down. Present plans call for a loan from an association underwritten by the government; thus although the state does not directly support the project of a private association, it does underwrite the necessary expenses.

Like the mayor of Saint-Lambert, few of the old people in Chanzeaux will admit the need for an old-age home. When they are asked about existing homes, the answer is always vague — they think there must be something in Angers and something in Gonnord, but "Chanzeans never enter such a home unless they live alone and cannot care for themselves." They themselves have never considered going into such a home, for they will live with their children. M. Vinconneau of Beaulieu, who serves as doctor in Chanzeaux, attributes this reluctance to the reputation of old-age homes as places where the sick and dying are thrown in with the healthy, often in one dormitory-like room. Dr. Vinconneau himself avoids visiting the homes whenever possible, never having been to the old-age home in Gonnord and going to the one in La Jumellière only because he is the private doctor of one of the patients.

The growing independence made possible by the social-security system is another factor in the breakdown of traditional family bonds. A system of sorts has existed since 1930 for most salaried workers, but agricultural lobbies in the government have kept the agricultural workers and farmers separate from the general social-security system. Present compromise legislation has been in effect only since 1952. Social-security taxes are now obligatory for agricultural workers and farmers, but they are allowed to organize their own semiprivate insurance association (the Mutualité Sociale Agricole) with over half its funds coming from the government.

The case of Jean Bourgeaud readily illustrates the procedure and potential effect of the present social-security provisions. Unable to do a normal amount of work because of ill health, Bourgeaud applied for his pension in December 1963 although he had not yet reached his sixty-fifth birthday, when he would normally receive the pension. At the townhall he was given an application form on which he had M. Delaunay put down the necessary legal information to establish the validity of his claim. He himself outlined the dates and places he had worked as a nonsalaried agricultural worker and informed the Mutualité of his current financial situation. M. Bourgeaud was eligible for a full pension because he had been a farmer for at least fifteen years and had paid all his social-security taxes since 1952 — a per capita tax of 25 francs and a percentage (26 percent in January 1964) of the cadastral value of the land under cultivation. His completed application then had to be checked by the departmental office of the Mutualité against their record of his tax payments and their special social-security land census. By August 1964 the Mutualité had calculated Bourgeaud's pension. The basic pension is 450 francs a year ($90) and is awarded to all farmers who have paid social-security taxes. But the Mutualité takes other factors into account when calculating the total benefits. Because Bourgeaud farmed a large property, his social-security taxes had been higher than many of his neighbors', and his benefits were increased in proportion to these taxes. Even counting these benefits, however, Bourgeaud's income still was not higher than the minimum income for an elderly couple of 4,700 francs a year (around $940), and he therefore receives a supplementary allowance from the government and a complementary allowance from the Mutualité. The total benefits are then increased by 10 percent because his wife lives with him and has no outside income. Bourgeaud's total pension amounts to a total of 1,800 francs a year ($360) paid to him by postal check every three months. At sixty-five his pension will be revised and increased if necessary.

M. Bourgeaud's pension is only slightly above average for the benefits of the eighty retired farmers now living in Chanzeaux. Very few people are wealthy enough to receive no pension at all. Yet even with a pension the old person must have some outside income, for social-security benefits will not support even a person who limits his wants within reason. Social-security benefits, however, have steadily become a larger part of the old person's income and have benefited more people.

To be eligible for a pension, according to the law, one had to have paid one's taxes for at least five years since 1952, and many of the farmers over seventy had retired before 1957. To include these people in the social-security system a recent law, which came into effect in 1963, allowed retired farmers to pay now for the years they worked without paying social-security dues. Not all of the old people have taken advantage of this legislation. M. Tessier readily saw its advantages and immediately paid 110 francs for his back years; if he had waited a year, he would have had to pay 140. But others through ignorance or prejudice refused to make back payments: Jean-Pierre Gardais cites the case of a farmer who, with less than six months to make up, refused to listen to reason.

To combat such attitudes and to judge cases where people fail to make their payments, all agricultural workers, salaried and nonsalaried, elect representatives from each commune. The authorities of the Mutualité in Angers then keep these representatives up to date on social legislation and current rates of taxes and benefits. Besides these four, Chanzeaux's representative is Gardais, who is a prominent member in the bureaucracy of the Mutualité and very willing to speak with local farmers about problems they have with social security. At first these representatives were often called on by the central agency in Angers to make sure that people were making their payments, but today the local representatives have little to do, as people become accustomed to social security.

An important function of these local representatives is to determine incomes of those applying for supplementary benefits, for, although the Mutualité has established sixty-five as the retirement age, many farmers continue to work and earn an income. A recent survey of the whole department of the Maine-et-Loire shows that a more reasonable estimate of the average retirement age is seventy-four. In Chanzeaux retirement is so nebulous that no such estimate has been made. M. Guérin retired recently as postman at the age of sixty-five; yet now he not only works in his potato patch and fishes in the Hyrôme, but he also works as the custodian of the camping ground. Retirement is a gradual and individual process. The height of professional activity comes between thirty and sixty, but two thirds of the people in their sixties and one third of those in their seventies still consider themselves professionally active.

Support naturally has to come from the family or from whatever other ties replace the family but, to help out, the old person will do all he can to curtail his expenses. A faded black or grey dress is almost a uniform for older women; while always neat, it is worn until useless. Nor do the old travel often. When M. Forget handed over his tailor shop to his son, he stopped traveling to Chemillé and Angers for material and customers. For longer trips the old are sometimes organized into groups, which lowers the expense. The war veterans, the firemen, and the farmer's association (CGA) sponsor a longer trip each year, and some of the older people make the trip with their families. Even M. Sage, who could not hear a word of the tour, went on the veterans' trip to Normandy in 1964. Because the old do not expect entertainment, they rarely spend money for it. At the annual kermesse to raise funds for the Catholic school, few of the older members of the community were present. Some explained that they thought the price — 5 francs — exorbitant and some protested that it went on too late at night, but most said they just were not interested.

To cut expenses further for their families, many of the aged have gardens or other small enterprises. M. Guérin catches enough fish to supplement the food supply and in addition tends his potato patch. Mme. Amelin, when she can tear herself away from watching passersby in the bourg, can often be seen carrying a basket of greens up the road to Chanoiseau in order to feed her rabbits. On the farms some of the old men have their own small vegetable gardens, while during the summer many of the old women supplement the family income by working in either the family's or someone else's patch of camomile.

Just as professional work is curtailed in old age, so the social life of most of the old is slowed down. In the main social concerns of the citizen of Chanzeaux — politics and religion — the activity of the old is not different from that of younger people, but it has decreased. Politics is the traditional prerogative of men, and the mayor and most of the leaders of the town council have, until the past election, been the elders of the town. Aside from these leaders, few of the old men become actively involved in local political haggling, but almost all have an opinion on politics. Although the older men are more conservative than the younger men, both groups supported de Gaulle in recent elections. The voting behavior of the old people reflects the slowdown in their social activity. Of the population as a whole, three out of five people have voted in all eight elections since 1958. Chanzeans in their sixties, however, gradually become less consistent voters, and only one out of ten people in their eighties voted in the last eight elections. Men continue to vote regularly until late in their sixties, whereas women discontinue voting earlier.

While politics remains the sphere of men, religion is the domain of the women. The decline in religious activity is gradual as a person becomes older, but women still keep more active than men. In the population as a whole, more than eight out of ten inhabitants, including those in their seventies and eighties, attend church every Sunday, and only one out of ten never attends Mass. This is true for men and women alike. The elderly women are the most faithful at communion. Elderly men, on the other hand, receive communion less often even than the younger men. The proportion of women to men who receive communion on common holy days is two to one. Men, on the other hand, greatly outnumber the women in the group of those who take communion only three or four times a year.

Distance from the bourg and increasingly poor health are the largest factors in the decreasing social activity of Chanzeans over sixty. The large number of old women, especially widows, in the bourg helps to explain both the religious and the political activity there, as well as the difference between men and women in the consistency of voting. Thus while M. and Mme. Forget can vote steadily because they are in the bourg itself, M. Tessier now finds it impossible to come to the bourg either to vote or to go to church.

Health also becomes an increasing problem with age. Mme. Ditière, who can no longer walk, moves about with the help of a wheelchair. Yet she says she is very religious, and the curé comes to her at La Brosse to hear confession and give communion as often as six times a year. Those who boast about the hardiness of the Chanzean in his eighties and nineties tend to forget about the large number who die young. There is a popular myth that the old men are able to consume a bottle of *eau de vie* a day; but people forget the many who died young of bad livers or weak hearts brought on by excessive drinking.

For the most part the old people simply wear out, and heart failure appears to be the major cause of death. Many also have trouble with varicose veins. Moreover, resistance to colds and grippe decreases with age, and a common cold sometimes turns into pneumonia. Tooth decay makes life miserable and sometimes painful. M. Tessier, for example, who walks with a stick because of varicose veins, must also limit himself to a liquid diet, because his teeth — or rather his tooth — hangs by a thread. For his legs M. Tessier made a trip to the clinic in Chemillé and to the hospital in Angers. These consultations were time-consuming and inconclusive, but Tessier paid only a nominal fee. Under the present system a patient normally pays the whole of a doctor's fee and is reimbursed 80 percent by the government. The Agricultural Mutualité has introduced a new insurance policy that covers the insuree 100 percent for a fee of 50 francs a person. Although some of the older farmers distrust the new laws, most are sensible about calling the doctor. The old people have never had more or better medical attention than under the present social system.

There is no doubt in the minds of most old people that they are materially better off today. But few are aware how material benefits for the aged, such as old-age homes, social security, and medical care, are breaking down the traditional pattern of family interdependence.

Increasing material welfare may also break down the demographic balance in the commune, for the percentage of old people is growing as the younger people leave for work elsewhere.[5] Such an exodus affects the balance of the active and inactive members of society, which in turn depends on the economic growth of the commune and ultimately of the country as a whole. The present generation of old people may be the last in a system of strong family ties.

* * *

Learning how to live in the community of Chanzeaux takes a lifetime of training. The concepts and habits characteristic of Chanzeaux's family relations, religious practice, and social organization have to be reemphasized at each stage of an individual's life.

The family maintains its traditional role as the organizing institution of the community by making itself indispensable at every stage of a Chanzean's life. It surrounds children as they grow up; it determines the occupational and marriage choices of adolescents; it strengthens the position and security of adults in the community; and it takes care of old people. Religious behavior also develops throughout a lifetime. The devoutness expected of young girls continues through adolescence into adulthood and old age. While women of all ages fill the church, the men from age fifteen to eighty stand at the back of the church or sit in the café.

Finally, in each stage of life Chanzeans are aware of their place in the social structure of the community. Small children from the extreme social groups — the deviants and the Catholic militants — may learn their position from the way they are treated by other children. Adolescents from these groups may sense their separation from others of their age because they went to the public school or to secondary school. And young people from the middle of the social structure identify their place by distinguishing themselves from the deviants they are not supposed to be and from the militants they are not prepared to be. Yet it seems likely that the distinctions based on education, devoutness, residence, and occupation, by which these groups identify themselves and each other, may begin to break down. There is no longer a public school to set apart children of deviant families. The bourg is dying as a center of commercial activity, and young people who were born there are drawn to other communes or to the city, where it hardly matters who their fathers were in Chanzeaux. Nor does it matter in what part of the Chanzeaux commune farm adolescents were born when they move away.

The training for participation in a traditional community is effective because the continuity of behavior is unbroken from childhood to old age. Chanzeans of all ages depend on their families, associate with their own sex, and tend to accept without complaint what is given, whether it is a scolding in primary school, a career in adolescence, or a place in their children's homes in old age. This quality of acceptance may maintain the conservative character of the community, but it also permits the acceptance of change, if change is what is given from outside or above. Chanzeans may not be able to prevent modernization, but they are not unable to adapt to it.

Many of the changes that affect Chanzeans of all ages have come from the outside. The new education laws, not the wishes of Chanzeaux's parents, will keep children in school till the age of sixteen. The aspirations of adolescents for marriages and careers that are scarcely possible in Chanzeaux derive from contact with the outside world. Social security and old-age homes have been introduced not in response to the desires of Chanzeans but by government or private agencies. So far Chanzeaux's adolescents have allowed their aspirations to remain unlinked to their planning for the future. And old people have resisted what they consider the least desirable of the welfare services, old-age homes. But there are also pressures for change indigenous to the community. There are now even fewer job opportunities for young people in Chanzeaux. Better medical care has increased the life expectancy of old people, and there is no room for them either. Because of demographic pressure, both young and old are being forced to take advantage of the opportunities for supporting themselves, growing up or growing old outside their families and the commune.

What happens to the life cycle in the process of change? Most significantly, it becomes less and less a continuous process of training for the life patterns of the previous generation. For one thing, the community itself is changing; for another, young and old are increasingly drawn outside the commune and the family. There are more sharp breaks, such as leaving the community, during the process of growing up than there were before. The three-generation family, which encased the life cycle of an individual, is becoming a thing of the past. It is not that each generation today lives much differently from the previous one; but the close relationships among the generations, which allowed traditional values to be passed on from parents to children, are slowly lessening and opening the way for acceptance of change.

Conclusion

FROM the beginning we have been concerned with a problem of definition. Exactly what is the Chanzeaux we are studying? Geographically there is no question: on a map one can easily see its precise boundaries and in a few hours actually trace the circumference of the commune on foot. Administratively Chanzeaux is not so neatly defined, but still its limits are sufficiently clear for the state to know which of its citizens are accountable to the mayoralty of Chanzeaux.

As a social unit Chanzeaux at first seemed clear to us, too. Even the people of Chanzeaux themselves spoke of the community as an entity with its own particular characteristics: "The people of Chanzeaux are hospitable," "Chanzeaux is more conservative than Saint-Lambert," "Every summer the Chanzeans have a school festival," "Chanzeaux is not so pious as it used to be." Our problem began with the difficulty we had whenever we tried to be precise about this social unit; its definition seemed to elude us. We found that, in order to study the structure of the ever-evolving society known as Chanzeaux, we were forced to ignore its mobility and to assume that the Chanzeaux with which we were concerned was made up of the individuals recorded in the townhall files in August 1962. This has been our statistical unit, but we have always known — and have always been troubled to know — that it was not identical to the Chanzeaux so often assumed to be a clearly defined social unit.

We originally assumed, as most students of communities do, that the human beings associated in a geographical and administrative unit necessarily form a significant social unit, but in studying the structure of Chanzeaux we have repeatedly seen that the inhabitants of the commune may be considered a social unit in only the most artificial administrative sense. In truth, the so-called Chanzeans represent many antagonisms as well as allegiances, forces that divide whether by restricting or enlarging the social boundaries of the group. Besides these fluctuating and varied Chanzeauxes, one must not forget the many — less important for us, perhaps, but nonetheless real — Chanzeauxes based on single impressions, personal experiences, and mythical half-truths. It is a mistake to equate all these Chanzeauxes and to assume that they are a single unit to which all Chanzeans feel they belong.

In trying to clarify our conception of the community, we realize that disunity seems to have characterized Chanzeaux for as long as we have been able to study its history. The expressions frequently used to describe rural life — *stability, simplicity, homogeneity* — have never applied to Chanzeaux at any point in its history. To our eyes, more characteristic expressions have been *flux, conflict, diversity*. Well aware that the Chanzeaux of the 1830s was not the ideal community, Théodore de Quatrebarbes assumed that the ideal had existed before the Vendée Rebellion: "If it had not been for the unanimous battle cry which shook the Vendée, the simple recitation of the virtue of Chanzeaux's curés, the foundation of its chapels, the magnanimity of its seigneurs and the pure customs of its peaceable laborers would have formed the sum of its history." [1] As we have shown, however, Chanzeaux in the eighteenth century was characterized by disunity.

Today it is often assumed that the Chanzeaux of Quatrebarbes' time was a more ideal community, but this is not true either. All of our studies indicate that division has been a constant factor in Chanzeaux life. It is common knowledge that the "wine people" and the "cow people" have always felt their separateness. We began to see even more the importance of the differences when we learned that the marriage and kinship patterns differed considerably between bourg and campagne. We became further impressed when we found that people living in hamlets were markedly distinct in certain ways from the people living on isolated farms. Finally, we realized that the population of Chanzeaux is separated into identifiable groups that in some cases have only the most tenuous connections. In this sense, the population as a whole does not form a significant social unit.

This does not mean, however, that no unity can be found. Curiously, it may even be that by seeing the disunity we have found the key to understanding what the basic social unit in Chanzeaux is. Coming to know Chanzeaux consists largely in learning to identify the various social and economic networks that exist, to recognize the individuals belonging to them, and to see the relationship of the local network to a larger whole. These groups, we learn, tend to perpetuate their distinctive characteristics, sometimes for generations. The Bertrands are bourg people and have business ties only with farmers. The Duvals are strictly farm people. The Jouberts and Ditières are vintners; the Plancheneaus and Chaillous are dairy farmers. The Chauvins are freethinkers; the Plancheneaus are conventional Catholics; the Brichets are devout. Many of the priests (including a bishop and a canon) and the nuns whose birthplace was Chanzeaux have come from the descendents of the Piniers, a devout family that lived in Chanzeaux a hundred years ago. These networks have been identified by family names, but of course there are exceptions and not every member of a family participates.

It is through the networks that new ideas are best introduced into the commune and tested for acceptance by the general population. Most important, however, is that the sense of unity we attribute to Chanzeaux at any period of its history is in fact a reflection of the strength of one network, or set of allied networks, which gives the impression that their characteristic behavior, values, and symbols are those of the community as a whole. Much of the feeling and thought and conversation of the Chanzeans is concerned with the question of what Chanzeaux is and what it could be — if only the other networks did not prevent its full self-realization. If a given group has sufficient power and energy and an active leadership, it will try to force Chanzeaux as a community into its own mold, to shape the commune to its own ideal. The 1793 conflict in Chanzeaux seems to have resulted from the efforts of the wealthy, city-minded bourgeois network to impose its ideas and identity on the parish through the power newly given it by the government in Paris and Angers. In opposition was a network led by the Blanchard-Bureau-Forest group, which was accustomed to setting the tone in the community. It appears that many people in Chanzeaux were indifferent to the conflict, but eventually most of them were forced to take sides. At the outbreak of the Vendée Rebellion the traditionalist group overcame its rivals and gave to the community as a whole a mythical identity that still persists: that of a community of peasants rising unanimously to strike down the persecutors of priests and king.

Once a network comes thus to dominate a community, many factors work to help it maintain and even reinforce its power to impose its image on the community. Kinship and land-tenure patterns are both important conservative forces, as we have seen elsewhere in this book, but when they are in conflict, one cannot be certain which will be the conserving force and which the force working for change. For instance, even though Quatrebarbes had tremendous economic power, he was unable to impose his views on a community still dominated by the Blanchards and Forests, who had even greater control through the kinship pattern they represented.

Migration also exerts a conservative force on the community. Deviants who remain in the commune strengthen the dominating networks by forming the nuclei of opposition networks which do not threaten the controlling elements but actually help them to clarify their identity. Stronger deviants, potentially a threat, usually emigrate. We have seen that the places of the emigrants have always been filled by a steady flow of immigrants. Some of these immigrants leave, some stay, their decision largely determined by their attitude toward the currently dominant networks. Those who stay are usually those who marry into the networks or espouse their spirit so enthusiastically that they perpetuate and even intensify the image of Chanzeaux to which they have given their new loyalty. We have seen that a surprisingly large number of town councilors were born elsewhere. Converts are very often the most intense followers.

Traditionally, then, the domination and persistence of the network system make radical change difficult in Chanzeaux. Change does take place, of course, and the networks even favor certain change, but any effort to create a radically new identity for Chanzeaux has failed. This was true in 1793 and again in the middle of the nineteenth century with the Comte de Quatrebarbes. Even today, when there are strong currents favoring change in Chanzeaux as elsewhere in France, we see that radical solutions are rejected.

Because of the economic crisis facing Chanzeaux, it is generally acknowledged that change must come. In his remote house at the end of an all but impassable lane, even M. Catrou talked to us of the need for "changement dans les structures." The question is what the change should be and how it should come about. There are two networks represented locally in Chanzeaux that have thought seriously about the subject, the Catholic activists of the bourg (formerly members of the JAC and now leaders in the MFR) and the Jeunes Agriculteurs (primarily farmers). The former would like to see Chanzeaux become an ideal Catholic community so that God's kingdom might be realized on earth — at least in Chanzeaux. The latter are economically motivated syndicalists. The men and women in both groups are among the most intelligent and best informed of the commune, and certainly some of the reforms they suggest have a wide appeal and approval — the need for scientific farm operations, for cooperative efforts, for pressure on the government. But the ideological fervor of both groups is rejected. André Blond, former departmental president of the Jeunes Agriculteurs, is dismissed with the nickname "Robespierre." The devout Catholic activists sit at the front of the church as an example to others to do more than passively attend Mass. The majority react by sitting farther and farther back in the church. The question is whether they will not eventually just slip out the back door, leaving the Christian activists alone with their radical solution to the problems of modern life.

The same reaction was seen in the municipal elections of 1965. Most of the voters agreed that there was need to rejuvenate the town council, and the leaders of the Jeunes Agriculteurs and Catholic activists were obvious candidates — though because of the election system no one was officially a candidate. Each voter simply writes down the names of the thirteen men he wants on the council. The most active leaders of the two groups — André Blond, Henri Amelin, and Joseph Brée — were all passed over by the voters. Less extreme men, though representing the same network, were elected.

On the previous council the only representative of the younger liberal group was Jean-Pierre Gardais. Since he was re-elected, he naturally became the leader of the new moderate liberal group; the moderate conservatives recognized as their leader the former deputy mayor, Paul Guitière. The two groups were evenly divided on the new council, so the question was whether Guitière or Gardais should be mayor. With a vote of six to six, the decision fell to the thirteenth councilor, a new man and not committed to either group. This was Louis Faligand, the prototype of the Chanzeaux town councilor — born outside the commune, marrying into a strong, local kinship group, fermier of one of the largest farms in Chanzeaux, independent but still representative of the dominant network. At first he was inclined to vote for Guitière because of his uneasiness at Gardais' pietist tendencies, even though he would rather have favored the new ideas Gardais would bring to the council. He talked to both candidates and was won finally by one thing especially that Gardais said: "Il ne faut pas trop bousculer les gens." Reassured, Faligand cast the deciding vote for Gardais, thus continuing the Chanzeaux tradition of accepting change if it is gradual and if it is sponsored by dominant groups.

We could learn much more about the networks and their relation to social change if we were to investigate the history of several innovations that have been accepted by the people of Chanzeaux. We know, for instance, that Faligand successfully introduced a new fertilizer. Curiously enough, he learned about the technique in the communist peasant paper, *La Terre,* which is the last source one might expect a Chanzeaux farmer to consult. Undoubtedly this paper has its lowest circulation in such conservative Catholic communities, and it would be revealing to know how Faligand came to read *La Terre.* At any rate he was convinced by the article, tried the system on his own wheatfields, and was so successful that other farmers adopted the fertilizer. If we could know exactly how this knowledge spread, much about the nature and function of the networks would certainly become clearer.

It would be equally revealing to compare Father du Boulay's experiment in changing farm patterns with Curé Alleaume's method of introducing church reforms. Father du Boulay, professor at the Jesuit agricultural school in Angers, wanted to teach modern accounting techniques to the farmers to make them aware of the deficiencies and potentialities of their operations. Victor Guibert, one of his graduate students, secured a list of thirty typical Chanzeaux farmers from Bourdelle, the regional representative of the farmers' union. Each farmer was given an elaborate questionnaire concerning his past operations and his plans for the next five years. The only farmer who filled out his questionnaire was Henri Amelin, who had taken a three-month farm-management course in Paris and was therefore prepared to think of his operation in abstract, long-range terms. A few others completed the schedules with the aid and insistence of Guibert, but most of the men simply withdrew from the project and it had no real influence on farming in Chanzeaux.

Contrasted to this is Curé Alleaume's attempt to make certain reforms in the church service. He wanted among other changes to give up the old custom of renting chairs and pews to specific persons each year so that whole families might sit and worship together.

It was inevitable that sharp objections would be raised. Some of the older parishioners, holding the same places for years, had so proprietary a feeling that they had upholstered their kneeling benches and kept cushions in their chairs. There was indeed turmoil after the first Sunday of the reform, when some of the younger people dared to occupy the comfortable seats that "belonged" to older women. But in spite of the grumbling, Curé Alleaume won out because he had made sure in advance that he had the support of two powerful networks — the Catholic activists and the devout and conservative mayor. Exactly how had Alleaume chosen the individuals to back his reform? Certainly he had an accurate idea of how this phenomenon we call the networks functions.

Alleaume's predecessor in the nineteenth century, who assigned Théodore de Quatrebarbes's pew to a commoner when the count had arrogantly neglected to attend the annual pew auction, was less fortunate in his reform. Although the curé had local support, the count included in his reliance network the bishop himself, who intervened in his favor. From a methodical analysis of cases like these, we could learn a great deal about the wider social networks in which Chanzeans are included, and about the function of networks as obstacles to or vehicles for social change.

We now realize how important the system is to understanding much of the behavior we have observed in Chanzeaux, for traditionally one of the main features of rural life has been the relationship among networks and their constant evolution. Even today much of the conversation concerns rivalry among groups, the virtues of one's own network, the vice and stupidity of opposition groups, and shifting allegiances. Certainly weather and health come first chronologically in any conversation, but actually the principal subject always concerns these other questions. The liveliest topic seems usually to be novelties introduced into the commune by local people acting as agents for wider groups to which they belong. In these conversations we see how social change is introduced, tested, accepted, or rejected: a new farming technique, a proposed sewage system, novel adolescent behavior — all such possible transformations are introduced through the network systems and tried for their fit to the local patterns. Changes that are inevitable — war and taxes — must be rationalized, but optional changes — farm techniques and women's hats — if accepted by a dominant network come to characterize the community even though they may not be unanimously approved or adopted.

If we look at the nature of the networks over the historical period covered in this book, we see that there have been important changes, especially in the last few years. There are fewer networks, but they are more extensive. The differences among them are less extreme and less charged with hostility. The system is simpler and more unified. The implications of these changes are important for our understanding of Chanzeaux as a community.

There are fewer networks because there is less economic and social differentiation in Chanzeaux today than two hundred years ago. This is most evident in a comparison of the ways people made their living then and now. There used to be many kinds and levels of farmers, artisans, and merchants. More professions were represented: there were doctors, midwives, notaires, real-estate agents, tax collectors, innkeepers, governesses, monks. Today only a handful of artisans remains. There are no important merchants, and few professions are represented in Chanzeaux now. There is no longer so complicated a hierarchy of farmers with *journalier* at the bottom, *laboureur* at the top. Some of the distinctions have counterparts today, but most of them have disappeared. We must remember, too, that the total population is only two thirds of what it used to be in Chanzeaux.

The change in land tenure and in attitudes toward it is an example of how the leveling process reduces the number as well as the distinctiveness of existing networks. There is now in Chanzeaux no one with the power and wealth of Quatrebarbes, who in this one commune alone owned twenty-four farms. Today even the chatelain owns only two farms — and we have seen how unimportant a role he has in the community. Furthermore, ownership of land is not so important as it used to be. Because of advantages given a fermier by government legislation, he is often better off than a landowning farmer. He has the coincidental advantage of operating a farm with efficient grouping of fields. Between the chatelain and his fermier, too, the enormous social difference has been reduced. Typical is the relatively egalitarian relationship between Dr. Massonneau, the Parisian functionary who owns the Paperie farm, and Paul Guitière, his tenant. Their equality is increased by the fact that Guitière is also proprietor of a farm a few miles north of Chanzeaux. He has very much the same relationship with his own tenant that Massonneau has with him.

As the social networks in Chanzeaux have diminished in number, they have, mostly because of the revolution in transportation, greatly increased their geographic spread. Whenever the people of Chanzeaux are not working, they are on the move, usually in order to visit friends, relatives, acquaintances of far-reaching networks. Eight years ago if we wanted to talk to a farmer, we would be sure to find him at home on Sunday afternoon, and our visit was welcome since he seemed to have nothing else to do. Now people are rarely at home when they have leisure time. If they stay at home, it is because they expect visitors. The traffic on all the roads of the Maine-et-Loire, especially the back roads leading to hamlets and farms, is surprisingly heavy on Sunday nowadays. Sometimes farmers — and townspeople — go even farther away for the weekend. Faligand visits his cousins in Paris. Bourdelle visits a friend with whom he has kept up since army days in Lille. The Massonneaus drive down from Paris to visit the Guitières. Only the ill stay at home — and they have visitors. It used to be that on Sunday afternoon the Chanzeans who wanted to get away from home would walk along the Hyrôme River to stop and drink with friends at the little wineshops along the way. Today one can walk the length of the path and see only an occasional fisherman. The people of Chanzeaux have broader contacts and interests.

These new networks are no longer exclusively rural. The processes of urbanization, the standardization of life through education and mass media, the technological revolution in farming, have made social ties between farmers and city people more intimate. When the republican soldiers in 1793 mentioned their dread of venturing into "le pays des boeufs," they were expressing the traditional urban fear of the simple man of the soil whose close contact with nature kept him ignorant and gave him a savage strength. The fear of a peasant revolt was deep in France and often still lingers in the minds of literary people. In reality, of course, the distinction between farmer and citydweller is fast vanishing. The farmer (please note that the word peasant has been avoided in this book, since it is used now only by politicians seeking to activate old antagonisms) is today a trained technician and feels himself less the slave than the master of his land.

When one of us was invited to lunch with the Faligands and their cousins at the cousins' apartment in the suburbs of Paris, we saw enacted the 1965 version of the tale of the country mouse and the city mouse. Being from the country turned out to be no disadvantage. We were at the table from one o'clock until well into the evening to celebrate Faligand's first trip to Paris — an unusual thing, for most Chanzeaux men have been to Paris, if only during their *service militaire*. In the presence of his two Parisian cousins, Faligand at first seemed somewhat subdued. The two young men had been born and raised in Cholet, but had come to Paris to work as soon as they finished school. One is a master tool-machine operator with his own little shop. The other is a technician at IBM. Both of them are obviously intelligent, energetic, ambitious. Though they were kind to their cousin, whom they had not seen for several years, they seemed somewhat condescending toward him. The young men did most of the talking at first, but gradually Faligand began to take a more active part in the conversation. Little by little it became obvious that he was just as much a scientific technician as either of his cousins — perhaps more. He was skilled in auto mechanics, soil chemistry, botany, husbandry, accounting, marketing. He was also well informed on politics, problems of social security, questions of farm policy and the Common Market. Besides, he was a member of Chanzeaux's town council and chairman of its finance committee. As all this became clear, the country-mouse city-mouse situation faded. These three men were much more on a level than they had thought. If anything, Faligand had the edge over his city cousins, and at the end of the evening one felt the Parisians' pride in their kinship to their cousin from the country.

Because people have come to think of their problems more in economic and scientific terms, there has been a considerable lessening of the ideological conflicts that used to keep the social networks in a state of constant suspicion and hostility. Of course, economic factors were always basically important in ideological conflicts — 1793–1795 is a case in point — but, because people did not think of the problem in economic terms, they felt the need to justify the conflicts in ideological terms. Today there is almost no overt ideological tension among Chanzeans. People say that the few socialists and communists in the commune have a right to their own opinion. The devout Catholics (except for the old women, who have traditionally not taken part in such conflicts) feel that their evangelism should be carried out mostly by demonstrating the superiority of the Christian way of life. They have less concern with converting the socialists and communists than with persuading the passive Catholics to participate more actively in the complete Christian life. Even among the few gentry people, where one sees some vestige of religious and political hostility, it is recognized that the old life could not be brought back even with the restoration of the monarchy. "Everyone today thinks in terms of money and food and having a good time," they say. "The old ideas are gone."

The election of 1962 was striking evidence of the disappearance of the old ideological conflicts. All the candidates felt obligated to dissociate themselves from traditional parties and disputes. Only Poujade, who as it happened was the candidate for the district in which Chanzeaux is located, resorted to old-fashioned ideas, even though he rejected any traditional party affiliation. The talk Poujade made in the Chanzeaux townhall was a compendium of clichés from outworn ideological arguments. He tried to resurrect the old fears against the enemies of the little people — the too-powerful state, dictatorship, corrupt government-industry alliances, trusts, bands, Jews, old men, America, Russia. In 1956 this line had been effective, and Poujade had received 21 percent of the vote in Chanzeaux. He won the support of artisans, merchants, and small landowning farmers who, with their limited power, felt that Poujade might save the old way of life. By 1962 these same voters were disabused; they represented networks that were then — and still are — culturally the most traditional and economically in the most desperate position. Poujade's talk in Chanzeaux was attended by a single artisan — the least respected of bourg artisans — and on election day Poujade received only 29 votes from the 721 cast in the commune. The Gaullist candidate, Hauret, won an easy victory over all the other candidates. The old clichés had obviously lost their magic.

As we have seen, then, there seems to be mutual agreement among the different networks that change is inevitable. This feeling is reinforced because the traditional culture-maintaining institutions in Chanzeaux have to a considerable degree reversed their influence. The way children are brought up, their experiences in school, or their participation in church activities are no longer uniquely conservative forces. Of course, socialization is to a certain degree inevitably a conservative process. Parents cannot help raising their children to a large extent as they themselves have been raised, as they see other parents in their group raise children and in opposition to the way they see them raised in outside groups. Now, however, parents also realize that the traditional way of life is finished, and they feel unable to predict the future needs of their children in a world that will certainly be very different from theirs and their parents'. So the modern parent turns to magazines, newspapers, and television for ideas. Catholic activist parents in Chanzeaux attend section and regional meetings where child training is frequently discussed. One finds the Brées raising their children according to progressive principles suggested by church specialists on family life. But even when parents accept these new principles, old ways persist. One very "modern" family still punishes its small children by locking them out of the house in the dark of night. It is important not to forget, though, that children are increasingly less under the tutelage of their parents. They begin school at an earlier age, and more of them go away to school. Children, and especially adolescents, escape parental supervision more easily and more frequently. Far from home on their mobylettes on Sunday afternoons, they know they are not watched so carefully by family and society.

Outside forces are also responsible for introducing progressive principles into the educational experience of the children. Since teaching the catechism is relatively simple and since its program was generally recognized as hopelessly deficient, that change has been easier and more successful than school reforms. In Chanzeaux it was facilitated by the acceptance of a school contract with the national government, which stipulated that no religious instruction could be part of the school curriculum. Consequently a new system had to be devised. Catechism was concentrated in a few hours outside the schoolday, and the teaching burden was distributed among lay catechists — Catholic activists, untrained as teachers and ready to accept new pedagogical methods and materials. The catechist in Angers sent instructions, and through Catholic bookstores special progressive teaching materials were made available.

The school itself, however, remains the most conservative force in the community. Progressive parents are more and more frequently sending their brighter children to city schools by bus; their interest in the Chanzeaux school and their effect on it inevitably diminish. The teachers — like teachers everywhere — find it hard to change the point of view and methods they have used for years. Finally the schoolbooks themselves work against change. Once a teacher chooses a given class text and once the school committee and town council have bought the books, it takes a major political effort to make a new investment in schoolbooks. The books in Chanzeaux's schools, like those in many schools, are undoubtedly twenty years out of date — a conservative estimate of a conservative phenomenon.

Traditionally the church has been a reactionary influence in Chanzeaux. Sunday after Sunday the burden of the curé's message was to exhort his flock to live up to the virtues of their ancestors. Prevailing social and value systems were constantly bolstered by the church, which generally preached charity and acceptance of injustice in this world in order to prepare for the ideal life in the next world. The church supported the gentry morally, and the gentry supported the church financially. Now that the influence of the gentry on the church has disappeared, a few of the older priests are nostalgic for the past regime, but essentially the message of the clergy and activist laymen today is to accept changes of all sorts — in the ritual, in the setting of the Mass, in any new Christian activities. It is also implied that, by living well, one will glorify God in his earthly creation. Most of the statues of the saints have been put in the church storerooms; it is considered more pious to concentrate on active participation in Mass than on lighting candles. The old devotional societies and practices are forgotten. These changes in attitude and practice mean that the church in Chanzeaux is now an accelerating force for change.

The more conservative church networks have been left behind. They realize this and resent it, but are unable to compete with the dynamic network of activists. It is a question now whether the latter can convert other networks to their point of view, or whether their insistence on mixing religion with practical living will alienate the rest of the population. It may be that the Chanzeans in general may become more like the rest of the French people and satisfy their religious inclinations with the perfunctory, seasonal practice characteristic of Catholicism in France. In any case the church is no longer primarily a pattern-maintaining force. Symbols of this reversal are the great carved pews where the gentry used to sit and dominate the parishioners as they did the parish. For years the pews remained empty after the de Kerdouecs and the Jourdans had moved to the city, and the commoners still did not dare to move into the vacant places. With the reform of the seating arrangements, those parishioners who arrive earliest for Mass now have the privilege of sitting in the best pews. Social distinctions have been replaced by distinction for active participation in the service.

Although networks remain the essential social units, they themselves have been transformed. The dominant networks, still being reinforced by the process of immigration, have nevertheless become a vehicle for social change. The networks extend farther and farther beyond Chanzeaux's borders. There is a closer relationship between urban and rural strands of the networks. This strengthening of ties outside Chanzeaux, and especially with city people, will certainly lead some observers to conclude that the sense of community which they insist on attributing to traditional, rural communities has still further deteriorated. But we find the opposite to be true. There is probably a greater sense of community in Chanzeaux today than there has ever been, and this is possible only through changes in the system of networks. We have seen that there are fewer networks represented in Chanzeaux and that their members are more homogeneous socially and professionally. There is greater consensus regarding social change. People think more in economic than in ideological terms. There is in general less hostility among segments of the population.

In the face of today's severe economic crisis, people in Chanzeaux are cooperating as they never have before. Farmers now purchase equipment jointly, or they consult each other so that their purchases can complement each other's needs. Traditionally they gave each other a hand only in special circumstances, at harvest time or when there was illness, for instance; entr'aide is now a common phenomenon. Cooperation has been formalized in the creation of the Groupe d'Entr'aide at Le Plessis. Membership and participation in voluntary associations, credit unions, mutual-insurance programs, and cooperatives have increased tremendously. It seems to us that these developments would not have been possible when the networks inhibited rather than fostered the acceptance of new ideas. With the lessening of the barriers among social networks a greater will — and ability — to work together has developed. The formation of the Syndicat d'Initiative to "put Chanzeaux on the map" and the election of a town council and a mayor willing to broaden their community services are significant developments. Just as the town is showing more concern for a larger number of its citizens, so at the same time it is working more closely with neighboring communities to achieve greater benefits for all.

As an administrative unit Chanzeaux has lost much of its independence. The surrounding region and France as a whole have gradually absorbed it. But as a sentimental unit Chanzeaux is much stronger than it ever has been. We know that myths have hidden the diversities and conflicts of the old Chanzeaux. There was little real sense of community. Today the Chanzeans are less divided, less hostile toward each other than they were in the past. They have more significant and a wider range of human relationships outside their families and narrow social networks.

There is a general tendency to lament the passing of the traditional rural community because it is assumed that in such a social unit people lived in the greatest harmony. Perhaps this belief is based less on reality than on nostalgia for a past that never existed — like Quatre-barbes' vision of eighteenth-century Chanzeaux. To us it appears that the sense of community among Chanzeans grows stronger as Chanzeaux turns away from its past and seeks to face the problems of modern life.

APPENDICES

Chanzeaux and Saint-Lambert

Americans in Chanzeaux

NOTES

INDEX

Appendices

There is a natural tendency to generalize from findings about a particular village. We have not been immune, at times, from thinking that what we have seen in Chanzeaux is a microcosm of all of rural France. Yet many of the essentials of Chanzeaux's social and economic structure are not even representative of a limited surrounding region. Comparing Chanzeaux with the next-door commune of Saint-Lambert will help to put our study in perspective. Although Saint-Lambert shares a common border with Chanzeaux, it does not share Chanzeaux's devotional tradition. It is part of the wine-growing Layon Valley. Its land-tenure pattern and its political history are considerably different from Chanzeaux's.

Just as we must recognize the limited generality of many aspects of our study, so we have tried to be aware of the weaknesses of our own research methods, as well as the possible consequences for Chanzeaux of our stay there. For these reasons, the first appendix contains a short description of Saint-Lambert, comparing it with Chanzeaux; the second describes how we approached Chanzeaux and how we fitted into it while we were there.

The people of Chanzeaux's region have always recognized that each village in the area had its own peculiarities. For us Chanzeaux has always been "the place where traditions persist." Ironically enough, Chanzeaux is now known to the people of the region as "the place where the Americans are."

Chanzeaux and Saint-Lambert

A few minutes in any direction from Chanzeaux take one to another community. North and east, dotted along the Layon, are the wine towns of Saint-Lambert du Lattay, Beaulieu sur Layon, Rablay, and Le Champ sur Layon. To the south and west are the farming towns of Gonnord, Joué-Etiau, La Jumellière, and the market center for the region, Chemillé.

Saint-Lambert is the closest of all Chanzeaux's neighbors. It shares a larger boundary with Chanzeaux than with any other commune. Because of the awkward shape of that boundary, the villages of La Brosse and La Jutière, though they are legally in the commune of Chanzeaux, are closer to Saint-Lambert's bourg than to Chanzeaux's. The people of those two villages — who go to church, do their marketing and send their children to school in Saint-Lambert, and declare their wine harvests and vote in Chanzeaux — are a source of continual contact between Chanzeaux and Saint-Lambert. Saint-Lambert is, of all Chanzeaux's neighbors, the commune that has received most of its emigrants. The distribution of voters alive in 1962 who were born in Chanzeaux but who had moved to a neighboring commune was:

Saint-Lambert	33	Joué-Etiau	13
Chemillé	32	Le Champ	10
Beaulieu	20	La Jumellière	10
Rablay	19	Gonnord	7

Indeed, almost as many had gone to Saint-Lambert as had gone to Angers (39).

Chanzeaux is mainly wheat and cow country, while Saint-Lambert is mainly wine country. The face of the land is very different. If one looks at aerial photographs of the Layon Valley taken during the summer, one can distinguish a definite line dividing light, bright-green areas (ripening grapes) to the north and east from somber, dark-green areas (hedges, trees, pastures, and wheatfields) to the southwest. The political boundary between Chanzeaux and Saint-Lambert coincides with that line. On the Chanzeaux side of the line, the land is broken up into myriads of enclosed fields and peppered with four- and five-house hamlets. On the Saint-Lambert side and all along the Layon, the strips are much smaller and they are not separated by hedges.

Wine growing requires much less land than raising cattle or growing wheat. In the Layon region an average acre under *vigne* is considered to produce the same average revenue as three acres under wheat. It requires as much labor as five acres under wheat. Consequently settlements are closer and population is denser in wine country. Saint-Lambert has 85 people per square kilometer, while Chanzeaux has only 37.

Saint-Lambert has fewer isolated farms and small hamlets than Chanzeaux. The villages of La Vieillère, l'Olulière, Sainte-Foy, and Le Layon all have populations of over twenty people. They are also physically more like little bourgs than the hamlets of Chanzeaux; they have more flowers and more vegetable gardens. In a house in l'Olulière of Saint-Lambert, cooking is done on a stove and the floor is made of tile, as it would be in an average house in the bourg. In a house in Saint-Ambroise, Chanzeaux, the floors are of brick and some of the cooking is done on the fire. Moreover, there is nothing in Chanzeaux to compare with Saint-Lambert's two largest villages, Le Plessis and Les Grandes Tailles (1962 populations, 77 and 107). Les Grandes Tailles has a grocery store of its own. Further into the Mauges both settlements would be bourgs in their own right.

Saint-Lambert and Chanzeaux differ radically in the physical appearances of their bourgs. Saint-Lambert's is not as closely knit as Chanzeaux's; it is larger; and it is crossed by a national highway. The highway differentiates Saint-Lambert from Chanzeaux even more than its vineyards. The Paris-Sables d'Olonnes highway is one of the main routes of France. It was being paved when the Revolution came in 1789. This was one of a number of measures in the second half of the eighteenth century which opened up the area of the Mauges to the more commercialized parts of France. Under Louis Philippe, another big road was built from Saint-Lambert to Saint-Laurent de la Plaine. It was known then as a *route stratégique*, built to facilitate troop movements for putting down the sporadic remnants of Vendean guerrilla fighting.

The bourg of Saint-Lambert is stretched out along these two roads. Its drab, monotonous rows of gray houses suggest the outskirts of an industrial city or the residential stretch of a small summer resort. By contrast, Chanzeaux is quiet and compact. Its bourg is screened from long vistas of road by the bushy crevices of the Hyrôme. The street by which one enters Chanzeaux bourg is small and sinuous; one feels enclosed by it. Houses are bunched up in a heterogeneous fashion right on the street. At the entrance to the bourg there are no sidewalks, and one is expected to walk in the street. The Place de l'Eglise is very large in Chanzeaux, and most of the bourg seems set around it. In the entire bourg there is only one street corner (where the roads to Joué and Rablay meet) where two people could stop to talk without being in sight of the Place de l'Eglise. The Place, in a sense, is a stage — and the bourg is a theater in which there is but one auditorium. If one has the Chanzeaux type of square in mind, Saint-Lambert has no Place de l'Eglise. The bit of a square that is there is dwarfed by the enormous church, a late nineteenth-century edifice so big that it leaves room for nothing around it. It is out of proportion with everything but the straight and endless *route stratégique* which lands at its front door.

In Chanzeaux, the church, the townhall, the postoffice, and the parsonage are all in one spot. By contrast, in Saint-Lambert each one of these centers is located in a different place. You have to walk a quarter of the way up the Saint-Laurent road to reach the curé's house, halfway up to reach the town-hall, and halfway up the Chemillé road to find the postoffice. The separation of the church and the townhall is suggestive of Saint-Lambert's history of church-state rivalry. In Saint-Lambert the procession on All Souls' Day leaves the church first, goes to the townhall, where the mayor waits for it, and then goes to the cemetery. From the townhall the procession has to retrace its steps about twenty yards to find the path to the cemetery.

Chanzeaux and Saint-Lambert had different reactions to the church-state crisis of 1905. The reaction in Saint-Lambert was violent, first unanimously in support of the church, later polarized for and against. In 1910, Saint-Lambert's Curé Brémond raised the money for and built an independent Catholic school for boys, separate from the public school. He insisted that every parent remove his children from the public school. He is even said to have refused confession to some parents who did not wish to interrupt the last years of their children's studies, and, indeed, the pressure he exerted split the community in two. Henri Coulon, now in his sixties and a self-styled "Chouan," remembers getting into fist fights regularly over the matter, between 1911 and the war of 1914. At the end of the war the majority of the families quietly sent their children to the Catholic school. But a staunch minority remained in the public school. Those left of that minority now live principally in the villages of Le Plessis and Les Grandes Tailles. Several are people struggling to make ends meet, whose adherence to the Amicale Laique, a republican mutual-aid society, is mixed with resentment for the successful *bien pensants* of the bourg.

Today about one fifth of the families send their children to public school and do not go to church. This lay minority is much larger than in Chanzeaux. In the political realm, the communist and socialist vote is somewhat larger as well (though it is small in both communities). Surprisingly, the ardent Catholic minority is also relatively larger in Saint-Lambert than in Chanzeaux. Saint-Lambert has relatively more people who do not attend church at all and relatively more people who receive communion every Sunday. Both extremes are strong (see the figures below, based on parochial and diocesan archives in 1960, for adults over age twenty).

	Saint-Lambert	Chanzeaux
Never or rarely attend Mass	20%	7%
Attend Mass irregularly	10%	8%
Attend Mass every Sunday	70%	85%
Receive communion every Sunday	25%	16%
Total no. in sample	783	501

The highway through the bourg of Saint-Lambert carries a continuous stream of traffic. Even after midnight from a street-side room in the Hotel du Lion d'Or, one can count at least one car every fifteen minutes. Inside the door of the church of Saint-Lambert, there is a small poster assuring visitors that none of the benches is reserved. On Sunday, Curé Chevalier occasionally asks his parishioners to sit farther toward the front of the church in order to leave room for passing motorists. This flow of people supports a considerable number of the inhabitants of Saint-Lambert. There are three service stations in the bourg. The owner of one of them also operates a roadside wine stand. There is one other such wine stand at the entrance to the bourg. Another of the service stations is the local distributor for Simca. In the heart of the bourg, where the road turns around the church, there is a souvenir shop, a café, the Centre de Dégustation run by the village wine cooperative, and a roadside hotel, Boussion's Lion d'Or. During the peak month of August, Boussion is busy — two or three families of motorists at lunch, from time to time a busload of vacationers, and two or three families of pensionnaires for dinner. The pensionnaires are typically middle-aged working people from Paris, spending their two weeks' vacation "à la campagne."

The people of Saint-Lambert appear to have adapted to this steady flow of strangers by developing an uncanny sense for who is and who is not "passing through." They quickly sense the difference between someone who has come to stay for a while and a Parisian on his way to Sables d'Olonnes. While they are there, the transients are only superficially in Saint-Lambert. There are areas just fifty yards to either side of the main road never visited by people who are passing through. There, the presence of a stranger is an event. One morning one of the Americans was taking a walk on the side street that goes from the butcher's shop on the tiny square to the cemetery. When he reached the first crossing, he passed a grandmother with glasses, carrying a milk pail, and he said hello. She started to pass by, stopped in her tracks, took off her glasses, stared, and exclaimed, "Mais je ne vous connais pas!" On the Place de l'Eglise she would not have taken a second look.

The national highway has other, more profound effects on Saint-Lambert. For one, it brings the city, Angers, closer to the village. "Saint-Lambert is on the national highway and has a regular bus service," Mme. Cerqueus wrote to one of the Americans. "On ne craint pas d'aller en ville." Angers in fact has a strong drawing power on Saint-Lambert, stronger than on Chanzeaux. The city takes people away: about one out of every five natives of Saint-Lambert who leave the commune goes to Angers, and 7 percent more go to Paris. The corresponding figures for Chanzeaux are 8 percent and 2 percent.

The city also takes commuters out of Saint-Lambert for work. In 1954, forty-four nonagricultural, nonartisan wage earners who lived in Saint-Lambert left at regular intervals to work outside the commune. Many worked in Angers. Almost all the men of the village of Le Layon (population 30) on the northern frontier of the commune work in factories in Angers, commuting by bus or motorcycle. (The village of Le Layon is reputed to vote communist and is referred to sarcastically as "la commune libre du Layon.") Every weekday evening, the six or seven o'clock bus from Angers brings ten to a dozen young commuters from the city back to Saint-Lambert. There are always clusters of friends waiting in front of the hotel for the bus's arrival. By contrast, when the bus reaches Chanzeaux, it has few passengers to discharge. Even if one takes it regularly, once a day, between Angers and Chanzeaux, as some of the Americans did, one is not likely to see the same Chanzean face twice.

The city takes away Saint-Lambert's industry as well as its people. The only two operations in Saint-Lambert which could be called industry are Mme. Blanchard's bottling shed and a small shop making regional dolls that employs a dozen girls. There has been talk recently about bringing local industry to Saint-Lambert; the village leaders, however, believe that, unlike Chanzeaux, Saint-Lambert is too close to Chemillé and Angers to attract industry. The city also competes with local shopkeepers in offering goods and services to the people of Saint-Lambert. The typical Saint-Lambert housewife goes to Angers herself, or sends a member of her family, about once every ten days. Her counterpart in Chanzeaux rarely goes to Angers. This may explain why there is a shop for yarn and a tailor's shop in Chanzeaux, but neither in Saint-Lambert. Even the other shops appear more efficient in economic terms in Saint-Lambert than in Chanzeaux. There are four groceries and one dry-goods shop in Chanzeaux bourg. By contrast, there are only three groceries in the bourg of Saint-Lambert, one large one on the Place that distributes newspapers, another on the Chemillé road, and a minuscule one in a side wall of the same building that holds the hotel.

A different, somewhat contrary influence that the highway has on Saint-Lambert is that it makes it something of an urban center in its own right. For people in the region, Saint-Lambert is a more accessible place. Wholesalers can make their rounds to Saint-Lambert more easily than to Chanzeaux. Saint-Lambert has a minor but real role as a point of distribution for some services for which it would not pay to have outlets in every commune. Saint-Lambert has a pharmacy, which Chanzeaux does not. It had, until four years ago, barracks for an outpost of the highway police. It has a full-time barber-shop (*hommes, femmes, et chiens* — the wife clips dogs). In Chanzeaux, Lambert the café owner works as a barber only part-time.

Saint-Lambert's wine-based economy combines with its highway location to make it something of a cosmopolitan town. Vintners have a reputation for being more in contact with the outside world than farmers are. One inhabitant of Saint-Lambert emphasized the civilizing qualities of wine growing: "From the intellectual and cultural point of view, I think Saint-Lambert is more advanced. . . . In any case, the people of Saint-Lambert have a little feeling of superiority, which I feel is justified. It is because wine growing forces people to go to town to sell their wines and to entertain clients from different regions who come to buy the wine. I think wine growing provides more contact with the outside than farming, which is limited to the market at Chemillé." Maître Grellier in Rablay, the notaire for the region, adds that Chanzeans are easier to deal with than the people of his own town, because they are less suspicious. Chanzeans bring fewer cases into court than the people of Rablay. When a conflict arises, pressure is put on them to solve it "en famille." Group pressure is reputedly stronger in the Mauges than in wine country.

The Chanzeans themselves concede that Saint-Lambert is "plus evolué," and many of them will say that Chanzeaux is, in comparison, "un trou" (a hole). Another word that is used to describe Saint-Lambert is "bourgeois" (as different from "paysan" or "ouvrier"). Angers is definitely "une ville bourgeoise"; Saint-Lambert is also "un peu bourgeois." People who are bourgeois have fancy, citified houses and manners. They generally also have the defect of being "guindé," stuffy.

The people of Saint-Lambert are singularly concerned with not being outdone by the city. By 1963, the "twist" had hit Saint-Lambert. When the twist was played at a dance at about the same time in Chanzeaux, only three couples danced, and they were all from Saint-Lambert. At the dance of the Amicale Laïque in Saint-Lambert a week later, the dance floor was crowded during the twist numbers, and there were encores.

When the Americans left Saint-Lambert after the summer of 1963, the mayor was arranging for the installment of new road lights on the portion of the highway through the bourg. "Comme à la ville," he said with a mix-ture of satisfaction and amusement. The commune of Saint-Lambert also had running water almost twenty years (since 1948) before Chanzeaux (which started piping in water from the Loire in 1966).

Saint-Lambert is culturally as well as geographically between Chanzeaux in the rural Mauges and the city of Angers. Some of the themes that we have encountered in the historical development of Chanzeaux itself reappear in the differences between Saint-Lambert and Chanzeaux today. Despite its limita-tions, the analysis in depth of one village makes comparisons between villages more meaningful.

Americans in Chanzeaux

Americans have been a part of the life of Chanzeaux since 1957, and it is clear that in some respects the community has changed in the eight years we have been there. It has also become clear that much of our research is based on information from a relatively small and distinct part of the population. There is an obvious possibility that our research is biased, or at least that it holds true for only part of the Chanzeaux community.

To discover if this were so, we devised and filled out questionnaires on how we conducted our fieldwork, how we fitted into the community, and on whom we relied in Chanzeaux as informants and friends. From these questionnaires and from the extended discussions of them, there emerged a fairly coherent picture of our common method and relationship to Chanzeaux. Specifically, we attempted to answer these questions:

1. What were our sources of information, and why did we go to these sources and not to others?
2. What was our method of doing fieldwork, and why did we choose it?
3. What effect have we had on the community?

Sources of Information

From our questionnaires and discussions we discovered that our informants, especially our best informants and friends, were atypical Chanzeans:

	Average age	Type of residence	% of religious leaders	% of secular leaders
Major informants	44	50% in bourg 31% in villages, hamlets 29% on isolated farms	22%	21%
All Chanzeaux adults	48	25% in bourg 46% in villages, hamlets 29% on isolated farms	6%	6%

We found that we could agree on a group of roughly 70 Chanzeans — about 45 men and 25 women — whom we had come to know as friends or informants. (Most of our best informants were also friends, and our best friends were good informants.) These 70 people represent 10 percent of the adult population of the commune, which in 1962 was 703 people. They follow at least the outward forms of Chanzeaux's social customs: by sending their children to the Catholic school, by going to church each Sunday, by frequenting the bourg cafés after Mass, and by voting conservatively. But comparing them with the larger community, we discovered that our informants tended to play a more active role in community life than average Chanzeans. Also, as a group they were distinctly different from those people in the commune who did not participate in the activities of the community at all or, often, who did not share the community's basic values.

We also discovered that we did not know these "nonparticipants" very well at all. They include the wine growers on the edge of the commune near the Layon River, who are only administrative members of Chanzeaux; the hamlet dwellers, who associate mostly with other hamlet dwellers in their own subcommunity; the border families, who are often isolated by distance from the centers of community life in the bourg or who prefer other communities closer by; the population flowthroughs and the deviants of one kind or another, who participate in the life of the community but not on an equal level. From time to time, we had sensed that these gaps in our information existed and had tried to correct them. One fieldworker spent his summer living in a hamlet precisely for this reason, while others made attempts to meet the local "lower class" and the few socialists and communists in the community. But still, proportionately, these people remain little known. This gap is not important if it is recognized as such; though interesting in themselves, none of these groups plays a great role in the larger community we are primarily studying.

Making divisions along lines of age, religious practice, and social activism, we discover five types of Chanzeans we have come to know.

The first is the group of young, religious militants, the Catholic activists. These men and their wives hold key positions in the community life of Chanzeaux. Not only are they aware of what is happening throughout the commune, but — what is perhaps more important — they are interested in outsiders and sympathetic to our aims. They are thus easy to talk to and get to know, easily accessible since they usually live in or near the bourg, and extremely important sources of information about modern rural life.

The second group is similar to the first but even more powerful in the leadership circles of the commune. Men like Paul Guitière and Eugène Bourdelle, both farmers, are older than the young militant group by ten to twenty years. They have been around longer and have become the senior leaders of the commune, in religious organizations and in agricultural, educational, and welfare groups. They also have ties in the town council and in the Société de la Rue Bourgeoise.

The third group of informant-friends is characterized as secular activists. Ranging in age from thirty to eighty, they are farmers interested in bettering their position through cooperatives, welfare, and political organizations. André Blond is a good example of a farmer who is active in community life and even in regional affairs. Another is Jean Arrial who, with a small farm, nevertheless maintains a relatively prosperous life by hard work, modernization, and specialization in tobacco, which brings a high return. What sets him apart from a traditional farmer is not the size of his holdings, but his desire to participate in modern life and his recognition that the only way to survive and to improve is to keep abreast of the times.

The fourth group comprises what we can call the "establishment" of

Chanzeaux, those longtime residents who used to be on the town council and who provide the bulk of the members of the Société de la Rue Bourgeoise. These men and their wives represent an older generation and an older way of life. The former mayor, Jean-Baptiste Courcault, is an example of a man of this generation, on whom we usually paid a call early in the summer but rarely visited later on. As Mme. Courcault put it, "I have noticed the other American students during the summer, but they call and then prefer the company of younger people; it is natural." Because of their age, some people in this group have been valuable informants on the history of the community or on the problems of growing old, but very few have been particularly close friends of the Americans. There is probably too great a gap in age, in culture, and in spirit for close friendships to develop.

The last group is a more motley collection of people whom we have come to know for special or institutional reasons. In terms of age, religious practice, wealth, or activism, they are strictly average; they do not stand out as leaders in organizations, as prosperous farmers, or as pious churchgoers. Included here are Roger Asseray, the constable of Chanzeaux; Emile Bertrand *fils*, local plumber and electrician; Georges Lambert, café owner, barber, journalist, and patron of the Americans; and Armand Coulon and Emile Boutin, who work at the basket factory. Americans became acquainted with each of these men for different reasons: because they lived nearby in the bourg and were accessible, because they were relatives of other friends, because they worked at the factory, or because their position in the community as dispensers of needed services brought us inevitably into contact with them. In many ways, these relationships were more spontaneous or unplanned than our friendships with leaders or with experts on local lore, whom we tried to cultivate.

In general terms, then, it is clear that we have come to know only certain types of Chanzeans, those who participate in the web of community life that surrounds the church, the school, and the bourg cafés. Because we were primarily interested in community life, we know relatively little about those who do not participate in it and who have their own lives apart from it.

Fieldwork Methods

Our method of fieldwork leaned much more toward the pole of participant than the pole of observer, although the exact formula varied from student to student. Most of us tried to minimize our formal role, once it had been made known to the community, in favor of promoting friendships and opportunities for informal interviewing in depth. This approach came naturally to the Americans in the Chanzeaux project, because this was the way Laurence Wylie had gathered his information both in Roussillon and in Chanzeaux, and because those who became part of the project usually shared his personal interest in Chanzeaux. Most of the students worked fairly regularly somewhere in the community: in one of the cafés as bartender, on an isolated farm, or at the summer kindergarten held out of doors. Beyond fostering the close rapport so invaluable in gathering information and determining attitudes, this approach provided valuable personal experience for the students themselves.

With the exception of the statistical information that had to be copied from the townhall files or the historical information that could be gleaned from the archives in Angers or the chateau library in Chanzeaux, we found that we could best get information about almost all aspects of village life by participating in the life of the people and by asking questions in an informal way. There are, nevertheless, real barriers to *complete* participation which must be borne in mind. Not only were the Americans obviously outsiders, but in addition they were mostly non-Catholic, middle-class, and social scientists. Although they were accepted because of their interest and friendliness, the Americans could not adopt all the customs of the community. Thus even while trying to include them in as many activities as possible, the Chanzeans were aware of the observer as well as the participant roles of their visitors.

American Influence on Chanzeaux

What has been the effect of our presence, for almost eight years now, on the people of Chanzeaux? Reflecting on the differences between Chanzeaux today and in 1957, it seems to us that we have not had a major effect on the underlying social institutions of Chanzeaux but that we probably have had some effect on certain attitudes — specifically, Chanzeaux's ideas of Americans and Chanzeaux's ideas about itself.

Chanzeaux has two images of Americans that exist side by side: the old stereotype of America, which is basic, enduring, and undoubtedly a French cultural trait; and the new image of the local Americans in Chanzeaux. The Chanzeans, when they speak of Americans in general, think of them as materialistic, rich, a bit undisciplined, and possibly irreligious. These traits are quite unrelated to the Americans they know and probably persist in spite of personal contacts. They know us now as individuals, so they realize that Americans are people more or less like them — but it is difficult to generalize from the few they know to a whole country. If the traditional stereotype remains unchanged and disagreeable, however, the image of the Chanzeaux-Americans is friendly and accepting. With the exception of a few spy rumors that have circulated from time to time, we were warmly received by nearly all the Chanzeans we met. Religious and social differences have not only been generally accepted, but may at times even have served as an added source of amusement. When there have been conflicts, tact, a recognition of different cultural values, and a warm personal relationship have usually helped to overcome them.

There are many reasons why Chanzeaux was willing to allow the Americans their special niche in the community. We came expecting to make friends, and those of us who came after 1957 had the benefit of Laurence Wylie's strong friendships and prior acceptance by the community. At the same time, we also benefited from favorable coverage in the press, locally in the *Courrier de l'Ouest* and even nationally in short articles in *Le Figaro* and *Le Monde*, which gave details of Wylie's research in a "commune témoin" of France. Early in his research, Wylie made friends with the editors of the local newspaper in Angers, who reciprocated by helping him find his commune for study and by assuring their readers that he had no evil intentions: "Professor Wylie, whom numerous articles in this paper have already presented to the public . . . is a sincere friend . . . for the whole region"; "we know that with Professor Laurence Wylie, Anjou has in America a faithful friend"; and "we know that each door he knocks on will be opened to him in a friendly manner." In addition, the *Courrier* kept the region abreast of all the major American activities in Chanzeaux — from Wylie's arrival to the *vin d'honneur* given for him, and finally to the marriage of two Americans that took place in Chanzeaux in the summer of 1964.

Indeed, perhaps the best example of the type of relationship the Americans have with Chanzeaux is that marriage of 1964, between Suzanne Textor, a Radcliffe student who was spending a year on a French government scholarship studying in Angers and Chanzeaux, and Preston Tollinger, a Harvard law student who was spending the summer working in an Angers law office. The wedding illustrates the friendships we have formed; the newspaper coverage we were given — the *Courrier* ran a long article complete with photographs and best wishes; and the effect we have had on the Chanzeans. The form of the wedding was both American and traditional French. All the Chanzeans of the bourg turned out to watch the wedding procession as it made its way from the Lambert café to the townhall for the civil ceremony. Leading the procession were René and Yvonne Lambert, the children of Georges Lambert who had provided room and board for Suzanne during her stay. The younger Lambert children were followed by the bride and groom, the witnesses (the older Lamberts), the bride's grandmother, the groom's parents, and the entire group of Chanzeaux Americans.

The civil ceremony inside the townhall was the regular French ceremony as prescribed by law; when it was completed, the bridal party and a large group of Chanzeaux friends headed for Angers and a Protestant religious ceremony. For most Chanzeans this was the first time they had ever been to a Protestant wedding, and there was a great deal of speculation about how it would differ from a Catholic wedding in Chanzeaux. After the religious ceremony, Americans and Chanzeans returned for a *vin d'honneur* to celebrate the wedding. In keeping with local tradition, wine played a prominent role in the festivities. But otherwise there were two important breaks with tradition. In deference to the Americans, the local nobility attended a celebration with the "common" people probably for the first time in Chanzeaux's history. Equally unique was the presence of the Protestant minister from Angers who, with his wife and child, mingled with the members of the overwhelmingly Catholic community.

Chanzeaux's image of itself and consciousness of its own character have also been affected by our presence. Getting used to having friendly strangers around has made people aware of their own willingness to be hospitable to newcomers. It had always been somewhat of a myth in the community that Chanzeans were *accueillants*, friendly to strangers. Mme. Pinier, however, who migrated to Chanzeaux to marry a native, says that when she arrived the community could not have been more unfriendly. No one talked to her for two years, she maintains, except other outsiders like herself, who were also lonely. When Wylie first arrived, he too encountered an initial reserve and even suspicion, for there were some people who were not sure but that he was some sort of spy.

Yet today Chanzeaux seems conscious of the need to be and to appear friendly. Not only have Chanzeans proved friendly to Wylie's students, but some at least have attempted to make of their friendliness a tourist attraction. When the Syndicat d'Initiative printed a small folder about the glories of Chanzeaux as a vacation spot, they included on the second page a long testimonial by Wylie (complete with his full professorial title) emphasizing the friendliness of the commune. The image that Chanzeaux had held of itself implicitly is thus becoming more explicit in the hands of those who are capitalizing on the Americans to spur the tourist trade. Even Chanzeans who are not interested in the business benefits of the Americans are undoubtedly proud of the fact that their community, of all the others in the Maine-et-Loire and other parts of France, is the one being studied by a professor and a team of students from a famous American university. The publicity that has been generated around Chanzeaux as a "picturesque hyphen between the Loire and the Mauges," that "country of history," had probably also the effect of making Chanzeaux more self-conscious and aware of its unique history. In all these subtle and basically unmeasurable ways, our presence has served to change some attitudes of Chanzeans about the commune in which they live.

In addition to affecting attitudes, the Americans have probably had an effect on the local power struggles within the commune. Because our basic sympathies lie with the progressive element of Chanzeaux, we have sometimes been used by them in the furtherance of their own aims. The Syndicat d'Initiative is the best example. According to its founders, the original idea for the group came from Wylie himself, although he cannot remember having made the suggestion. But whether he did or not, it is significant that by linking the group to his name, the progressives have gained for it a measure of respectability and acceptance it might not have had otherwise. In the summer of 1963, the originators of the Syndicat held a *vin d'honneur* for Wylie to which they invited the town council. Had the meeting not been in his honor, these town councilors would undoubtedly not have come and would not have had to listen to André Blond give a speech praising the Syndicat. We suspect Blond and the progressives of being well aware of this situation, and of planning the *vin d'honneur* to persuade the town council to appropriate money for the Syndicat.

A similar incident occurred in the summer of 1964. The Syndicat had conceived and carried out the idea of installing a camping ground in Chanzeaux to attract more tourists. The day for the opening of the grounds was set, and many invitations were sent out to different families. A ribbon-cutting ceremony, followed by a *vin d'honneur*, was to celebrate the occasion. As luck would have it, the family of one of the American students was planning to drive to Chanzeaux to visit and would probably be camping out in the area for several days. An hour before the ceremony, the father, mother, and three children arrived in Chanzeaux. Seizing on the occasion, members of the Syndicat pressed the father (who is in the diplomatic corps) into service as the key speaker — in rusty French — at the ceremony and later as the principal figure at the *vin d'honneur*. The head of the Syndicat pointed out how much Chanzeaux owed to its other distinguished visitors, the American students. Interestingly enough, the mayor of Chanzeaux, not a particularly good friend of the Syndicat, "unfortunately could not be with us today."

Thus the presence of the Americans has widened a gulf that is present in any community — the gulf between hope for the future and nostalgia for the past. Chanzeaux has its share of citizens who militate for change and its share of citizens who fight to preserve the old ways. Simply by our presence, we bring to mind the fact that life as it now exists in Chanzeaux is not the only form of life that society can produce. We bring to mind that there are alternatives, and thus we force the debate as to whether these alternatives have value.

There have been long hours of discussions between the Americans and their friends about religion, dating, politics, and cultural patterns generally. These may have had the effect of broadening the horizons of at least some

Chanzeans and of making them more aware of America. Certainly the map that Georges Lambert keeps in his café — a map of America with pins for the home towns of each American student — is an indication of an increased interest in and awareness of another part of the world. It is not that this interest in the outside never existed, but simply that in this one case we have helped to make it more concrete. On the whole, we feel that our presence has not been a major factor in changing the nature of Chanzeaux's social fabric, but that it has changed certain attitudes and deepened already existing conflicts.

Notes

Introduction

1. Gabriel Le Bras, "La Religion dans la société française," in André Siegfried, ed., *Aspects de la société française* (Paris: Librairie Générale de Droit et de Jurisprudence, 1954), p. 226.

1. Chanzeaux at the Time of the Vendée Rebellion

1. The account of March 12 is reconstructed from testimonies given by town officers on March 15 and April 30, 1793, Departmental Archives of Maine-et-Loire, series 1 L 1028.

2. Departmental Archives of Maine-et-Loire, series 1 L 2018.

3. Paul Bois, *Paysans de l'ouest* (Le Mans, 1960); Charles Tilly, *The Vendée* (Cambridge, Mass., 1964).

4. This intrusion of industry into the Mauges was, however, of critical importance in the outbreak of the civil war. The entrepreneurs of the mills were among the most stalwart supporters of the Revolution, and their cities were the principal targets of the counterrevolutionaries. (See Tilly.)

5. Departmental Archives of Maine-et-Loire, series C 192.

6. The parish registers of Chanzeaux suggest that the process was reversible: more than half of the natives of other parishes who married into Chanzeaux were domiciled in Chanzeaux at the time of their marriage. They had undoubtedly been working there as domestiques and apprentices.

7. Slightly more than half of the marriages that took place in Chanzeaux during this period were between two Chanzeans. But since marriages involving Chanzeans also took place in other parishes, more than half of the marriages joined a Chanzean with a non-Chanzean. The parish register from Saint-Lambert shows one or two marriages a year involving a Chanzean. Whereas in the twentieth century most marriages take place in the bride's home town, there seems to have been no such rule in the eighteenth century. The parish registers indicate that less than half of the Chanzeans who married did so with outsiders; if half of the marriages involved one non-Chanzean spouse, only a third of Chanzeans married outside.

8. Le Champ, bordering Chanzeaux on the east, broke away from the parish of Thouarcé in the nineteenth century. Most of the people referred to in the eighteenth-century parish registers were thus from the contiguous parish of Le Champ.

9. Departmental Archives of Maine-et-Loire, July 4, 1790, series 12 Q 67: "soumission de municipalité de Chanzeaux, pour l'acquisition des biens des Ecclesiastiques. Pour 60,000 livres." Signed by: François Pinier, Charles Jean Fougeray, François Blouin, Jean-Pierre Blond, François Jean-Nicolas Coustard, Julien Picherit.

10. These towns were Saint-Lambert, Notre Dame de Chemillé, Sainte-Foi, Gonnord, and Joué.

11. Departmental Archives of Maine-et-Loire, series 1 L 65.

12. Males between the ages of 18 and 25 were eligible for the draft. The number of males born between 1767 and 1775, excluding those who had died before 1793, was about 160. The population did not vary during these years, and the emigration must have about equaled the immigration.

2. Chanzeaux under Quatrebarbes

1. The arrondissement is a subdivision of a department, administered by a subprefect. In the 1840s, as at present, Chanzeaux was included in the canton of Thouarcé within the arrondissement of Angers. However, the village lay on the southwestern border of both canton and arrondissement and, because most of the village was in the bocage (the hedge country southwest of Angers), it actually had as much in common with the villages in the neighboring canton of Chemillé, which was in the arrondissement of Beaupréau, as with other villages in its own canton.

2. The source of this and most other detailed information on agriculture in the Maine-et-Loire in this period is O. Leclerc-Thouin, *L'Agriculture de l'ouest de la France* (Paris, 1843), a comprehensive study written at the request of the Ministry of Agriculture.

3. Henri Sée, *La Vie économique de la France sous la Monarchie censitaire* (Paris, 1927), p. 44.

4. Letter of subprefect of arrondissement of Beaupréau to prefect of Maine-et-Loire, 1837, in F. Uzureau, ed., *Andegaviana*, XXXII (Angers, 1938), 347, 350.

5. This was obligatory by the 1833 Guizot Law. Half the salary was paid directly by the commune, and the other half was obtained by charging a monthly fee for each pupil: 1.50 francs for boys learning to read and write, 1 for those learning only to read, and a special bargain rate of 1 apiece for three brothers attending school. From these figures, it appears that between 50 and 75 boys attended school three or four months out of the year. In addition, 17 children of indigents were admitted to school without charge. This means that about 4 percent of the population, or perhaps half the boys of grade-school age, were attending school for some part of the year. The percentage compares favorably with that in the neighboring departments of the west, especially in Brittany, where only about 0.5 percent of the population was in school. In northeastern France, the proportion was about 10 percent. Emile Lavasseur, *La Population française* (Paris, 1891), II, 481.

6. Departmental Archives of Maine-et-Loire, series 10 M, dossier on Chanzeaux.

7. Philippe Ariès, *Histoire des populations françaises et de leurs attitudes devant la vie depuis le dix-huitième siècle* (Paris, 1948), pp. 420ff.

8. This was the case throughout France. In the second half of the nineteenth century, the ratio of farm servants to fermiers and proprietors declined steadily, and the total rural population declined absolutely, as landless laborers migrated to the towns. See J. H. Clapham, *Economic Development of France and Germany*, 4th ed. (Cambridge, Eng., 1936), pp. 162–170.

9. *Une Paroisse Vendéenne sous la Terreur* (Paris and Angers, 1837), pp. 271–274.

10. *Moniteur Universel,* April 25, 1847.

11. Procès Verbal of the Chanzeaux municipal elections, July 31, 1848; in the Departmental Archives of Maine-et-Loire, series 10 M, dossier on Chanzeaux.

12. The results of the election by canton were published in the *Journal de Maine-et-Loire,* April 29, 1848.

13. Extract from a decision of the civil tribunal of Angers, December 5, 1848; in the archives of the chateau of Chanzeaux.

14. *Note sur l'organisation de l'ouest* (1850); in the archives of the chateau of Chanzeaux.

3. *Chanzeaux at the Turn of the Century*

1. February 5, 1906, series 8 M 105.

2. May 12, 1910, series 8 M 108.

3. Quoted in A. Latreille et al., *Histoire du Catholicisme en France, la période contemporaine* (Paris, 1962), p. 468.

4. See André Siegfried, *Tableau politique de la France de l'ouest* (Paris, 1913), chap. 44.

5. Departmental Archives of Maine-et-Loire, series O, dossier on Chanzeaux.

6. Diocesan Archives of Angers, dossier on Chanzeaux.

7. Departmental Archives of Maine-et-Loire, series O, dossier on Chanzeaux.

8. *Almanach paroissial de Chanzeaux,* 1912, p. 3.

9. T. L. Houdebine, *Histoire religieuse de l'Anjou* (Angers, 1926), p. 283.

10. *Almanach paroissial de Chanzeaux,* 1912, p. vii.

11. *Almanach paroissial de St. Lambert du Lattay,* 1907.

4. *Land Tenure*

1. The requirement still holds today, even though the successor of those same republican notables, Mme. Thibault, is an arch-conservative Catholic. This is why the children of M. Lorseau, one of her Chanzean tenants, go to Saint-Lambert's public school.

2. A number of Chanzeaux fermiers have bought land from their landlords. A few now own as much land as most proprietors.

3. Numerical measures of the change in composition of Chanzeaux's farms are difficult to come by. Definitions in French censuses change from year to year, and the distinction between fermier and proprietor has been either nonexistent or hazy. These figures compare the results of an agricultural survey made in 1851 with our own survey of Chanzeaux farms in 1962:

	1851	1962
Proprietors	27	59
Fermiers	107	60

In the *Enquête Décennale de 1852* (actually made in 1851), Chanzeaux's proprietors were counted under the heading "propriétaires habitants leurs terres et faisant faire-valoir soit eux-mêmes, soit par régisseur ou maître-valet." There were no *régisseurs* or *maître-valets* listed; so we may assume that all the men counted were *propriétaires exploitants.* In our 1962 figures, enumeration of farms is divided according to legal tenure (over half of the land owned versus over half of the land rented). In the rest of the chapter we define a fermier as one who rents noble and bourgeois land; a proprietor, as any other farmer.

4. The Napoleonic Code requires equal inheritance. Historians are debating whether the code introduced this practice into France or simply formalized existing custom. Post-World War II reforms have modified the effect of the law.

6. The Farm Problem

1. The Chanzeaux estimate was made by the town secretary and the grain merchant. The urban family estimate is based on average monthly earnings of a sample of wage earners taken in Angers, Caen, and Rennes, December 1961. Nicole Tabard, "Précisions des Estimations et Durée de l'Enregistrement des Comptes dans les Enquêtes sur les Budgets Familiaux," *Consommation*, X.2 (April–June 1963), 53. That figure was converted to an annual average and then increased by 36 percent, the rate of increase of the national average hourly wage rate for all industrial employees from 1961 through 1965. Institut National des Statistiques et des Etudes Economiques, *Annuaire Statistique de la France*, 1965 (Paris, 1965), p. 471.

All current francs mentioned throughout are new francs.

2. The postwar period has been characterized by inflation. All prices have risen. In judging the strength or weakness of a particular market, one must compare the trend increase in its price to the trend in other markets.

3. Ministry of Agriculture, *Statistique agricole, retrospectif, 1930–1957* (Paris, 1959), p. 14, and *Statistique agricole, 1963* (Paris, 1964), p. li.

4. Quoted in "La Loi d'Orientation Agricole 5 ans après," *Chambres d'agriculture*, May 1–15, 1965, p. 6.

5. See Gilles Arfeuillère, *L'Organisation des marchés de la viande et des produits laitiers en France* (Toulouse, 1964).

6. This drop cannot be traced to the fall in the birthrate during the war years. Adolescents who were between 15 and 21 in 1954 were born before the war. Adolescents who were between 15 and 21 in 1964 were born from 1942 to 1949. Only the first three of those years were war years; the rest were years of exceptionally high birthrate.

7. Personality plays a part. The first tractor to appear in Chanzeaux was bought by René Lusson with Marshall Plan aid. Lusson has only 30 acres. However, he is an innovator. He specializes in commercial pig raising, was an early member of the medicinal plants cooperative, and is one of the freest spirits on the town council.

8. One Chanzeaux farmer recently made the following estimate of the advantages of tractor power over horse power:

	1 tractor	2 horses
Fuel consumption	6 liters of gas per hr. at .60 nf per liter	hay and grain
Time required to plow 5 hectares (1 man)	5 hrs.	20 hrs.
Time required to spread fertilizer over 5 hectares (1 man)	2½ hrs.	7½ hrs.

Purchase price of a gasoline tractor capable of performing as specified above is 9000 francs. Purchase price of a more powerful diesel tractor is 20,000 francs. Yearly wage of a full-time agricultural laborer (300 twelve-hour days) is 4230 francs.

9. The following figures are based on a representative sample of 24 farms. Excluded from the sample were (1) farms occupied by a retired man and operated by no one else, and (2) farms in the wine-growing areas of the commune.

	Less than 62.5 acres	*More than 62.5 acres*	*Unknown*
Exchange chiefly labor	9	3	2
Exchange chiefly machines	3	7	

7. Residence Patterns

1. Throughout this chapter "religious" means "church-attending," "irreligious" the opposite.

8. Migration

1. Our information about residents of Chanzeaux — both those born in Chanzeaux and those born elsewhere — comes from a file kept by Jean Delaunay, the *secrétaire de mairie*. Delaunay makes a card for every family or unattached individual who stays at least a year in Chanzeaux. Information on emigrants comes from voting lists, which in France are organized by place of birth. The Institut National des Statistiques et des Etudes Economiques has given us a list of all the voters living in France, outside of Chanzeaux (as of September 1962), whose place of birth was Chanzeaux. Talks with Delaunay and interviews with some of the friends and relatives of people who left furnished more information.

2. This figure, which comes from a 1962 voting list, is probably too high because it does not take into account any of the emigrants younger than twenty-one in 1962. Of the three types of migrants — flowthroughs, immigrants, and emigrants — we are limiting our attention in this section to the last. For all the emigrants, departure from Chanzeaux is the first displacement in their lives. This makes them the most stable group, and the best for studying whatever recurrent patterns there are in migration.

3. W. Christian and W. Braden, "Rural Migration and the Gravity Model," *Rural Sociology*, March 1966, pp. 73–80.

4. Furthermore, during the period 1954–1962, more flowthroughs left Chanzeaux than the total number of people who came in. This seems to show that prospective flowthroughs accumulated in less prosperous times and that, in the boom since 1953, they have been leaving en masse.

5. L. M. Goreux, "Les Migrations agricoles en France depuis un siècle et leur relation avec certains facteurs économiques," *Etudes et conjonctures*, April 1956.

13. Religious Behavior

1. The sample of persons rated as to church attendance by the curé covers only 502 of the 703 adults living in Chanzeaux in November 1962. The people not covered in the sample include 61 very young adults who still lived with their parents, 22 persons who were invalids, 23 persons who no longer lived in Chanzeaux, and 17 persons who were recent immigrants. Of these people, 70 percent were unmarried or widowed. (See the population pyramids in this chapter.) They were just as likely to live in the bourg as on farms. It is probable that people not included in the sample were more irreligious than religious. Most of them were people who were to all intents and purposes outside of Chanzeaux in community affairs.

14. Political Behavior

1. Jean-Paul Grousset in *Le Canard enchaîné,* November 21, 1962.
2. Prefect of Maine-et-Loire, memo to Minister of the Interior on the legislative elections of 1910, Departmental Archives of Maine-et-Loire, series 8 M 108.
3. *Journal de Maine-et-Loire,* February 17, 1876; quoted in André Siegfried, *Tableau politique de la France de l'ouest sous la troisième république* (Paris, 1913), p. 59.
4. Prefect of Maine-et-Loire, memo to Minister of the Interior, Departmental Archives of Maine-et-Loire, series 8 M 108.

15. Childhood

1. The young couples are distributed about the commune in much the same manner as older couples: about 26 percent in the bourg, 30 percent on isolated farms, 27 percent in the hamlets, and 17 percent in the farming villages. In occupation, too, these young parents are representative of the whole adult population: about 75 percent of the families make their living from farming of one sort or another. Significantly fewer young men are proprietors than the average for the commune, but many are expecting to inherit farms. In religious practice, these couples also follow the traditions of the village: there is a smaller proportion of the devout group (those taking communion every Sunday) among the young couples than in the commune as a whole, but this has more to do with their age group than with a decline in faith in Chanzeaux.
2. Billebault, *Au temps de* . . . . (standard Catholic-school text).
3. Personne, Ballot, and Marc, *Histoire de France* (standard public-school text).
4. Since the government has been helping to support the Catholic schools, by law no catechism may be taught during school hours. For this reason, class convenes a quarter of an hour late each day so that on Wednesdays an hour and a quarter may be taken off for a catechism class at the parish house.

17. Old Age

1. As a matter of convenience, the group known as "the old" throughout this chapter are all inhabitants of Chanzeaux born before 1900. Most of the

data on which the figures are based were drawn from information received after 1960; an inhabitant born before 1900 will be at least sixty — the minimum age for old-age pensions. The figures below show the age of Chanzeaux's population in selected years (1960 figure is not comparable with 1962 census):

	1851	1901	1926	1960
Over 60 years	11.8%	15.3%	18.2%	15.3%
20–59 years	52.7%	56.0%	49.7%	46.3%
0–19 years	36.5%	28.7%	32.1%	38.4%
Total no.	1,733	1,334	1,225	1,121

2. From the record of the inhabitants who died in 1953–1963, the following calculation was made of life expectancies: At birth, men could be expected to die at age 70.6, women at 74.4; men who reached age 65 could be expected to die at 78.5, women at 80.9. The average age at death of inhabitants in the middle of the nineteenth century, on the other hand, was only 52.

3. Even such an exponent of modernity and progress as Georges Lambert explains that the younger generation is less hardy because their food is over-processed. He cites as proof of the hardiness of the older generation the ability of many of the older men to drink as much as a bottle of *eau de vie* a day and still live to be eighty-five or ninety.

4. In the early 1900s the French government, in an effort to suppress religious organizations and associations, passed a law making members' contributions to these associations voluntary.

5. Dividing the population in three age groups — from birth to nineteen, from twenty to fifty-nine, and from sixty on — one sees that the demographic pattern has followed certain historical trends (see also the demographic charts in Chapter 7). From 1851 to 1901 the great strides taken in health and sanitation helped to increase life expectancies. The percentage of old people went up 3.5 percent, which meant that, although Chanzeaux's population as a whole dropped by 399 persons during these years, the absolute number of inhabitants over sixty remained the same. Even more striking was the large increase of the percentage of active workers between twenty and sixty and a corresponding decrease in the percentage of potential workers under twenty. When the census of 1926 was taken, therefore, many of these formerly active workers had retired, and the First World War had accounted for a great decrease in the number of active men, directly through casualties or indirectly by exposing agricultural workers to urbanized society. The result was that the percentage of people over sixty went up almost 3 percent, which in absolute figures meant that, despite a drop of 109 inhabitants in the population as a whole, the number of old people actually increased by 23. The percentage of children was growing, however, for despite the drop in population the absolute number of children under twenty remained virtually the same. Since 1926 the percentage of old people has gone down considerably, until in 1960 they represented the same proportion of the population as a whole as in 1901. At the same time, the percentage of children has increased almost 10 percent since that date. Hence, although the balance of active workers to inactive mouths to be fed places a heavy burden on the worker now, the future looks good because the proportion of old people should remain fairly constant as the

younger generation — discounting migration — replaces the presently active generation.

Conclusion

1. Théodore de Quatrebarbes, *Une Paroisse Vendéenne sous la Terreur* (Angers, 1837), p. 20.

Index

Abellard, Emile, 175, 238
Abstention from voting, 243, 271–276. *See also* Political behavior
Adolescence: careers after age 14, 302–303; choice of marriage partners, 305–308; dissatisfactions of, 303–304; emigration during, 314–316; force for tradition, 314, 315; formal education after 14, 301–302; ideals defined for, 310–311; importance of reputation, 308–310; occupational uncertainties, 304–305; persistence of childhood teachings, 312–314; social relations during, 308
Age: and farm closures, 133; in farming villages, 150; related to farm innovations, 117; and religious behavior, 247; and residence in bourg, 139–141, 147, 247; of town councilors, 238. *See also* Old age
Aged, distribution in commune, 318
Agriculture, present-day: crops, 93–103; income from, 104–107; labor for, 101–102; land tenure, 77–92; market reform, 109–114; mechanization, 114–122; population devoted to, 107; and technological change, 107–108; two case studies, 122–132. *See also* Crops; Farms; Land
Aides-familiales, 217, 218, 303
Allaire, René, 122
Allaire, René, *fils*, 237, 238
Alleaume, Curé, 209–211, 255, 286, 338
Allocations familiales, 91–92
Altar boys, 199–200
Amelin, Henri, 211, 213, 222, 338; and town council, 232, 234, 237, 337
Amelin, Mme., 328
Amelin, Monique, 213, 214
Amelin, Paul, 238
Amelin, Pierre, 77, 83, 118–120
Americans in Chanzeaux, effects and methods, 358–364
Amicale Laïque, 354, 356
Ancenis cooperative, 111
Angers: American wedding, 362; Catholic college, 245; Chanzeaux land owned

by residents of, 81; migration to, 173, 353; old-age home, 323, 324; relation to Chanzeaux, 1, 6, 68, 134, 356; relation to Saint-Lambert, 356; religious practice, 182; republicanism, 260; road to, 18–19, 39; in Vendée war, 16; *une ville bourgeoise*, 356
Anjou, province, 1–2, 28
Anticlericalism, 64–65, 69; effect on Chanzeaux, 71; and politics, 271; present-day, 267, 355. *See also* Church; Education
Arrial, Catherine, 124, 126
Arrial, Jean, 172; candidate for town council, 232, 233–234, 237; case study of farm, 122–129 (Tables 21–23); as innovator, 235; *propriétaire exploitant*, 84, 92; secular activist, 359
Artificial insemination, 121
Artisans, 142–143
Asseray, Paul, 122, 143, 144
Asseray, Roger, 360
Association d'Entr'aide du Plessis, 76, 117–120 (Table 20), 128
Association de l'Aide Familiale, 214, 217, 218, 233
Association de Bienfaisance, 324
Association Familiale (AF), 214, 215, 216–217, 233
Associés du Rosaire, 201
Attendance at church, 243, 249–257; related to voting abstention, 274–275. *See also* Religious practice
Automobiles, 104, 129, 131, 256
Avrilla, dairy, 111

Baignon, André and Gabrielle, 164
Ballu, Auguste, 127
Barbat, Louis, 122
Barbot, Joseph, 77
Basketball, 203
Basse Lande, La, 23
Bazantay, Chantal, 296
Beaulieu, 21, 24, 39, 151, 167, 324, 325, 352
Beaupréau, 16, 37, 245, 259